Securing Village Life

Development in Late Colonial Papua New Guinea

Scott MacWilliam

Securing Village Life

Development in Late Colonial Papua New Guinea

Scott MacWilliam

Australian National University

E PRESS

ANU
E PRESS

Published by ANU E Press
The Australian National University
Canberra ACT 0200, Australia
Email: anuepress@anu.edu.au
This title is also available online at http://epress.anu.edu.au

National Library of Australia Cataloguing-in-Publication entry

Author: MacWilliam, Scott

Title: Securing village life : development in late colonial Papua New Guinea /
                Scott MacWilliam.

ISBN: 9781922144843 (paperback) 9781922144850 (ebook)

Notes: Includes bibliographical references and index.

Subjects: Economic development projects--Papua New Guinea.
                Australia--Foreign economic relations.
                Papua New Guinea--Foreign economic relations.

Dewey Number: 338.9009953

Cover design and layout by ANU E Press

Cover image: Smallholders from the Nimai Group of Sinasina, Chimbu District, near Koge village
pruning and rejuvenating 20-year-old coffee trees in 1973 at approximately 1850 metres altitude.
Photograph by Robin Hide.

Contents

Acknowledgements

The research and thinking upon which this book is based has, in many aspects, taken over 40 years. During the early 1970s in East Africa, I became acutely aware of the academic and political tussles regarding colonialism and indigenous peoples. In particular two early intellectual mentors, Mike Cowen and Nicola Swainson, introduced me to the most controversial dimensions of what became known as 'the Kenyan debate': exploring the nature and contemporary condition of households in the countryside and indigenous capital. I have since had the good fortune to continue researching these dimensions of what Ernest Mandel optimistically termed 'late capitalism'.

On moving to Papua New Guinea (PNG) in 1983, and over the subsequent 30 years working in the Pacific, I have been assisted by many people with similar interests. Throughout my time as a teaching academic, countless students in Australia, PNG and Fiji have contributed to the further development of my thinking about development. Academic colleagues, government and corporate officials, as well as a wide range of knowledgeable informants have instructed, advised and informed my research and been unsparingly generous with their time and knowledge. To the many who have been important in shaping this study, 'Thank You'.

There are some people who I would like to single out for particular contributions. Dick Bryan, Robert Foster, Robin Hide, Michael Rafferty and Tony Smith remain constant guides, sources of advice and comradeship. Geoff Kay has been an important intellectual influence. Dave Roberts, a generous and wise counsellor, has always been available to help. In the United Kingdom, my recently deceased cousin Iain MacWilliam kindly provided accommodation, companionship and encouragement over many years. Huntley Wright also wrote a thesis about late colonial development in PNG and generously shared his notes, references, drafts and friendship.

Dedicated librarians and archivists have provided documents and other material, as well as given sound advice. The most important support came from staff at the Robertson Library, Curtin University of Technology, and in particular from the inter-library loan sections of the National Archives of Australia, the Noel Butlin Archives, the Chifley and Menzies libraries at The Australian National University (ANU), the PNG National Archives and the New Guinea collection in the Sir Michael Somare Library at the University of Papua New Guinea (UPNG). Mrs Joan Humphries at the former Burns, Philp archives provided an important starting point for research into that company's operations in PNG.

My PhD supervisor Rick Kuhn is an exemplary academic, who not only guided me through the sometimes difficult process of completing the thesis, but also found other ways to continue providing support for its publication. Rick was responsible for the successful nomination to the Australian Political Studies Association (APSA), which resulted in the thesis being awarded the 2011 PhD Dissertation Prize. He also was responsible for the nomination of the Humanities and Creative Arts Award from the Research School of Humanities and the Arts, ANU College of Arts & Social Sciences (CASS) which provided for copy editing of this book. Two other members of the thesis supervisory committee at ANU, Peter Larmour and John Ravenhill, were in right measure critical as well as encouraging. Three anonymous thesis examiners provided telling suggestions as to how the thesis could be turned into a book. Hopefully the final product warrants the generous support I have received from these academics, the APSA and the Humanities Research Centre of CASS, ANU.

I am deeply indebted to Mary Walta for her patience, enthusiasm and wise counsel as a copy editor. Duncan Beard at ANU E Press has provided invaluable advice and assistance. I would further like to thank Sinclair Dinnen of the State Society & Governance in Melanesia Program in the College of Asia & the Pacific (CAP), ANU and am indebted to the Multimedia Services in CAP for assistance with the presentation of maps that appear in this book.

The book is dedicated to the late Mike Cowen for nearly 30 years of wisdom and comradeship, who was physically there at the beginning and remains present in my mind. And to my sons, Hugh, Michael, Ewan and Lachlan, who have given me more by way of support, good humour and affection than I had ever thought possible.

Abbreviations

ALP	Australian Labor Party
AN	Accession Number
ANGAU	Australian and New Guinea Administrative Unit
ANGPCB	Australian New Guinea Production Control Board
ANU	Australian National University
ANZAAS	Australian and New Zealand Association for the Advancement of Science
AO	Agricultural Officer
AusAID	Australian Agency for International Development
BCL	Bougainville Copper Limited
BDC	Bougainville Development Corporation
CILM	Commission of Inquiry into Land Matters
CMB	Coffee Marketing Board
CPC	Constitutional Planning Committee
CPO	Central Planning Office
CRA-RTZ	Conzinc Riotinto of Australia-Riotinto Zinc
DASF	Department of Agriculture, Stock and Fisheries (Territory of Papua and New Guinea)
DC	District Commissioner
DEA	Department of External Affairs, Commonwealth of Australia
DET	Department of External Territories
DoT	Department of Territories
DO	District Officer
DPI	Department of Primary Industry
ENB	East New Britain
F/N	File Number
IBRD	World Bank International Bank for Reconstruction and Development
ICA	International Coffee Agreement
ICO	International Coffee Organisation
LGC	Local Government Council
LPA	Liberal Party of Australia
MA	Mataungan Association
MHA	Member of the House of Assembly

NAA	National Archives of Australia
NCDS	National Centre for Development Studies
NGDC	New Guinea Development Corporation
NGIP	New Guinea Islands Produce Company
NGRU	New Guinea Research Unit
NIC	Newly Industrialized Country
NLA	National Library of Australia
OPC	Office of Programming and Coordination
PM	Prime Minister
PNG	Papua New Guinea
PNGNA	Papua New Guinea National Archives
POC	Office of Programming and Coordination
PNGNA	Papua New Guinea National Archives
RAO	Regional Agricultural Officer
RSPAS	Research School of Pacific and Asian Studies
SAE	Senior Agricultural Economist
SAO	Senior Agricultural Officer
TCP	Tolai Cocoa Project
TPNG	Territory of Papua and New Guinea
UN	United Nations
UPNG	University of Papua New Guinea
UNDP	United Nations Development Program
UPNG	University of Papua New Guinea
VSD	Vascular Streak Dieback

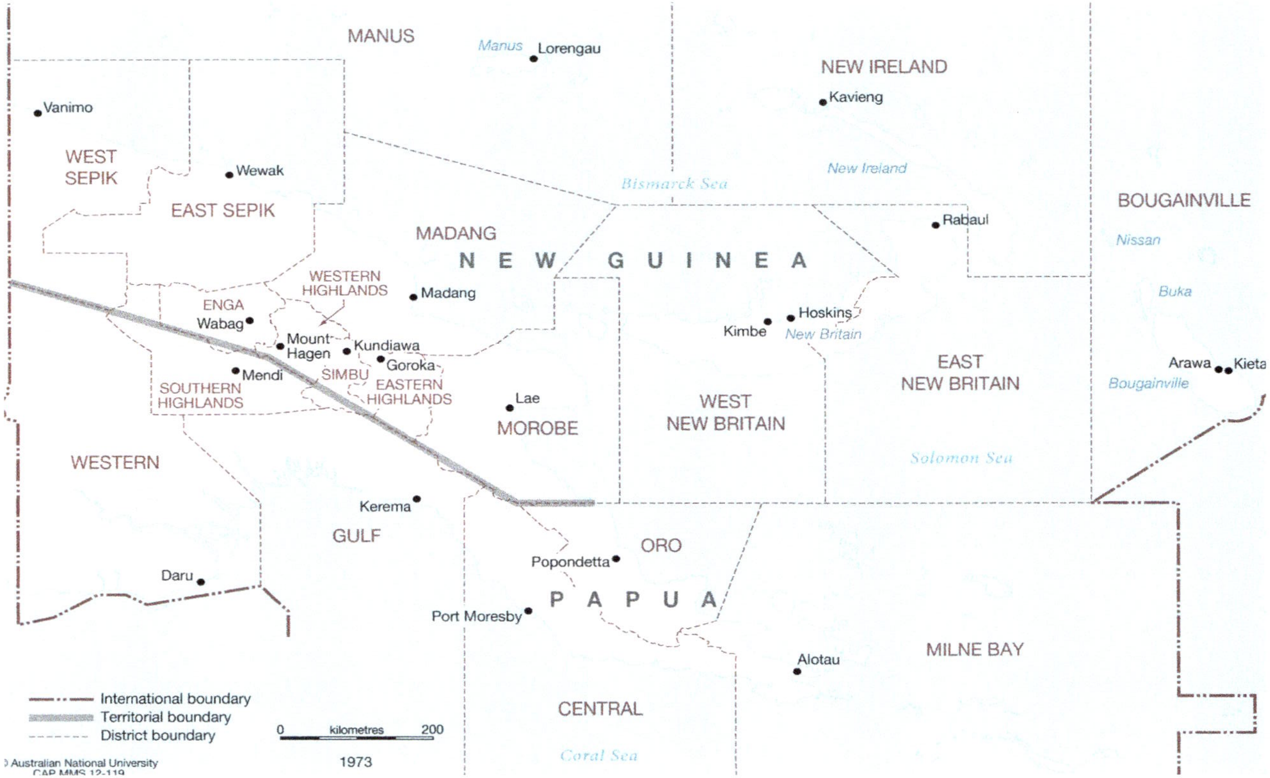

Map 0-1: Papua New Guinea

Source: Adapted from Government Printer of Australia 1976, redrawn by ANU Multimedia Services, 2012.

Introduction

The 'Badness' of Colonialism

There is now almost universal agreement 'that colonialism was bad'.[1] Even if there has been a degree of revisionism in recent years, as documented by William Easterly in favour of neo-trusteeship and 'postmodern imperialism', it is still common to find condemnation of colonial rule. Accounts abound of brutality by colonial officials against indigenous populations. There are numerous assessments which purport to have found a lack of growth, improvement in living standards and generalised political repression. Where colonial rule continued after World War II, the consequences are included in what another economist asserts is 'the failure of post-war development policy'.[2] While more measured accounts appear they are less influential.

The near-universal assessment of colonialism's damaging effects also is applicable to accounts of the South Pacific and particularly late colonial, post-World War II, Papua New Guinea (PNG). The views of influential former academic and ex-World Bank economist Helen Hughes are typical. Hughes is scathingly condemnatory, concluding that the colonial powers, particularly Australia, failed to bring growth and development. Hughes has asserted that although the South Pacific region 'has been stalled at the communal stage of development', nevertheless:

> the violence that was endemic in Pacific societies was held at bay during the colonial era by the imposition of security and probably more importantly, by rising living standards.[3]

How stalling at the communal stage was or could be associated with colonial authority and an improvement in welfare is not explained. Hughes also proposed that nostalgia about the colonial legacy is entirely misplaced. This is in part because:

> Colonial administration was almost entirely carried out by expatriates. Kiaps, other local administrators and Christian missions treated local populations as children. Roads, airfields, ports, water and electricity

---

1   William Easterly *The White Man's Burden: Why the West's Efforts to Aid the Rest Have Done So Much Harm and So Little Good* (New York: Penguin, 2006) p. 271
2   Dambisa Moyo *Dead Aid: Why Aid is Not Working and How There is a Better Way for Africa* (New York: Farrar, Strauss and Girou, 2009) p. xix
3   Helen Hughes 'Aid has failed the Pacific' *Issue Analysis* 7 May 2003, no. 33, p. 11, Ex-Kiap Network Forum, retrieved 12 September 2005 at <http://exkiap. net?articles/cis20030507-failed-aid/ia33.htm>

serviced urban areas where expatriates lived. Production and productivity were neglected except for expatriate plantations .... The prospects for independence were long denied (as they still are in the French colonies) so that when independence came to the Pacific as the result of global anti-colonisation agitation, Pacific populations were unprepared for it. Unpreparedness was a major cause of the difficulties the Pacific has encountered.[4]

Leaving aside for the moment the obvious internal inconsistencies in these two conclusions about colonialism in the region, of which PNG is the largest and most populous country, there is nothing original in Hughes' recent assertions. Indeed, as is shown later in this study, many of them were made during the 1950s and 1960s by critics of Australian rule and from a range of political positions. Then as now, critics located at distinct and distant places on the political spectrum borrow lines of argument from each other with a promiscuity that is striking.[5]

Against the current obsession with so-called evidence based policy, it needs to be recognised that assessing the nature and effects of colonial rule is not primarily an empirical matter. Undoubtedly there are difficulties and shortages of data, some of which are sketched in the Appendix of this book. Nor is it a matter of pointing out that Hughes, to continue with this critic, is simply empirically wrong. As is easily shown, late colonial authorities did not ignore smallholder production and pay attention only to plantations. Due in substantial measure to the work of colonial extension officers, by 1959 smallholders in the PNG Highlands had planted a greater area with coffee than had occurred on expatriate-owned large holdings. At least until the mid-1960s, the principal focus of Administration attention was directed at expanding household production of immediately consumed, locally and internationally marketed crops. This attention was largely successful. By 1965, the favourable results of the efforts to increase indigenous smallholder 'production and productivity' were known in Canberra and at the World Bank.

Across the late colonial period, intellectual and political contests were conducted about the nature of Australian rule over an indigenous population

---

4 Hughes 'Aid has failed the Pacific' p. 12. For a contrary and minority view of post-war Australian rule in PNG during some of the years covered in this book see Peter Ryan 'Papua New Guinea: the almost broken country' Keith Jackson & Friends: PNG Attitude 6 September 2012, retrieved 11 September 2012 at <http://asopa.typepad.com/asopa_people/2012/09/papua-new-guinea-the-almost-broken-country-nearing-90-peter-ryan-reflects-on-his-association-with-pn.html?cid=6a00d83454f2ec69e20177448bee17970d> which includes the sentence: 'For the 12 years from 1951 to 1963 it was possible to feel up-beat (rather than "sombre") about PNG's prospect of a successful transition from colony to thriving, independent modern state'.
5 Easterly *The White Man's Burden* commences Chapter Eight 'From Colonialism to Postmodern Imperialism' citing favourably FA Hayek, with whom he clearly empathises. Within a few pages he also draws upon the work of Mahmood Mamdani to bolster an anti-colonial argument, without even pausing to note that this ostensible similarity is nearly all the two have in common politically or ideologically (see pp. 269 onwards).

spread across a physically attractive as well as intimidatingly rugged land and sea scape. Many of the disputes are placed in their context later in this book. However the central purpose of the study is not to go over old ground but to re-examine the objectives and outcomes of the exercise of colonial rule during the approximately 30 years from 1945 until 1975 in contemporary terms, including the claims of Easterly, Moyo and Hughes.

As much as deficiencies in the assertions of anti-colonial critics can be shown to be empirically incorrect, there is a more important basis for re-considering the nature and effects of late colonial rule in PNG. Much of the disagreement has revolved around the terms of the assessment, of which there is a no more often applied expression than development. Did colonialism bring development? This remains a topic sure to provoke extreme reactions, most of them determinedly negative. Further, to argue against the predominant view may lead any proponent of such a position to being described as nostalgic, the ultimate form of condemnation along with romantic and utopian.

Yet if late colonialism in PNG did not bring development, there is an obvious paradox to be uncovered, a paradox which probably extends well beyond the PNG case. Throughout the entire period from 1945 until PNG's Independence, no term appeared more often than development as the objective of state policies. Australian officials intended to bring development through policy and practice. Further the same officials, from successive governments in the metropole, ministers of the responsible departments, through to the Administration in PNG held state power. Even their critics acknowledge the strength of the grip when making the claims that these same governments, departments and officials failed to make development happen. If development was perhaps 'the idea of the twentieth century',[6] late colonial officials in Australia and PNG inscribed this idea at the centre of what they aimed for and did. So having placed bringing development to the colony at the centre of state policy, and holding state power to effect the objective, the paradox at the centre of accounts which condemn colonialism lies in why did all the efforts over nearly three decades fail.

The short answer to these questions, provided in greater detail in the following pages, is that much of the difficulty of assessing what occurred in late colonial PNG lies in the idea of development itself. The continuing nostalgia surrounding development as a potential liberating force stifles understanding of what it represents: even such expressions as alternative development, balanced development and gender development remain imprisoned in a multitude of ways.

---

6   Ed Brown 'Deconstructing development: alternative perspectives on the history of an idea' *Journal of Historical Geography* 1996, vol. 22, no. 3, p. 333

Papua New Guinea as International Exemplar

For the purpose of examining wider issues about the nature and effects of postwar colonialism, PNG provides an especially instructive example. Indigenous existence had been substantially changed prewar in both the Australian colony of Papua and the former German colony, New Guinea, administered since the end of World War I by Australia as a League of Nations Mandated Territory. Particularly in the latter, the establishment and operation of plantations and mines had already transformed villages where the bulk of the indigenous population lived. The industrial requirements of these enterprises for unskilled and semi-skilled workers threatened household agricultural production heavily dependent upon family labour processes, for which male labour was especially critical in tasks that included clearing land. Large areas of unutilised and under-utilised land on plantations owned by international firms and European settlers testified in part to the extent of labour shortages. As the 1930s Depression passed and even before the war commenced the consequences for Papua New Guineans' lives of the demands for more workers was already of concern for colonial policy. The destructiveness of the military conflict elevated the apprehension regarding the indigenous population's future even further.

As a consequence of the Allied military victory and the establishment of the United Nations, in 1945 Australian authority was re-established over the colony of Papua and the now UN Trust Territory of New Guinea (see Map 0-1). In 1949, the two territories were united administratively, even though for international legal and political purposes the separate entities remained. Australian governments submitted separate reports on Papua and New Guinea to the United Nations. In 1973, the territories attained self-government as PNG, and two years later became the independent nation-state of that name. Over the 30 years after World War II, the population probably increased from about 1.5 million to less than double that number.

During the war, a particular phrase became central to official considerations of what was to be Australian policy for PNG once the fighting ended. That phrase, 'the paramountcy of native interests' had been borrowed from a major policy document on Kenya, the 1923 Devonshire White Paper. The Paper prioritised the trusteeship responsibility of the British Government for African welfare against the competing claims of European settlers and Indians, especially over land for large holdings. After the 1940s the expression faded from official use for PNG, and the central purpose of Australian colonial trusteeship became guardianship. Even in the 1950s and 1960s, as colonial rule ended in other colonies, Australian officials continued to invoke this purpose.

However guardianship was an idea which retained the primacy and sharpened the meaning of 'native interests', while also maintaining Australian government responsibility for what occurred. Households occupying smallholdings with increased output of crops and improved living standards became the embodiment of the 'natives' whose 'interests' became central for colonial policy. Explaining why guardianship took this particular meaning for colonial trusteeship policy, as it did in PNG, assists in overcoming continuing tendencies to treat colonialism as a uni-dimensional phenomenon along the lines favoured by critics.

Just as importantly, as the Conclusion to this account argues, the outcomes associated with guardianship invite consideration of Australian rule and the late colonial state in PNG in an even broader context. That context is the current extended debate over whether the advance of capitalism is facilitated, even accelerated, by a particular relationship between specific holders of state power and the character of the capitalist state. The shorthand employed to describe the continuing controversy is the developmental state debate.[7] Was the postwar colonial state in PNG developmental? Should late colonial PNG be considered part of the developmental state lineage which so far has been confined to independent nation-states—Japan, South Korea, Taiwan, Mexico and others—engaged in rapid manufacturing expansion?

The emphasis upon smallholder agriculture was not, of course, confined to Australian colonial policy for PNG. It was elevated in French policy from the 1920s and by British officials after World War II, as with the 1954 Swynnerton Plan for Kenya. Aware of instances from other colonies, Australian officials even employed knowledge gained from these attempts to expand smallholder production. However nowhere else, to my knowledge, was the focus upon expanding smallholder agriculture so dominant and determinant. In Kenya, to cite one case where planning for increased smallholder production was prominent at the same time as in PNG, these efforts nevertheless had to contend with the Mau Mau revolt in central Kenya. In that colony the political force of African nationalism was not always supportive of Administration aims to expand household production and considerably dampened the effectiveness of colonial government efforts in this direction during the run-up to Independence.

In this study of Australian policy and its consequences for late colonial PNG, the concentration upon smallholder agriculture as the principal focus of efforts to bring development receives most attention. The account of the centrality of rural households centres upon three major propositions. The first is that the colonial state during much of the period played an important part in bringing

---

7   For a brief explanation of the purpose behind the original argument by its originator, see: Chalmers Johnson 'The Developmental State: Odyssey of a Concept' in Meredith Woo-Cumings (ed.) *The Developmental State* (Ithaca: Cornell University Press, 1999) p. 32.

development, conceived as securing village life, where the bulk of the population lived, at higher living standards. Despite some current empirical and other difficulties associated with establishing the validity of this proposition, it is shown here how the bulk of the population was secured upon 'their land' where increased production and consumption occurred. The importance of colonial policy and practice for this outcome is demonstrated.

The second proposition is contrary to the predominant view that colonialism necessarily leads to under-development or just non-development, and acts in favour of 'foreign interests'. Until the mid-1960s at least, officials quite deliberately refused to provide support for those forms of commerce, mainly international and expatriate owned which were regarded as potentially destructive of village life. Barriers were constructed against their operation. In simple terms, there was no favourable bias toward plantations, as Hughes and others have claimed. The intention to anticipate and block what were considered as negative dimensions of capitalism's spontaneous development, including landlessness, was an especially important basis for postwar colonial policy.

The third proposition relates to contemporary arguments about the consequences of colonial trusteeship. Again contrary to existing literature which is derogatory toward colonial officials, bearers of the 'white man's burden',[8] this account suggests the need for a re-examination of the developmental impact of trusteeship. Australian colonial officials, some of whom were trenchant anti-colonial nationalists, were early advocates of the need to develop a strong economic base for an independent nation-state. Almost until the end of the 1960s, Australian policy did not advocate any 'rushing to elections before economic growth ... got underway'.[9] If anything, the criticisms were that too much emphasis was placed on the increases in production and consumption and not enough on political reform.

Trusteeship or guardianship also was critical to secure village life dominated by smallholder households against threats posed by the emerging class of indigenous capitalists, today's much vaunted and valued entrepreneurs. The threat these posed to development became apparent during the transition to Independence in 1975, when securing village life became a more contested objective of government policy as Papua New Guinean representatives of the capitalist class came to power.

However as I argue in the Conclusion to this book, the PNG case presented here has an even wider significance than simply providing the location for an examination of development in a relatively small, low population South Pacific country. It is well known that particularly after World War II, under domestic

---

8   Easterly *The White Man's Burden*
9   Niall Ferguson 'Foreword' in Dambisa Moyo *Dead Aid* p. xi

and international pressures, colonial administrations tried to speed up economic growth and reform governing institutions in some colonies. However so far there has been no attempt to link what occurred under late colonial authority to another argument about the nature of the capitalist state and development in 'newly industrializing countries' (NICs). This argument is characterised by the expression the developmental state, and has been used mainly to examine a number of sovereign East Asian countries. This study concludes with the proposition that late colonialism in PNG should be characterised as belonging within the lineage of developmental states. The changes wrought in the colony make possible an extension of the argument about the capitalist state's role to circumstances where the principal form of bringing development was through agriculture, not manufacturing as in the other cases previously considered.

The Meaning and Influence of Development

The idea of development which influenced colonial officials and Papua New Guineans was not synonymous with, nor reducible to, other descriptors of change, including improvement, progress and economic growth. While the history of development's distinctiveness is provided elsewhere,[10] in order to understand the specific argument which follows it is necessary to briefly summarise the main features of this highly influential modern idea.

As a response to the disorder and unemployment which followed the Napoleonic Wars in Western Europe, the modern idea of development was invented. The aim of development's creators was to transcend earlier thought which described the process of change that early industrialisation brought in positive terms, especially progress. Identifying negative consequences of this process of change was intended to provide the basis for ameliorative action. In recognising both positive and negative effects of industrialisation, the modern idea of development was invented as a description of, and prescription for joining what were understood as two processes of change. The first process was considered to be spontaneous, as in the spontaneous development of capitalism moved by 'the invisible hand' or market forces. The second process was intentional, the appropriate subjective or willed response to the negative consequences of spontaneous development. Intentional development meant the application through the state of deliberate, intended policies, to counter what was negative, destructive in the first process. Disorder, including unemployment and impoverishment, which had come

---

10   Robert A Nisbet *Social Change and History: aspects of the western theory of development* (New York: Oxford University Press, 1969); Robert Nisbet *History of the Idea of Progress* (New York: Basic Books, 1980); Heinz W Arndt *Economic Development: The History of an Idea* (University of Chicago Press, 1987); MP Cowen and RW Shenton *Doctrines of Development* (London: Routledge, 1996); and Scott MacWilliam *Development and Agriculture in Late Colonial Papua New Guinea* PhD thesis, ANU (2009)

to be seen as inherent in the process of spontaneous development was to be counteracted, negated through intentional development without overturning what is best described as the external authority of capital.[11] From the outset, development was an idea of reform not revolution.

Because the modern idea of development was formulated as a unity of the two processes, spontaneous development and intentional development, it has retained the positive as well as negative components of the former process. The positives, increases in production and the potential for improvements in living standards remain central to the current popular usage of development as meaning economic growth. However other necessary but negative consequences of spontaneous development, including unemployment and various forms of disorder, continue to appear. Their presence provides a major force underlying the intention to overcome such effects, thereby extending development to include both spontaneous and intentional forms of change.

As this study shows, both dimensions of development were highly influential for Australian officials, academics and others, whether or not these people were based in the metropolitan country or the colony. By the 1960s and early 1970s, the idea of development also had become central to the thought and policy prescriptions of the most ardent nationalists, indigenous and expatriate, in PNG. In the passage to Independence in 1975, as the hold on state power passed from the Australian Government and colonial administration officials to Papua New Guineans, development continued to influence state officials and policy. The idea had become so entrenched among the indigenous population that school children in Bougainville described the effect of the European presence on the island in terms of its contribution to development.[12]

In order to make development happen it is necessary to move from intention to design. In the explanation employed by Cowen and Shenton:

> An intention to develop becomes a doctrine of development when it [the intention: SM] is attached, or when it is pleaded that it be attached, to the agency of the state to become an expression of state policy.[13]

A doctrine or codification of development provides the structure by which a particular design is shaped to direct policy. In the case of late colonial PNG, an agrarian doctrine underpinned the postwar colonial administration's efforts to bring development.

---

11   Cowen & Shenton *Doctrines* pp. 1–59
12   Alexander Marmak and Richard Bedford 'Bougainville's Students' *New Guinea* 1974, vol. 9, no. 1, pp. 4–15
13   Cowen & Shenton *Doctrines* p. xviii

Securing Village Life and the Agrarian Doctrine for PNG

The role of agriculture in thought about development was especially important during the late colonial period. Increasing agricultural production was envisaged as the main form which economic growth should take in order to satisfy the output increases and improved living standards, both objectives of development thought. For the Australian colonial authorities, the principal basis for the increases was to lift output by households occupying smallholdings, parcels of land usually from less than one to three hectares in size. One positive dimension of development, growth in production, was to be attained by utilising household labour processes upon smallholdings to grow crops for immediate and marketed consumption at raised levels of production. Exchanging income earned from marketed crops for goods, either grown locally or manufactured through industrial processes in other countries, was intended to lift living standards, improve welfare and maintain what was conceived of as rural community or communities. To achieve such ends, state coordination and supervision of households were placed at the centre of the colonial agrarian doctrine of development.[14]

Postwar development thought envisaged a major break with the previous orthodoxy in Papua and New Guinea. It was also to distance 'native agriculture' in the colony and trust territory from that which Australian colonial officials understood to be predominant in other colonies, including Ghana in British West Africa. In these territories, production of export crops, particularly cocoa, was envisaged as taking an especially disorganised, spontaneous form of peasant farming. This farming was considered to have resulted in low productivity, vulnerability to crop diseases and the production of inferior quality bulk cocoa.

The smallholders or household producers in postwar PNG were to be distinct from peasant farmers elsewhere on two principal grounds: the first being the object of production and the second, the methods of production. The latter included the labour processes employed and the relationship of the indigenous producers to the state, in the form of the colonial administration. When framing policy for PNG, peasant farmers in other countries were conceived first and foremost as driven by the objective of meeting immediate consumption needs as a form of simple reproduction, subsistence production and consumption. What marketed production or purchased consumption as did occur in peasant households was envisaged by colonial officials in PNG as only fulfilling low levels

---

14 Huntley LR Wright *State Practice and Rural Smallholder Production: Late-Colonialism and the Agrarian Doctrine in Papua New Guinea, 1942–1969* PhD thesis, Massey University (1999) provides an exemplary treatment of the doctrine.

of need. Household producers, instead, would engage in marketed production for local and international markets, while also growing food and other crops for immediate consumption. Both would occur to meet continuously increasing levels of need, or higher living standards.

Secondly, for peasant farmers, relatively undifferentiated family labour processes were the principal forms of labour employed, and the state's role was largely confined to facilitating the maintenance of subsistence at low levels. In the agrarian doctrine of development formulated for postwar PNG state coordination and supervision was a prerequisite for systematically increasing household production and consumption. Improved welfare would follow primarily through commercialised production and consumption, including of crops marketed locally and internationally. Unlike the peasant farming envisaged by Australian officials, which was deemed to be incapable of further improvement, household production was not to be a terminal stage.[15] Instead with close coordination and supervision through the colonial state, in PNG households were expected to be capable of continuous development, resulting in increased incomes and consumption of purchased goods.

During the 1950s, colonial officials and the policies they constructed framed the distinction between household producers and peasant farming in an especially sharp form. According to one of the key colonial officials responsible for emphasising the difference, villages, as the previous focus of administrative attention, were too small and an inadequate basis for moving the indigenous population beyond the mythical ideal of 'the sturdy peasant farmer', unrealised 'anywhere in the world'.[16] Instead the movement required a reshaping of the colonial administrative structure and official roles so as to more closely coordinate and supervise household production to further raise output and consumption. A central feature of the policy was to further encourage a shift away from 'communal farming' toward individualised household production, even if it was politically and administratively difficult to change the legal basis of land ownership from the existing customary tenure.

Because the prevailing idea of development also sought to deal with the negative consequences of growth, colonial thought and the agrarian doctrine

---

15   For arguments which cast household production in PNG as peasant farming, see: Diana Howlett 'Terminal development: From tribalism to peasantry' in Harold Brookfield (ed.) *The Pacific in Transition: Geographical Perspectives on Adaptation and Change* (London: Edward Arnold, 1973) pp. 249–273; Rolf Gerritsen *Groups, Classes and Peasant Politics in Ghana and Papua New Guinea* PhD thesis, ANU (1979) p. 20; Peter Fitzpatrick 'The Creation and Containment of the Papua New Guinea Peasantry' in E Wheelwright and K Buckley (eds) *Essays in the Political Economy of Australian Capitalism* vol. 4 (Sydney: ANZ Book Co., Sydney, 1980) pp. 85–121; L Grossman *Peasants, Subsistence Ecology and Development in the Highlands of Papua New Guinea* (Princeton University Press, 1984) p. 14; Barry Shaw *Agriculture in the Papua New Guinea Economy* Discussion Paper no. 20 (Port Moresby: Institute of National Affairs, 1985).

16   NAA: M331/1 35 *D. Fienberg—Correspondence* 17 April 1956, Fienberg to Director of Department of Native Affairs, p. 12

paid attention to the need to restrain international and local manifestations of the spontaneous development of capitalism. For colonial officials in post-World War II PNG, constraining plantations and other commercial enterprises which employed wage labour was necessary to check the formation of a landless proletariat. Particularly in the 20 years after the military conflict ended, this meant preventing further increases in the area of land occupied by large holdings which employed labour under wage and other arrangements.[17] Securing village life as the desired form of (classless) community remained the favoured objective,[18] which later came to have wide support among educated and politically active Papua New Guineans.

Development requires developers. Colonial officials subject to international scrutiny, imbued with the idea that a central purpose of holding state power was to bring development were well placed to act as trustees, or developers. That they were also barred by policy and regulations from holding state positions and engaging in private accumulation further increased their capacity as developers. The 1960s and 1970s accession to power of Papua New Guineans who joined holding senior public service positions with private commercial activities brought to the fore what had been central to the developmental capacity of their colonial counterparts, who had been barred from straddling between public employment and private accumulation. What is now almost universally condemned as corruption among PNG's politicians and other state officials indicates that the passage from colonial authority to Independence included a reduced capacity of the holders of state power to be trustees, developers making development happen.

Outline of Argument

The book commences with a brief description of the origins of the modern idea of development. Chapter One also shows how the idea was reformed during the first half of the twentieth century in Australia and for colonial rule in PNG. 'Positive Australianism', with the 'paramountcy of native interests' foremost encapsulated the change of direction for policy makers in Canberra and the

---

17   The establishment during the 1950s of coffee plantations on leasehold land in the Eastern and Western Highlands provinces is the most important exception to the general point. Even here, expatriates acquired the bulk of the leaseholds in a very short period, from 1952 to 1954; cf. Paul Hasluck *A Time for Building Australian Administration in Papua and New Guinea 1951–1963* (Melbourne University Press, 1976) pp. 118–25; Ian Downs *The Australian Trusteeship Papua New Guinea 1945–75* (Canberra: Australian Government Publishing Service, 1980) pp. 174–186.
18   The most substantial treatment of this objective remains Wright *State Practice*; see also Huntley LR Wright 'Contesting community: the labour question and colonial reform in the post-war Territory of Papua and New Guinea 1942–1946' *The Journal of Pacific Studies* 2001, vol. 25, no. 1, pp. 69–94.

colony. The change also signalled that postwar policy would emphasise making development happen rather than letting the spontaneous process of development which gave primacy to private enterprises regain the ascendancy.

However postwar circumstances internationally, in Australia and PNG combined to make the application of development intent especially problematic. The Allied military victory confirmed that recovering from the effects of the 1930s Depression and the military conflict in the South Pacific would take place under the external authority of capitalism. Production and trade for most of the world's population was governed by profitability, the re-assertion of the private accumulation of capital. While steps could be taken to rebuild where wartime damage had been especially severe, and attempts to revert to the prewar dominance of plantations blocked, how the new policy direction giving primacy to indigenous smallholding agriculture could be implemented was both more and less certain. Chapter Two documents the uncertainties involved in re-establishing accumulation and giving development a new shape.

In these circumstances, colonial policy and practice came to be determined by politicians and other public officials wedded to a particular view of development. With a Liberal-Country Party coalition holding power in Australia from 1949 until 1972, the view was primarily that of liberal developers. Committed to the extension of private property rights, and suspicious of the tendencies inherent in capitalism to centralise and concentrate property in fewer hands, these developers took the internationally determined conditions of trusteeship in a specific direction, emphasising guardianship. Chapter Three shows how this direction, which became known as uniform or even development, was framed and implemented during the 1950s as state policy.

Chapter Four extends the examination of what happened under uniform development, with reference to both the spontaneous and intended processes of change. This is done mainly through a detailed consideration of the expansion of two crops, coffee and cocoa, which were successful outcomes of colonial policy. This policy aimed to increase production and consumption by smallholders in some of the most populous areas of the country. The third crop examined more briefly is rice, where despite a major commitment of official resources, little increase in production occurred. Instead imported rice, primarily grown by farmers using irrigation and industrial machinery in Australia, became a more important item for household consumption. This change indicated how the reproduction of labour power in the colony was determined by international industrial as well as by domestic household processes.

Chapter Five documents how during the 1960s the success and constraints of uniform development provided a platform for a major change in colonial policy, from uniform to accelerated development. Although by the late 1950s some of the limits of the already substantial increases in household production were already obvious and forcing changes in official policy, capitalism's 'growth obsession' demanded even more.[19] Using what could be construed as support from the World Bank, and the departure of the main political and administrative advocates of uniform development from colonial policy-making circles, a new direction was plotted by the Australian authorities. Even as the effects of the continuing major expansion in smallholder plantings of export crops were becoming apparent with trees and bushes yielding fruit, emphasis shifted to new crops and a major mine on Bougainville.

Change also occurred in a political direction, as electoral and other reforms necessary for the transition to self-government and independence became important. There was increasing criticism of official policy and stronger expressions of indigenous political and commercial ambitions. The postwar international anti-colonial mood extended to PNG, including in terms which challenged accelerated development's benefits for indigenes. The chapter continues the examination of what was occurring in the production and marketing of coffee and cocoa, in the international and domestic arenas.

Chapter Six shows how from the late 1960s until Independence in 1975 Australian colonial authority passed to indigenous politicians and other officials. At the surface it appeared that as had happened after World War II, there was uncertainty about the meaning of development and how it could be made to happen. From the surprise 1972 election victory of a coalition led by Michael Somare until Independence in 1975 there were continuing political and administrative tussles over the shape the new nation-state would take. There was also uncertainty about the main components of government policy, as accelerated development became unfashionable and advice was provided along lines that followed a change occurring internationally in development thought.

However of greater significance for these years and after Independence than the obvious tussle over policy direction was the change that had become apparent in political and state power. Until the 1960s, development policy had been predicated on the need to reign in private accumulators, expatriate as well as indigenous. Keeping both in check commercially and politically was central to uniform development. Some of the constraints were lessened during the 1960s. The continuing growth in smallholder production and consumption also opened more space for indigenous capitalists, including in processing as well as trading crops. The political representatives of the indigenous bourgeois and would-be bourgeois became especially prominent with their anti-colonial utterances facilitating success particularly at the 1972 House of Assembly elections.

---

19   Elmar Altvater 'The Growth Obsession' in Leo Panitch and Colin Leys (eds) *A World of Contradictions Socialist Register 2002* (London: Merlin, 2001) pp. 73–92

Although all sides in the political tussles still emphasised their intention to bring development, during the pre-Independence period uncertainty did not indicate the postwar conditions but increasing conflict between indigenes, particularly over land. In the main agricultural areas of the country, notably the Highlands and the Gazelle Peninsula, landless, smallholders and indigenes with ambitions to acquire large holdings from departing expatriates battled over the terms of the post-colonial settlement. While the government and officials struggled to resolve these conflicting demands, other ambitious indigenes injected both separatist and secessionist claims into the process of setting the territorial boundaries of the new nation-state and the terms of the National Constitution.

The Conclusion joins a particular condition that characterised PNG's population at Independence, and continues to be of importance, with an international argument about development. Over the postwar years discussed in this book, even as the population almost doubled most people remained rural dwellers, secured on small holdings. Numerous commentators, expatriate and indigenous, have noted this feature of PNG and spoken of it favourably. The 'survival of the village as a viable and attractive, or potentially attractive, social and economic unit in many rural areas' seems to need no explanation for many who comment on this characteristic.[20] As PNG's first Prime Minister, now Grand Chief Sir Michael Somare explained: 'Whenever I went home on leave, I regarded myself not as a teacher but as a village man, and I behaved like everyone else'.[21] However the nature and effect of colonial development policy is rarely noted as having been a substantial factor in (re)securing village life, immediately after the destruction of World War II and subsequently.

Yet as shown in this book, for at least two decades after the war colonial policy intended both the development of capitalism in the form of commercialised production and consumption for the indigenous population, and secured attachment to land at improved living standards for smallholding households. Only in the 1960s was this direction challenged. Even then the weight of the earlier uniform development drive remained powerful. The shift to towns of the mid to late 1960s was a significant change but one which only involved a relatively small proportion of the population. How did the increased commercialisation of production and consumption with sustained occupation of smallholdings by the bulk of the population occur?

In the Conclusion I suggest that understanding postwar PNG can be enhanced by drawing upon an explanation constructed for industrialisation in several

---

20   Ross Garnaut 'The Framework of Economic Policy-Making' in John A Ballard (ed.) *Policy-Making in a New State: Papua New 1972–77* (St Lucia: Queensland University Press, 1981) pp. 161–162
21   Sir Michael Somare *Sana: an autobiography of Michael Somare* (Port Moresby: Nuigini Press, 1975) p. 41

East Asian countries and more recently Mexico.[22] While this argument so far has been concerned to explain capitalist development through manufacturing industry in independent nation-states, here several of the central propositions are enlarged through consideration of what occurred as agrarian development under colonial rule in PNG. The lineage of the developmental state should be extended to this colony, at least, and perhaps to others where capitalism was advanced by locking households upon smallholdings. If this is the case then there would seem to be implications for other studies of colonialism, and also for the formalistic Marxism against which Jairus Banaji and others have cautioned.[23]

---

22   John Minns *The Politics of Developmentalism: the Midas states of Mexico, South Korea, and Taiwan* (Basingstoke: Palgrave Macmillan, 2006)

23   Jairus Banaji *Theory as History: Essays on Modes of Production and Exploitation* (Chicago: Haymarket Books, 2011) esp. ch. 2 'Modes of Production in a Materialist Conception of History', which originally appeared in *Capital and Class* 1977, no. 3, pp. 1–44.

1. The International Idea of Development Reformed

Introduction

The idea of development which became so important for late colonial PNG has a lineage extending back at least to early nineteenth century Europe. The first part of this chapter outlines the most important elements of the idea of development and its evolution before becoming influential for PNG.

From the late nineteenth century the idea of development had begun to affect policy in Australia, Papua and New Guinea. The second section of the chapter shows how, from the late nineteenth century until the outbreak of World War II, Australian colonial policy was informed by an idea which emphasised the importance of immanent, spontaneous development led by private firms and expatriate planters. With this continuing focus, Australian policy toward PNG lagged behind changes that had begun to occur in British and French colonies, where intentional development was becoming more important.

Australian thinking about colonial development in PNG—as distinct from their official policy towards—began to change in response to the economic and political turmoil of the 1930s and early 1940s. In the process Australia was catching up with international trends in thinking about development. Part three describes the nature of the shift in official Australian thinking from the 1930s. During World War II, when the description 'positive Australianism' was first coined, the changes—particularly regarding trusteeship—helped shape international thought about postwar reconstruction and development.

During and immediately after World War II, the official Australian idea of what development policy would constitute for PNG and the indigenous population was sharpened. Part four of the chapter describes the outcome and process which was central to further defining and implementing 'positive Australianism'. Deliberate steps were taken to ensure that development would not resume along prewar lines. The Australian reformulation was largely settled even when the immediate capacity of the postwar administration to advance the development objectives was limited.

The Modern Idea and Doctrines of Development

Invention and Design

Development refers to both an idea about how change should occur, and to a process by which change could be made to happen in a desired, positive direction. The onset and advance of industrial capitalism in Western Europe produced enthusiasts about the changes, including Adam Smith, for whom the process was immanent, spontaneous and the basis of progress. There were also critics who came from a range of political-ideological positions, and included the English radical conservative, William Cobbett.[1]

However for present purposes, by far the most significant objection to the idea and process came at the end of the eighteenth and beginning of the nineteenth centuries from a group of French intellectuals who would be known by the name of their leading figure, Henri de Saint-Simon. The Saint-Simonians, including Auguste Comte:

> posed the same problems that had inspired Adam Smith: the creation of order in a society undergoing radical transformation and the nature of that transformation itself. The answers they provided were, however, markedly different.[2]

In early nineteenth century Europe, ideas about specific undesirables or negatives of growth and progress were especially prominent. The unemployment and disorder of post-Napoleonic Europe prompted the initial formulation of the modern idea of development in response to these conditions.

That is, development was invented to express the need and the basis for framing a solution to that which appeared desirable as well as undesirable. Because unemployment and disorder were seen to arise as necessary, objective features of spontaneous development, which also brought the increases in productivity and welfare that were seen as progress, any response had to counter the former while retaining the advances. A positive, intended response could provide a means to overcome that which was negative without rejecting spontaneous development's benefits. Accordingly development as an idea had two components, spontaneous development and intentional development.

While the Saint-Simonians were not alone in their diagnosis of capitalism's ills, they were, in Cowen and Shenton's words, important because of the extent to

---

1 I have previously documented the empathy felt by Australian Territories Minister Paul Hasluck (1951–1963) for Cobbett's objections to the effects of industrialisation. See Scott MacWilliam 'Liberalism and the End of Development: Partington against Hasluck and Coombs' *Island* July 1997, Issue 70, pp. 79–91.
2 Cowen & Shenton *Doctrines* p. 22

which they 'attempted to impose constructive order upon what they took to be industrial disorder of the present'.[3] By rejecting metaphysics, and emphasising the connection between empirical methods for understanding the past and the capacity to predict the future, the Saint-Simonians formulated the positivist basis of the idea of development.

Two features of this history of the idea of development need to be emphasised here and placed in the circumstances of colonial PNG. Firstly, at its invention development did not represent an objection to the positive or desirable consequences of growth, including improved living standards. Development was not framed to supplant that which Smith and others regarded as an essential feature of industrial advance, its spontaneous or immanent character. Secondly, the purpose of intentional development was to make productive that which had become unproductive or under-utilised because of growth's negative consequences, including unemployment and disorder.

As a result of the earlier experience elsewhere and the influence of the idea of development, Australian officials emphasised the importance of anticipating the possible negative consequences of industrial capitalism, particularly in the forms of plantation agriculture and mining. However their thought also retained an emphasis upon the perceived benefits of spontaneous development, increased productivity and raised living standards. While development policy, including for PNG, was framed in anticipation of the possibility, even certainty that if left unchecked the spontaneous process of industrial capitalism would result in unemployment, policy also placed a major emphasis upon encouraging further growth. Thus while there was continuing concern that industrialisation would lead to unemployment and the destruction of 'village life', which was idealised as the local form of classless community, there was also a policy emphasis upon encouraging productivity increases through other, mainly smallholding agricultural, forms of production.

As a reforming idea constructed during industrial capitalism's rise, development accepted, indeed was even framed to secure 'the external authority of capital'.[4] In the PNG case, capitalism as incessant accumulation and persistent competition between capitals was always present. Development policy endorsed the logic of capital accumulation while encouraging a specific form of production, namely smallholder agriculture. The power of capitalism's focus upon accumulation ensured that the possibility of intentional development being effected to counter the negatives of spontaneous development, including the tendency to create unemployment, was always uncertain.

---

3   Cowen & Shenton *Doctrines* pp. 24–25

4   Cowen & Shenton *Doctrines* p. xv. This acceptance was of course the basis of Marx' and Engels' criticism of the Saint-Simonians as utopian socialists.

However, the process of accumulation is itself always conditional since it is driven by the struggle between capital and labour to raise the rate of surplus value,[5] and the competition between capitals over the appropriation of shares of that surplus.[6] Even in the absence of generalised, substantial threats to accumulation, including depressions and wars, the continuous pressure on capitals to accumulate also generate conditions, including unemployment, which may justify the pursuit of intentional development.

That is, the process of immanent, spontaneous development may set off a political reaction either favouring or against constructive development. If the latter reaction occurs, then non-development, spontaneous development unmodified by intentional development prevails. One such occasion, when non-development was dominant, was of considerable importance for the twentieth century shaping of development as idea and doctrine. But before exploring this moment, two other central features of the modern idea of development need to be outlined.

Firstly, how are development policies formulated and by whom? Secondly, once intentional development has been designed, how is it implemented? Trustees are an important element in the answer to both questions. Instead of individual capitalists, driven solely by the imperative of accumulation, intentional development necessitates trusteeship exercised by holders of political power. To make development happen such trustees must be able to bring state power to bear in accordance with a vision of what is required to deal with the negative consequences of the spontaneous process of development.

The existence of the intent to develop and powerful trustees are the necessary conditions for the construction of a doctrine of development, a systematic form of intentional development.[7] The two most substantial forms which a doctrine of development has taken thus far are agrarian and manufacturing.[8]

After development's initial formulation in early nineteenth century Europe, the idea of development travelled back and forth between metropolitan countries and their colonies, linking conditions in each to the other. Unemployment in industrial Britain, as during the last decades of the nineteenth century, could be resolved through the expansion of markets in the colonies for British

---

5   Karl Marx *Capital: A Critique of Political Economy* vol. 1 (Harmondsworth: Penguin, 1976)
6   Marx *Capital: A Critique of Political Economy* vol. 2 (Harmondsworth: Penguin, 1978); Dick Bryan 'Monopoly in Marxist method' *Capital and Class* Summer 1985, no. 26, pp. 72–92 makes the point that 'monopoly is to be regarded as a form of competition rather than its antithesis' (p. 72). Geoffrey Kay *Development and Underdevelopment: A Marxist Analysis* (London: Macmillan, 1976) provides the seminal account of the effect of the tussle between industrial and merchant capital for the process of development and under-development.
7   Cowen & Shenton *Doctrines* p. viii
8   Cowen & Shenton *Doctrines* pts 2 & 3, ch. 4–7

manufactured goods. For some influential officials, including British Colonial Secretary Joseph Chamberlain (1896–1903), state-sponsored development of agriculture and manufacturing at home also meant constructive development of colonies. Rural unemployment and urban impoverishment as well as fears about Britain's long-term decline as an industrial power, prompted rethinking about colonies as outlets for investment and as markets.[9]

As this book shows, during the twentieth century development as an idea continued to be transformed by the intersection of concerns in industrial metropolitan countries and primarily agrarian colonies. The international shaping of development as an agrarian doctrine became of critical significance. The next section outlines the process by which further change occurred.

Fabian Development and Agrarian Priority

After the 1906 electoral defeat of the British Government in which Chamberlain was Colonial Secretary successive British governments refused or failed to apply Chamberlain's imperial development project. The antipathy toward intentional development lasted into the inter-war years and during the Great Depression. The parallels with the dominance of spontaneous development and the weakness of developmental intent in colonial policy during the late nineteenth century and into the inter-war years in Papua and New Guinea are striking, as indicated below.

However, during this period circumstances including war and economic turmoil also began to change in favour of a new phase of developmental intent, which had a strong Fabian influence. During the late nineteenth and early twentieth century, Fabians had focused upon Britain as their field for development. However during the inter-war years Fabians extended their interests beyond the metropolitan terrain to a concern for colonial development. That extension influenced Australians formulating late colonial development policy in PNG. An especially clear expression of the shift in development thought, from concern with metropolitan to colonial conditions, occurred in relation to Africa, and particularly Kenya.

After World War I, the growing conflict over land and labour between indigenous Africans, European settlers and Asians (Indians) with aspirations to extend beyond commerce into large holding agriculture in Kenya forced the British Government to explicitly spell out the basis of its colonial policy. A 1923 White Paper, known popularly as the Devonshire Declaration after the British noble who lead a mission to examine conditions in Kenya provided direction for policy makers. The Paper set out the central principle, declaring that British

---

9   Cowen & Shenton *Doctrines* p. 274

policy for land and labour should follow a direction expressed by the phrase 'the paramountcy of native interests'.[10] This expression subsequently travelled widely, including as will be shown, into Australian policy for PNG. The White Paper concluded that both Europeans and Asians were only to be allowed to advance to the extent that 'native interests' were not damaged. This effectively blocked Asian capital from moving into large holding agriculture and restrained further European settler expansion. Although it took a further 30 years to change the pronouncement of policy intent from an essentially negative injunction into a positive direction promoting African smallholder agriculture, the White Paper was nevertheless important for Kenya, and became so for PNG.

In 1925, at the British Labour Party's twenty-fifth annual conference, for the first time a major debate was conducted on colonial policy. This debate marked an important step for Fabians trying to influence the holders of state power. The outcome meant that the Fabian sense of trusteeship was inserted into Labour policy, 'to socialise' rather than 'to smash' the British Empire.[11] Garnished with the claim that it was socialist, this new trusteeship aimed to provide a moral basis for colonialism, and colonial development. To distinguish this trusteeship from earlier forms, leading Fabians identified a third British Empire distinct from the two previous 'old' empires, of the white colonies, India and the Caribbean. According to Sidney Olivier, leading Fabian, member of the Labour Party and Secretary of State for India, the third Empire:

> was created according to two motives: Firstly, to secure on economic grounds, sources of materials and minerals which would have been appropriated by other powers: Secondly, to protect Africans "from destruction and exploitation".[12]

The reformulated focus for trusteeship, which justified the retention of colonies, also brought the matter of land ownership and distribution in the metropole and the overseas territories to the fore. Colonial trusteeship, in the hands of a British Labour Party guided by Fabian precepts, made it possible to imagine a political alliance of working people extending from the industrial working class of Britain to the peasants of the colonies. The alliance, *its advocates intended*, would be united against oppression and exploitation by capitalism which was considered to be the major barrier to development. Importantly, colonial trusteeship was informed by an opposition to the further extension of wage labour and capitalist exploitation. Indigenous land rights were to be

---

10   JH Oldham, Secretary of the International Missionary Council may well have coined the phrase. See Carl G Rosberg Jr and John Nottingham *The Myth of "Mau Mau": Nationalism in Kenya* (Nairobi: East African Publishing House, 1966) pp. 68–69.

11   MP Cowen and RW Shenton *The Roots of Trusteeship: The Moral Basis of Fabian Colonialism; Development and Agrarian Bias* Working Paper 18, Department of Economics, Faculty of Business, City of London Polytechnic, 1992, p. 1

12   Cowen & Shenton *The Roots of Trusteeship*, p. 3

protected and secured as the basis for colonial development. At the same time, by securing peasants upon land in the colonies, it would not be possible for *one set of workers* to be used as a source of cheap labour to undercut the wages and conditions of *other workers* in the industrialised metropolitan countries, including Britain. Thus Fabian colonialism provided a moral basis for imperial and colonial development.

Fabian colonialism also implanted a very strong agrarian orientation at the centre of schemes for metropolitan and colonial development. Rural colonisation became an important element of development which extended beyond planning to deal with unemployment in Britain, into colonial schemes for settling households that neither employed nor sold their labour upon smallholdings to deal with disorder, even the threat of revolution. This emphasis upon smallholder agriculture for agrarian development doctrine subsequently became especially significant.

By the late 1930s, British officials recognised the need for a revitalisation of their African colonies. In Nigeria, the failure of the colonial policy of non-development was acknowledged by no less important a colonial official than Governor Bernard Bourdillon, who urged an end to the 'exploitation theory' of colonialism and its replacement by 'the development theory'.[13] Thus the connection which Chamberlain previously had drawn between conditions in the metropolitan centre and those applying at the colonial periphery re-appeared in the idea of development embraced by Fabians and non-Fabians alike.

The economic and political crisis of the 1930s also gave considerable impetus to further modifications of the idea of development, including in its application to Britain's colonies. One consequence of this impetus was the passage of the Colonial Development and Welfare Acts of 1939 and 1945, even though these had 'an overwhelmingly welfarist [rather than developmental: SM] agenda'.[14] However the shift from welfare, including state-sponsored means to deal with diseases, to development, making productive what had been rendered unproductive during the military conflict, awaited the end of the military conflict for British colonial policy, as it did for Australian colonial policy towards PNG.

When the Labour Party came to power in 1945, followed by the sterling crisis of 1947, another British Government attempted to couple national interest with colonial development, along the lines proposed by Chamberlain at the

---

13   Cowen & Shenton *Doctrines* pp. 294–295
14   Cowen & Shenton *Doctrines* p. 296

turn of the century. On this occasion, anti-Marxist Fabians acting in the name of socialism and through the Labour government resuscitated development doctrine.[15] However according to Cowen and Shenton:

> This was a late-imperial doctrine to maximise production in African colonies to meet British national material need. The intention to develop schemes for the large-scale production of primary products—from eggs in Gambia to groundnuts in Tanganyika—was guided by a national need to swiftly expand exports to Britain and to save the need to spend dollars on imports of food and other immediate needs.[16]

The exceptional character and brevity of this moment needs to be emphasised. This was the 'only occasion on which there was concerted British state effort to make colonial populations do the work of generally maintaining subsistence, and therefore productive capacity, in Britain itself'.[17] In other words, there was no consistent imperial practice that sought to tie the production of colonial peoples into development in and of Britain. As will be shown later, this conclusion is only slightly less appropriate for Australian rule in PNG. The account now turns to the chapter's second theme, thought about development and its effect on policy in the earliest phase of Australian colonial rule over Papua and New Guinea.

Development in Early Colonial Papua and New Guinea

An important proposition of this book is that the late colonial idea of development which informed Australian policy for PNG represented a major break with pre-World War II thought about the colony. Understanding the extent and significance of the shift is facilitated by an outline of the earlier, displaced idea of development which initially influenced colonial officials and policy.

Development in the spontaneous sense was 'a word much used in the discussions about Papua in the first decade of [the twentieth: SM] century'. Further, the term contained little ambiguity, resting as it did 'upon two assumptions common to the men of that day and generation'. The assumptions were the right

---

15   Colin Leys 'Socialism and the Colonies: Review' *Fabian Journal* July 1959, no. 28, pp. 20–24: a review of Arthur Creech Jones (ed.) *New Fabian Colonial Essays* (London: Hogarth Press, 1959). See in particular Creech Jones' essay 'The Labour Party and Colonial Policy 1945–51' pp. 19–37. Creech Jones, founder of the Fabian Colonial Research Bureau, was British Secretary of State for Colonies between 1945 and 1950.

16   Cowen & Shenton *Doctrines* p. 296. As discussed in Chapter Two, the late 1940s and early 1950s was also when Australian officials considered linking expanded production of agricultural crops in PNG to Australian domestic needs, for consumption and exports, and to British imperial objectives of constructing a sterling bloc of countries to defend Britain against US ascendancy.

17   Cowen & Shenton *Doctrines* p. 297

of private European entrepreneurs to accumulate and the potential of Papua as a 'profitable (colonial) possession'. The role of government was to realise the potential by making the colony 'attractive to white settlers and entrepreneurs exercising their undoubted rights'.[18]

Similarly, as Stewart Firth has noted regarding German New Guinea, the drive to extend trade and establish agricultural large holdings, whether company or individually-owned, dominated in the north-east mainland and islands territory.[19] Albert Hahl, in charge of the German Protectorate of the New Guinea Company from 1896 until 1898, subsequently acting governor, then governor of German New Guinea until 1914 'had no doubts about the aim of German colonisation. It was to open up the country to European planters and traders'.[20] Indeed, according to Firth, '[w]ith the exception of the Dutch, the European powers in Melanesia before 1914 all wanted their possessions to become plantation colonies'.[21]

West locates the place of the indigenous population in the schema, in terms which could also be applied to New Guinea:

> There were, of course, obligations to native races involved in development, but in 1906 in Papua they could be stressed more lightly because the duty of the government to Europeans had scarcely begun to be discharged. The first and most urgent task, which Hubert Murray fully accepted, was to ensure that development took place. [22]

Drawing in part upon experiences in other colonies, the authorities recognised that spontaneous development posed a threat to the indigenous population.[23] In the *Preface* to his autobiographical *Gouverneursjahre*, first published in 1937, more than 20 years after he left German New Guinea, Hahl stressed that:

> In New Guinea, the native problem was and still is of first importance. The clash of two cultures, ours and that of stone-age man, inevitably led to dislocation and friction. It was imperative to avert these, and

---

18   The quotations in this paragraph are from Francis West *Hubert Murray The Australian Pro-Consul* (Melbourne University Press, 1968) p. 122. That plantations at least in Papua turned out to be generally unsuccessful does not make any less relevant this understanding of development: see DC Lewis *The Plantation Dream: Developing British New Guinea and Papua 1884–1942* (Canberra: The Journal of Pacific History, 1996).
19   Stewart Firth 'The New Guinea Company, 1885–1899: A case of unprofitable Imperialism' *Historical Studies* 1972, vol. xv, no. 1, pp. 361–377
20   Stewart Firth 'Albert Hahl: Governor of German New Guinea' in James Griffin (ed.) *Papua New Guinea Portraits. The Expatriate Experience* (Canberra: ANU Press, 1978) p. 30
21   Stewart Firth *New Guinea under the Germans* (Melbourne University Press, 1982) p. 66
22   West *Hubert Murray* p. 122
23   See James Griffin, Hank Nelson and Stewart Firth *Papua New Guinea: A Political History* (Richmond, Victoria: Heinemann, 1979) p. 8; Roger B Joyce *Sir William MacGregor* (Melbourne: Oxford University Press, 1971) p. 205

appropriate means had to be found, on the success of which hinged both the expansion of economic penetration and the cultural development of this island domain.[24]

The tension between profit 'forc[ing] the pace'- to use Bill Gammage's explanation for the Hagen-Sepik Patrol of the late 1930s into the New Guinea Highlands and north coast[25]—and finding a means of averting 'dislocation and friction', continued to underpin much that happened during the inter-war years in each colony. Murray's pre-World War I recognition that demands from European plantation owners for workers threatened to turn the indigenous population into a landless proletariat was significant. In Papua, finding positive means to safeguard the position of the indigenous population took modest steps,[26] including Murray's largely unsuccessful drive to establish 'native large holdings'.[27] However from the 1920s in New Guinea, the Australian administration had little trouble 'put [ting] business first',[28] with a substantial increase in the number of indigenous labourers recruited for work on plantations and in gold-mines.[29] Despite Administration efforts in both territories to limit the worst effects of wage employment on the indigenous population, West argues that:

> [t]he demand for labour always pressed heavily on the sources of supply, and a high proportion of labour was drawn from the relatively backward or recently opened up areas of the country, like the Sepik river district.[30]

In 1939, a commission was established by the colonial administration to investigate what was believed to be the growing shortages of labour to work land already alienated for large holdings, but not yet developed. The investigations revealed that an increase in the total potential labour force from 60,000 to 85,000 would be required, without any known reserves available to meet the likely demand.[31] Even without the deaths and other deleterious effects of the

---

24 Albert Hahl *Governor in New Guinea*, edited and translated by Peter G. Sack and Dymphna Clark (Canberra: ANU Press, 1980)

25 Bill Gammage *The Sky Travellers: Journeys in New Guinea 1938–39* (Victoria: The Miegunyah Press & Melbourne University Press, 1998) p. 17

26 Griffin, Nelson & Firth *Papua New Guinea* ch. 3; cf. Charles Rowley *The New Guinea Villager: A Retrospect from 1964* (Melbourne: FW Cheshire, 1968) p. 90

27 Cf. L Lett *Sir Hubert Murray of Papua* (London: Collins, 1949) pp. 184–185 (esp. p. 188, with West *Hubert Murray* p. 132). For a specific consideration of Murray's emphasis on native plantations, see Ron G Crocombe *Communal cash cropping among the Orokaiva* New Guinea Research Bulletin no. 4 (Port Moresby and Canberra: New Guinea Research Unit, ANU, 1964) pp. 4–20

28 Griffin, Nelson & Firth *Papua New Guinea* p. 55; see also Charles D Rowley *The Australians in German New Guinea 1914–1921* (Melbourne University Press, 1958), esp. pt vii, 'The Sacred Trust'.

29 Hank Nelson *Black White & Gold: Goldmining in Papua New Guinea 1878–1930* (Canberra: ANU Press, 1976)

30 Francis J West 'Indigenous Labour in Papua-New Guinea' *International Labour Review* 1958, vol. 77, no. 2, p. 91

31 West 'Indigenous Labour' p. 91. West (p. 95) emphasises that the shortages were particularly substantial in the Mandated Territory of New Guinea. Most large holdings were located in this territory and considerable areas of alienated but not yet planted land were available.

prolonged military conflict which was to come, existing production relations were under severe strain. War rendered the previous emphasis on spontaneous development untenable.

Inventing 'Positive Australianism'

The Metropolitan Australian Influences

During World War II, particular emphasis was given to redefining the basis of Australian colonial authority. Senior Australian officials specifically rejected what they understood as the Japanese-formulated Greater East Asia Co-Prosperity Sphere model of development as undesirable because of its exploitative character.[32] The phrase which came to embody the principal thrust of Australian postwar policy toward PNG was 'positive Australianism'. It was used publicly in early 1944 by the Minister for External Affairs Dr HV Evatt when castigating critics of the recently signed Australia-New Zealand Agreement.[33] The Agreement changed previous consultative arrangements between the two countries into a formal treaty, one of whose effects was to influence negotiations between major wartime allies over reforms to international trusteeship conditions.

The treaty contained a chapter entitled 'Welfare and Advancement of Native Peoples of the Pacific'. The chapter specified that 'the main purpose of the trust is the welfare of the native peoples and their social, economic and political development'.[34] In order to bring this aim, or intention, to fruition colonial policy should cease to be negative, merely reducing the deleterious effects of existing colonial policy. Instead government policy and state agency should make development happen as a positive consequence of the reformed international trusteeship arrangements.

It has previously been pointed out that the Australian-New Zealand emphasis also was influenced by changes in international thinking about development which had commenced in the 1920s.[35] It is less often noted that conditions prior to the outbreak of the war in the metropolitan country were also important in changing how powerful and influential Australians envisaged the future *for Australia and for PNG* after World War II ended. The Depression deeply

---

32   See Wright *State Practice*; Huntley LR Wright 'Protecting the National Interest: The Labor Government and the Reform of Australia's Colonial Policy, 1942–45' *Labour History* May 2002, vol. 82, pp. 65–82

33   See HV Evatt *Foreign Policy of Australia: Speeches* (Sydney: Angus and Robertson, 1945) pp. 183–184

34   William Roger Louis *Imperialism at Bay: The United States and the Decolonization of the British Empire, 1941–1945* (Oxford University Press, 1997) p. 290, citing from the original text of the Agreement.

35   Wright *State Practice* ch. 3; Wright 'Protecting the National Interest'; Scott MacWilliam 'Papua New Guinea in the 1940s: Empire and Legend' in David Lowe (ed.) *Australia and the End of Empires: the impact of decolonization in Asia and the South Pacific, 1945–1965* (Victoria: Deakin University Press, 1996) pp. 25–42

affected Australians who were to become central in defining what 'positive Australianism' meant, in particular its agrarian emphasis. The early 1930s crash in agricultural prices which drove individual European large holding owners off their plantations in PNG, leading to greater concentration of ownership in the hands of the large firms, especially Burns, Philp and Carpenters,[36] had a parallel in Australia. Rural and urban unemployment reached nearly 30 per cent in 1931–32. '[G]reat pockets of poverty in the cities and in the countryside',[37] had a lasting effect and not only on those who were impoverished and unemployed. While some so affected became politicians and government ministers,[38] others were employed as senior bureaucrats and advisers. Reducing unemployment by various means, including resettling households on small farms became a central element of the positive approach to postwar circumstances.[39] In addition to the Fabian reformulation and advocacy of intentional development outlined above, the demand management economics of JM Keynes increasingly influenced these politicians, policy advisers and senior administrators who began to meet regularly, including at the Commonwealth Bank in Sydney.[40]

Two of the attendees were Dr HC (Nugget) Coombs, and (Sir) John (Jack) Crawford. Coombs' part in shaping the role of governments in the conduct of war and reconstruction, especially under Labor governments, with a focus upon placing security of employment at the centre of policy, is well known.[41] So too is the extension of this policy direction to PNG.[42]

Crawford's significance for this account lies in the emphasis he placed upon post-Depression agricultural reform, emphasising the need for positive state involvement, a need which also was transferred to his view on PNG's development and the coffee industry in particular (see below). The death of *laissez-faire* liberalism in Australia,[43] and the increasing emphasis in liberal thought upon the state's role in dealing with the economic crisis was especially important for Crawford. His personal experience of the Depression also

---

36   For the advance during the 1930s of Burns, Philp in particular, see Ken Buckley and Kris Klugman *"The Australian Presence in the Pacific": Burns Philp 1914–1946* (Sydney: Allen and Unwin, 1983) ch. 12–16, pp. 213–325.

37   DH McKay 'Post-War Agriculture' in LT Evans and JDB Miller (eds) *Politics and Practice Essays in Honour of Sir John Crawford* (Sydney: Australian National University Press and Pergamon Press, 1987) p. 34

38   David Lee *Search for Security: The Political Economy of Australia's Postwar Foreign and Defence Policy* (St Leonards: Allen and Unwin, 1995) p. 8 notes that: 'The circle of Australian Labor Party (ALP) ministers who made Australian foreign policy in the 1940s had come to the fore as critics of social injustice in the depressed conditions of the 1930s.'

39   Lee *Search for Security* p. 9 includes among the 'gifted bureaucrats' who assisted these ALP ministers, John Burton, head of External Affairs and HC Coombs.

40   Heinz W Arndt *A Course through Life: Memoirs of an Australian Economist* History of Development Studies, no. 1 (Canberra: National Centre for Development Studies, ANU, 1985) p. 28

41   Tim Rowse *Nugget Coombs: A Reforming Life* (Port Melbourne: Cambridge University Press, 2002) pp. 116–121

42   Rowse *Nugget Coombs* pp. 178–181 'Reconstructing Papua New Guinea' provides a brief summary of Coombs' war and immediate post-war role most relevant to this account.

43   FW Eggleston *Reflections of an Australian Liberal* 2nd edn (Melbourne: FW Cheshire, 1953) ch. 1, pp. 2–5

reinforced 'broad sympathy with underdogs'.[44] During appointments as an economist with the Rural Bank of New South Wales (1935–42), as Rural Adviser to the Commonwealth Department of War Organisation of Industry (1942–43), and as Director of Research in the newly formed Department of Post-War Reconstruction, headed by Coombs, Crawford drew upon this experience to influence development in Australia and PNG.[45]

While working in the Department of Post-War Reconstruction, Crawford commenced an association with the Rural Reconstruction Commission. The Commission played an important role in stressing the importance of maintaining 'family farms' as 'the basic units of the most natural form of society'.[46] Because farmers' incomes had been cut substantially during the Depression, and increased agricultural production was required to meet war and postwar demand, Crawford and the Department of Post-War Reconstruction became heavily involved in devising means of raising prices and finding other ways for improving rural livelihoods. A self-declared 'interventionist', Crawford's principal significance was to place agricultural expansion and farmers' living standards at the centre of government considerations on international relations and the domestic economy. Government policy on full employment, as expressed in the 1945 White Paper on the subject, was intimately related to rural policy.[47] Most importantly for Australia and, as will be shown below, for PNG the connection meant an emphasis upon increasing agricultural exports for a 'hungry world—especially in the United Kingdom and Europe'.[48]

Another key figure for late colonial development in PNG with close connections to Crawford and agricultural policy in Australia was CR Lambert, who was subsequently appointed by Coalition Minister Hasluck, as Secretary for the newly constructed Department of Territories, formerly External Territories. Like Crawford, Lambert had worked in the Rural Bank of New South Wales (1933–48), and was Chairman of the Rural Reconstruction Commission (1943–46). Immediately prior to becoming Secretary for Territories, Lambert had been Commonwealth Director of Regional Development. With this background in designing and implementing state action to expand agriculture in Australia, it is unsurprising that Lambert and Hasluck forged a lengthy working relationship aimed at bringing agrarian development to PNG.

---

44 Max Crawford 'My Brother Jack: Background and Early Years' in Evans & Miller (eds) *Policy and Practice* p. 14
45 McKay 'Post-War Agriculture' pp. 36–37 stresses how Crawford continued to see post-war agriculture and its problems through the prism of pre-war conditions.
46 McKay 'Post-War Agriculture' p. 35
47 McKay 'Post-War Agriculture' pp. 37–38
48 McKay 'Post-War Agriculture' p. 38

HV Evatt and British Colonial Influences

An especially important figure in the reformation of the idea of development, giving it a particularly Australian flavour, was Dr HV Evatt. In Evatt's case, championship of 'the underdog' extended domestically and overseas. This support was expressed for individuals facing injustice and small countries threatened by major powers' domination.[49] Evatt's role as Minister for External Affairs from 1941 onwards is of special significance for the international reshaping of trusteeship (see below). Evatt's knowledge of and sympathy for the welfare of people in countries other than Australia grew during the inter-war years, when he was an academic, lawyer and judge of the High Court of Australia. The most important dimension of Evatt's personal development for this account involves Kenya and the Devonshire Declaration. Another Australian, Edmund Piesse, a senior official in the Prime Minister's Office also had seen the parallels between British policy for Kenya and the Australian situation in the Mandated Territory of New Guinea.[50]

The argument that the Kenya White Paper provided the basis for British trusteeship appeared in a monograph Evatt prepared and published in 1935 while a judge of the High Court of Australia.[51] The central proposition that Evatt took from the White Paper on Kenya was that British governments exercised:

> a trust on behalf of the African population, and they are unable to delegate or share this trust, the object of which may be defined as the protection and advancement of the native races.[52]

Evatt highlighted the above phrase from the White Paper and then extended trusteeship beyond British concerns. For Evatt, responsibility exercised by His Majesty's Government was as 'trustees *before the world* for the African population [emphasis added: SM]'.[53] That is, trusteeship should be practised according to international, and not simply imperial, principles, a conclusion Evatt constantly pushed during the 1940s at a series of conferences and during negotiations about the future of postwar arrangements.

There is no need to repeat here how Britain and the United States, in particular, disagreed about the terms of colonial authority after the military struggle ended. Nor is it necessary to document again the role played by Australian and

---

49   This sense of sympathy was particularly evident in the belligerence of Minister for External Affairs Dr Evatt when dealing with British and US officials over the meaning and terms of trusteeship. Louis emphasises how Evatt 'championed the cause of the underdog', a stance that he stretched to include 'small powers' internationally as well as 'dependent peoples', *Imperialism at Bay* p. 291.

50   Wright *State Practice* p. 100

51   See HV Evatt 'The British Dominions as Mandatories' *Proceedings of the Australian and New Zealand Society of International Law* 1935, vol. 1, pp. 27–54

52   Evatt 'The British Dominions as Mandatories' p. 29; also cited in Louis *Imperialism at Bay* pp. 108–109.

53   Evatt 'The British Dominions as Mandatories' p. 29; also cited in Louis *Imperialism at Bay* p. 109.

New Zealand representatives in persuading the major powers to acknowledge the specific importance these two British Dominions placed upon postwar arrangements, particularly but not solely for the colonial territories of the South-West Pacific. It is sufficient to note Dr Evatt's dogged belligerence, backed up by persistent support from Australian officials. One key figure was Paul Hasluck, then working in External Affairs and who attended many of the most important meetings. Evatt played a substantial part in changing the terms of trusteeship to include international supervision, but not international control or administration of colonies.

Tied together by their anti-colonial nationalism, the US, Australia and New Zealand worked against any easy re-assertion of British colonial rule. But suspicious of US ambitions in the South Pacific, the representatives of the last two countries also allied with British Labour Party supporters to establish a form of international accountability and a postwar trusteeship arrangement distinguishable from prewar imperialism. Working together was facilitated by personal agreement, including between Arthur Creech Jones, then a Fabian Labour MP and Parliamentary Secretary and Hasluck, an adviser to Australian Labor Minister Evatt who had developed a close association.[54] As well as formulating a means for closer international scrutiny over colonial powers, the emphasis in the justification for continuing colonial rule shifted considerably toward a responsibility for promoting indigenous welfare and hastening self-government, even national independence.

Deliberations on Australia's Postwar Defence

Wright emphasises how the appeals to a new form of internationalism by leading Australians was associated with, even driven by, a need to protect what was conceived as the Australian national interest.[55] Not surprisingly at a time of war, one conception of interest involved territorial occupation with a direct military presence. But a second view of territorial security was also influential, and ultimately prevailed. Its foremost advocate was the Australian military commander General (later Sir) Thomas Blamey.[56]

As the Australian Labor Government prepared its plans for the Australia-New Zealand Conference of January 1944, the Defence Committee of Cabinet drew up and submitted a report. The document argued that 'the "best means of securing Australia from invasion" was "by taking strong offensive action

---

54   Wright 'Protecting the National Interest' pp. 68–69; MacWilliam 'Papua New Guinea in the 1940s' p. 33
55   Wright 'Protecting the National Interest' notes that from the late nineteenth century a concern for national defence was central to the Australian 'imperial presence, first in Papua and later in New Guinea' (p. 65) and proceeds to show how the terms of this concern changed during World War II.
56   David Horner *Blamey: The Commander-in-Chief* (St Leonard's: Allen and Unwin, 1998) esp. ch. 19, pp. 436–438

from established and well-defended forward bases"'. While Australia would be responsible for maintaining the bases '"the naval commitment should be regarded as an Imperial obligation"'.[57]

In a letter to the Secretary of the Department of Defence (Sir) Frederick Shedden, Blamey disagreed with this position. He argued that Australia's strength lay in its '"strategic isolation"', the preservation of which should be '"our strategic aim"'.[58] Blamey asserted that not only could Australian garrisons in the Pacific be bypassed by an attacking enemy, maintenance of the bases would be a problem when defence expenditures were cut during peacetime. Blamey preferred a close alliance with Britain and conditional encouragement for US bases in the Pacific.[59]

Devising a defence strategy for Papua and New Guinea located so close to northern Australia, and over which military authority already existed—in the form of the Australian and New Guinea Administrative Unit (ANGAU)[60]—posed questions distinct and separable from the proposal for maintaining forward bases that Blamey opposed. As the Australia-New Zealand Agreement was negotiated, Blamey placed his views on the record about 'the long-term strategic problems connected with the present military and future civil, administration of Papua and the Mandated Territory'.[61]

Blamey had a lengthy document prepared by his Director of Research, Lieutenant-Colonel Alf Conlon, and submitted to Prime Minister John Curtin on 4 February 1944. 'The Situation of Australian Colonies as at January 1944' presented to Curtin provided another early official application of the phrase 'the paramountcy of native interests' to postwar colonial policy for Australian colonies. It envisaged a long-term program of development for the territories and 'point[ed] to the necessity of a sustained interest by military officers in developmental projects'. Development in PNG should have two objectives, as far as Australia's strategic interests were concerned. First, there was a need to forestall 'a sudden and uncontrolled [postwar] rush of competitive interests' into the South-West Pacific, where the interests were both of rival nation-states and commercial concerns. The second objective reflected the changing focus of trusteeship outlined above, to place native welfare at the centre of economic and political development, rather than allowing a return to prewar conditions.

---

57 Quotes are from Horner *Blamey* pp. 436–438.
58 Horner *Blamey* p. 437
59 Horner *Blamey* p. 437
60 See Peter Ryan 'The Australian and New Guinea Administrative Unit' in KS Inglis (ed.) *The History of Melanesia* 2nd Waigani Seminar, Port Moresby, 30 May–5 June 1968 (Canberra: ANU and UPNG, 1971) pp. 531–548
61 Horner *Blamey* p. 438

The document lent complete support to the position being developed elsewhere in the Australian civilian administration that domination by the trading and plantation interests should not be restored after the conflict ended.[62]

Most importantly, as Wright notes, the position adopted by Blamey made it possible to combine 'wartime idealism … with the executive power of the Army'. The circumstances, by Blamey's reckoning, 'presented the Labor Government with a unique, "epoch making", opportunity to exercise policy on the "highest moral level as a justified weapon of power politics to protect not only the future of the native peoples of the Pacific but the strategic security of Australia'''.[63]

Within a few days of Blamey's letter to Curtin, from February 7 to 12 a conference of the ANGAU HQ officers and district staff was held in Port Moresby.[64] While some of those who attended may not have envisaged major changes in the terms of colonial rule as a consequence of the war, the general thrust of the published papers asserted the importance of improving the welfare of the indigenous population. Nor were the proposed future directions outlined by the ANGAU personnel at the conference ever distant from the approach being formulated by civilian and military authorities in Australia.

When Major JL Taylor said at the conference: 'I take it that you all agree that a higher standard of living is necessary for the native people',[65] he was advocating something which would have found no dispute at either military HQ or in the Curtin Labor Government. Further, when stating that this standard should be reached through 'the development of native agriculture, greater native production, and hence greater wealth', and not by further increases in plantation production, Taylor was in step with what was fast becoming the dominant position in development thought about policy for postwar Australia and PNG. He also espoused the increasingly popular view that:

> Plantations in this country exist to a considerable degree by virtue of the low standard of living of the native employees-that is, by cheap labour. It is essential to raise this standard of living in an endeavour to reduce the high death rate of indentured labourers, the pick of the community, which stood at between 15 and 20 per 1,000 before the war. This is an extremely high death rate and is the answer to those who contend that labour conditions [on plantations: SM] were satisfactory.

---

62 NAA: CP637/1/1 no. 65 *The Situation of Australian Colonies as at January 1944, General Sir Thomas Blamey to PM Curtin, 4/2/1944*; see also Wright 'Contesting community'; Wright 'Protecting the National Interest'
63 Wright 'Protecting the National Interest' p. 73; quotes in Wright's document are from Blamey to Curtin *The Situation of the Australian Colonies as at January, 1944* pp. 3–4.
64 NAA: A9372 *ANGAU* [*Australia and New Guinea Administrative Unit*] vols 1–3 *Conference of Officers of Headquarters and Officers of District Staff, Port Moresby, 7–12 February 1944*; cf. Gammage *The Sky Travellers* p. 225, who gives the venue of the conference as Melbourne.
65 See Taylor 'A Paper on Native Welfare' in NAA: A9372 *ANGAU*

While it has been suggested that the conference exposed a major divide between Papua and New Guinea officers on 'native welfare' with the latter less supportive of the position Taylor emphasised, the divide is not apparent in the published papers.[66] The final stage in the formulation of 'positive Australianism' during and immediately after World War II is now considered.

Planning Postwar Development: Defence, Reconstructing Community and Paying a Debt

Through settlement schemes and other forms of state assistance, family farms were to provide the basis for postwar agricultural expansion and employment for returning soldiers in Australia. But in PNG, the urgency of the global food shortages initially appeared to favour reconstruction and expansion on another basis altogether, the rehabilitation of plantations owned by expatriates and overseas firms that employed indigenous labour. In 1943 centralised produce marketing, particularly for copra, was established under National Security Regulations and support from the ANGAU. In the same year the Australian New Guinea Production Control Board (ANGPCB) had taken over plantations operated by the ANGAU, and become the central marketing authority for these and privately owned and operated plantations in areas where the Japanese army had not been a sufficient threat to force the departure of owners.[67]

As the conflict ended, large holding owners chaffed at any restrictions which slowed their return to plantations abandoned in the face of the Japanese military's rapid advance.[68] Initial assistance to returning planters, including through the ANGPCB, prodded Coombs' concern, expressed in a letter to Treasurer Ben Chifley, as a member of a government committee formed in February 1944 to determine policy for postwar PNG. The concern was that without proper consideration the Government would acquiesce in the re-establishment of an economy dominated by large holdings. Their owners' aspirations for a quick return to prewar conditions now confronted government and administrative opposition to plantation agriculture and international companies hoping to expand their landholdings and plantings.

As noted above, even prior to the start of the war, there were concerns about the effects on the indigenous population of plantations and their demands for labour. Wartime changes internationally and in Australia in the idea of trusteeship made dealing with these concerns even more important. During the

---

66   Cf. Gammage *The Sky Travellers* p. 225
67   Harry H Jackman *Copra marketing and price stabilization in Papua New Guinea: A history to 1975* Pacific Research Monograph no. 17 (Canberra: NCDS, ANU, 1988) pp. 82–97
68   See Rowse *Nugget Coombs* p. 179; Wright 'Protecting the National Interest'; Wright 'Contesting community'

war, the potential for conflict between plantation operations and indigenous welfare became a central focus for government officials working in Australia. Opposition to 'development by Europeans with native labour', strengthened in Canberra, although renewing the importance of plantations remained the direction favoured by JR (Reg) Halligan, the most senior official in the Department of External Territories.[69]

As the destructive effects of the military conflict, particularly on indigenes and village life, worsened and became better known, this opposition to European use of native labour increased. The September 1943 appointment of Minister for External Territories EJ (Eddie) Ward who fervently opposed the continuation of the prewar direction of colonial policy, gave the opponents of large holding agriculture their most prominent representative. While Ward was never alone in his antipathy to the re-assertion of plantation and trading company dominance, his particular combination of populism and labourism placed the Minister at the forefront of the opposition. Wright correctly concluded:

> The vehemence with which Ward attached the labels of exploitation and non-development to the so-called "vested interests" operating in the Territory created a climate in which more interested parties [than Ward on colonial development: SM] could insert demands for expanded indigenous welfare into the domain of intentional development.[70]

As already noted, officers in the ANGAU were among the interested parties in PNG. These officials had the advantage of holding administrative authority at the critical moment as the Japanese forces retreated and before civil administration was re-established. Whatever the extent of disagreement among senior ANGAU officials about how the 'paramountcy of native interests' could be effected, there seems to have been little dispute that this should be the organisation's primary concern. While acknowledging prewar differences between conditions in Papua and New Guinea, and recognising that the ANGAU was not in a position to determine postwar arrangements, Chairman of the 1944 ANGAU Conference Brigadier DM Cleland nevertheless emphasised the need for policy 'applicable to both Territories' which represented 'a progressive development on rational lines'. For Cleland, rejecting 'retrogression' and embracing 'progression' meant 'betterment' in 'the best interests of the country [i.e. PNG] and its people'.[71] Other speakers left little doubt which people's interests were of concern for many ANGAU officeholders.[72]

---

69   Wright 'Protecting the National Interest' p. 74, cites a memo of November 1943 prepared by the Second Secretary of the Department of External Affairs (DEA) that described the plantation system as a form of production 'doomed from the beginning'.
70   Wright 'Contesting community' p. 76
71   Cleland 'Summary of Chairman's Address on "ANGAU Organisation and Policy" and of his final survey of the Conference Papers and Discussions' in NAA: A9372 *ANGAU*.
72   In addition to Taylor's paper on 'Native Welfare' already cited, see also papers by: Lt-Col. JM Mack 'Preventive Medicine'; Capt W Trembath 'ANGAU Dental Services'; Major L Austen 'Native Welfare'; Lt-Col

The dominant view neatly combined Australian defence interests with the 'paramountcy of native interests' development thrust. Officers most concerned with the deleterious effects of pre-war indentured labour and wartime military demands upon the indigenous population sang from the same song sheet as General Blamey and government officials in Australia regarding the principal objectives behind postwar reconstruction in PNG. The close ties between senior ANGAU personnel and key Directorate of Research officials go some way to explaining the coincidence of views.[73] Taylor stated the underlying purpose of postwar colonial development neatly in his conference paper:

> Leaving sentimental and moral reasons aside, it is vitally necessary for Australia, because of her geographical position, to have a large and contented native population in New Guinea as a buffer between Australia and Asia. This is of paramount importance, and our aim should be 10,000,000 New Guinea natives with an Australian culture and Australian sympathies, so that in the wars of the future a vigorous native race unaffected by any Pan-Asiatic movement will stand with Australia a bulwark against the Orient.[74]

Other interested parties, including religious denominations, trade unions and academics, easily supplied the 'sentimental and moral reasons'. At the November 1943 Anglican Archbishops and Bishops Conference held at Cheltenham, Victoria, a 'Native Charter' for the South-West Pacific was adopted. Drafted by Sydney University anthropologist AP Elkin and Bishop JW Burton, the Charter re-asserted the '"paramountcy of native interests"' doctrine, and 'urged "that every effort be made to establish native community enterprises … and to develop peasant proprietorship"'.[75] In February 1944, when Blamey was setting out his preferred position to Curtin and the ANGAU conference was taking place in Port Moresby, the Anglican missions prepared and sent a submission to External Affairs Minister Evatt. The submission explicitly tied the destruction and disruption of the military conflict, the effect upon the indigenous population and Australia's strategic security together in moral terms as a debt owed which should be repaid at least in part by the abolition of the indentured labour system.[76]

E Taylor & Lt-Col S Elliott-Smith 'Native Labour'; Major DH Vertigan 'Native Labour'; Lt JB McAdam 'Land Tenure'; REP Dwyer 'Agriculture'; Capt WR Humphries 'A Review of Native Plantations'; Major WHH Thompson 'Rice Cultivation'; and Lt-Col. WE Stanner 'Broad Aspects of Colonial Administration' in NAA: A9372 *ANGAU*.

73 See Gammage *The Sky Travellers* p. 224; Horner *Blamey* p. 466

74 Taylor 'Native Welfare'

75 Wright 'Contesting community' p. 82, citing AP Elkin *Wanted—A Charter for the Native Peoples of the South-west Pacific* (Sydney: Institute for International Affairs, 1943) p. 10.

76 Griffin, Nelson & Firth *Papua New Guinea* pp. 102–112, ch. 8 'Paying a Debt 1945–1949' details the strength of this moral purpose, especially in the immediate post-war years.

In December 1944, Minister Ward organised a Native Labour Conference in Sydney. To representatives of various interested parties, and in the absence of representation from either Papua New Guineans or the large plantation companies, Minister Ward's purpose in calling the conference was made clear. External Territories Department Secretary Halligan, the man regarded in official circles as most enthusiastic for a 'return to the past', was given the task of reading the Minister's conference opening statement expressing the Government's commitment to abolishing the indenture system that formed the legal and administrative basis for hiring indigenes. The indentured system under which workers were employed for up to three years was to be replaced by an as yet undefined arrangement. The revised terms of employment would be those '"best suited to the people"', and would '"cause the least upset to [the] village economy, [and] permit ... native peasant production"'.[77] Conference deliberations were to assist the government and colonial administration in finding a new arrangement, not to debate whether indenture should be preserved.

In July 1945, a further clear and defining public expression of the shift in development thought and policy was given. Speaking to the Australian Parliament on the Papua-New Guinea Provisional Administration Bill, Ward emphasised the principal connections between 'positive Australianism' and postwar rule. There would be a break with the past, when not enough had been done, and a future of 'better health, better education, more participation in the wealth of their country and eventually a say in its government' for the indigenous population.[78] Ward signalled a major overhaul of the Native Labour Ordinance with a substantial increase in legislated minimum pay rates, reduced working hours and indentures cut from three to one year, with indentures to be abolished altogether 'as soon as practicable'.[79]

In late 1946, as expatriate planters anxious to re-establish holdings pressed the UK Government to intervene and overturn the newly introduced labour laws, Ward spelled out how 'native development' would affect large holding and other similar commercial interests. Without acknowledging the lineage of the idea 'paramountcy of native interests', this most anti-British Australian Labor Party politician stressed once more how development would change in PNG in terms which replicated those that had appeared in the 1923 British White Paper.[80] Ward emphasised that:

---

77 This and other quotations in the paragraph are from Wright 'Contesting community' p. 94, citing NLA: EJ Ward Papers MS239 6/12/260-346 *Native Labour Conference, Sydney 1–2 December 1944.*
78 Griffin, Nelson & Firth *Papua New Guinea* p. 102
79 Griffin, Nelson & Firth *Papua New Guinea* p. 102
80 On Ward's anti-British views, see John Kerr *Matters for Judgement: An Autobiography* (South Melbourne: Macmillan, 1978), p. 122.

> Non-native expansion must ... be governed by the well-being of the indigenous inhabitants of the Territory as a whole ... [and] while as in the past the basis for the economy will be native and non-native working side by side: [now] the limit of non-native expansion [would be] determined by the welfare of natives generally'.[81]

Ward's statement summarised just how far Australian official thinking about development had travelled since the start of the twentieth century, and particularly during World War II. Previously dominant expatriate settler interests now had every reason to be 'unsettled', in Edward (Ted) Wolfers' phrase.[82] While the major commercial firms had less reason for concern, given their dominance and critical role in trade which would become central for postwar reconstruction and beyond, nevertheless they too were major employers of indigenes. As substantial plantation operators, these firms also had to adjust to the shift in thought and policy towards the primacy of smallholder agriculture. Clearly for both settlers and international firms, as well as for colonial officials, the immediate issue would be how an administration short of skilled personnel and essential equipment could transfer the shift into detailed policy that secured 'the paramountcy of native interests'.

Conclusion

For decades colonial rulers in PNG paid only minor attention to the negative consequences of growth driven by plantation and mining operations. During the inter-war years Britain and France[83] had begun to adopt the idea of intentional development for colonial policy but Australian thought about development for PNG lagged behind. Despite the pre-war awareness of some officials about changing international thinking and policy, it took wartime conditions to accelerate the process by which these changes were inserted into Australian thought about and policy for PNG.

By 1945 a major transformation had begun in thinking about the policies necessary to make postwar development happen. The priority of officials became shaping further commercialisation in a manner which satisfied defence needs and international demand for agricultural commodities while maintaining

---

81   NLA: MS2396 *Statement by the Honorable EJ Ward, MP, Minister for Territories, December 6, 1946;* 'External Territories of the Commonwealth', also cited in MacWilliam 'Papua New Guinea in the 1940s' p. 37
82   Ted Wolfers 'The unsettled settlers: New Guinea in Australia, 1942–1946' *Journal of the Papua and New Guinea Society* 1967, vol. 1, no. 2, pp. 7–15
83   Monica M van Beusekom *Negotiating Development: African Farmers and Colonial Experts at the Office du Niger, 1920–1960* (Portsmouth, NH, Oxford and Cape Town: Heinemann, James Curry and David Philip, 2002)

indigenous attachment to 'village life' with higher living standards. Initially however, little progress was made towards these objectives. The account now turns to the years immediately after the military conflict ended.

2. Postwar Development's Uncertainties

Introduction

Once the war ended in 1945, and over the next two years as the administration of Papua and New Guinea passed from military to civilian hands, defining and applying 'positive Australianism' was especially difficult. It was one thing for colonial officials to propose that the 'paramountcy of native interests' should occur on the basis of development policy aiming to bring about a major expansion of household production. It was quite another matter to work out what the policy meant and how it could be achieved. The overarching theme of this chapter is that the difficulties faced during the late 1940s produced uncertainty, tensions and debates but also resulted in responses which began to shape development policy.

One source of difficulty was the Australian Government and the Department of External Territories. Previous accounts have emphasised how the Minister for External Territories, Eddie Ward and the priorities of the Department Secretary Halligan did not assist officials in PNG to define what 'positive Australianism' might mean in practice. The first section of the chapter briefly considers this explanation.[1] The second section focuses on how uncertainty arose out of the distinct circumstances faced in PNG because of widespread and substantial destruction during the protracted military conflict. The third section of the chapter outlines some of the postwar challenges faced by the Administration, which heightened the uncertainty about how to bring development. The final section shows how in the late 1940s, increases in indigenous production began even while colonial development policy remained vague.

Political and Administrative Uncertainty

In 1949, the Ben Chifley-led Labor Government lost the second postwar election to a Liberal-Country Party coalition headed by RG (Bob) Menzies. For the previous six years, Eddie Ward had been Minister for External Territories. He was also the Minister for Transport, and heavily involved in internal Labor Party and trade union politics. Apart from making general proclamations which emphasised

---

1   See Wright *State Practice* pp. 126–163

the changed direction of development thought and policy, Ward provided little guidance for either the Department in Canberra or the Administration in PNG. Ward's principal preoccupation was domestic Australian politics, which included tussles over his own political survival.

The External Territories Department did not offer clear guidelines either. Headed by Secretary JR (Reg) Halligan, who favoured the re-establishment of the primacy of plantations and other large private enterprises, the department was small. Staff shortages meant it was unable to engage in detailed planning, even had the specifics of policy been settled. Consequently, when Colonel JK Murray assumed office in late 1945 as the first postwar Administrator at the head of the Provisional Administration, he did so with little more than general advice from Canberra and the lingering influence of the military administration which determined the availability of personnel and equipment.[2]

Insufficient personnel and the different backgrounds and expectations of staff exacerbated continuing tussles about how to bring about development. To make matters worse, the personnel shortages continued into the 1950s and affected attempts to make planning more precise and detailed. The shortages of skilled personnel were repeatedly emphasised in communications between the Administration and the Australian Government. Such shortages were felt worldwide, as the Administration soon realised when attempts were made to recruit staff in the UK.[3] To increase the size and range of activities undertaken, critical local departments, including Public Health, needed personnel who were flexible about the tasks they could and would undertake.[4]

The staff shortages were particularly serious because one of the central tasks taken on by the postwar administration was to extend colonial rule over areas and people not yet subject to the Administration's authority. Military victory over Japan entitled Australia to international recognition as the governing power over both territories. As Hank Nelson correctly pointed out, with the Territory of New Guinea under the International Trusteeship System, by Article 76, the Australian Government was committed to '"promote [the inhabitants'] progressive development towards self-government or independence"' in accord with '"the freely expressed wishes of the people concerned"'. Although Papua was an Australian colony, 'under the joint administration it was generally

---

2 Downs *The Australian Trusteeship* p. 19
3 ToPNG *Report of the Economic Development Committee of the Provisional Administration* (Port Moresby: TPNG, September 1948) pp. 14, 16–21; NAA: A518/1 AQ800/1/1 Part 1 *Administration—Territory of Papua-New Guinea, Coordination Plans for Development. Inter-Departmental Committee. 1947* JK Murray to Chairman, Inter-Departmental Committee on the Planning and Development of New Guinea p. 3; and NAA: A518/1 AQ800/1/1 Part 2 *Administration—Territory of Papua-New Guinea, Coordination Plans for Development. Inter-Departmental Committee. 1947* 1/10/1947 Minutes of Sixth Meeting of Inter-Departmental Committee, p. 13
4 Donald Denoon, K Dugan and L Marshall *Public Health in Papua New Guinea: Medical possibility and social constraint, 1884–1984* (Cambridge: Cambridge University Press, 1989) pp. 72–73

accepted that what applied to one Territory, applied to the other'. Over the entire late colonial period, from 1945 until 1975, what ambiguity existed in this commitment was mainly over the pace of moving towards and the timing of national independence.[5]

However internationally bestowed authority was in advance of internal rule, particularly in parts of the most populous Highlands region of mainland Papua and New Guinea. In the immediate postwar years, warfare between indigenes and attacks against the officials trying to assert authority still marked the colonial frontiers, particularly in the Highlands. A limited number of officials had to be spread more thinly, often over terrain that was difficult to traverse by frequent and sometimes lengthy foot patrols. Experienced as well as inexperienced officials, supported by indigenous carriers and police, had to move cautiously in case of attack.[6]

From 1945 the civilian administration supplanted military authority region by region. In 1947, the takeover extended to the Highlands which was gazetted as a separate area, the Central Highlands District, with its headquarters at Goroka where the Allies had built a substantial airstrip. While the District was divided into ten sub-districts, only five (Kainantu, Bena Bena-Goroka, Chimbu, Hagen and Wabag) were allocated assistant district officers. The other five sub-districts were 'administered in a theoretical rather than real sense'.[7]

Securing colonial law and order requirements over a larger area and more people was an easily defined basis for administration efforts. It was more difficult to prescribe how smallholder production could be expanded. While some of the uncertainty arose from conditions within PNG, considered below, others involved relations between the colony and the metropolitan country. In particular, the general objective of increased agricultural production did not specify to what extent development in the colony should be subordinated to development in Australia where postwar reconstruction was also a government priority. One early area of tension, which highlighted the more general difficulty, arose over which markets should be the focus for PNG agricultural exports.[8]

Global postwar reconstruction rapidly increased international and domestic demand for labour and materials. Worldwide shortages of food and other

---

5   Quotes from Nelson 'A Comment On' Unpublished Paper, May 2005; cf. Hugh White and Elsina Wainwright *Strengthening Our Neighbour: Australia and the Future of Papua New Guinea* (Canberra: Australian Strategic Policy Institute, 2004) p. 22.
6   August Kituai *My gun, my brother: the world of the Papua New Guinea police, 1920–1960* (Honolulu: University of Hawai'i Press, 1998)
7   Charles M Hawksley *Administrative Colonialism: District Administration and Colonial "Middle Management" in Kelantan 1909–1919 and the Eastern Highlands of Papua New Guinea 1947–1957* PhD thesis, University of Wollongong (2001) p. 308
8   See ToPNG 'Introduction: Scope of Enquiry' *Report of the Economic Development Committee* pp. 1–2

agricultural produce resulted in considerable pressure for the rebuilding of plantations, especially coconut producing large holdings where there were relatively easy output increases available from previously planted trees. Under trees, large piles of nuts lay awaiting collection and processing, providing cash-flows for further rehabilitation if sufficient unskilled labour was available. In the case of Burns, Philp's plantations on Bougainville, the firm's managers reported stacks of nuts 15 and 20 feet high under trees which would be accessible once elementary clearing up had been done.[9] International shortages extended beyond copra to a wide range of crops which could be grown in PNG. However the shortages also affected Australian manufacturers and traders trying to rebuild production and meet the demand for agricultural goods in Australia.

While there was easy initial agreement that there should and could be substantial increases in agricultural production, particularly of crops in demand in Australia, there was uncertainty about the relationship between production in PNG and in Australia. The uncertainty arose especially clearly when an early premise of postwar reconstruction was that production of crops in PNG could be 'integrated' with supply of and demand for agricultural produce in Australia. However it was more difficult to determine the appropriate policy response if there were barriers to 'integration' of the two economies.[10]

In the late 1940s and early 1950s, one of these barriers was international, including United States' Government objections to preferential trading agreements. Another difficulty for policy formulation arose when there was a greater advantage for colonial revenues and grower incomes in PNG by fitting production in the country to the wider international, rather than Australian demand. This possibility arose over cocoa production, which was solely an export crop. Soon after the war ended when decisions were being made about the type of cocoa trees to be planted on small and large holdings, there was an immediate tension over priorities (see below for more detail). This tension was expressed as a clash between colonial and metropolitan nationalism, with Australian colonial officials likely to be found on the former side. Immediately after World War II anti-colonialism was expressed by some cargo cults (see below). However also from the 1940s, the most important advocates of future national sovereignty and national self-sufficiency for the colony, against an unquestioning primacy of Australian concerns, were expatriate settlers and colonial officials. Among the latter were some who resided in Australia. The terms of the United Nations Trusteeship, noted above, were important for these colonial nationalists. That is,

---

9   Scott MacWilliam 'Post-War Reconstruction in Bougainville: Plantations, Smallholders and Indigenous Capital' in Anthony J Regan and Helga M Griffin (eds) *Bougainville before the conflict* (Canberra: Pandanus Books, 2005) p. 232

10   See the minutes of the first meeting of the Inter-Departmental Committee for the Coordination of Plans for the Development of Papua-New Guinea held on 29 April 1947 in the Office of the Secretary of the Department of External Territories, Canberra. NAA: A518/1 AQ800/1/1 Part 1 *Administration*

colonialism was not conceived as antithetical to nationalism, but as supportive of its development, even if the support was provided by people not indigenous to PNG.[11]

Major shortages of food crops on international markets encouraged officials in PNG who were looking to expand agricultural production for export markets particularly, but not solely, by smallholders to look beyond the Australian market. In these circumstances, local officials could and did argue that their first priority was maximising colonial income and revenues. Producing and selling crops that yielded the greatest return, wherever the markets could be found was their priority. Restricting exports from PNG to the small Australian market was not in the colony's best interests, according to some senior officials.

The choice of priorities was made more difficult by the fact that as far as PNG agricultural exports were concerned, Australia and its colony also belonged to the sterling currency area. Postwar reconstruction in both was fastened to British imperial needs for agricultural commodities and as a means of overcoming Britain's indebtedness to the USA.[12] Access to US dollars influenced official thinking on a wide range of matters, including how to obtain Caterpillar tractors for road construction and preparing flood-prone land for rice production in PNG (see below). Increasing copra exports could meet PNG and Australian requirements as well as the British requirement for sources of supply within the sterling area.[13]

Although the tension between colonial and metropolitan priorities came to the fore more and more in the 1950s and 1960s, it was nevertheless also present immediately after the war. While cocoa production and marketing provided a more substantial long-term test of administrative commitment to maximising export income (see Chapters Four and Five), the appropriate priorities regarding exports of timber needed to be settled almost immediately after military hostilities ended. In this initial instance, officials in Australia including Minister Ward were decisive in establishing policy which prioritised needs in the colony.

Commercial timber harvesting, mainly carried out by international and expatriate firms in a small number of areas, required the local administration and colonial government to rank possible markets for PNG produce. The Inter-Departmental Committee of the Australian Government, formed in April 1947

---

11   For a history of colonial nationalism in Britain's 'white colonies' relevant for the PNG case, see Norman Etherington and Deryck Schreuder (eds) *The Rise of Colonial Nationalism: Australia, New Zealand, Canada and South Africa first assert their nationalities, 1880–1914* (Sydney: Allen and Unwin, 1988) esp. ch. 2, Schreuder 'The making of the idea of colonial nationalism'. See also Luke Trainor *British Imperialism and Australian Nationalism: manipulation, conflict and compromise in the late nineteenth century* (Melbourne: Cambridge University Press, 1994).
12   MacWilliam 'Papua New Guinea in the 1940s'
13   Jackman *Copra marketing* ch. 5

to 'report to [External Territories Minister Ward] on plans for the rehabilitation and reconstruction of the territories to accelerate their development' spent much of its time debating how to 'exploit [the] softwood timber stand at Bulolo for plywood manufacture'. The controversial matter had been referred to the Inter-Departmental Committee by the Commonwealth Cabinet Sub-Committee on Secondary Industries. The reference was a response to 'Australia's urgent need for plywood'. Queensland, as the principal source for plywood supplying 70 per cent of domestic requirements, was believed to have only enough timber for a further six to seven years.[14]

There were international trade agreement barriers to giving PNG timber preference in the Australian market. Opposition from the USA to 'discrimination' was specifically cited by the representative of the Commonwealth Department of Trade and Customs as a reason why preference could not be given to PNG timber veneers imported into Australia.[15] However the principle established in June 1946 for the forest policy approved by Minister Ward asserted an even more important limit upon giving the metropolitan market priority. While holders of pre-war harvesting permits were to be encouraged to re-establish their operations, they were required to first meet 'immediate Territory requirements', then meet Australian 'shortages of sawn timber and logs' and finally supply the larger 'export market as shipping becomes available'. However where a specific timber produced in PNG was either not required in the colony or Australia, there was no objection to selling the surplus to the United States, particularly as this would earn US dollars.[16] In short, not only was there no automatic subordination to Australian requirements, there was a deliberate strand of development thought about and in the colony which gave primacy to PNG's immediate postwar rebuilding needs.

Because the war had been especially destructive for many Papua New Guineans and for the colonial economy, in one direction meeting rebuilding needs was especially clear-cut. The needs shaped the Administration's first phase of giving priority to 'native interests' and also affected future development policy.

---

14 All quotes in this paragraph are from NAA: A518/1 AQ800/1/1 Part 1 *Administration* Minutes of Fourth Meeting, 25/6/1947.
15 NAA: A518/1 AQ800/1/1 Part 1 *Administration* Minutes of Second Meeting. Opposition from the United States of America to 'discrimination' was specifically cited by the representative of the Commonwealth Department of Trade and Customs as a reason why preference could not be given to PNG timber veneers imported into Australia.
16 NAA: A518/1 AU800/1/1 *Administration general. Subjects to be dealt with by Inter-Departmental Committee on co-ordination of plans for development of the Territory of Papua-New Guinea* 22/5/47 'Exports of timber in the log from Papua and New Guinea.'

Reconstruction and Rehabilitation

Prolonged modern warfare had disrupted indigenous existence in PNG on a scale far beyond that wrought pre-war by plantations and mines. The effect of the conflict had also been more severe in PNG than in other British colonies, specifically Nigeria and Fiji which made using the development plans formulated for these territories of less relevance.[17] The military conflict had wrought havoc in some areas but done little damage in others. As Worsley indicates, where the war 'did touch it destroyed utterly' although about one-third of the country's population was unaffected.[18] At least 15,000 indigenes and an estimated 100,000 pigs had been killed.[19] In rural areas, houses, food gardens, roads and bridges suffered extensive damage.

Bombing and other forms of fighting had been severe and especially destructive in their effects in the areas of the country where plantation agriculture had been substantial, including the Gazelle Peninsula, Bougainville, New Ireland and Madang. Some idea of the effect upon plantation agriculture can be gauged from the following figures. Prior to the outbreak of the military conflict there had been about 370 and 130 plantations operating in New Guinea and Papua respectively. Within two years, when the Australia New Guinea Production Control Board was formed and took over the operation of plantations in areas not controlled by the Japanese from the military-run ANGAU, this number had been reduced to 121 producing large holdings.[20] At the end of the war, there were very few undamaged buildings in the main towns of north coastal and island New Guinea. Rebuilding 'village life' absorbed scarce resources, even as the Australian Government increased revenues provided for colonial administration.

In addition, thousands of people had left rural holdings to perform various war-related tasks, most prominently as soldiers and carriers. As Worsley concludes: 'After the physical devastation of people and livestock, huts and gardens, the large-scale dragooning of native labour was the most shattering effect of the War upon the lives of the native people'.[21] At its peak, the Allied forces probably employed about 55,000 indigenes, and many more worked without signing-on.[22] Griffin, Nelson and Firth also note indigenous employment by the Japanese military, concluding: 'The total number of Papua New Guineans employed by

---

17   ToPNG *Report* pp. 13–14

18   Peter Worsley *The Trumpet Shall Sound: A Study of "Cargo" Cults in Melanesia* (New York: Schocken Books, 1968) p. 195. See also Griffin, Nelson & Firth *Papua New Guinea*, esp. pp. 91–99.

19   Worsley *The Trumpet Shall Sound* p. 195

20   Jackman *Copra marketing* p. 96

21   Worsley *The Trumpet Shall Sound* p. 124

22   Griffin, Nelson & Firth *Papua New Guinea* p. 96

the Japanese is unknown'.[23] Initially, the health of many workers suffered, with sickness among the indigenous carriers on the Kokoda Trail up to 30 per cent. Of long-term consequence for postwar recovery, malaria and dysentery were introduced into the Highlands.[24] However in the last years of the war, as rations increased, conditions of service improved for those employed by the Allies, although the ANGAU plantation overseers were criticised for their brutality toward indigenous workers.[25]

The recruitment of males for military service and associated work reduced the labour available for cultivating household gardens, increasing the burden on women and children of producing food and other consumption goods. Forced removal of many villagers from their existing homes and gardens for safety as well as military purposes made the task of maintaining consumption levels even harder.[26] Adding to the effect of war damage, immediately after the fighting ended thousands of indigenes, mainly males, employed as carriers and other military assistants were demobilised. The numbers of indigenes employed on wages plummeted dramatically. Responsibility for meeting the needs of large numbers of people returning to rural villages was transferred on to households, resulting in at least short-term deficiencies in many items of necessary consumption.

One of the first priorities of the postwar colonial administration, and especially the Department of Public Health under its newly appointed Director John Gunther,[27] was to deal with the health concerns of the indigenous population. The welfare consequences of the military conflict and the withdrawal of the civilian administration from important if limited pre-war activities dealing with indigenous health and welfare, posed urgent problems. The concerns of public officials about the state of indigenous health, and their efforts to assess conditions, neatly illustrate not only how the postwar welfare of the native people was evaluated, but also how the assessment reinforced the importance of planning to make development happen.

---

23 Griffin, Nelson & Firth *Papua New Guinea* p. 97

24 Worsley *The Trumpet Shall Sound* p. 125

25 Griffin, Nelson & Firth *Papua New Guinea* p. 96; Geoffrey Gray 'Stanner's War: W.E.H. Stanner, the Pacific War, and its Aftermath' *The Journal of Pacific History* 2006, vol. 41, no. 2, pp. 145–163, esp. p. 155, citing anthropologist Herbert Ian Hogbin, 'Report of an Investigation of Native Labour in New Guinea' (Unpublished document).

26 Major L Austen 'A Paper on Native Welfare' in NAA: A9372 vol. 2 *ANGAU*

27 Hasluck *A Time for Building* p. 103. For more on Gunther's appointment and personal qualities, as well as the operations of the Department of Public Health in the immediate post-war years, see also Downs *The Australian Trusteeship* pp. 43–49; James Griffin '"Someone Who Needed No Pushing": The Making of Sir John Gunther' in Sione Latukefu (ed.) *Papua New Guinea: A Century of Colonial Impact 1884–1984* (Port Moresby: National Research Institute and UPNG, 1989) pp. 223–246; Denoon, Dugan & Marshall *Public Health in Papua New Guinea* pp. 67–84, pt 2, chs 8–9; Sir John Gunther 'Post-war medical services in Papua New Guinea: a personal view' in Sir Burton G Burton-Bradley (ed.) *A History of Medicine in Papua New Guinea: Vignettes of an Earlier Period* (Kingsgrove NSW: Australasian Medical Publishing, 1990) pp. 47–76.

The medical, non-nutritional characteristics of health attracted immediate attention. Malaria, hookworm, tuberculosis and leprosy as well as other primarily tropical illnesses seriously affected many Papua New Guineans. They also undercut long-term welfare, including the physical characteristics of stature and strength, key ingredients of the capacity to labour. Reducing the prevalence of these illnesses, which were of little significance to populations in industrial countries, had priority.

In 1946, Gunther decided that:

> his first task was to provide basic health care as quickly and as widely as possible. Needs were greatest among those communities that had become dependent [pre-war] upon government or mission health services and then been cut off from all aid during the war. [The apparent] signs of ill-health were the numbers of people suffering from skin diseases, yaws, enlarged spleens resulting from malaria, and respiratory diseases.[28]

However ill-health soon acquired a more comprehensive conception than particular infections and diseases, to include nutrition and other medical characteristics of the indigenous population. Systematic data collection began on these dimensions, initially through fact-finding visits by individual officials, including by Gunther to war-torn Bougainville.[29]

In 1947, the Department of External Territories and the Provisional Administration responsible for the Territories of Papua and New Guinea commissioned a Nutrition Survey.[30] This Survey, conducted with 13 field staff and seven staff of the Institute of Anatomy in Canberra, operated under the direction of a Planning Committee. The Committee included the directors of the three departments which were at the centre of postwar reconstruction for the colony, Health, Education and Agriculture, Stock and Fisheries. The Director of Agriculture, W Cottrell-Dormer, had previously outlined a policy and plan for indigenous agriculture which linked the Administration's goal of a 'stable social structure based on a family unit' with the improvement of 'the nutrition and the standard of living of the native peoples of the Territory'. Cottrell-Dormer advocated an 'ideal form of production' of mixed farming on individual smallholdings which combined production for immediate consumption with cash cropping.[31] The Survey was part of a continuing drive to reduce or eliminate the most debilitating conditions faced by the indigenous population,

---

28 Griffin, Nelson & Firth *Papua New Guinea* p. 106
29 Murray 'In Retrospect 1945–1952: Papua-New Guinea and Territory of Papua and New Guinea' in K.S. Inglis (ed.) *The History of Melanesia* Canberra and Port Moresby: RSPAS, ANU and UPNG, p. 198
30 CoA, Department of External Territories *Commonwealth of Australia Report of the New Guinea Nutrition Survey Expedition 1947* (Sydney: Government Printer, 1950)
31 Wright 'Contesting community' p. 87

envisaged as protein shortages and a range of diseases. The low level of protein consumption became an immediate target for colonial officials, who were aware of the war's effects on indigenous herds and flocks.

For pigs in particular, the military conflict had been especially destructive.

> Pig populations in many parts of the country were almost entirely annihilated during the Japanese occupation. As the pig is one of the chief sources of meat to most natives, a serious unbalancing of the native diet has been brought about in such areas.[32]

Consequently colonial officials paid particular attention to increasing meat production by importing and distributing chicken and pigs. Small studs of pure breed imported pigs were established at Lae, Aitape, Rabaul and Sohano, to make possible the distribution of better quality animals to indigenes. Cattle numbers too, which had been reduced from around 30,000 head pre-war to almost nil during the fighting, were slowly increased by a similar process of importation and distribution.[33] Similarly day old chicks and quality cockerels were flown into the colony for distribution.

Previously the Institute of Anatomy in Australia had been advising the Administration, through the Department of External Territories, regarding the appropriate ration scales for labourers employed on plantations, mines and other occupations. Preparing this advice had not required data about consumption patterns of villagers and particularly not of locally produced and immediately consumed produce. However the first objective of the postwar Survey indicated the shifting focus of official efforts, stating that:

> As the Administration was anxious to use as much native grown food as possible it was considered desirable to collect information relative to the food patterns of native groups living exclusively on indigenous foods, and at the same time ascertain the nutritional status and health of these same groups.[34]

The second objective involved locating areas where 'conditions were known to be normal', so that 'abnormal conditions [that is, the localised areas where food shortages did occur: SM] would not give a distorted picture'. By collecting

---

32   CoA *Report to the General Assembly of the United Nations on the Administration of the Territory of New Guinea-From 1st July, 1947 to 30th June, 1948* (Canberra: Commonwealth Government Printer, 1949) p. 23

33   Robin Hide *Pig Husbandry in New Guinea: A Literature Review and Bibliography* Monograph no. 108 (Canberra: Australian Centre for International Agricultural Research, 2003) pp. 8–9; PNGNA: AN12 3,893 F/N 1-1-84 *Planning and Development Part 1 5/11/52 1949–1952* REP Dwyer, Director, DASF to Government Secretary, Port Moresby 'Recommendations made by Senator A.M. Benn after a visit to the Territory of Papua and New Guinea' p. 3

34   CoA *Report of the New Guinea Nutrition Survey* p. 13

'quantitative data on food production and food consumption' where conditions were normal, a base set of data could be established as a yardstick for future 'investigation of food shortages'.

So far, the Survey's terms might seem to suggest only the aim to maintain the status quo in household production. However the third objective pointed to a potential for change being considered, which was in line with Director of Agriculture Cottrell-Dormer's 'ideal form of production' noted above. For the Survey had:

> A third purpose, of perhaps lesser importance, [which] was to ascertain whether it would be possible and desirable to recommend a policy of native agriculture which could combine the production of "cash" and native food crops without detriment to the latter.[35]

The phrase 'without detriment to the latter' is especially important. It stresses the primacy of 'native food crops' over household production of cash, mainly export crops, in the initial postwar phase of fleshing out the details of thinking about development for PNG. That is, while faced with the immediate problem of how to remedy the war affected state of indigenous existence and to overcome immediate welfare deficiencies, by 1947 the colonial administrative priority of information collection as a guide for health policy was also suggesting a direction which an expanded postwar scheme of smallholder agriculture could take.

The terms of the Survey implied a specific developmental objective for indigenous health. To understand why, it is important to recognise the Survey proposed that household living standards needed to be raised, and not simply returned to pre-war levels in order to match those prevailing in industrial countries, especially Australia. As a 1948 Report of the Provisional Administration emphasised:

> Australia offers a rich prize to the teeming Asiatic millions. Australia's nearest friends are at a considerable distance in America and South Africa. Apart, then from the ethical obligations to develop her dependant peoples which Australia accepted when she accepted the trusteeship of the Territory of New Guinea, it is of extreme strategic importance to her that she has control of this buffer area. But, to ensure that this area does function as buffer state and not a festering wound in the Australian way of life, it is essential to extend that way of life to the peoples of this Territory as rapidly as they can absorb the changes.[36]

'[N]ormal areas' within PNG provided the base for domestic comparisons. But in order to define these areas, the Survey constructed the appropriate yardstick

---

35   CoA *Report of the New Guinea Nutrition Survey* p. 13; see also WR Conroy and LA Bridgland, 'Native Agriculture in Papua-New Guinea', in CoA *Report* pt 3, pp. 72–91.

36   ToPNG *Report* p. 10

of adequacy, in nutritional and other terms, by reference to standards found outside the colony. The idea of welfare took on a precise nutritional basis, and one which permitted easy international comparisons. Summarising the Survey findings, the Report stated:

> When the intake of foods is expressed as nutrients it is seen that the calorie intake is slightly lower, and the protein intake much lower than amounts recommended as desirable to ensure adequate nutrition amongst people of Caucasian origin.[37]

In this instance, the specific Caucasians were from Sydney, while other comparisons were made using 'National Research Council Recommended Dietary Allowances ... based solely on North American data'.[38] That is, data derived from mainly urban populations in leading industrial countries, formed the basis of major comparisons for the Survey. Most importantly, the comparisons made it possible to re-emphasise what was deemed necessary if development was to occur and indigenous living standards lifted. '[A]dequate nutrition' at Australian and US levels was the necessary basis for raising the indigenous capacity to labour.

According to the Survey,[39] there were important exceptions however, where the indigenous population was not always worse off than the overseas comparators. Due to the availability of regular sunshine and the wearing of fewer clothes, rickets frequencies were fewer than for children attending Sydney hospitals in the 1930s. The incidence of dental caries was also much lower than usually observed among 'civilised' peoples.

The Survey thus reinforced, through specific dietary and other health conditions, the demarcation between undeveloped and developed peoples and territories which was so important for colonial development planning. In so doing, it also set terms for the subsequent emphasis upon improving welfare by increasing production and raising productivity through reformed agricultural practices.

The postwar drive emphasised by the Survey did not immediately eliminate the most important components of the detrimental health conditions, including tropical diseases and malnutrition, which continued to exist into the 1950s at least. In 1958, Gunther, who had become Assistant Administrator, could still state:

---

37   CoA *Report of the New Guinea Nutrition Survey* p. 23
38   CoA *Report of the New Guinea Nutrition Survey*. In the case of calcium, the use of the North American data was accepted only as a temporary measure (p. 107) 'realizing that these figures are probably well in advance of the actual calcium requirements of the natives'.
39   CoA *Report of the New Guinea Nutrition Survey* pp. 154–155; 248

The population is not healthy: the expectation of life is half of what it should be; the infant mortality rate twice to ten times what it should be …. These indigenous people of the Territory are only 80 per cent well …. This [is] the physical condition of the people which has to be improved so that their country may progress, for they are the only labour force available to achieve development.[40]

Hasluck subsequently made much of his continuing preoccupation, when Territories Minister, with 'the physical welfare and the physical needs of the people', as well as expressing his contempt for 'parliamentary buffoons' in Australia who mocked when told of medical campaigns, including to overcome yaws.[41]

However, by 1948 some reconstruction and rehabilitation had been completed. The official assessment was that:

Despite the shortages in material and personnel, much has been achieved in the two and a half years since the return of the Civil Administration [in 1945]. Most of the villages disturbed by war have been rebuilt, the natives settled and the gardens re-established on pre-war levels …. It is only the European establishments and that part of the native economy which is dependent on imports that has not reached prewar levels.[42]

This ordering of restoration priorities, indigenes in occupation of smallholdings over plantations and other expatriate-owned enterprises was in accord with official objectives. Further, in their initial attention to reconstruction and rehabilitation, officials understood that the process of rebuilding was not simply a technical matter, fixing bridges and roads, and eliminating diseases by the application of medicines. They recognised that dealing with the damaging and deleterious effects of warfare upon the indigenous population also had consequences for the future social relations of production. As much as the first response of officials seemed to be determining and meeting the welfare needs of Papua New Guineans, this occurred with an awareness of the future implications for 'the paramountcy of native interests'. As Administrator JK Murray explained in 1947:

In the carrying out of its policy, the Administration has so far been hampered by the requirements of rehabilitation in this country—the major victim in the Australian theatre during the recent war. It has

---

40   See Sir John Gunther 'The People' in J Wilkes (ed.) *New Guinea and Australia* (Sydney: Angus and Robertson, 1958) p. 49

41   Hasluck *A Time for Building* pp. 101–102. Chapter 11 on health services includes some of the most intensely emotional as well as revealing passages in anything Hasluck wrote or spoke about while Minister for Territories. See, on the same point, Robert Porter *Paul Hasluck: A Political Biography* (Nedlands: University of Western Australia Press, 1993) pp. 112–113.

42   ToPNG *Report* pp. 11–12

been suggested that this task could be more readily accomplished if all new features of policy were postponed until it was completed. The Administration has not accepted this view. It does not believe it either possible or desirable to make such a separation between rehabilitation and future development; the Territory must be reconstructed and developed now on lines in keeping with our intentions for the future. What is done now determines in a large measure the future pattern.[43]

However beyond improving indigenous health, rebuilding roads and bridges, and re-establishing household gardens growing food crops for immediate consumption and local markets, little was settled on what development policy was to be and how policy could be implemented. As shown in section one of this chapter, the lack of detailed direction provided from the Minister and Department in Australia was one impediment to determining what development policy and practice might be. There was also a particular conjunction of international conditions and circumstances in the colony which affected the Administration's capacity to bring development.

Postwar Challenges Affecting Development Policy

Despite the limitations of staff shortages and the difficulties of postwar conditions, Administrator Murray was certain about some aspects of the direction the Administration should take. He and other officials continually stressed the importance of their trusteeship role for securing 'native interests' against the potential for harm, including the breakdown of community. In late 1947, the Administrator argued that economic growth would inevitably mean the transformation of 'the way of life of native people', but 'native tradition' could be preserved as long as the attachment to land was maintained. The Administration acting as trustee could adjudicate on what was 'still vital in native tradition and what [would] become obsolete …. Continued progress will, in the last analysis, be dependent on a simultaneous development and conservation of economic resources'.[44]

Or to cite Murray again from the same document:

In this economic advance, the way of life of the native people will inevitably be transformed. Regret will be felt for the passing of much

43 JK Murray 'Memorandum on the Policy of the Administration' 8 September 1947, sent to the Chairman of the local Administration's Economic and Development Committee on Planning and Development of Papua and New Guinea, subsequently forwarded to the Commonwealth Inter-Departmental Committee for the Coordination of Plans for the Development of Papua-New Guinea. NAA: A518/1 AQ800/1/1 Part 2

44 Wright 'Contesting community' p. 80, citing from NAA: A1838/283 F/N 301/1 *8/9/1947 JK Murray Memorandum on the Policy of the Administration*.

that is admirable and gracious in the traditional life of the people. But the very presence of existing institutions in the country has doomed much of the old order to attenuation and extinction; the choice now lies, in great part, between inaction or development-that development must be directed upon lines calculated to produce the greatest human happiness.[45]

What was obsolete? Determining vitality, what should be preserved and extended in 'native tradition' was difficult for colonial officials, even if stopping local fighting and attacks against administration patrols were obvious 'traditions' which had to be made obsolete. Several postwar conditions threatened the Australian Government's major policy guideline, that the pre-war dominance of plantations and mines would be supplanted by a concentration on raising smallholder output to improve 'native welfare', and secure the 'paramountcy of native interests'. The responses of the colonial administration to each threat further defined what was to occur under this guideline, while also creating space for other obstacles to arise. Officials established key policy parameters, including for labour and land, which were to become central to 'uniform' or 'even' development in the 1950s. The present section details the most substantial challenges which were faced and how officials responded.

Some difficulties arose from the consequences of the war itself, including the worldwide food and other material shortages which encouraged immediate restoration and expansion of plantations. Other challenges resulted from the efforts of colonial officials to overcome the worst effects of the conflict on the indigenous population. With improved health and better food supplies, many indigenes—especially males—could leave smallholdings in home areas to work for commercial enterprises and the Administration. In the immediate postwar years, the out-migration of potential labour threatened the colonial objective of expanding household production. Extending colonial authority to new areas, particularly of the Central Highlands, and reducing the importance of warfare could either make possible the recruitment of increased numbers of labourers or provide the opportunity for more leisure activities. Neither possible outcome satisfied the principal objective of colonial policy and so had to be prevented or at least limited where possible.

Even with a drive to increase production and marketing of copra in the last years of the war, by 1946 only 13 per cent of all plantations had returned to production. A large number of the plantations, 160 of which were in the Territory of New Guinea, had been so badly damaged during the war that it was uneconomic to re-open them. However high prices and a nine year purchasing contract

---

45   NAA: A1838/283 F/N 301/1 p. 3

for copra with the British Ministry of Food,[46] led to the rapid resuscitation of many other large holdings. Between 1945–46 and 1948–49 production of copra increased from 11,000 to 46,000 tons.[47]

After 1945, the wartime turn in government policy against the large firms and owner-occupiers who had operated plantations pre-war was also extended to international companies looking to set up similar operations in PNG. While the principal barrier was the refusal to allow the expropriation and consolidation of land for an expansion of large holdings, the focus upon the rehabilitation of household agriculture also limited the supply of labour for plantation agriculture. Australian Government policy was supported by important officials in the colony.[48]

When political and commercial connections between Australia and Britain were being refashioned, the British Government and major UK firms were searching for areas within the sterling bloc to expand agricultural production under their direct control. The failed Tanganyika Groundnut Scheme remains probably the best known instance of this search. Conceived in 1946 by an official of the United Africa Company, subsidiary of Unilever, the project was taken over by the British government-owned Overseas Food Corporation until closed in 1951.[49] PNG was a focus of attention too, with some colonial officials holding out limited hopes that either the Overseas Food Corporation, or a major international food company, would be able to successfully expand production. The hopes were never realised.

Even before the war, international supplies of cocoa had been threatened by a major outbreak of the swollen shoot virus in West Africa. The virus was especially widespread among the extensive plantings in the British colony of the Gold Coast, later Ghana, the largest exporter in the world. Soon after the war, representatives of cocoa and chocolate manufacturing firms in the UK and Australia began to press their governments for assistance in establishing new areas of supply. PNG's production had been decimated by the war, with an estimated 80–90 per cent of sole planted bushes and approximately 60 per cent of bushes inter-planted with coconuts destroyed.[50] (In the inter-war period PNG was distinct as one of the few places in the world where cocoa was inter-planted with another tree crop, in this case coconuts.) However with climatic and soil

---

46   Jackman *Copra marketing* p. 107

47   NAA: A518/1 H927/1 and Attachment *Development of the Territories. Organisational. Report on Present Conditions in Papua & New Guinea (February 1950)* p. 11

48   See the mid-1946 exchange of correspondence between the Director of DASF, W Cottrell-Dormer and Minister Ward, NAA: A518/1 A58/3/3 *Commodities—Cocoa Papua and New Guinea Proposals for Development.*

49   See also Michael Cowen 'The Early Years of the Colonial Development Corporation: British State Enterprise Overseas during Late Colonialism' *African Affairs* January 1984, vol. 83, no. 330, pp. 63–75

50   NAA: A518/1 A58/3/3 8/1/48 REP Dwyer Acting Director DASF to Government Secretary 'New Guinea Cocoa Industry'. In the inter-war period PNG was distinct as one of the few places in the world where cocoa was inter-planted with another tree crop, in this case coconuts.

conditions in many parts of PNG regarded as extremely favourable for growing cocoa, the colony was considered a potential major source to fill a substantial portion of international demand at a time of serious postwar shortages.

Private firms in Australia and the UK, as well as representative organisations of merchants and manufacturers exerted pressure on the colonial administration and Labor Government for rapid action to support expanded production. The pressure was exerted at a time when world demand exceeded supply and quotas limited the availability of cocoa for Australian manufacturers. Over 80 per cent of cocoa imports into Australia came from West Africa, where a combination of disease and political turmoil was making supply even more uncertain. One proposal, outlined when production in PNG was negligible, envisaged the planting of 175,000 to 200,000 acres, yielding around 25,000 tons to 'produce, close at hand, sufficient Cocoa Beans for both Australia and New Zealand'.[51]

The Australian Government and the British Overseas Food Corporation briefly flirted with a project to assess how increases in major agricultural crops, particularly cocoa, might be achieved. Concerns for the effects upon the indigenous population, including the need to move large numbers of people to provide sufficient labour featured prominently in the Australian scepticism regarding such a large project using mass-production methods.[52] More seriously, Cadbury Brothers, the UK parent company of Cadbury-Fry-Pascall Ltd, based in Claremont Tasmania, sought a large land grant to develop a cocoa plantation on a scale which would dwarf all the existing large holdings in the colony. Consideration of this venture was only finally terminated in 1956, when Cadbury gave up on establishing a plantation, settling instead for a role as major purchaser and exporter of PNG cocoa.[53] In addition to the Administration's opposition to substantial increases in the land occupied and operated by plantation firms, there were also fears that more large holdings would further increase the demand for labour.

These fears were grounded in postwar changes. While an initial substantial reduction occurred in the numbers of Papua New Guineans in wage employment, within five years of the war ending the flow of labour away from smallholdings had been reversed. Between August 1945 and February 1946 the number of employed indigenous labourers fell from 34,000 to 4,100, with most returning to their villages. Subsequently, postwar reconstruction demands resulted

---

51 NAA: A518/1 B58/3/3 *Commodities—Cocoa. Papua and New Guinea. Proposals for Development, Commonwealth Chocolate and Confectionery Manufacturers Association;* NAA A518/1 A58/3/3 21/11/47 Gordon L McLure to EJ Ward, Minister for External Territories

52 NAA: A518/1 C58/3/3 *Commodities—Cocoa. Papua and New Guinea, Proposals for Development* British Overseas Food Corporation. Department of External Territories File memos 17/8/1949 and 11/10/1948

53 NAA: A518/1 A58/3/1 *Cocoa—Papua and New Guinea, Research General*

in increases of around 10,000 workers per year. By mid-1950, the number of indigenes in wage employment had become over 48,000.[54] There was also more labour militancy over working conditions.[55]

One immediate effect of the increase in commercial and government activities was raised concerns about the consequences for village life. These concerns were heightened by other indigenous responses to the war and the postwar re-establishment of civilian colonial authority.

'Cargo Cults', Political Stability and Development Thought

Cults had flourished in some areas prior to World War II.[56] In other areas, including the Highlands, there were cargo—inspired movements during the war, particularly in recently pacified locations from which the Administration's presence had been removed or reduced. The most prominent areas where cults flourished immediately after the war and even into the early 1960s were in the Sepik, Madang and Morobe Districts, although they were also active in Papua, Manus, New Ireland and Bougainville, particularly on Buka Island.[57]

The international warfare, carried out by militaries using equipment of types and quantities never previously seen, unsettled indigenous existence beyond the effects of actual destruction and loss of life. Downs notes:

> Uncertainty and suspicion [of the colonial authorities: SM] were not diminished by the extent of the allied armadas that ended the Japanese invasion. The massive use of men and material was in extra-ordinary contrast to the small penurious pre-war administrations .... When the people saw the extent of the allied war effort they could not help making comparisons.[58]

Where wartime experience had included contact with Australian and US troops, including black Americans, the effect was often profound. The experience sometimes strengthened a distinction between 'Australians' who as

---

54   Worsley *The Trumpet Shall Sound* p. 196
55   Worsley *The Trumpet Shall Sound* p. 197, citing Lucy Mair *Australia in New Guinea* 1st edn (London: Christophers, 1948) p. 216.
56   The complexities involved in describing what is meant by the expression 'cargo cult' are discussed at length in Worsley's, *The Trumpet Shall Sound*, including in the 'Introduction to the Second Edition: Theoretical and Methodological Considerations' pp. ix–lxix and 'Introduction to the First Edition' pp. 11–16.
57   Downs *The Australian Trusteeship* pp. 61–65. See also: Hugh Laracy '"Imperium in Imperio"?: the Catholic Church on Bougainville' p. 131; Albert Maori Kiki *Ten Thousand Years in a Lifetime A New Guinea Autobiography* (Melbourne: Cheshire, 1971) pp. 104–125; Eugene Ogan *Business and Cargo among the Nasioi of Bougainville* New Guinea Research Bulletin no. 14 (Port Moresby and Canberra: New Guinea Research Unit, ANU, 1972); James Griffin 'Movements Towards Secession 1964–76' in Anthony J. Regan and Helga M. Griffin (eds) *Bougainville before the conflict* pp. 291–299
58   Downs *The Australian Trusteeship* p. 61

military personnel were admired for their friendly egalitarianism, and officials plus employers who were classified as 'English' because they maintained discriminatory practices and attitudes towards indigenes.[59]

Comparisons reinforced previous puzzlement about the basis for the wealth or cargo possessed by Europeans, which had been present almost from the start of colonial rule. Comparison and conjecture combined with unemployment and impoverishment fuelled the formation of organisations that speculated about and became committed to finding the source of the now so obvious wealth. For many cults and their leaders, the abundance of goods associated with the European presence—military and civilian alike—did not appear to be a consequence of labour. Cargo came into the colony with no labour and other means of production seemingly involved, except by the largely indigenous labour force which unloaded ship and aircraft cargoes. One official assessment provided in a February 1950 secret report, concluded that the cults in part represented a 'definite misappreciation of the ramifications of production and supply'. Accordingly: 'These manifestations [of cargo cultism] are dealt with tactfully and every effort made to acquaint the people with the lack of foundation for the cult and to instruct them in the processes of manufacture and supply, including incidental labour, by which the outside world acquires its "cargo"'.[60] Not only was its production 'hidden' because the goods were manufactured elsewhere, but ownership within the colony passed into the hands of those who did not labour—the plantation owners, government officials and company managers whose wealth could not be associated with any productive labour they carried out.

In some cases, the increased supplies of goods not obviously connected to labour produced leaders who garnered support by promising to find their source, 'capture it' and bring wealth to an organisation's members. Unsurprisingly, and especially potent in the areas where postwar impoverishment was most severe, cult activities were often directed at finding and identifying the seemingly mysterious source of wealth which arose without labour.

Wartime experiences and postwar hopes fuelled by the cessation of military conflict provided suitable conditions for revitalised and reshaped cultist activities.[61] Unemployed or underemployed villagers and increased commercialisation of consumption opened further space for the rise of cargo cults. For Australian officials countering cults played an important part in shaping development

---

59   Worsley *The Trumpet Shall Sound* p. 126
60   NAA: A518/1 H927/1 *Development of the Territories* p. 9
61   Worsley's *The Trumpet Shall Sound* remains the most comprehensive account of these activities. For an assessment of the significance of cults during and after World War II, from the position of a former senior Administration official, see Downs *The Australian Trusteeship* pp. 61–65, 201–206. See also Peter Lawrence *Road Belong Cargo: A Study of the Cargo Movement in the Southern Madang District, New Guinea* (Manchester: Manchester University Press and Humanities Press, 1964).

thinking along colony-wide lines. In countering the claims of cult leaders that increased consumption could occur without a concomitant increase in labour, colonial officials were also forced to re-emphasise how increased production by households was central to their development plans.

The initial Administration efforts to co-opt cult leaders showed concern over a different kind of threat. Postwar cults and their leaders sometimes developed as centres of opposition to continued colonial rule, challenging the legitimacy of administrative authority, including its Christian basis. Between 1946 and 1950 the Paliau Movement 'established control over most of southern Manus ... organized a boycott of the Administration, and [its leader Paliau] is said to have urged the expulsion of the Europeans and the Asians'.[62]

When cult leaders became anti-mission and/or opposed to the colonial government in word and deed, they were either turned or jailed. The case of Yali, the most significant Cargo leader on the Rai (Madang) Coast in the late 1940s and early 1950s, is exemplary in this respect. At first the Administration sought to temper his anti-mission views, persuading him to encourage followers to form cooperatives and other acceptable development projects. However as the Letub Cargo movement grew in importance, its activities were associated with threats against missionaries and cult non-believers. Illegal taxes were levied. In 1950, the Administration arrested Yali, charged him with incitement to rape and extortion. He was tried and sentenced to six and a half years in gaol.[63]

A favoured Administration response was to attempt to co-opt cult leaders in postwar reconstruction efforts as well as to try to explain the ways goods were produced. To cite Downs, a senior official:

> Administration efforts to stop objectionable cult practices included moral persuasion, economic aid, better education, social reconstruction, better communication and, as a last resort, police action. Most cult situations were resolved by a judicious combination of all these methods. Some cult leaders were taken on conducted tours of Australia to see the source and manufacture of goods. The tours proved popular, but the tourists were not easily convinced. For example, the Mint in Canberra was beyond explanation and had to be dropped from the itinerary.[64]

Of greater long-term importance, cult activities:

> compelled the attention of the Government and resulted in closer and more intensive Administration support. The evidence is clear

---

62 Worsley *The Trumpet Shall Sound* ch. ix, pp. 170–194, 'From Millenium to Politics' captures the post-war shift in Solomon Islands and PNG. The quote comes from pp. 186–188.
63 Worsley *The Trumpet Shall Sound* pp. 216–218
64 Downs *The Australian Trusteeship* p. 62

that all the major cult movements and disturbances were followed by more favourable Administration treatment of the areas in which they occurred.[65]

In calling attention to the more impoverished areas, the cults were important in forcing officials to emphasise that development should be 'even' across the colony. During the 1950s, tackling cults contributed to the construction of a more precise official direction for late colonial development, uniform or even development (see Chapter Three).

The Threats of Leisure and Wage Employment

Improving indigenous welfare required lifting household output, which under conditions of a relatively simple division of labour mainly involved increasing the numbers of workers and lengthening working hours on smallholdings. However the provision of compensation for damage to housing, livestock and gardens made increased leisure an enticing and realistic possibility which particularly arose in lowlands and islands areas. By the end of 1949, almost one million pounds Australian had been paid to indigenes in war damage compensation, with more than one million yet-to-be paid. A Committee of Enquiry formed in July 1945 by the Administration to recommend an appropriate basis for compensating indigenes was concerned about how money would be spent, stating that:

> The leisure thus made available is largely spent in gambling, and it seems inevitable, unless the flow to the Islands of goods of a type which are necessary to native subsistence—garden tools, fishing tackle, etc.—is considerably increased, that the money which was intended to enable natives to replace these losses will have been frittered away before it is possible for them to do so.[66]

Changes in consumer preferences, toward purchased rather than domestically produced goods, affected some Papua New Guineans' propensity to labour in household gardens. This was particularly the case among younger indigenes living close to urban centres with shops and markets, with Hanuabada village adjacent to Port Moresby one focus for official attention because residents were

---

65   Downs *The Australian Trusteeship* p. 65; see also Huntley Wright 'Economic or Political Development: The Evolution of "Native" Local Government Policy in the Territory of Papua and New Guinea, 1945–1963' *Australian Journal of Politics and History* 2002, vol. 48, no. 2, p. 198, fn. 34, who cites an August 1953 letter from anthropologist Margaret Mead to Hasluck regarding the establishment of a Local Government Council on Baluan Island, Manus District that rescued 'the constructive elements in the Paliau movement [ie. 'cargo cult': HW] and arrested what might—under other policies—be a focus of trouble and destructive activity'.
66   NAA: A518/1 H927/1 *Development of the Territories* pp. 8–9; Mair *Australia in New Guinea* pp. 219–224. Mair notes too that compensation also furthered commercialisation, as well as early attempts by indigenes to enter commerce, transportation and related activities.

'aping' European consumption habits and not growing their own food.[67] Early signs that postwar conditions had opened up the possibility of more leisure rather than labour were the substantial numbers of young men seen in rural villages and some urban centres, playing cards or simply visiting friends. Some indication of the liquidity of indigenous households is given by the amount of money in Commonwealth Savings Bank accounts. In 1950, there were 33,415 accounts with AU£466,050 deposited. The popularity of as well as official antipathy toward gambling, sometimes for large amounts of money continued into the mid-1950s.[68]

The prospect of more leisure rather than productive labour was especially strong in the Highlands, but for different reasons. The Highlands had provided few plantation and mine workers before World War II so the basis of concern was not that workers returning from war-service or the recently abolished indentured employment would select leisure rather than re-entering wage labour. Instead in the region where 'first contact' had only occurred within the last 20 years,[69] the establishment of the colonial peace reduced the uncertainty arising from warfare as well as the amount of labour time needed to prosecute combat. Downs, a kiap or colonial official, who subsequently became District Commissioner, Eastern Highlands, notes how in the immediate postwar years his predecessor George Greathead had reported that: 'Something had to be done to provide opportunities for a huge population in desperate need of some outlet to fill the vacuum which pacification had created'.[70] The increasing availability of steel tools especially axes and shovels also lessened the time required for many domestic tasks, particularly clearing trees and bush from land prior to cultivation and planting of crops.[71] Again potential working age males were most affected as these activities tended to be performed by males.

An immediate if limited solution to the problem of unemployment and underemployment was labouring in public works, directed by administration officials. This fitted with the increased provision of public revenues for expenditure on roads and other facilities. In 1939–40, the Australian Government

---

67   PNGNA: AN12 3,875 F/N 1-1-4 *Plans for Native Welfare, Social Development and Economic Development, 1947–1951* 8/8/51, Minutes of Meeting of Inter-Departmental Committee on Native Development and Welfare held in Conference Room of Department of District Services and Native Affairs. However the minutes also noted the view that there was little land available to till in Hanuabada.

68   NAA: A518/1 H927/1 *Development of the Territories* pp. 8–9; MacWilliam 'Post-War Reconstruction in Bougainville' pp. 229–230

69   Michael Leahy 'The Central Highlands of New Guinea' Royal Geographical Society, published in *Geographical Journal* vol. 87, no. 3, pp. 229–260; Michael Leahy and Maurice Crain *The Land That Time Forgot* (New York: Funk and Wagnalls, 1937); Anon. '"A Second Kenya" in Central New Guinea: Return of Hagen-Sepik Exploring Party' *Pacific Islands Monthly* 15 August 1939, vol. 10, no. 1, pp. 19–20; Bob Connolly and Robin Anderson *First Contact: New Guinea's Highlanders Encounter the Outside World* (New York: Viking Penguin, 1987); Gammage *The Sky Travellers*

70   Ian Downs 'Kiap, Planter and Politician: a Self-portrait' p. 243

71   Richard F Salisbury *From Stone to Steel: Economic Consequences of a Technological Change in New Guinea* (Melbourne University Press, 1962)

provided a mere AUD90,000 to administer Papua. In the first year after the war ended, this had increased to AUD1.1 million for the two territories. Five years later the allocation was almost AUD18 million. However from 1945 to 1950, administration expenditure on all activities in PNG increased much less, from AUD1.2 to over AUD11 million. The gap between allocation and expenditure is striking and suggests much about Administration capacity.[72]

Hawksley notes that:

> Peace therefore created a relatively large population of surplus male labour. The administration's fear was that boredom would set in and … it attempted to soak up some labour for public and private works to prevent highlanders from reverting to warfare.[73]

However, as Hawksley also emphasises, the numbers employed by the Administration were relatively small by comparison with the large populations in the Highlands. The imbalance between the number of waged jobs and the number of idle potential workerswage employed and potential labour force became ever greater as colonial authority was extended into more and more areas.[74] During 1947/48, in the Bena, Chimbu and Kainantu sub-districts, with an estimated population of 250,000 people, only 2,017 were employed on a permanent and casual basis.[75] Not until the 1950s, as the road and bridge building program gathered pace in the Highlands through the use of unpaid gangs of workers from nearby villages, did the public works program draw more upon the available labour force (see Chapter Three).

Before this program could take effect and an expansion of smallholder coffee growing occurred, however, there was a rapid exodus of Highlanders, primarily males, from the region. Other changes occurring within the Highlands increased the attractiveness of waged employment. Due to the extended commercialisation of Highlanders' existence, which had begun before the war and further accelerated during the conflict, previously valuable goods lost their appeal. The gradual introduction of a colonial currency as the principal medium of exchange increased buying and selling of recently introduced products, whose uses spread rapidly across the region.[76]

---

72   Griffin, Nelson & Firth *Papua New Guinea* p. 102; Downs *The Australian Trusteeship* pp. 37, 122, Table 6.2. See also JK Murray 'In Retrospect' p. 206. I have converted pounds into dollars at the rate of 2:1 for convenience, even though Australia did not switch from the former measure into dollars until 1966.

73   Hawksley *Administrative Colonialism* p. 339

74   For a detailed consideration of the process of extending colonial authority, see Hawksley *Administrative Colonialism* pp. 317–319, and below.

75   Hawksley *Administrative Colonialism* p. 340

76   Ian Hughes *New Guinea Stone Age Trade: The Geography and Ecology of Traffic in the Interior* Terra Australis 3 (Canberra: ANU, 1977); Ian Hughes 'Good Money and Bad: Inflation and Devaluation in the Colonial Process' *Mankind* 1978, vol. 11, no. 3, pp. 308–318

Under the Highlands Labour Scheme, which formalised the movement of workers out of the region, plantations and mines in particular came to depend upon these workers. Commencing in January 1950, by June over 4,000 workers had left Goroka, the collection point from which labourers departed. A further 5,000 were assembled, waiting to leave. By June 1951, of the 8,400 workers who had left the District, less than 1,000 sought employment with the colonial administration while the remainder went to work on plantations, primarily in Madang and New Britain.[77]

Recruitment continued during the 1950s and 1960s. As smallholder production of crops expanded, recruiters had to move further into more remote Highland areas, where no coffee or other commercial crops were grown, to sign up workers. Going away to work on plantations for a contracted period, usually two years at-a-time, became a rite of passage for many young Highlanders, and a means of acquiring consumption goods, including bride price payments.[78] The attraction of leisure and ceremonial activities added to the challenge that wage employment posed for a colonial administration attempting to bring development. Neither leisure nor migration as wage workers suited official plans for increasing smallholder production. In the 1950s, a more desirable solution was found through the rapid expansion of smallholder coffee growing and processing.

Turning the Highlands into the next major labour frontier threatened household existence and the dissolution of community, especially if males left the region for employment in coastal and islands areas.[79] Highlanders leaving for coastal and island areas of the colony where illnesses were found which were not common at higher altitudes also caused official concern. The threat increased the already substantial attention being paid by the postwar colonial administration to indigenous health. In early 1950, the Department of Public Health noted that: 'The greatest advance [in prophylactic health measures: SM] was to establish an active anti-tuberculosis team who are using the BCG vaccine on a mass scale in the Central Highlands, thus allowing the recruitment of labour and so increasing the economic potential and doing as little harm to these completely non-immune people'.[80]

However not all the uncertainty about the most desirable direction of development policy arose because of the indecisiveness of the colonial government, the extent of the war damage and the pressure for a further

77   The figures are from Hawksley *Administrative Colonialism* pp. 341–342.
78   See Paula Brown *The Chimbu: a study in change in the New Guinea Highlands* (London: Routledge and Kegan Paul, 1973) p. 27; also cited in Hawksley *Administrative Colonialism* p. 342.
79   Francis J West 'Colonial Development in Central New Guinea' *South Pacific* September-October 1956, vol. 9, no. 2, p. 308; Worsley *The Trumpet Shall Sound* p. 196 makes the same point.
80   NAA: A518/1 H927/1 *Development of the Territories* Appendix E 'A Report on the Present Position of the Department of Public Health' p. 1. See also Hawksley *Administrative Colonialism* p. 341.

expansion in plantation production. The war and some postwar conditions also stimulated shifts in indigenous agriculture, including by ambitious indigenes who wanted to expand their activities further using wage and other forms of employed labour. During the initial postwar years, sorting out which 'native interests' would be 'paramount' and which form of indigenous production should receive administration backing was not settled quickly or easily.

Changes in Indigenous Agriculture

Pre-war indigenous growers had produced copra for international markets, as well as sold coconuts and other produce into village and nearby urban markets.[81] The European administrative, mission and commercial presence had begun to encourage major changes in production and exchange, not least by increasing supplies of shells used as a medium of exchange and store of value.[82] One effect of this pre-war increase in commerce was to enlarge the space occupied by indigenous capitalists, who traded locally produced crops for sale to the colonial administration, missions and expatriate plantations.

For areas of the country outside the immediate war zones, the military conflict accelerated commercialisation of indigenous agriculture. Military bases and administration centres populated by Allied and ANGAU personnel required large amounts of food, not all of which could be imported. With substantial numbers of indigenes removed from villages for employment as carriers, soldiers and other essential personnel, the demand for purchased food supplies expanded. Where the occupying Japanese military engaged in growing rice and other produce, a demonstration effect in agricultural practices developed and new crops were adopted by village producers.

Indigenous growers responded in two intersecting ways to postwar shortages and increased demand for their produce locally and abroad. Firstly, there was a spontaneous surge, which was especially prominent in but not confined to vegetable production for missions, administration centres and remaining military bases. In late 1952, an Australian Senator who toured PNG and subsequently made recommendations to Department of Agriculture, Stock and Fisheries officials in PNG pointed out that:

---

81   See MA Wheeler, MA Sackett and DRJ Densley *Coconuts Agriculture in the Economy. A Series of Review Papers* (Konedobu: Department of Primary Industry, n.d.) p. 5.

82   Hawksley *Administrative Colonialism* p. 263 notes how from the end of the nineteenth century Tolai growers supplied German plantations with local produce, including vegetables. On the inter-war years, see Hughes *New Guinea Stone Age Trade*, and Hughes 'Good Money and Bad'; AJ Strathern 'Political development and problems of social control in Mt Hagen' in RJ May (ed.) *Priorities in Melanesian Development* (Canberra and Port Moresby: RSPAS, ANU and UPNG, 1973) pp. 73–82, esp. pp. 73–74.

The vegetable production on the Highlands for such areas as Port Moresby, Lae and Madang, has already reached their peak and many thousands of pounds come out weekly. The Armed Forces personnel in Manus are also supplied from the Central Highlands and the local islands there.[83]

While initially distinctions among indigenous growers were not critical for colonial policy, this soon changed even as the activities of wealthy indigenes were vital for the postwar increases. Many accumulated capital from their return on growing and processing crops for domestic and international markets. The early efforts by administration officials to encourage and supervise indigenous growers were also important in propelling indigenous accumulation. These efforts in turn accelerated recognition of the fact that there were two principal forms of indigenous production and the Administration would have to restrain one while advancing the other. As part of the general drive against extending plantations and increasing wage employment, indigenous large holdings would subsequently have to be restrained. The early postwar growing, processing and marketing of rice and cocoa illustrate how indigenous ambitions and initial colonial efforts to encourage 'native interests' intersected.

Rice

Prior to World War I, plantations and missions in New Guinea were already heavily dependent upon rice to feed labourers and others.[84] While there had been minor attempts to grow the grain in Papua, commencing in 1891 and in New Guinea as early as 1903,[85] most rice consumed was imported from Asia. In 1918, the Native Plantations Ordinance came into effect in Papua with the intention, in part, of 'mak[ing] the Territory self-supporting as regards rice'.[86] In reporting another, largely unsuccessful, drive during the 1920s, Lieutenant Governor of Papua, Sir Hubert Murray, also stated that the aim had been to make the 'Territory self-supporting in rice'.[87]

Between the wars, 'rice cultivation [in the Mekeo area] was encouraged by the Papuan administration and the Roman Catholic Mission of the Sacred Heart'.[88] Initially production increased under considerable administration supervision

83 PNGNA: AN12 3,893 F/N 1-1-84 REP Dwyer, Director, DASF to Government Secretary 'Recommendations made by Senator AM Benn after a visit to the Territory of Papua and New Guinea' p. 3
84 Rowley *Australians in German New Guinea* p. 6
85 Peter R Hale *Rice Agriculture in the Economy. A Series of Review Papers* (Konedobu: Department of Primary Industry, n.d. c. 1977) p. 7; Firth, 'Albert Hahl' p. 100
86 Hale *Rice Agriculture* p. 7
87 Gordon Dick and Bob McKillop *A Brief History of Agricultural Extension and Education in Papua New Guinea* Extension Bulletin no. 10 (Port Moresby: Department of Primary Industry, 1976) p. 17
88 FJ Jeffreys *The Mekeo Rice Project* MA thesis, Port Moresby: Economics Department, UPNG, 1974, p. 20. Bryant Allen 'The North Coast Region' in Donald Denoon and Catherine Snowden (eds) *A time to plant and a*

and enforcement of Native Regulations requiring agricultural production. Although official supervision was withdrawn in the 1934–35 production year, the Catholic Mission stepped in to purchase rice that was surplus to domestic consumption and paid spot cash. Production peaked at between 300 to 400 tons in 1936–37, and slumped thereafter.[89]

During World War II, the military controlled ANGAU attempted to produce much needed supplies in the Mekeo floodplain, north of Port Moresby. The Japanese also tried to increase local supplies of rice, with substantial compulsory schemes in New Britain and New Ireland,[90] and small plots on Bougainville.[91]

In February 1944, Major WHH Thompson, District Officer Lakekamu who was responsible for increasing rice growing in the ANGAU-controlled territory, noted how labour intensive was the method currently being employed on village holdings in the Mekeo. Thompson also indicated the extent to which mechanisation was employed, how this increased output and how the ANGAU had made limited use of compulsion. In 1944, mechanisation was extended from planting to harvesting,[92] and rice growing provided not only food for household consumption but also for trade. Thompson concluded optimistically:

> [I] cannot see why in the future perhaps a district, or the whole Territory, should not be self-supporting as far as rice is concerned.[93]

However with the end of hostilities, a 'sharp decline both in interest [regarding rice growing in the Mekeo] and acreages occurred in the 1945–46 and 1946–47 seasons'.[94] Revitalisation of rice growing in the Mekeo flood plain did not occur until 1948 when Administration concerns and indigenous efforts were at least temporarily united in a brief period of high prices and global shortages. However the union brought to the fore tensions over how substantial the administration's role should be and whether there should be a simple household or a complex division of labour, increased by mechanisation. Also in dispute was whether yields could ever be substantial enough on a flood plain with unpredictable rainfall using dry land cultivation methods, distinct from the wet land, flooded irrigation methods employed for growing most of the world's rice.

---

time to uproot: a History of Agriculture in Papua New Guinea (Port Moresby: Institute of Papua New Guinea Studies for the Department of Primary Industry, 1981) p. 112. See also Crocombe Communal Cash Cropping p. 11.

89   Jeffreys Mekeo Rice p. 22

90   Hale Rice Agriculture p. 7; TS Epstein Capitalism, Primitive and Modern: Some Aspects of Tolai Economic Growth (East Lansing: Michigan State University Press, 1968) p. 60

91   John Connell Taim bilong mani: The evolution of agriculture in a Solomon Island society Development Studies Centre Monograph no. 12 (Canberra: Australia National University, 1978) pp. 67–68

92   Hale Rice Agriculture p. 13 concludes that as a result of the war-time experience: 'The Mekeos have never looked back to manual production'.

93   Major WHH Thompson 'A Paper on Rice Cultivation' in NAA: A9372 vol. 3 ANGAU; also noted in Jeffreys Mekeo Rice p. 134.

94   Jeffreys Mekeo Rice p. 27

While these tensions became more apparent from the early 1950s, the initial postwar revitalisation of rice growing took place in a manner which contained all the elements of the later turmoil.

John Connell has described how in 1948, in Siwai in southern Bougainville, there was the 'first government effort at agricultural extension' in the area. The actions involved supervising rice plantings at two villages in order to produce seed for further plantings.[95] The 1949–50 estimates for the colony's Department of Agriculture Stock and Fisheries (DASF) indicate the scope and nature of the Administration's postwar ambitions regarding research and extension activities designed to increase rice production. Eight district agricultural stations and two sub-district agricultural stations had either commenced and were intended to continue activities, or were initiating work. At Madang, Sohano, Popondetta, Beipa and Aitape work had begun, while at Lae, Bainyik via Maprik, Manus and Buin the estimates projected that 'rice experiments [were] to be initiated' or 'rice [was] to be introduced'.[96] Emphasising the importance given to dry land rice growing, Michael Bourke has noted that official trials on rice (234) constituted between one-fifth and one-sixth of all trials (1228) conducted on food crops between 1928 and 1978, and exceeded the trials on any other crop.[97] These figures do not include the extensive experiments conducted in the first five years after the war on rice, which would substantially increase the proportion of all trials devoted to this one food crop.

In each case where substantial efforts were made to produce rice, it was the local class of capitalists and would-be bourgeois that initially led moves to expand indigenous production. While these moves fitted within the general rhubric of 'the paramountcy of native interests', colonial officials were cautious about encouraging any advance of such a class. Shifting indigenous rice growers from Rural Progress Societies to cooperatives with close official supervision of financial contributions from members, other income and expenditure, became one means of limiting the siphoning off of funds for individual accumulation. But it was harder to supervise the uses to which administration-provided machinery, tractors, harvesters and mills were put.

Initially rice played a significant role in the commercial advance of local businessmen,[98] including in southern Bougainville, where linking trade and

---

95   Cf. Connell *Taim bilong mani* pp. 92, 100

96   See NAA: A518/1 G927/4 *Economic Development of the Territories—Commodities—Rice* 11/5/50 FGG Ross to First Assistant Secretary, Department of External Territories 'Rice Production: Papua New Guinea'

97   See RM Bourke *Agronomic field trials on food crops in Papua New Guinea 1928 to 1978* Technical Report 82/3 (Port Moresby: Department of Primary Industry, 1982) pp. 7–8

98   Bryant Allen 'The Importance of Being Equal: the Colonial and Post-Colonial Experience in the Torricelli Foothills' Paper prepared for the Wenner-Gren Foundation for Anthropological Research Symposium no. 95 *Sepik Research Today: the Study of Sepik Cultures in and for Modern Papua New Guinea* held in Basel, Switzerland 19–26 August 1984, p. 16

production was integral to their postwar activities.[99] However by the mid-1950s, rice growing declined as a cash crop in southern Bougainville. The decline occurred in the face of crop disease, the rise of a superior source of income and revenue, cocoa growing, and ultimately the long-term decline in world prices for the grain. However even as it ceased to provide income or revenue returns commensurate with those available from other produce or wage labour, rice entered into necessary consumption to such an extent that households continued to grow it for immediate non-marketed purposes.[100]

Straddling, between higher wage and salaried employment, and accumulation through rice production was also a feature of indigenous efforts in other regions of the colony. A well known instance occurred in the Sepik, according to Hale 'a result of self-help agricultural extension'.[101] Bryant Allen explains the origins of postwar rice growing in East Sepik as a consequence of men from the region serving in carrier lines, plantation and vegetable garden labour gangs, as well as police and military units which for the first time meant mixing with other indigenes from Papua and New Britain. Allen explains one consequence thus:

> Men from the Sepik who served in these units heard talk about "Kampani", a new form of organisation which was thought to resemble the social and political organisation of Europeans who "worked together" to achieve wealth and did not fight among themselves as did Papua New Guineans. "Kampani" also seems to have been closely associated with rice.[102]

A similar impetus behind postwar Sepik rice growing came from Pita Simogun of Dagua village, west of Wewak. Having trained during the war in Australia for guerrilla fighting in New Britain, Simogun encouraged police in Port Moresby to 'return to their villages after the war to initiate "bisnis" enterprises, using whatever cash crops would grow best in their respective areas'. With funds contributed from war damage compensation, in 1947 he established the Dagua Rural Progress Society. Concludes Allen: 'Simogun planted rice, peanuts and coffee at Dagua, but rice grew better than peanuts and became the major annual crop of the cooperative in 1948 and 1949'.[103]

This venture had considerable influence in nearby and distant areas. By using the ex-policemen network, Simogun was able to affect activities beyond the

---

99 NSPGA: Buin Patrol Reports *Report No. 4, 1952/53 Patrol to Kono Paramountcy* p. 2; also cited in MacWilliam 'Post-war Reconstruction in Bougainville'; see also Connell *Taim bilong mani* pp. 199–200

100 NSPGA: Buin Patrol Reports *Report No. 10, 1959/60 Patrol to Eastern Paramountcy of Buin Sub-District* p. 9

101 Hale *Rice Agriculture* p. 9

102 Allen 'The North Coast Region' p. 115

103 Allen 'The North Coast Region' p. 116

Sepik District, including the Erap Mechanical Farming Project in the Markham Valley, where the main crops grown and marketed became—after a failed attempt to grow and sell rice—sweet potato and peanuts.[104]

In 1948, the same year as government extension activities began in southern Bougainville, officials in Port Moresby received a request from a prominent indigene in the Mekeo. An official of Inauaia village asked for government assistance to obtain a rice mill, in order to 'start their industry'. The request was made to the first postwar Director of the DASF, Cottrell-Dormer, who was on an inspection tour of the area.

Rice production at Inauaia, and at least another six adjoining villages, was tied to the first flowering of Rural Progress Societies in the area. Extension centres were created at Anabunga and Beipa to facilitate hiring out of machinery to the Rural Progress Societies 'to enable them to cultivate commercial holdings of rice'. For the 1950 season about 80 acres of indigenous plantings were harvested, with about half of this area planted using machinery.

> The native people were enthusiastic at first, but were disappointed when the monetary return from the first season's crop was small .... By 1951 rice mills had been set up in six villages and an agricultural research station had been established to investigate mechanisation, variety selection and to carry out research into pests and diseases.

Although there was further expansion over the next two seasons, by 1953 'it was apparent ... that the project was rapidly declining', and needed reform.[105]

The official departmental analysis used by the Territories Minister Hasluck understates the extent to which mechanisation requirements increased for the postwar Mekeo Rice Project. A more accurate assessment was made by Cottrell-Dormer, who resigned in 1950 as Director of Agriculture to become Regional Agricultural Officer in charge of the project. In a bitter critique of an article about the Mekeo Project being prepared by Professor OHK Spate of ANU,[106] Cottrell-Dormer succinctly explained why the project had taken the direction of greater mechanisation. He said:

---

104   RG Crocombe and GR Hogbin *The Erap Mechanical Farming Project* New Guinea Research Bulletin no. 1 (Port Moresby and Canberra: New Guinea Research Unit, ANU, 1963) reprinted July 1968
105   Quotations are from NAA: A452/1 1958/628 *Mekeo Rice Project P & NG* 11/61 Paul Hasluck to Master Roger Barker, which was a letter the Minister wrote to a schoolboy who had asked for information about rice production in PNG.
106   OHK Spate 'Changing native agriculture in New Guinea' *The Geographical Review* 1953, vol. 43, no. 2, pp. 151–172; with an extract from this original article published as: Spate 'The Rice Problem in New Guinea' *South Pacific* November-December 1953, pp. 731–736.

Full mechanisation in rice production is the objective because only in this way can the great potentiality of the fertile flood plain be exploited with the existing population density and available labour.[107]

Attempting to utilise a fertile flood plain, subject to extensive flooding as well as long periods of hot weather without rain, brought its own special problems if mechanisation was to be extended to soil preparation, planting, and harvesting as well as milling. The Mekeo people were disinclined to work in collaborative endeavours, for either Rural Progress Societies or later for cooperatives, because of the availability of preferable alternatives. These included paid employment in Port Moresby, growing other better yielding and higher priced crops, or simply extending leisure activities. Hiring of equipment became necessary for nearly every aspect of rice growing on even the smallest holdings. In 1954, the Agronomist-in-Charge of the Epo Experiment Station pronounced that as far as rice production in the Mekeo was concerned 'the impetus has … shifted from peasant to mechanised production'.[108]

As is shown later in this study, even this shift and the associated substantial administration resources involved did not bring a major continuing increase in the production of rice. Rice growing elsewhere in PNG did not raise the same problems for the colonial administration, or receive as much attention and resources as in the Mekeo, but in these areas output also remained low. Instead imports increased substantially to meet a rapidly growing demand, and the objective of colonial, then national self-sufficiency was never achieved.

Spate claimed that:

> the Mekeo has to some extent primed the pump for other schemes. Indeed, the Mekeo and the Gazelle Peninsula rank as the Territory's experimental forcing houses for native agriculture.[109]

The rider 'to some extent' is critical. As will now be shown for cocoa, the parallels between the crops, the populations and areas of the country are very limited. Most importantly, compared to its promotion of rice production the Administration's subsequent role in extending smallholder production and fitting the growing, processing and marketing of cocoa and also coffee into the agrarian doctrine of development was much more effective.

---

107   PNGNA: AN12 3,901 F/N 1-2-6(D) *Mekeo Rice Project* 4/7/52 W Cottrell-Dormer to Professor OHK Spate
108   NAA: A518/1 AR927/4 *Development. Papua & New Guinea. Rice—Research*, 7/9/54 T Sorensen, 'Rice Improvement in Papua and New Guinea'
109   Spate 'The Rice Problem in New Guinea' p. 735

Cocoa

Since at least the beginning of the twentieth century, cocoa has been grown as a plantation crop in PNG.[110] During the inter-war years, some plantation owners began to inter-plant the crop with coconuts. The leaves of the tall palm trees reduce the amount of sunlight that reaches the ground, which in turn checks the growth of weeds around the cocoa bushes and cuts maintenance costs. Inter-planting spread among plantations, although the availability of unplanted land on many large holdings before the war meant that some of the largest firms engaged in sole planting of bushes as well. While there was little planting of cocoa by indigenes before World War II, the ability to inter-plant bushes subsequently made the crop especially suitable to indigenous growers with limited land who retained coconut palms for immediate consumption needs as well as cash incomes from marketed nuts and copra.[111]

An early indication of the extensiveness of the Administration's aims for cocoa growing in PNG was given in a 1947 report which assessed suitable growing areas. Drawing upon plantation experience growing cocoa as well as research conducted in the inter-war years, an agricultural official concluded that cocoa grew best up to 1,400 feet above sea level, in areas protected from strong winds. Geologically newer soils found on New Britain, Bougainville, Witu Islands, and Kar Kar Island were especially well suited. But cocoa could be expected to thrive also on areas of mainland New Guinea, including the Markham Valley and in Papua at Dobodura. Even soils derived from raised coral, where some existing plantations grew cocoa were suitable.[112]

During World War II, most of the cocoa bushes were destroyed and there was widespread damage to coconut trees. Some stock survived and soon after the military conflict ended, administration officials began to distribute planting material collected from the Lowlands Agricultural Experiment Station at Keravat, from Rabaul Botanic Garden and Asalinga Plantation to plantations and some indigenous growers.[113] The stock was of the Trinitario type, higher yielding and more vigorous by comparison to the Forastero type then growing in West Africa. By using local stock, officials were aware that the postwar expansion would not be affected by the swollen shoot disease which had already substantially reduced cocoa output in Ghana and other nearby countries.

---

110   Cf. Firth 'The New Guinea Company' p. 367; DRJ Densley and MA Wheeler *Cocoa: Agriculture in the Economy A Series of Review Papers* (Port Moresby: PNG Department of Primary Industry, n.d. c.1978) p. 2
111   Richard Salisbury *Vunamami: Economic Transformation in a Traditional Society* (Berkeley and Los Angeles: University of California Press, 1970) p. 14
112   REP Dwyer *Cocoa Production Territory of Papua-New Guinea* Part 1 *The Economics of Cocoa Production* (Port Moresby: DASF, 3 July 1948) p. 1
113   Anon. *Lowlands Agricultural Experiment Station Keravat, Papua New Guinea 1928–1978* (Rabaul: Trinity Press, 1978) p. 2

Furthermore Trinitario formed the basis for fine and flavour cocoa, for many years regarded as superior to the bulk Forastero cocoa, which was used for milk and drinking chocolate.

The decision to use Trinitario stock for the postwar expansion was not solely due to availability and its swollen shoot free status. It has already been noted above that colonial officials in Australia were in regular contact with cocoa traders and manufacturers. The Australian manufacturers sourced most of their cocoa from West Africa. With the swollen shoot disease and anti-colonial eruptions in Ghana adding to postwar shortages, they were concerned to secure other sources of cocoa. In 1946, it was predicted that shortages in international supplies would reach about 200,000 tons and a price increase for 1947 of 150 per cent. The prediction prompted Australian manufacturers to raise the possibility that employment in the local confectionery industry would decline. It was in these circumstances that proposals were advanced for the major expansion of large holding production in PNG, as previously outlined. Neither the recommendation to extend plantations, nor the attempts by Australian manufacturers to influence what type of cocoa would be grown in the postwar expansion, were welcomed or acted upon by the Australian Government which was strongly supported by Administration officials in PNG. One particular official, Cottrell-Dormer, the Director of Agriculture was strongly opposed to indigenes becoming 'a race of wage-earners dependent upon European industry for their livelihood and losing the greater part of their native-self-reliance'.[114]

The manufacturers, who had imported very little PNG plantation cocoa pre-war, wanted the postwar administration to push the production of bulk cocoa for their requirements.[115] In an early instance of a clash between Australian manufacturing and colonial administration objectives, agricultural officials in PNG rejected this proposal. Not only did Trinitario 'trees come into bearing 6–12 months earlier than is usually experienced in any other country' but on the light pumice soils around Rabaul, yields were considerably higher than for Forastero, the basis of 'Accra cocoa'.[116]

Strengthening the local officials' position even further, there was a price advantage to be gained by selling into continental Europe rather than to Australian markets. In European markets fine and flavour cocoa formed the base for bitter chocolate which was preferred to the sweeter milk chocolate. Although only forming a small proportion of the world market, fine and flavour

114 NAA: A518/1 A58/3/3 Undated W Cottrell-Dormer, Director, DASF to Secretary, Department of External Territories p. 1
115 NAA: A1422, 12/2/11 Part 1 *New Guinea and Papua—Cocoa 1938–52* 19/3/51 Fred B Richardson, for Cadbury-Fry-Pascall 'Type of Cocoa Which Should be Grown'
116 Dwyer *Cocoa Production* p. 3

cocoa—then produced from Trinitario—was in high demand. Selling to this important potential market would also reduce PNG producers' reliance upon and subjection to the Australian manufacturers.

The position taken by local officials, to target the fine and flavour market with the use of Trinitario stock was strengthened by support received from Colyer Watson, one of the principal exporters of PNG cocoa. At a time when only a small number of indigenes had bearing bushes, the firm was characterised as mainly a purchaser of plantation cocoa. However the firm was already looking to a future of substantially increased production and exports. In October 1950, five months before the letter from Richardson, just cited, the exporting firm's principal RA Colyer wrote to the Secretary, Department of Territories about a recent successful trip to the UK. Drawing attention to previous unsatisfactory treatment of PNG cocoa by 'Australian users', Colyer stressed the importance of making:

> our beans better known to the world … where New Guinea beans … had a considerably higher value [than that placed on them previously by the Australian Confectioners' Association]. We must keep on shipping these beans so that the world's markets will get to know them as a "special bean" so that when production increases the planter will derive the benefit of their full value.[117]

As an especially astute commodity trader, Colyer is likely to have known not only that plantation owners were beginning to include cocoa in their postwar rehabilitation plans, but also that the Administration was giving priority to increasing indigenous production of the crop. With the company's main buying office located in Rabaul where this increase was especially strong, Colyer could hardly have missed the attraction of the crop for wealthy Tolai on the Gazelle Peninsula, East New Britain, who were adding another dimension to their already substantial commercial activities.

Important accounts of the early postwar move into cocoa by Tolai growers, provided by Salisbury and T Scarlett Epstein, provide very similar descriptions for Vunamami, near Rabaul, and Rapitok, also on the Peninsula but at the frontier of Tolai settlement.[118] With the encouragement of DASF officials, wealthy and influential Tolai were the first to embrace cocoa. These individuals often had unplanted land and the capacity to mobilise labour from 'clan dependants'.[119] While there were important differences in the sources of the wealth for these Tolai in Vunamami and Rapitok, their similarities are what matters for this account.

---

117   NAA: A518/1 A58/3/1 22/10/1950 RA Colyer to Secretary Halligan
118   Michael H Lowe *Smallholder Agrarian Change: the experience in two Tolai communities* PhD thesis, ANU (2006) esp. chs 4–6.
119   Salisbury *Vunamami* p. 136

In the case of densely populated and relatively affluent Vunamami, with a long history of contact with European owned plantation and administration personnel, the first planter was a senior political figure who grew cocoa on his own and his wife's clan lands in the neighbouring Balanatam and Vunamami villages. Apart from the first planter, Salisbury notes that:

> The early growers were for the most part landed and progressive older men; others were drawn in only after 1953–1954 when the early planters began reaping large returns from cash sales.[120]

In Rapitok, the critical initial source of wealth utilised for cocoa cultivation had been previous migration to work on plantations. Once again, there was a flow-on effect from the activities of the first planters to other returned migrants and then more widely to other indigenes. As TS Epstein states:

> One of Rapitok's migrants, who is the most enterprising and also the wealthiest man in the parish, was the first prepared to experiment with planting cocoa [in 1948] … before the first trees began to bear, a number of migrants had followed the example and also planted cocoa. The Rapitoks were selling copra in the meantime and encouraged by these earnings they were prepared to extend their investment in perennial cash crops.[121]

The rapid adoption of cocoa by Tolai who planted substantial acreages and others who grew a few trees meant that Director of Agriculture Cottrell-Dormer's preferred position for the best form of indigenous production became irrelevant for official policy toward cocoa growing on the Gazelle. His preference was for 'the development of Government plantations on behalf of the natives, i.e. on the natives' land and for the purpose of handing over to native ownership in the shape of co-operative societies in the future' utilising European management. Even though Minister Ward agreed with the rejection of proposals for more large holdings, Cottrell-Dormer's favoured direction was never applied, for cocoa or any other crop.[122] Instead the spontaneous process of development, with Tolai bourgeois and would-be bourgeois to the fore, initially out-ran official planning and capacities. Only in the 1950s, under a new Minister and strengthened state machinery was cocoa production placed at the centre of the scheme of smallholder production.

---

120   Salisbury *Vunamami* pp. 135–136
121   Epstein *Capitalism, Primitive and Modern* pp. 60–62
122   NAA: A518/1 A58/3/3 Undated W Cottrell-Dormer, Director, DASF to Secretary, Department of External Territories p. 1

Conclusion

The immediate postwar period in PNG was marked by a particular form of uncertainty. While by 1945 the Australian Government and influential colonial officials were agreed on a general direction for postwar development, 'positive Australianism' was little more than a vague statement indicating a preferred direction. Subsequently, between 1945 and 1950–51, in the circumstances of postwar reconstruction and rehabilitation, it continued to be hard to shape development in ways which would flesh out what was intended. Instead securing barriers against the return of what had been seen as destructive in the circumstances of pre-war PNG, and surmounting some of the most deleterious effects of the military conflict dominated official activities. Despite the best of intentions to bring development, only tentative moves along the intended route had been made, including in areas of the country and among populations previously only loosely included in the colonial territory.

All this was to change from the early 1950s, to the extent that just over a decade later the dominance of smallholder agriculture was firmly established. The colonial administration's part in securing this ascendancy, which improved living standards for most of the population, was central. Of particular importance for the change was the political dominance of the Australian Minister for Territories, Hasluck, and the Department in Canberra. Unlike Ward, ideologically certain but little involved in giving effect to his beliefs, Hasluck focused his energies on gaining control of, and revitalising the colonial administration. With power centralised, and detailed consideration given to how the main premises of development thought could become policy, the Minister drove major reforms. The change from uncertain development to the central policy direction of even or uniform development was pronounced, as the next chapter shows.

3. Uniform Development Framed, Implemented and Challenged

Introduction

During the 1950s uncertainty was replaced by a well-defined strategy to make development happen. The most important consequence of colonial development policy over the decade was a substantial expansion of smallholder agriculture and commercialised consumption by households. The change from the uncertainty of the immediate postwar years occurred through an enlarged, better resourced administration following a policy direction which came to be known as uniform or even development.

Uniform development built upon the policy priorities established during and immediately after World War II, discussed in the previous chapters. While the language of development policy changed, to the extent that the terms 'positive Australianism' and 'the paramountcy of native interests' largely disappeared from official discourse, the central elements of each remained influential. Making development occur, rather than letting it happen spontaneously, remained the central premise of official policy. Neither the December 1949 defeat of the Labor Government nor a decade of Liberal-Country Party governments resulted in the shift against 'native interests' anticipated by some. Instead the important changes which occurred during the 1950s expressed considerable continuity in the idea of development which informed Australian policy for PNG.

The first section of this chapter shows how even as a major political change occurred in Australia, there was no break in the previous emphasis upon the importance of state action for intentional development. The principal focus of government plans did not change either. Emphasis continued to be placed upon increased production and consumption by indigenous households attached to rural smallholdings.

The second section of this chapter considers how, during the 1950s, intentional development was defined as even or uniform development. While I have been unable to find a specific document which sets out what was intended as uniform or even development, nevertheless the policy position which became synonymous with Minister Hasluck's period in office evolved during the early to mid-1950s.[1] This evolution corresponds to the unity of idea and process, discussed

---

1   See also Downs *The Australian Trusteeship* pp. 126–163, ch.7 'Achieving uniform development'.

in the Introduction and Chapter One, by which the idea of development was formed, reshaped and attached to colonial policy. The policy had three inter-connected policy pillars. The first emphasised measures to encourage greater homogeneity among the indigenous population. The second focused upon the comprehensiveness of administrative action throughout the colony, particularly coordinating and supervising smallholder agriculture using household labour processes to increase production. An instance among many of the priorities of the Minister appears in a File Note of June 1954 on food supplies in which Hasluck stated:

> In communicating the decision please stress again that the advancement of native agriculture—for local food supply and improved land use in village gardens, as well as for economic production of crops for sale—has a high priority in Government policy for the Territory.[2]

Thirdly, linked with the first two, administrative effort was to be applied to all regions and populations to check inequalities between and within areas of the country, rather than concentrating state resources upon smallholders in the most advanced areas. Even development also meant continuing barriers against international firms and expatriate enterprises, as during the initial postwar period, and checking the advance of an indigenous capitalist class which had already emerged in some parts of the colony.

The final section of the chapter shows how while even development was highly successful in expanding smallholder production, by the mid-1950s the colonial government was concerned that the pace of growth had slowed. Considerable thought was given to the problem of achieving further increases in the rate of growth while maintaining the emphasis upon colony-wide uniformity, rather than encouraging greater unevenness which was becoming apparent in the most successful export crop growing areas of the colony. Increased revenues plus reforms to the administration which included further expansion in the number of agricultural extension officers were directed at plans and projects designed to raise output of locally consumed as well as internationally marketed produce. The decade ended with the Administration still determined to maintain the primacy of smallholder agriculture.

Change Within Continuity

Some thought the electoral defeat of the Ben Chifley-led Labor Party Government in 1949, and the victory of the Liberal-Country Party coalition would pave the way for a major shift in thinking about development in PNG. There were hopes

---

2   NAA: M1776/1 vol. 5 *Minister for Territories Instructions to Department 1/1/1954 to 30/6/1954*

as well as fears that the new Minister for External Territories, the Liberal Percy Spender, would support a change from 'socialism' toward 'free enterprise'. The Planters' Association in the colony sent a congratulatory cable to PC (Percy) Spender, who became Minister for External Territories and Minister for External Affairs, which urged him to make an 'early visit to Territory to gain first hand information difficult problems confronting planters due former Government's negative policy'.[3] In particular, it was anticipated that in order to take advantage of worldwide food shortages, the Minister would encourage more favourable treatment of the demands arising in the colony, Australia and the UK for a major expansion of large holdings.

During his only visit to PNG in early 1950 and in a subsequent statement to parliament, as well as in a substantial policy document prepared in the Department, Spender disappointed those hoping for a major shift.[4] He continued to emphasise two principal interlocking objectives. The first was improved indigenous welfare and the second, development of the colony's resources. Spender maintained the connection which had appeared in the first years after the war between resource development and making the colony self-supporting. The latter would, in the Minister's view, include the ability 'to supply the needs of Australia and the world generally with the valuable commodities that the Territories are capable of producing'. Spender also accepted the established view that the size of the available labour force was a limiting factor. His position, that the colonial administration should be given a major role in securing 'a generally improved standard of living for the native peoples', was also in line with previous thought about how to give effect to 'positive Australianism'.[5]

Like Ward, Spender held responsibility for another, more substantial ministerial post. While Ward had been Minister for Transport as well as Minister for External Territories, Spender held the latter office and that of Minister for External Affairs. Each Minister only visited PNG once, whereas Hasluck became a frequent visitor, who would have travelled to the colony more often had parliamentary and other official responsibilities not prevented him from doing so. During a visit of Administrator Murray to Sydney, Spender finalised some 30 submissions which had been awaiting decisions, although he contributed little new or original about development.[6] Futhermore, before leaving the Menzies Government in April 1951, Spender did not manage to make his substantially enlarged Department noticeably more effective in determining

---

3   Downs *The Australian Trusteeship* p. 69

4   Cf. Administrator Colonel Murray 'In Retrospect' p. 179; Downs *The Australian Trusteeship* p. 70.

5   Cf. NAA: A518/1 I927/1 *Development of the Territories. Organisational. Minister's Policy Speech, June 1950* 'Australia's Policy in Relation to External Territories' p. 2 for quotations in this paragraph; PC Spender *Politics and a Man* (Sydney: Collins, 1972) pp. 271–279.

6   Murray 'In Retrospect' p. 178

how development could occur.[7] Spender's main contribution, however, was to emphasise the importance of an instrumental role for private capital, as a means of obtaining additional resources to supplement those provided by the Australian Government so that indigenous welfare goals could be pursued more effectively.[8]

A New Minister—Hasluck Takes Office

After a one month interregnum, from April until May 1951 while (Sir) Richard Casey also occupied both the ministerial positions of External Affairs and External Territories, Hasluck was appointed Minister for Territories. Simultaneously, the department was revamped from the previous External Territories, to include responsibility for both internal (the Northern Territory and the Australian Capital Territory) and external territories. Hasluck remained in the position until December 1963, and held no other ministerial duties as part of his permanent portfolio.

Hasluck came to office with extensive experience at the international political-administrative level, including as a participant at major meetings on postwar development. His employment in the Department of External Affairs between 1941 and 1947 working on the formation of the United Nations and in particular the trusteeship protocols,[9] had prepared him far better than either Ward or Spender for the task of colonial minister. Hasluck's intellectual heritage included knowledge of, as well as admiration for, the English radical Tory objections to the destructive effects of early industrialisation upon rural life.[10] As a person who came to maturity in the early twentieth century, Hasluck was an Australian liberal who did not believe in *laissez faire* but in a positive role for the state and the importance of trusteeship, along the lines advocated by earlier Australian liberals (see Chapter One). He was also sympathetic toward indigenous Australians whose impoverished condition he regarded as a consequence of European settlement.[11]

Hasluck concluded that the destruction of indigenous life was so complete in Australia that 'today there is nothing that can be recognised as a homogeneous

---

7 Downs *The Australian Trusteeship* pp. 83–84
8 Cf. NAA: A518/1 I927/1 'Australia's Policy in Relation to External Territories' p. 3; NAA: M335/1 2 *Australia in New Guinea. The Post-War Task. A Paper prepared in the Department of Territories During the Term of Office of the Hon. P Spender* p. 9. The document is dated October 1951, six months after Spender left office, but was prepared during late 1950 and early 1951. The paper had an earlier title 'Australia's Bastion. The Post-War Task in Papua and New Guinea' which disappeared in the process of final preparation.
9 Murray 'In Retrospect' p. 178–179 states 'I have often wondered whether he (Hasluck) devised the Trusteeship provisions'. Louis *Imperialism at Bay* pts iii and iv provides a more substantial account.
10 MacWilliam 'Liberalism and the End of Development' p. 90
11 Paul Hasluck *Black Australians. A Survey of Native Policy in Western Australia, 1829–1897* (Melbourne University Press, 1942)

and integrated aboriginal society'.[12] As the Minister whose Department also held responsibility for the Northern Territory where substantial numbers of indigenes lived, European responsibility for this condition and National Government obligations for its amelioration was thought best resolved by assimilation of the indigenous population. For Hasluck, assimilation meant incorporation into what he construed as the mainstream of Australian life, primarily through becoming wage workers. He advocated a specific form of positive state agency—development through assimilation—to overcome the deleterious consequences of capitalism's advance in Western Australia, about which he had researched and written, and the Northern Territory, for which he now held ministerial responsibility.

Hasluck drew a separate conclusion about what was required for development in PNG, as MacWilliam noted:

> Assimilation required trusteeship, where the indigenous population were in the minority, as in Australia, just as the paramountcy of native interests required trusteeship where the indigenous population were in the majority, as in Papua New Guinea.[13]

If the overall premises of international trusteeship were known to Hasluck, he had no direct experience of, or much knowledge about, PNG before taking ministerial office. At the beginning of his tenure, these lacunae pushed him to temporarily accept existing policy.[14] The secretary of the newly constructed combined Department, CR Lambert, who was appointed soon after Hasluck became Minister, also lacked knowledge of PNG. However as already noted in Chapter One, Lambert was another senior Australian official with a predilection for agrarian development as an appropriate response to the effects of the 1930s Depression and in postwar conditions.

Two months after being sworn in, and accompanied by Lambert, Hasluck made his first visit to PNG. Experiences on the trip reinforced some of his predilections, including the strong anti-British colonial bias he shared with Ward. As he subsequently recorded:

> although I trotted around the Territory on my best behaviour and trying to smile like an innocent friend, I came away from that first trip revolted at the imitation of British colonial modes and manners by some of the Australians who were there to serve the Australian government.[15]

---

12 Hasluck 'Some Problems of Assimilation' Address to Section F of ANZAAS, 34th Congress, Perth, 1959, p. 1
13 MacWilliam 'Liberalism and the End of Development' p. 91
14 Hasluck *A Time for Building* p. 25
15 Hasluck *A Time for Building* p. 14

The combination of his political views, and what he as Minister encountered on the initial tour of PNG, greatly influenced several of the immediate political and administrative changes Hasluck made. The first involved terminating Murray's tenure as Administrator, the need for which had been previously flagged by Spender. Murray was replaced by DM (later Sir Donald) Cleland. Hasluck also returned to Australia convinced of the importance of obtaining increased funding for PNG from the Commonwealth. The removal of Murray produced some personal bitterness, and allegations that the former Administrator's departure represented a continuation of the shift toward 'private enterprise' begun by Spender.[16]

For the remainder of his term in office, Hasluck's thoughts about what development should constitute for PNG changed little. The changes that did occur in his thinking were largely refinements of policy within the parameters laid down by the Australian adoption and adaptation of international trusteeship, discussed in Chapter One. In 1952, he enunciated what would remain his understanding of the relationship between Australia and PNG, as one of 'guardianship'. The emphasis upon guardianship is particularly important in the light of subsequent attempts by others to suggest the need for a partnership between Papua New Guineans and Australians. The significance arises partly because for Hasluck a principal task of the colonial government's trusteeship was to act as guardians. Guardianship included containing the ambitions of expatriates, particularly those who sought to acquire more large holding land and an important place in the colony's political economy as partners with the ascending class of indigenous capitalists.[17]

Hasluck distanced himself from two features of the policy position he had inherited, the emphasis upon 'planning' and 'private enterprise'.[18] He cancelled the intended distribution of the policy paper prepared at Spender's direction which mirrored the latter's June 1950 statement to parliament.[19] Of more immediate consequence for bringing development were the steps taken by Hasluck to counter the political tendencies and administrative indecisiveness which had arisen, even flourished during Murray's term as Administrator. Important political-administrative changes were required, as well as better defining and shaping the policy needed to bring development. However Hasluck's initial efforts to gain more financial and personnel support for the

---

16   Wright *State Practice* pp. 222–228 canvasses the alternative interpretations given for Murray's departure.
17   Hasluck *A Policy for New Guinea* Address by the Minister for Territories to the William McGregor Club, Sydney, 20 November 1951; also cited in *South Pacific* Jan-Feb 1952, vol. 5, no. 11, p. 225; and in Hawksley *Administrative Colonialism* p. 418; cf. Downs *The Australian Trusteeship* p. 165.
18   Administrator Murray's enthusiasm for overall planning is evidenced in numerous files and documents: see NAA: A518/1 K927/1 *Development Papua and New Guinea. Administration's Seven Year Plan for Development* 2/10/50 JK Murray Administrator to Secretary, Department of External Territories 'Plans for the Development of the Territory'; cf. Hasluck *A Time for Building* p. 128.
19   NAA: M335/1 no. 2 *Australia in New Guinea*

colonial administration illustrates how his thought about the importance of the colonial state's role in making development happen was akin to Murray's view. The two men also approached the matter of indigenous political representation in a similar manner. Their approach to state coordination and supervision, as well as the political advance by Papua New Guineans is now examined.

Prior to Hasluck taking office there had already been an increase in funding allocated for the colony, which by 1950–51 was over AU£A8.7 million, compared to only AU£90,000 in 1939–45.[20] Even this increase was regarded as unsatisfactory by Murray, who pressed for the establishment of a Territory Development Fund of AU£100 million, to be expended over ten years and supplementary to annual budget commitments. Inspired by the United Kingdom example of a UK£120 million colonial welfare and development fund, Murray received support in Australia from the Minister, Spender, and the Secretary of External Territories, Halligan. The request for a major funding increase was justified in terms of PNG's defence purpose for Australia, international trusteeship obligations and the inability to fund development from local resources.

The Commonwealth Treasury, supported by the Prime Minister's Department, opposed the proposal, stressing financial stringency, the difficulty of managing such a large fund, and political accountability matters, including the inadvisability of a government committing its successors in advance. Instead Treasury insisted that the existing budgeting terms of three years maximum should be maintained.[21] Murray subsequently noted that in 1951–52 the grant-in-aid rose to AU£10.5 million, up about 20 per cent on the previous year's amount.[22]

In December 1951, Hasluck persisted with Murray's proposal which was for the establishment of a Territories Development Fund of AU£100 million to become available at the rate of AU£20 million a year over five years. He also arranged for his Parliamentary Under-Secretary to visit the Colonial Office in October 1952 to ascertain whether the Colonial Development and Welfare Fund for British colonies would be a suitable model for Australia to adopt for its territories. As Hasluck subsequently explained:

> I took it for granted that, for a generation or so, services, utilities, amenities and the whole economic infrastructure would have to be provided by Australia and not from the earnings of the Territory itself.

---

20 Murray 'In Retrospect' p. 206 states, regarding this increase, that it represented '[t]he change from rhetoric to intent beyond question'.

21 See NAA: A518/1 J927/1 *Development of the Territories. Organisational. Development Programme*; A518/1 K927/1 *Development Papua and New Guinea*; A518/1 L927/1 *Financial methods of encouraging development—Territories—General*; see also newspaper coverage in *The News* (Adelaide) 26 August 1950; *The Daily Telegraph* (Sydney) 24 August 1950; *The Herald* (Melbourne) 26 August 1950.

22 Murray 'In Retrospect' p. 180

> Perhaps eventually the Territory would be able to service the long-term debts for such necessities, but even that would require Australian support.[23]

Hasluck's reasoning followed that of Murray's, in particular that the criteria which operated in Australia should not be applied to funding development for PNG.[24] Nevertheless the outcome remained the same: no major development fund was established. For the remainder of his term as Minister, Hasluck had to operate with the relatively short-term annual and triennial budgetary cycles, as applied to other Australian Government ministers and departments. The Minister's subsequent success can be measured by the fact that, despite this restricted process of obtaining funding for development, Australian grants-in-aid continued to increase. By 1963, when Hasluck left office, AU£40 million, approximately two-thirds of total Administration expenditure was paid out of Australian-raised revenue. Of the funds raised internally, import duties provided the largest component, while less than one-third came from income and company taxes.[25]

Murray and Hasluck also agreed that political development required direct representation by indigenes in a reformed colonial state. The legal basis for the Legislative Council was established before Hasluck came to office, by the *1949 Papua and New Guinea Act*. The Legislative Council's 29 members included the Administrator's representative, the Assistant Administrator as Council President, 16 officers from the Administration, and nine non-official members to be nominated by the Administrator. The principal purpose, to continue Administration dominance of the legislative process and marginalise expatriate settler representatives, was transparent. Of the nine non-official members, there were three expatriates representing Christian missions, three commerce, mining and plantation representatives and three indigenes from Papua, the New Guinea mainland and New Guinea islands. Three non-officials elected by expatriate voters rounded off the Council's membership.[26]

Nothing had been done about appointing members of the Council or holding elections before Hasluck became Minister. In mid-1951, Hasluck urged the Department and Administration to give priority to establishing the Council's

---

23   Hasluck *A Time for Building* pp. 11–12; Wright *State Practice* p. 215

24   NAA: M1776/1 vol. 1 *Minister for Territories* 11/12/51 Minister to Secretary 'Future Development of Territories' p. 2; Hasluck *A Time for Building* p. 129; see also NAA: M338/1 1 *Visit Papua and New Guinea 26th July to 8th August, 1951* 26/7/51, Copies of *ABC* News Broadcasts, Interview with Minister.

25   Downs *The Australian Trusteeship* Table 6.2, pp. 122–123. For the long battle from 1957 which surrounded the introduction of personal (head tax) and then income tax, see Downs *The Australian Trusteeship* pp. 138–147, 186–195 and Hasluck *A Time for Building* pp. 258–265.

26   Cf. the claim made by Yash P Ghai and Anthony J Regan *The Law, Politics and Administration of Decentralisation in Papua New Guinea* Monograph no. 30 (Boroko: The National Research Institute, 1992) p. 7: 'A legislative council was set up in 1951, but it was dominated by the administrators and expatriate interests'.

membership and setting an inauguration date. When the membership and the date of late 1951 were announced, a storm of criticism broke.[27] The *South Pacific Post*, which frequently espoused the expatriate settler version of colonial nationalism, immediately claimed that it:

> was the Eddie Ward clique that slipped into the Act the most objectionable provision that out of a Council of 29 members only three would be elected by the general public.[28]

As the editorial made clear, general public was a synonym for expatriate 'private enterprise'. Apart from the insufficient 'private enterprise' representation, the Planters' Association of New Guinea, based in Rabaul, also objected to the presence of three nominated indigenes.[29]

The Minister shrugged off the objections. He was supported by the Chairman of the London Missionary Society in Papua, who hoped that this Council was a first step toward a more representative structure for which indigenes could elect representatives on a District basis.[30] Hasluck pointed out that the composition was specified under the 1949 Act and before seeking an amendment, it should be given 'a trial in its present form'.[31]

Formulating and Applying Uniform Development

Countering Separatism, Centralising Power and Strengthening Administration

Apart from reinforcing his anti-colonialism, Hasluck left the colony after his first visit in mid-1951 with serious doubts about the local administration's capacity to bring about development, despite the considerable changes which had occurred already. In 1949, while the legal distinction remained between Papua as an Australian colony and New Guinea as a UN Trust Territory, from 1 July 1949, the Territory of Papua and New Guinea was administered under the *Papua and New Guinea Act*. Under the Act, the Administrator was the senior official in the Administration, who acted with the advice of the Executive Council of nine members. The nine were an acting Government Secretary and the Secretary, acting Secretary, Director, or acting Director, for eight departments

---

27   *South Pacific Post* 27 July 1951
28   *South Pacific Post* 3 August 1951
29   *South Pacific Post* 3 August 1951
30   *South Pacific Post* 3 August 1951
31   See NAA: M338/1 1 *Visit Papua and New Guinea* 6/8/51 Radio summary of talk between Minister and members of Wau Advisory Council. For Hasluck's version of the discussion that took place with Murray over the appointments; see Hasluck *A Time for Building* pp. 40–44.

(Planning and Development, Public Health, Education, Agriculture, Stock and Fisheries, Native Labour, Treasury, Lands, Surveys and Mines, and Forests). As well there were 11 Committees, Boards, and a Rural Production Advisory Council. Ten departments and seven branches were also established for a public service which had 1,272 personnel.[32] Some of the Minister's doubt arose from the level of funding available to sustain intended activities. The numbers and abilities of the personnel available for the Department of Territories and the PNG Administration also caused concern for the Minister.

Murray epitomised an even more serious problem for Hasluck, much deeper than simply a clash of personalities or the fact that Murray was not, in the view of Spender and Hasluck, a particularly good administrator. On his first visit, Hasluck had noted 'an underlying spirit of separatism and perhaps in some cases, of resentment against Australia'[33] which was 'also apparent' in Murray who had 'developed an argument [presented when Hasluck visited PNG in July 1951: SM] for self-government which meant government by himself and his staff, who were to be left free to do good as they saw it'.[34] Murray had developed a 'reticence' toward involvement by the Minister and Department in the administration of PNG. According to Hasluck, Murray 'regarded the rule of the Territory as a matter for him and not for the Minister to handle'.[35] If, as Hasluck had deduced, separatism and resentment were more widely held than simply by the Administrator, his removal and replacement would not overcome the deeper problem of how to define and impose colonial authority along the lines the Minister determined were necessary to satisfy international trusteeship conditions.

Hasluck's first steps involved the appointment of a like-minded Lambert as Department Secretary and Cleland as Administrator who had the additional advantage of substantial personal experience in PNG. From 1943 until 1945, Cleland had been effectively Chief of Staff of the ANGAU, the military administration of those parts of PNG not under Japanese control. Cleland had also been Chairman of the Production Control Board. Upon returning to Australia after the war, he again became active in conservative politics. He was appointed Director of the Federal Secretariat of the Liberal Party and played an active role in building the party machine, which was important for the 1949 campaign that resulted in the Liberal Party becoming the major partner in the governing coalition.[36] Cleland was a Western Australian, where Hasluck had won a federal parliamentary seat.

32   NAA: A518/1 H927/1 *Development of the Territories*; see also David M Fenbury *Practice without Policy: genesis of local government in Papua New Guinea* Monograph no. 13, 2nd edn (Canberra: Development Studies Centre, ANU, 1980) pp. 8–59.

33   Hasluck *A Time for Building* p. 14

34   Hasluck *A Time for Building* p. 15

35   Hasluck *A Time for Building* p. 15–16

36   HN Nelson 'Cleland, Sir Donald Mackinnon (1901–1975)' Australian Dictionary of Biography vol. 13 (Melbourne University Press, 1993) pp. 440–441, retrieved 18 September 2012 <http://www.adb.online.anu. edu.au/biogs/A130486b.htm>

Cleland, who had been Assistant Administrator since early 1951, and then Acting Administrator in June 1952 when Murray left, became Administrator in early 1953. Hasluck emphasised that this appointment did not represent a change of policy, which was 'to protect and advance the welfare of the natives'.[37] Until 1963, the triumvirate of Hasluck, Lambert and Cleland formed a powerful bloc at the head of the colonial administration.[38]

In order to ensure that the authority he intended to impose upon the Department and Administration had the appropriate basis in law, Hasluck also obtained advice about the constitutional-legal relationship between Australia and the colonial territory(ies). This advice supported Hasluck's view that the Minister, under delegation from the Governor-General, held ultimate authority over the Department, the Administrator and Administration in PNG. It also confirmed Hasluck's opinion that Murray held an erroneous view on the constitutional status of the Administrator, who, according to Hasluck, wanted to receive 'Instructions' from the Governor-General rather than directions from the Minister and Department.[39]

A change originally proposed in October 1950 regarding the structure of the Administration provided another early indication of Hasluck's determination to assert control. Before he became Minister, two positions as Deputy Administrator had been advertised publicly but were not filled. Instead, the role of Government Secretary was strengthened and one Assistant Administrator, Cleland, appointed and based in Port Moresby while Murray's own position was considered further.

Between Cleland's appointment as Assistant Administrator and Murray's departure, a request was made by a representative of European planter and commercial interests that the Assistant Administrator should be located in Rabaul, the centre of expatriate settler political activism. Hasluck rejected this proposal. In response to the demands for a degree of decentralisation, the Minister offered 'devolution of responsibility to the District Offices, and a raising of the status and responsibilities of the District Commissioners'.[40] As will be shown below, even the elevation of District Commissioners (DCs) quickly resulted in consequences which had to be checked. Nor was it the last time that the Minister rebuffed attempts to locate key officials where they could be subjected more easily to the demands of expatriates resident and commercially active in the colony.[41]

---

37 Hasluck *A Time for Building* p. 52
38 Hasluck *A Time for Building* pp. 53–57; Sir Donald Cleland 'An Administrator Reflects' in Inglis (ed.) *The History of Melanesia* pp. 209–228
39 Hasluck *A Time for Building* p. 16
40 Hasluck *A Time for Building* pp. 23–25; see also NAA: M338/1 17 *Notes for Minister's Visit to Papua and New Guinea May–June 1958* 9/2/52, Hasluck to WR Paul, General Secretary, Planters Association of New Guinea, rejecting the suggestion made in a letter of 23/1/52.
41 NAA: M338/1 17 *Notes for Minister's Visit*, see letter from 28/4/58 TM Wilton, President Rabaul Chamber of Commerce to Administrator.

Strengthening Ministerial authority gave the Australian Government, as trustee for New Guinea under the United Nations, greater capacity to fend off criticisms of its rule made in that forum. These criticisms were invariably along the lines that expatriate interests were being favoured and insufficient attention and resources were being committed to improving indigenous welfare.[42] At the same time, the Minister saw strengthening the local administration as a major priority, a priority which was maintained during his term of office, even as skilled labour shortages continued to plague efforts to improve standards.[43]

Another reason for strengthening administrative capacity in Australia and PNG arose from Hasluck's view of policy and policy formulation. The Minister wanted the colonial administration, in Canberra and PNG, to be active in further policy development. Policy to Hasluck was inseparable from administration.[44] Due to this close connection, the Minister believed that policy formulation was something engaged in by all officials of the Department and by extension of the colonial administration in PNG. As Hasluck stated:

> "Policy development" is something that takes place as the result of a succession of acts performed by a wide range of people. Policy is built up by a number of decisions taking place over a period of time on a number of submissions, and the development of policy is not a job which can be confided to any one person or group of persons. I think one of the most dangerous and improper tendencies that is growing up in the Commonwealth Public service is this idea that certain officers established in certain positions have a job of developing a policy. I want the contribution to policy to come from the activities of every officer in the Dept and the process to be a continuous one at all levels.[45]

This was not a populist view of policy formulation, where Jack is as good as his master. A prodigious worker and reader of correspondence, Hasluck was ever alert for officials in Canberra or PNG, who whether by personal inclination or as a result of immediate experience strayed from the main premises of his development policy. If all officials were to be involved in policy formulation, Hasluck had to have the capacity to initiate changes and adjudicate conflicts about policy and its implementation. Thus, despite his often fulsome praise of officials including Cleland,[46] Minister Hasluck invariably admonished the

42 NAA: M338/1 1 *Visit Papua and New Guinea* 6/8/51; WE Tomasetti *Australia and the United Nations: New Guinea Trusteeship Issues from 1946–1966* New Guinea Research Bulletin no. 36 (Port Moresby and Canberra: New Guinea Research Unit, ANU, July 1970)
43 Hasluck *A Time for Building* pp. 59–76, esp. ch. 7 'The Bid for Funds and Staff'; Downs *The Australian Trusteeship* pp. 108–125, ch. 6 'Building a more effective administration'; Porter *Paul Hasluck* pp. 125–132
44 Hasluck *A Time for Building* p. 23
45 NAA: M1776/1 vol. 1 *Minister for Territories* 11/12/51 Hasluck to Secretary of Department 'Proposed Staff re-organisation of the Department of Territories'
46 Hasluck *A Time for Building* pp. 53–55

Administrator as well as subordinate officials for proposing policy which did not follow what he regarded as basic premises. In particular, Hasluck was well aware that certain officials were more disposed to encourage private enterprise and respond to expatriate demands than he was. All activities undertaken by the colonial administration were assessed according to whether, in Hasluck's view, they helped to maintain household attachment to smallholdings at improved standards of living.

However on occasion Hasluck too contributed to uncertainty about the place of large holdings by seeming to adopt an instrumental approach similar to Spender's. A report of an April 1952 press statement by the Minister, which while stressing the importance of village agriculture, also pointed out that:

> it could not alone meet all the opportunities for agricultural development .... I was looking both to the individual settler and to the big plantation companies for a substantial contribution of capital, enterprise and effort to promote tea, rubber, fibre crops, coffee, cocoa and rice.[47]

Within two years the Minister would be forced to face the consequences of this seeming ambiguity and decisively resolve development policy in favour of smallholder primacy (discussed further below).

One instance among several involving disagreements between Hasluck and his senior officials was the major road building program which commenced soon after the Minister took office and which played a major part in empolying indigenous labour. Speaking in the late 1960s about roads built from late 1952 in the Highlands utilising state funds, Cleland claimed:

> That was the start of the real development of the Highlands .... These roads were not so much for administrative purposes, but more so to open up the country for development by private enterprise.[48]

Subsequently, against Cleland's version, Hasluck asserted that the initiative to upgrade existing tracks into roads and highways arose out of a conversation between Cleland and himself, as a consequence of failed efforts to get any support in Cabinet for 'our own loan works programme'.[49] The Minister claimed that: '[T]he upshot was a ministerial direction that each district commissioner was to be instructed to encourage and direct the building of roads in his district'.[50] By Hasluck's account, the Highlands roads were part of a wider program promoting even or uniform development for the entire colony using local labour and serving a different purpose from that specified by Cleland. As Hasluck stated:

---

47   Hasluck *A Time for Building* p. 136
48   Cleland 'An Administrator reflects' p. 223
49   Hasluck *A Time for Building* p. 147
50   Hasluck *A Time for Building* p. 148

> These roads are being built with amazing cheapness and speed because of the help of the natives. Their purpose is chiefly administrative and they are developmental roads only in the senses that they provide access.[51]

Hasluck also saw the potential for clashes between villagers, who regarded the roads as 'their roads' and 'Europeans [planters and traders] who had done nothing to build the roads [and] started to cut them up with vehicles carrying commercial loads'.[52]

Administrative reform and centralising power in the Minister was intended to strengthen Hasluck's capacity to rule over the Department in Canberra and the Administration in PNG, even as each was strengthened. He also wanted to build up the capacity of the Administration so it could check the inherent advantages of a department located in Canberra, the capital and administrative centre of Australian Government. He resisted attempts to integrate the Administration with the Department, taking what he regarded as 'perhaps ... [a] too classical ... approach to the structure of government',[53] that is insisting on the separate legal-constitutional entities under different acts of the Australian parliament. This separation, and the constitutional requirement that both the Department and the Administration in PNG reported to and took instruction from the Minister, placed Hasluck in an especially powerful position.

Nothing exemplifies the strength of the Minister's position more than how during the early 1950s, elements of the previous idea of development were taken and reformed into government policy. The account now turns to the detailed policy position, uniform or even development, which more than anything else came to define colonial development in the 1950s.

Taking Advice

Despite Hasluck's dominance, it is important to recognise that the process by which policy was formulated, as well as its direction, involved more than the views of the Minister. In the case of the role of local native councils or local government councils, a senior Administration official in PNG, David Fienberg was important (see below). Without much personal knowledge of PNG, the Minister also sought advice from others, including academics at the recently established ANU. In 1951 and 1953, the Department of Territories was provided

---

51   Hasluck *A Time for Building* p. 150; Dame Rachel Cleland *Pathways to Independence; Stories of Official & Family Life in Papua New Guinea from 1951–1975* (Cottesloe: self-published, 1985) pp. 68–69
52   Hasluck *A Time for Building* p. 149; cf. Downs *The Australian Trusteeship* pp. 181–184; Downs *The Last Mountain: A Life in Papua New Guinea* (St Lucia: University of Queensland Press, 1986) pp. 230–251, ch. 14 'The High Road'
53   Hasluck *A Time for Building* p. 55

with two documents prepared by senior ANU academics. In October–November 1951, *Notes on New Guinea* was written by Oscar Spate, Jim Davidson and Raymond Firth, an economic geographer, historian and economic anthropologist respectively, after a three week visit to the colony.[54] The *Notes* set out many of the themes followed in the later *Report of a Working Committee of the ANU*, prepared by Spate, anthropologist Cyril Belshaw and economist Trevor Swan.[55]

In the *Notes*, Spate dismissed the prospect of any substantial expansion of 'economic soldier settlement', in case it led to a 'poor white problem', and dismissed 'White Melanesia [as] a pipe dream'.[56] Spate and Firth both noted the extent of the growth of indigenous agricultural production, and its unevenness, just six years after the war ended. While Spate pointed to a specific instance of a Tolai cocoa grower with 4,500 trees planted, Firth indicated that '[t]he native entrepreneur-capitalist is beginning to be a recognisable figure'.[57] In the Sepik, Bougainville and the Gazelle, there were men with reported incomes of AU£1000 a year. Firth also made the point that the 'rise of native middlemen, of native petty capitalists, of native entrepreneurs organizing the labour of others' while just beginning, could be expected to result in competitive struggles 'with one another [and] with the cooperative organizations which aim at applying a different principle to economic affairs'.[58]

Davidson recognised the Australian Government's difficulty in administering PNG, as 'an example of old-style colonial rule—one of the last in the world … in an age of non-European nationalism'.[59] He also recommended defining and clarifying the authority of the Minister, the Department and Administrator, while stressing the need to reorganise and strengthen the central administration in the colony. The latter was necessary because of the slowness and difficulty of communications between officials spread over the colony.

The *Report*, described subsequently by Hasluck as, 'a basic document in any study of the postwar economic policy in Papua and New Guinea',[60] repeated much of the direction taken in the *Notes*. The later document also stressed the importance of fulfilling trusteeship obligations and ruled out any substantial expansion of large holdings or 'economic soldier settlement'. Under the 'paramountcy' of native interests, the academics instead urged a 'revolution' for indigenous agriculture so that households went beyond 'merely feed[ing] and

---

54   NAA: M336/1 2 *Notes on New Guinea October–November 1951*
55   NAA: M1775/1 6 *SPATE-BELSHAW-SWAN—Report on economic structure of Papua and New Guinea*; see Hasluck *A Time for Building* pp. 140–141, for information on the genesis and preparation of, as well as the reception accorded to, the Spate, Belshaw & Swan Report in the Department of Territories.
56   NAA: M336/1 2 *Notes* 'Resources and Economic Potentialities' p. 9
57   NAA: M336/1 2 *Notes* 'Some Observations: Native Social and Economic Change' p. 15
58   NAA: M336/1 2 *Notes* p. 17
59   NAA: M336/1 2 *Notes* p. 2
60   Hasluck *A Time for Building* p. 141

hous[ing]' themselves.[61] Such a change required 'intensification, diversification, and eventually more regional specialization'.[62] Swan, who produced the first detailed accounts for the colony, re-emphasised the need for continuing flows of funds from the Australian Government. Net private capital formation was very small, perhaps even negative, when plantations and mines were depreciating assets with little new planting or investment in up-to-date equipment.[63]

The academics also included a section on 'Possible Social Dangers', which stressed the need for anticipatory action to secure development, even if the dangers had not yet appeared in PNG. As they warned:

> Native economic development must be undertaken always with the prospect in view that specific social evils may emerge and may require counter-action …The emergence of an unproductive rentier group, of oriental-style landlordism, of a habit of credit or usury, of community leaders becoming local bosses, of sweated labour, and of unprotected machinery can be foreseen and avoided. It is important not to be too hasty in introducing western property concepts before local society is ready with the necessary controls. Payment of cash rents, primogeniture in inheritance, and the ability to alienate land individually, would, for instance, lead to social chaos if introduced overnight.[64]

Spate, Belshaw and Swan favoured 'action', and avoiding the 'inhibitory effect' of 'this planning-fixation', an expression for which they provided no specific reference or instance.[65] However in December 1952 Hasluck had fulminated against what he saw as a tendency of the colonial administration to produce proposals but little action. Hasluck noted on a proposal to expand indigenous rice production in the Madang and Sepik districts:

> This is lamentable. We keep on drawing up proposals and approving them in principle. I want to approve some action. I want people to start growing rice. Subject to the availability of funds in the current financial year, action should start not later than January 5, 1953.

So this specific advice from the ANU academics, as well as other recommendations, would have been music to the Minister's ears.[66]

The Minister was also capable of ignoring advice which did not fit with his view of development policy. A specific direction favoured by the ANU academics

---

61   NAA: M1775/1 6 *SPATE-BELSHAW-SWAN* par. 7.6

62   NAA: M1775/1 6 *SPATE-BELSHAW-SWAN* par. 11.3

63   NAA: M1775/1 6 *SPATE-BELSHAW-SWAN* pars 36.4, 37.4

64   NAA: M1775/1 6 *SPATE-BELSHAW-SWAN* par. 25.1

65   NAA: M1775/1 6 *SPATE-BELSHAW-SWAN* par. 2.5

66   NAA: M1776/1 vol. 2 *Minister for Territories Instructions to Department* 1/7/52 to 31/12/52 19/12/52 Minister to Secretary

went against the attention already being paid to more marginal areas of the country, and was rejected. Using the supposed template of Dutch colonialism in 'the Indies' especially Java, their *Report* advocated 'the full development of two or three favourable regions; the introduction and fostering to the full of two or three crops'. In short, there should be 'concentration on attainable objectives and firm priorities'.[67] Nevertheless, the overall contribution of the ANU academics, particularly Spate, toward the formulation of uniform development as colonial policy was considerable and is reflected in each of the principal pillars of the evolving policy.

The book now provides an outline of uniform development and shows how the main components arose. It also stresses their inter-connectedness. A scheme of smallholder agriculture including projects to expand rice, cocoa and coffee production for markets, as discussed in greater detail in the Chapter Four could, for example, also satisfy a principal priority of agrarian development. Growing marketed crops could also stimulate the production of immediately consumed food to such an extent that surplus beyond household needs soon appeared in local markets.

Uniform Development's Pillars

Homogeneity Through Law and Order, Justice and Education

It will be recalled from the previous chapter that after World War II colonial rule continued to be challenged by 'cargo cults'. Because cults often appeared in economically marginal areas, they pushed the colonial administration to pay greater attention to the evenness of development efforts. As well, it has been previously pointed out that there were areas of the colony, particularly in the Central Highlands, where colonial authority did not yet encompass all of the people. Extending colonial rule to these areas also spread Administration resources more widely among populations which were not as commercially or politically advanced as other indigenes.[68]

During Spender's term as Minister, the goal was established that by 1955 colonial authority, specifically law and order, would be extended to all areas of the colony. Hasluck retained the objective, which referred primarily to the headwaters of the Sepik River and populous parts of the Central Highlands. The establishment of law and order could be seen as the precondition for promoting welfare measures,[69] an objective shared by Spender and Hasluck. However, at least as importantly, the Minister also saw the absence of colonial authority as an

---

67   NAA: M1775/1 6 *SPATE-BELSHAW-SWAN* par. 2.5

68   See also Hawksley *Administrative Colonialism* chs 7–10

69   Downs *The Australian Trusteeship* pp. 98–99; Hasluck *A Time for Building* pp. 77–79

indication of the unevenness of development which had to be overcome. Despite opposition within the Administration to the policy of extending authority to all areas in a few years, opposition which eventually proved wise when the task was uncompleted at the end of the decade, the Minister's decision prevailed.[70] During the 1950s, when uniform development was most powerful as state policy the greatest reduction in the frontier 'restricted area' did occur. Between 1961 and 1966, there was a further substantial diminution in this area.

In an early rebuttal of the proposition that Australian policy was aimed at retarding political development in the interest of maintaining an indefinite period of colonial administration, Hasluck regarded the diversity of the indigenous population as an impediment to future independence. Instead, he claimed that:

> a sense of unity and some measure of homogeneity among this very diverse population was an essential foundation for any viable and equitable self-government.[71]

He also opposed what he described as a view held by some officials that 'the coastal peoples were the most enterprising and intelligent part of the population and were the "born rulers" of the land'. A similar intent, to secure a greater measure of homogeneity, lay in the design of the judicial system which was intended to combine justice and administration.[72] Courts for Native Matters in Papua and Courts for Native Affairs in New Guinea tried to apply local customs and join these with overarching rules, jurisdiction and procedures established centrally. While only applying to Papua New Guineans, and thus 'racially discriminatory', these courts 'provided an expedient way of taking the law to the people and enforcing the authority of the Administration over a wide range of affairs'.[73] As the drive to self-government gathered pace in the late 1950s, the necessity of replacing such a manifestly deficient judicial system became a major priority, but for the moment it served the objective.

The pursuit of homogeneity was also apparent in education, health and agricultural extension policies and programs. During the 1950s the unsatisfactory condition of indigenous education and the very limited number of public schools drew official attention. Furthering indigenous education had political as well as economic purposes. Emphasising the skills suitable for agricultural production and otherwise improving the indigenous capacity to labour was central to the expansion of primary education across the colony. Expanding

---

70 Hasluck *A Time for Building* pp. 78–79; Downs *The Australian Trusteeship* pp. 268–269
71 Hasluck *A Time for Building* p. 78; Downs *The Australian Trusteeship* pp. 126–128
72 Hasluck *A Time for Building* p. 78
73 Downs *The Australian Trusteeship* p. 148

primary education was also designed to meet the political purpose of ensuring that different people from a wide range of areas would have near-identical opportunities in a self-governing country.[74]

As Hasluck stated in the same Departmental Instruction, when establishing the Department of Native Affairs:

> I have made it an aim of our policy that the people in the outlying areas, such as the Sepik and the Fly River delta, have to be brought up to a level of education comparable with that of the natives of Port Moresby or New Britain so that they are not left behind in the eventual progress towards self-government and placed in a position of subservience to the more fortunate of their fellow countrymen. We are not labouring in Papua and New Guinea simply to hand over their destinies to a few "smart boys" and "shrewd heads" from Moresby and Rabaul. Similarly we have to make sure that the women are not left behind in the general progress.

The colony-wide emphasis on smallholder agriculture also had a homogenising effect, given that this priority was designed to improve living standards across the colony through increases in household productivity. Securing 'village life' on the basis of relatively undifferentiated family labour processes applied to smallholdings was intended to prevent the breakdown of community.[75] This was not a policy for economic and political stagnation, but of development through administrative effort which would increase production and improve living standards.

Administrative Action to Coordinate and Supervise Household Production

If smallholders in the Highlands and Sepik districts were to produce crops with a similar labour content applied to 'their land', state coordination and supervision to raise productivity of households while maintaining attachment to land was essential. So too was sustaining household family labour processes which involve(d) divisions of labour along age, gender, strength, skill, and other lines. For the late colonial developers who coordinated and supervised the scheme of smallholder production, these divisions were preferable to the divisions of industrialised production, particularly those requiring a landless proletariat, wage labour and a class of capitalists owning and operating large holdings. Since households were already producers of crops for immediate consumption, administration attentions were directed at raising this output by

---

74 NAA: M1776/1 vol. 8 *Minister for Territories Instructions to Department 1/7/55 to 31/12/55* 18/10/55 Minister to Secretary
75 Wright *State Practice*; Wright 'Contesting community'

providing advice about cultivation practices and soil fertility, crops grown—including the distribution of improved strains and new crops—and marketing. Considerable attention was given to the development of agricultural extension services and designing projects for particular crops.

In the earliest phase of uniform development, raising the production of food for local consumption, marketed and non-marketed was emphasised. Concern at the rapid increase in food imports, especially rice, and the implications for self-sufficiency stimulated an ordering of priorities.[76] The colonial administration was required to give equal importance to the production of non-marketed crops, including vegetables for immediate household consumption, as to the production of export crops. An early example of the success of this emphasis was provided in 1954 from the project for the expansion of indigenous production in the Madang and Sepik districts. In March 1954, one senior official reported to his superior that:

> In the Amele-Gogol area, which has been the longest under the influence of the project, we now have concrete evidence that in spite of the attention to crops, such as rice and cocoa, native food production is now at a much higher level than before the project was started. The Acting District Commissioner, Madang, told me during my visit last month that the market for native foods in the Madang area is now completely glutted and that he is exploring outlets for exports to other parts of the Territory.[77]

This supervision also meant revising the Native Labour Ordinance to deal with the undesirable as well as desirable consequences of wage employment for indigenes. The Minister emphasised the need for administrative attention to be paid to the problem raised by casual employment increasing at faster rate than contract (that is, longer-term) employment. Because of the threat that casualisation posed to community, the Minister sought to find a means of checking 'the whole position of casual labour and the growing number of natives who are being divorced from village life'. Hasluck was not the only powerful Australian concerned with this trend. 'Nugget' Coombs, Governor of the Commonwealth Bank, wrote to Hasluck on the importance of village life following from his observation that a 'proletariat' was being formed in and around Port Moresby. Coombs recognised the difficulties of formulating administrative action, asking for Administration plans for dealing with the:

> danger and source of deterioration in native standards as well as providing a medium in which difficult and anti-social influences

---

76 Hasluck *A Time for Building* p. 130

77 NAA: A518/1 C2/1/1 *Advancement of Native Agriculture—Papua & New Guinea 1954–1956* 27/3/54, WL Conroy, Acting Chief of the Division of Agricultural Extension to the Acting Director of DASF

could grow. On the other hand, an increasing native population close to major townships and "capitalist" enterprises is necessary for their development.[78]

Hasluck consistently refused to allow 'native labour policy' to be subordinated to the needs of private employers, emphasising the importance of fixed term agreements for 'regulated rotation' between smallholdings and wage employment. He also wanted state provision of technical education to increase the skills which would make it possible for Papua New Guineans to move out of low-paid unskilled labour positions.[79]

Coordinating and supervising smallholder production also required further development of native village councils, subsequently local government councils, which had been first established at the end of the 1940s. Their establishment followed a major change in British colonial policy after 1947. The Colonial Office abandoned what had been termed indirect rule, exerting colonial authority through appointed indigenes.[80] The change was closely followed by the Administration in PNG and especially by Fienberg/Fenbury whom Huntley Wright appropriately describes as 'the chief architect of the Local Government Council system' in the Australian colony.[81]

Fenbury had been present during the formation of the new postwar British colonial policy, visiting East Africa and on secondment to the Colonial Office when the change was occurring.[82] He intended to construct local councils as instruments of central administration control, not institutions for training indigenes in self-government.[83] Nor were the councils intended to be representative vehicles or sites for democratising administration to be captured by the 'rising class of more astute and realistic entrepreneurs (which) is slowly but surely wrestling leadership from the traditional elders'.[84] As much as councils had indigenous members, colonial officials—including DCs and District Officers (DOs)—supervised their activities closely. Wright's conclusion regarding the policy under which these institutions were first established is that:

---

78   NAA: M331/1 74 *Native Labour Ordinance Papua and New Guinea* 1/12/52 Minute from Minister Hasluck to Secretary, Department of Territories; NAA: A518/1 B822/1/6 *Papua & New Guinea Finance. Establishment of Banking Facilities 1945–1956* 1/10/53, HC Coombs Governor of Commonwealth Bank to Hasluck

79   Hasluck *A Time for Building* pp. 160–161

80   Hasluck seems not to have been aware of this change, retaining his own undergraduate 'prejudice' against what he termed 'the Lugard gospel of "indirect rule" as expounded and applied in West Africa', see *A Time for Building* p. 165

81   Wright 'Economic or Political Development' p. 194

82   Fenbury *Practice without Policy* p. 16

83   Cf. Wright 'Economic or Political Development' p. 194; Robert Waddell, 'Local Government Policy in Papua New Guinea from 1949 to 1973' *Australian Journal of Politics and History* 1979, vol. xxv, no. 2, p. 186.

84   NAA: M331/1 35 *D. Fienberg* 17/4/56, DF 'Notes on Native Policy' to Director, Department of Native Affairs, copy to Minister; cf. Ghai & Regan *The Law, Politics and Administration* p. 7

> The primary objective of local government policy was to maintain indigenous attachment to land under conditions of *intensified economic activity*. [Italics in original: SM][85]

As is noted below, this initial objective became less important by the late 1950s, when changes in smallholder agriculture and the Minister's greater concern for councils to play a political role in indigenous development shifted the emphasis away from councils being primarily economic instruments. However the extent to which almost from the outset councils became a forum for tussles between officials and members of the rising class of indigenous businessmen was soon apparent.

When the local government policy had been launched in 1950, the Gazelle Peninsula had been chosen as the chief testing ground, where the first three councils had been set up. Establishment of the councils was supervised by the Senior Native Authorities Officer, who was based in the area. Subsequently, as a start was being made to setting up councils in other locations, including Hanuabada in urban Port Moresby, the policy to establish councils was extended to other parts of the Gazelle Peninsula where Tolai lived.

Almost immediately, organised opposition appeared, with its leadership including a wealthy Tolai, one of the 'entrepreneurs'.[86] The continued opposition to councils and the introduction of a head tax to pay for their operations eventually led in August 1958 to a violent confrontation at Navuneram, where two Tolai villagers were killed.[87] Throughout the 1950s, as councils were set up in other areas, maintaining their economic role for the extension of smallholder activity under close official supervision rather than an arena for indigenous representative politics became more important, as is shown in the final section of this chapter.

As was the case with local councils, scrutiny and direction was provided for other organisations formed to extend commercialisation of household production and consumption. The need to check the rise of indigenous accumulators and limit the extent of anti-colonial activism were seen as necessary corollaries of higher production on smallholdings and improved welfare for the bulk of the population.

---

85   Wright 'Economic or Political Development' p. 200 [Italics in original: SM]
86   NAA: M331/1 35 *D. Fienberg* 17/4/56 'Notes on Native Policy' p. 10; cf. Downs *The Australian Trusteeship* pp. 137–147 and more recently Lowe *Smallholder Agrarian Change* ch. 6 'Social Innovation'.
87   Downs *The Australian Trusteeship* pp. 136–147; Lowe *Smallholder Agrarian Change* pp. 152–156

From the late 1940s, cooperatives and Rural Progress Societies had also been part of official plans for raising household production and consumption.[88] As Wright concludes: 'The postwar model of cooperation adopted in PNG drew extensively from British practice in Africa and Asia'.[89]

This model was central to the doctrine of colonial trusteeship, which rejected spontaneous indigenous activity as an adequate basis for cooperative operations and stressed the importance of administration efforts. While attempts were made to draw parallels between a supposed 'communal type of living common to all village life', and 'the idea of the co-operative effort',[90] the point of drawing the parallel was to develop another means, cooperatives, by which to increase household production and consumption without encouraging migratory labour, which would destroy communal living or community.[91]

Cooperatives flourished initially, and their formation helped in checking indigenous accumulation while spreading the availability of goods for purchase.[92] However their role in increasing indigenous production of export quality crops was very limited. Cooperatives also contributed little to extending the range of crops grown and marketed by smallholders, since most produce marketing was of crops, including coconuts and copra, already grown and processed by smallholders. Even where cooperatives in rural areas aimed to combine trading, providing consumer goods sought by households, with production the former activity invariably dominated.

As Wright notes, of the 134 rural cooperatives registered in 1953, 123 purported to be both producer and consumer co-ops.[93] However despite an initial important presence, with consumer-producer societies contributing to the first postwar increase in the indigenous marketing of copra, the societies had difficulties controlling the quality of the copra purchased for processing and competition from private traders. Consequently cooperatives were unable to attain a major position in marketing smallholder copra. When international prices declined from 1953, cooperatives became even less important for the processing and export of indigenous copra.[94] Most came to rely upon selling consumer goods to smallholders in order to survive.

---

88   Catherine Snowden 'Copra Co-operatives' in Denoon & Snowden (eds) *A time to plant* pp. 185–204
89   Wright *State Practice* p. 312
90   Wright *State Practice* p. 313, citing the Registrar of Co-operative Section within the Department of District Services and Native Affairs CJ Millar from a February 1950 document on the Native Co-operative Movement in PNG.
91   A point also made by Wright *State Practice* p. 314.
92   Wright *State Practice* pp. 317–322. Snowden 'Copra Co-operatives' p. 190 describes the blocking role in these terms: 'By the 1950s it seemed that the Administration had set up bureaucratic devices to restrict local business initiative rather than to encourage it'.
93   Wright *State Practice* p. 318
94   Cf. Wright *State Practice* pp. 322–328; Snowden 'Copra Co-operatives' pp. 194–204.

Cooperatives were also regarded unsympathetically by key officials, including the Minister and Fenbury. Hasluck had a more political-ideological opposition to cooperatives and the support these received within the Administration and from missions. While the Administration continued to support their expansion, the Minister doubted 'whether the co-operative movement was the whole answer to native participation in economic enterprises' in the face of the emergence of the 'exceptional native' as well as 'the native community produc(ing) its own tycoons, mobilising their own families or clans'.[95] Fenbury, however, had another concern, that these organisations could not deal with what had become the central problem of smallholder production, how to raise productivity, or levels of per capita production.

The final section of the chapter takes up the late 1950s shift in uniform development, a change which in some respects was forced upon the colonial government by the successful expansion of smallholder production and consumption during the first period of uniform development. However first it is necessary to deal with the third pillar of uniform development policy, the emphasis on applying administrative efforts comprehensively and in an egalitarian manner across the colony without favouring particular districts and peoples.

Comprehensive Development

Uniform development meant, as Wright has indicated, 'an implicit notion of gradualism'. Citing Hasluck from a 1954 statement on land settlement, Wright points out that '"gradual development"' meant the slowing '"down of economic development until the indigenous people could share in it on a more equitable footing"'.[96] The statement was made in the context of reforms to the administration pf land policy which arose out of the rush by expatriates to obtain land in the Central Highlands, but also represented a broader policy position.

As the Minister re-emphasised in the mid-1950s, comprehensiveness meant limiting unevenness across the colony, which required:

> distributing administrative activity widely over the Territory ... avoiding a concentration of expenditures in the established centres and of increasing the pace of welfare work among the women.[97]

---

95 Hasluck *A Time for Building* pp. 152, 268
96 Wright *State Practice* p. 220, quote from NAA: A518/1 A1927/2 30/7/1958 P Hasluck to Department Secretary Lambert.
97 See also NAA: M331/1 2 *Discussions with Administrator* Notes on Discussions held in the Office of the Minister for Territories, 1st and 2nd February 1956 pp. 13–15.

The uniformity of opportunity to which Hasluck referred regarding education policy, especially regarding women's education, had a liberal basis which also underpinned the intent to make uniform development comprehensive. As well as the advice Hasluck had received from the ANU academics about the dangers of producing a 'poor white problem', he also had been warned about the drive for economic and political advance by wealthy indigenes. The possibilities that administrative support would be provided to either or both phenomena struck at Hasluck's liberal concern for the rights of 'small property' owners.[98] In the PNG context, where the focus of concern was households in occupation of smallholdings, development policy intended that administrative effort would be applied across the whole colony to secure as well as extend rights to these particular Papua New Guineans.

Consequently, even if cocoa was first taken up by wealthy indigenes on the Gazelle Peninsula, agricultural extension services were directed to give substantial support to smallholder production of the crop in this area and also to the many other areas in the colony deemed suitable for growing cocoa. With food production for immediate and locally marketed consumption accorded equal importance to export crops, comprehensiveness required a similar colony-wide attention by DASF and other departments to a wide range of crops.

While one aspect of evenness was positive, to ensure that as much as possible households in all areas were provided with comparable services and resources, the second was clearly negative. There was an equally comprehensive application of state effort and resources to check the advance of particular peoples in specific areas. Hasluck's 1955 concern that education policy should not favour the 'smart boys' and 'shrewd heads' of Port Moresby and Rabaul has previously been noted. In the case of agriculture, areas of the country which were more advanced, including the Gazelle Peninsula, were not to be favoured. Instead colonial policy was to prioritise a process of catching up, which meant greater attention by the Administration to areas which were less developed commercially.

A Challenge to Uniform Development as Policy and Administration

While colonial policy from the 1940s until the mid-1960s, with few exceptions systematically prevented further substantial alienation of land for ownership by large plantation firms, there was less certainty regarding European settlement by owner-occupiers. Considerable official encouragement was given to European settlement in the decade after World War II.[99] These farmers and would-be farmers

---

98   Hasluck *A Time for Building* pp. 217–218
99   Wendy Timms *The Post World War Two Colonial Project and Australian Planters in Papua New Guinea: The search for relevance in the colonial twilight* PhD thesis, ANU (1996)

were often favoured by colonial administrators, from Colonel Murray onwards and including Minister Hasluck. While support provided was in part a response to political pressures in Australia, the expatriate owner-occupiers were also encouraged in the belief that their presence would have a demonstration effect for indigenous smallholder agriculture. While after the war the most important focus for further land alienation became the Highlands, comprehensiveness as one of the defining elements of uniform development meant that the settler demands in one region had implications for overall colonial policy.

With the prominent exception of freehold large holdings obtained before World War II, and alienated land utilised for administration purposes, the bulk of land in PNG was held under customary title.[100] This form of title, whose seeming vagueness was initially its principal advantage, met the general objective of agrarian development, namely to protect indigenous land rights through the exercise of colonial authority. As Hasluck noted, he commenced with an awareness of the importance of 'lands policy and administration' even though he 'knew little or nothing about lands administration except in the setting of the early Australian colonies'. Nevertheless, he 'endorsed without question the long-established policy of protecting native land rights'.[101] Restraining expatriate settlers' demands for land had two purposes. One, that present indigenous occupants would not be pushed off their land to satisfy expatriate ambitions. And two, that there would remain an adequate supply of land for future indigenous requirements, including from the migrant workers who left the highlands to work in coastal and islands regions and subsequently wanted to return home to take up coffee growing.

By the early 1950s, as land pressure increased particularly where cash cropping was taking hold, it became obvious that erecting barriers against removing land from customary tenure, providing 'safeguards against unlimited alienation of native lands' in Hasluck's terms, required further legal and administrative changes. In 1952, the Native Lands Commission was established under the previous year's Native Land Registration Ordinance to determine 'land rights as between natives themselves … [and to protect] native lands from encroachment by non-natives'.[102] Problems immediately arose from the complexity of indigenous ownership and occupation of land.[103] The administration of alienation in circumstances where a measure of decentralised authority over land negotiations

---

100   Peter Larmour *Land Policy and Decolonisation in Melanesia: A Comparative Study of Land Policymaking and Implementation before and after Independence in Papua New Guinea, Solomon Islands and Vanuatu* PhD thesis, Sydney: Macquarie University (1987); Peter Quinn 'Agriculture, Land Tenure and Land Law to 1971' in Denoon & Snowden (eds) *A time to plant* p. 171
101   Hasluck *A Time for Building* p. 114
102   Both quotes are from Wright *State Practice* p. 408, citing an internal Department of Territories memo of 16 April 1953 from Hasluck. Cf. Quinn 'Agriculture, Land Tenure and Land Law' p. 174; Hasluck *A Time for Building* pp. 114–118.
103   Hasluck *A Time for Building* p. 117

and purchase already applied also caused difficulties. The terms of indigenous smallholding ownership and occupation remained a running sore (see below), but alienation for expatriate settlement required an immediate solution.

Between 1952 and 1954, a 'land rush' took place in the Eastern Highlands District, particularly between Goroka and Kainantu. Nearly 3,500 acres was alienated for European settlement. Comprising about three-quarters of the total area alienated between 1949 and 1960, the major expansion occurred at precisely the time indigenous production also was increasing (see Chapter Four).[104] The early 1950s rise in the international price of coffee provided much of the impetus for the expatriate drive to secure land suitable for coffee growing, although land speculation was also a motive. With little previous agricultural experience and limited finances, many of the settlers had no success, failing even to plant a substantial proportion of the land acquired. By Diana Howlett's calculations, five years after the rush ended, undeveloped land accounted for 42.5 per cent of the holdings.[105] By the late 1950s, when international prices had fallen considerably from their earlier peak, centralisation and concentration of holdings had begun. Plantations moved from being operated by owner-occupiers into the hands of firms conducting operations as agricultural capital.[106]

This early 1950s land rush exposed the underlying conflict between spontaneous and intentional development, particularly, but not solely, over land policy. The conflict had to be resolved if the agrarian doctrine was to prevail. Resolution was necessary even though the movement of Europeans into the Highlands was not large in number, with only 26 'established on dispersed coffee farms in the [Eastern Highlands District] between 1952 and 1954', and 'another eighteen farms ... later established in the Western Highlands District, mainly in the Wahgi Valley'.[107] Nevertheless, the timing of the drive to acquire land by expatriates as well as the procedure by which land was being alienated from customary ownership forced Hasluck to re-emphasise his authority, including through the establishment of a new institution to oversee all future land alienation transactions in the colony.

Before the land rush, the procedure by which land was identified for alienation and subsequent sale/purchase had opened the way for considerable decentralisation of decision-making to the district level. Part of this decentralisation arose out of the Minister's own early decision, discussed above, to devolve more authority

---

104 Diana Howlett *A Decade of Change in the Goroka Valley New Guinea: Land Use and Development in the 1950s* PhD thesis, ANU (1962) p. 222, Table 4; Downs *The Australian Trusteeship* pp. 174–186; James Sinclair *The Money Tree: Coffee in Papua New Guinea* (Bathurst: Crawford House, 1995) pp. 66–210

105 Howlett *A Decade of Change* p. 235

106 Cf. Downs *The Australian Trusteeship* pp. 179–181; Downs *The Last Mountain* pp. 261–274, ch. 16 'Coffee and Politics'; Sinclair *The Money Tree* pp. 228–296.

107 Downs *The Australian Trusteeship* p. 179

to district level officials, including DCs. According to Ian Downs, who was appointed DC of the Eastern Highlands District in October 1952 where most of the initial expatriate attention was concentrated:

> (T)here were already enough potential European settlers in the highlands (some of them government officers developing land in their spare time) to make the façade of settlement restrictions threadbare of either moral virtue or administrative effect.[108]

The first phase of expatriate settlement in the region, beginning in the 1930s and 1940s, had taken place through individual transactions between expatriates and indigenes. In May 1952, under Cleland as Acting Administrator while Murray was on pre-retirement leave, restrictions on applications by expatriates were lifted by the Executive Council. Applications for not more than 200 acres were to be submitted to the Council, which would send these to the district office in Goroka for advice and formal application. 'Among applications later rejected by the DC at Goroka and not approved for further investigation were applications from Administration staff, real estate promoters and members of parliament in Australia'.[109]

Downs explained that much of the land offered for lease was in areas where ownership was disputed and the cause of fighting between indigenous claimants. He justified the sales by indicating that from 1952 until 1975, there was no case 'of a ground dispute between Highlands people and a settler occupying a "buffer" zone'.[110] However much this 'dispersed settlement preserved the social and ecological balance' and made it possible for 'a few Australians to give widespread assistance to thousands of people',[111] the process as well as the outcome immediately raised concerns in Australian academic and political circles.[112]

At first these expressions of concern were pushed aside in the rush for land. However it was not long before the Minister too became involved. Hasluck lauded what on 'the one side seemed good' but '(t)he real problem came over land and then over roads'.[113] Hasluck located 'the problem' as the side-stepping of the local land settlement board, established in 1952 to coordinate the actions of all departments involved in land development. In this version, out of the inabilities at the administrative centre decision-making had been devolved to the Highlands. There the DC took over.[114]

---

108 Downs *The Australian Trusteeship* p. 178
109 Downs *The Australian Trusteeship* p. 178
110 Downs *The Australian Trusteeship* p. 179
111 Downs *The Australian Trusteeship* p. 179
112 KE Read 'Land in the Central Highlands' *South Pacific* October 1952, pp. 440–449, 465; for more general concern over European settlement, see James McAuley 'White Settlement in Papua New Guinea' *South Pacific* 1952, vol. 5, no. 12, pp. 250–255.
113 Hasluck *A Time for Building* pp. 120–121
114 Cf. Hasluck *A Time for Building* p. 121; Downs *The Australian Trusteeship* pp. 178–179

While not impugning Downs' personal motives,[115] Hasluck was determined to put a stop to the localisation of decision-making on land alienation. He wanted to prevent DC Downs—and by implication all DCs—from being a 'local ruler' of the district. Decentralisation of responsibility would be limited. The Minister introduced a series of administrative reforms against 'the weight of advice both from the Department and the Administration favouring an easier policy in respect of the acquisition of native lands in order that agricultural development by Europeans might be facilitated'.[116] The Lands Department was strengthened and the formula by which lands could be assessed as surplus to indigenous requirements at present and in the future more tightly defined. Through a newly constituted Lands Board, the Director of Lands based in Port Moresby became responsible for receiving all applications, assessing and purchasing land for expatriate settlement.[117]

While applications previously accepted and in the process of being dealt with were allowed to proceed, and become part of the 1952 to 1954 increase of European farming in the Highlands noted above, there was no subsequent rapid expansion of large holdings. Despite vociferous criticism, especially within PNG, the Minister stood his ground, and rejected proposals to devolve land matters back to DCs.[118]

If checking the ambitions of particular Europeans was a relatively easy matter, the production and consumption increases of the first postwar decade raised more general and thus more intractable problems for uniform development. As well as trying to devise means to further increase smallholder output, especially by stopping fragmentation of holdings as populations increased, the colonial administration was under pressure from another anticipated direction. In particular, institutional arrangements intended to restrain local, particularly indigenous, capitalists were under challenge in those areas where cash cropping was most advanced. Uniform or even development was economically and politically threatened. Although the problem of maintaining the rate of growth while checking the advance of local, especially indigenous capitalists first appeared in the early 1950s, after the middle of the decade it became greater.

---

115 Cf. Hasluck *A Time for Building* p. 121
116 Hasluck *A Time for Building* p. 123
117 Howlett *A Decade of Change* pp. 223–224
118 Cf. NAA: M331/1 58 *Lands Policy (Papua and New Guinea)*; Anon. 'Land Systems Come Under Fire in NG: E. Highlands. Plain Talk to Official' *Pacific Islands Monthly* January 1955, pp. 19, 138.

Picking Up the Pace

Not 'Going Fast Enough'

In January 1958, Territories Minister Hasluck publicly assessed the colonial administration's performance during the seven years of his appointment. Summarising the discussion which had followed presentation of his paper to the Australian Institute of Political Science summer school, Hasluck suggested that comments had been based around an implicit question: 'Are we going fast enough?" He concluded:

> Broadly speaking, we are not and there are many things that ought to be done which we are not doing. … the limitation has not been on the intention to do more but has been based on the capacity to do more.[119]

While dissatisfaction with what was occurring was a constant feature of Hasluck's ministerial persona, from the mid to late 1950s the Minister's sense of urgency became more pronounced. Although there had already been major extensions of plantings, including of coffee, cocoa and copra bushes and trees, with some harvesting and processing increases already apparent (see Chapter Four), international and domestic pressures for further growth were building up. Despite the absence of colony-wide information on the extent of production increases for immediately consumed and locally marketed crops (see Data Appendix), however, as noted in Chapter Five, both academic opinion and the World Bank survey mission of the early 1960s agree that the increase since the end of the war was already substantial. Even with the rapid growth, the longstanding commitment to securing economic advance as a precondition for self-government was under growing pressure internationally. This advance, in the form of financial and other indicators of self-sufficiency, required even more attention to increasing agricultural production while retaining smallholder primacy. The extent to which into the early 1960s development policy for the colony continued to include the objective of 'primary production self-sufficiency' can be gauged from the materials provided to senior officers of the Administration in training courses.[120]

There were also indications that the previous emphasis upon 'village' agriculture would not form an adequate basis for further growth. While households retained security of land tenure under customary title, and the colonial administration remained ever alert to further attempts to accumulate land as large holdings,

---

119 Hasluck 'Present Tasks and Policies' in Wilkes (ed.) *New Guinea and Australia* p. 136
120 See The Australian School of Pacific Administration *Indigenous Economic Development and Its Relationship to Social and Political Change* no. 7, Course for Senior Officers of the Territory of Papua and New Guinea Mosman, Sydney 1st–26th April 1963, pt 15, ch. 6 paras 62–63

preventing fragmentation of smallholdings into ever smaller parcels was near impossible. Colonial officials, including the Minister, became more and more aware of the complexity of indigenous ownership, occupation and farming patterns. Wright locates 1956 as the seminal year when the object of development shifted from expanding household production of marketed crops utilising 'traditional patterns of land and labour usage'. Subsequently, without rejecting 'the assumption that labour effort remained fixed in land', attention turned to formulating means of lifting the 'low returns to labour' and to altering 'a system of land tenure perceived as incapable of ensuring the retention by households of minimum economic areas'.[121]

As is shown in more detail in Chapter Four, the highly successful expansion of indigenous cocoa growing in the Gazelle Peninsula and smallholder coffee production in the Highlands provided a template for broader colonial development policy. Although some substantial indigenous growers appeared early as planters of these crops, determined administrative action, as well as the increasing attraction of cash incomes to purchase consumption goods, also spurred major smallholder plantings. In the Highlands, out-migration to coastal and islands areas for wage employment became less attractive as households gained cash income from coffee. On plantations in the Eastern Highlands many wage workers came from adjoining areas where less smallholder coffee was grown.[122]

During the mid-1950s, officials recognised these changes and intensified their pursuit of uniform development. Emphasising the 'need for a spread of development effort', the Minister told Cleland during discussions in February 1956, that while:

> some local groups would outstrip all other groups in development; whilst there should be no conscious effort to hold back the rate of development in rapidly advancing areas the major effort should be concentrated on accelerating progress in other areas; and there always had to be kept in mind the responsibility which we had, to try to ensure uniform development.[123]

Two months later Fenbury reported that: 'A slow ferment is discernible in native society in most of the areas visited'. The ferment included the drive by the 'average villager' to find 'accelerated ways of bridging the obvious gap between his living standards and those of non-natives'. There was also a changing of the guard in indigenous leadership, with the 'native entrepreneurs' taking over

---

121   All quotations in this paragraph are from Wright *State Practice* p. 334.
122   Howlett *A Decade of Change* pp. 231–234
123   NAA: M331/1 2 *Discussions with Administrator* pp. 13–14

from 'the traditional elders and achieving a grip on the native economy'.[124] While applauding the 'existence of [a] reasonably effective administrative machinery with an economic bias [that] has largely resulted in the entrepreneurs confining their activities to the immediate field of production' among Tolais on the Gazelle Peninsula, Fenbury warned against entrepreneurs engaging in other activities. He illustrated the danger by reference to a particular Tolai leader who strengthened his position 'by political activity which is essentially anti-Administration in character and against both the long-term economic and social interests of the people he dominates'.[125]

Fenbury sought a solution to the problem of how to retain the primarily economic role of local authorities in intensifying supervision of household production, while shifting the focus of local government from a village to an area basis. For the architect of the local government policy, the principal objective was to stress the important role of the 'native local government system' in 'fulfilling [the] need for an integrating and implementing mechanism *at native area level'*. In order to put 'policy into effect', to raise living standards through increased smallholder production, Fenbury asserted that there was a need for 'some form of permanent area organisation'. This need was to be filled by local councils as the future embodiments of the 'hard headed practical administration' which had resulted over the previous three years 'in systematic progress'.[126] Villages, as the previous focus of administrative attention, were too small and an inadequate basis for moving the indigenous population beyond the mythical ideal of 'the sturdy peasant farmer', unrealised 'anywhere in the world' according to Fenbury.[127]

Against Fenbury's preferred position, the Minister now emphasised the political representative role of councils as a training ground for indigenous politics. That Hasluck held such a view, despite the increasing evidence that these and other local organisations including cooperatives were often an important base for the indigenous bourgeoisie, is further testament to the contradictions inherent in development, spontaneous and intentional, as a process.[128] The numbers of local government councils in the colony continued to increase during the 1950s and into the early 1960s. From four councils covering an approximate population of 15,400 people in 1951, by 1963 there were 50 councils, with 1,518 councillors covering over half a million people. Other figures Downs cites from a debate in the Australian parliament in May 1963, suggest an even greater increase to

---

124 NAA: M331/1 35 *D. Fienberg* 17/4/56 Fienberg to Director, Department of Native Affairs, copy to Minister, 'Notes on Native Policy' p. 10
125 NAA: M331/1 35 *D. Fienberg* 17/4/56 Fienberg to Director p. 10
126 Fenbury *Practice without policy* p. 279
127 NAA: M331/1 35 *D. Fienberg* 17/4/56 Fienberg to Director p. 12
128 Jackman *Copra marketing* p. 117 states of the decline of rural cooperatives: 'In retrospect, it is clear that the emergence of Papua New Guinean individual entrepreneurs from the late 1950s on has been the main cause of the gradual demise of the copra marketing and other cooperatives'.

78 councils with closer to 700,000 people. As more and more emphasis was placed on political development, the councils became an important forum for ambitious Papua New Guineans as well as a means of tying local populations of rural smallholders to electoral politics (see Chapter Five).[129] The tension between these organisations' economic and political roles increased further, especially in areas where indigenous accumulation was most pronounced.

The seminal year when the colonial administration made a decisive shift 'towards a policy of individual household production, as opposed to the development of communal ventures' may have been 1956.[130] However since the early 1950s the outcomes which provoked the shift had been intrinsic to the establishment of smallholder export crop production, particularly cocoa on the Gazelle Peninsula. By 1952, indigenous growers had planted more than half a million cocoa trees in that area.[131] While the case of cocoa is considered in more detail in Chapter Four, here it is sufficient to note that from the early 1950s there had been official efforts to shape the rapid expansion of cocoa planting and processing on an individual household basis. These efforts included legislation specifying a minimum number of 500 trees to be planted in one continuous grove as an attempt to prevent further fragmentation of indigenous landholdings and to make state supervision of plantings through agricultural extension services easier.

If low productivity smallholders on increasingly fragmented, smaller plots of land was undesirable, intentional development required even more substantial state coordination and supervision to raise productivity of households across the colony. In order to extend the developmental role of the colonial state, a further increase in state expenditure was required. The low proportion of revenues raised in the colony which limited expenditure from this source was an impediment to pressing the Australian Government for further funding.

Funding and the Increased Administrative Effort

Pressure to increase local revenues had begun in 1955, as the result of Hasluck's continuing but unsuccessful efforts to obtain substantial forward commitments for development funds from the Menzies Government and Commonwealth Treasury. He was directed by Cabinet to increase the revenues raised in the colony, including by taxing expatriates resident there. The target set for the colonial administration was that 'local revenues would be about 30 per cent

---

129 Downs *The Australian Trusteeship* p. 136
130 Wright *State Practice* pp. 333, 345; RJ Cheetham 'The Development of Indigenous Agriculture, Land Settlement, and Rural Credit Facilities in Papua and New Guinea' *The Papua and New Guinea Agricultural Journal* December/March 1962–1963, vol. 15, nos 3–4, pp. 67–78
131 NAA: M335/1 3 *Departmental Brief on Agriculture and Land. January 1954* 'Papua and New Guinea. Agricultural Production and Marketing' p. 6

of the total annual expenditures in the Territory'.[132] In 1956 Treasury and the Department of Territories collaborated in preparing income tax legislation for PNG. Delays occurred in drawing up the legislation, which also provided time for the opposition to the measure to become organised. Only in July 1959, after attempts by the Administration to raise revenues by other means, was the income tax legislation passed by the Legislative Council in PNG.[133] Between 1959 and 1963, when Hasluck ceased to be Minister for Territories, Administration expenditure increased from over AU$11 million to nearly AU$17.5 million.[134] Locally raised revenues as a proportion of total revenues had begun to increase. As Chapter Five shows, however, it was also in 1959 that Hasluck and the Department began to consider the possibility of obtaining World Bank advice on how to lift the rate of growth even further.

Despite the limits placed on alienation of land for large holdings, as discussed above, the extent of land shortages as a barrier to the continuous extension of smallholder agriculture rapidly became apparent. In 1956, Minister Hasluck instructed the Department, and through it the Administration to give 'urgent attention to future land policy'.[135] Efforts soon turned to acquiring unused or under-utilised freehold land on large holdings which had been established prior to World War II on alienated land. The possibility of compulsory acquisition was considered but not pursued until the 1970s.[136]

In order to increase the supply of land necessitated by the drive towards individualisation of indigenous smallholder agriculture which the colonial administration favoured, a series of settlement schemes continued to be implemented. These aimed to reduce the growing landlessness which followed from the expansion of smallholder agriculture in some areas. In 1952 the Administration had given the Rabaul Local Government Council (LGC) a 99 year lease for 1000 acres of land at Keravat, to provide a partial solution to increasing landlessness among Tolai. The settlement schemes were subsequently extended in 1956 to 800 acres purchased for the Amenob LGC in the Madang area, and to 390 acres obtained by the Vunamami LGC, on the Gazelle Peninsula, for land in the Warangoi Valley. The schemes were a deliberate attempt to combine household production of immediately consumed food crops with marketed produce, and were largely predicated on the premise that little or no wage labour would be employed on a continuing basis. From the late 1950s, some individuals were provided with loans.[137] These schemes were continued into the

---

132   Hasluck *A Time for Building* p. 261
133   As well as Hasluck *A Time for Building* pp. 258–265, ch. 23 'The Row Over Income Tax', see Downs *The Australian Trusteeship* pp. 186–195.
134   Downs *The Australian Trusteeship* p. 257, Table 9.1
135   Hasluck *A Time for Building* p. 320
136   Hasluck *A Time for Building* p. 322
137   Cheetham 'The Development of Indigenous Agriculture'; Quinn 'Agriculture, Land Tenure and Land Law' pp. 176–179; Sumer Singh *A Benefit Cost Analysis of Resettlement in the Gazelle Peninsula* New Guinea

1960s in other areas. By 1967, there were 'forty-nine land resettlement schemes in existence in different parts of the country. These schemes include(d) 1,768 blocks of varying sizes with 1,256 blocks allocated to settlers by the end of 1965'.[138] As was obvious from the relatively small acreages provided and the few individuals who obtained land, resettlement had a minimal impact on the increasing landlessness.

The attempts to reform land tenure also had minimal effect, coming up against continuous indigenous resistance as well as the ineffectiveness of administration efforts. Quinn noted that in the '10 years of operation [of the 1951 Native Lands Registration Ordinance] no systematic registration of ownership was undertaken and of 472 applications for individual registration 176 only were determined and none registered'.[139] A more damning conclusion was reached by Robin Hide, who stated that with constant disputes about land ownership and occupation 'the Native Land Registration Ordinance might as well not have existed as far as the Chimbu region was concerned, until after 1957'.[140] Even after this year, little changed, except for the occasional presence of a Native Lands Commissioner, based in Goroka, to whom major land disputes were referred but who rarely settled them.[141]

In any case, as was recognised by officials in Canberra and the colony, not only did formalisation of ownership have the potential to undercut community, it did not necessarily lead to increased productivity. Individual titles could just as easily lead to further fragmentation and declining productivity as to consolidation of holdings and higher output per unit of labour. Impoverishment and landlessness, along with destruction of 'village life' could arise out of individualisation of land tenure, even in the unlikely event that popular support could be gained for such a major reform. Unsurprisingly in the face of such potential difficulties, the sense of floundering during the mid to late-1950s among officials, including Minister Hasluck, over the appropriate direction to be taken in land reform was palpable.[142] In any case, as Wright notes, as long as the Native Lands Commission followed the earlier instruction to register landholdings in the name of clans

---

Research Bulletin no. 17 (Port Moresby and Canberra: New Guinea Research Unit, ANU, September 1967); Wright *State Practice* pp. 379–388

138   Singh *A Benefit Cost Analysis* p. 3; cf. Cheetham 'The Development of Indigenous Agriculture' p. 72, Table 1, who indicates that between September 1959 and March 1963, 634 leases were made available in 12 locations.

139   Quinn 'Agriculture, Land Tenure and Law' p. 176, citing Theo Bredmeyer 'The registration of customary land in Papua New Guinea' *Melanesian Law Journal* 1975, vol. iii, no. 2, p. 269

140   Robin Hide *The Land Titles Commission in Chimbu: An Analysis of Colonial Land Law and Practice, 1933–68* New Guinea Research Bulletin, no. 50 (Port Moresby and Canberra: New Guinea Research Unit, ANU, 1973) p. 25

141   Hide *The Land Titles Commission* pp. 25–28

142   Quinn 'Agriculture, Land Tenure and Land Law' pp. 176–179

and not individuals, there was a conflict between the process of registering indigenous ownership and the post-1956 shift in official practice to encouraging individualisation of land tenure.[143]

The shift to individualisation as the basis for lifting household production, and the increasingly political rather than economic role for LGCs, resulted in a heightened need for another section of the colonial administration to take up the coordinating and supervisory role of smallholder agriculture. Accelerating uniform development required a colony-wide mechanism: the agricultural extension services gained further importance under the turn to intensification after 1956.

In 1927 a Division of Agricultural Education had been formed within the Department of Agriculture. Soon after a Native Agricultural School began operations at Keravat, with a focus on teaching indigenes about 'the cultural practices of economic crops'.[144] In 1932 patrols by officials commenced with the aim of 'improv[ing] the maintenance of copra groves and to introduce new food crops, thus improving the native diet and preventing famine'.[145] Religious missions too 'played a direct agricultural extension role in encouraging local people to engage in cash cropping and by providing market services'.[146]

After the war, when the DASF was formed, Agricultural Extension became one of five divisions, with an establishment of 54 agricultural officers. With postwar reconstruction the foremost task, the Division focused on trying to raise food production by smallholders. As previously noted, activities to support this direction included importing improved pig and poultry strains to raise protein levels.[147] Extension officers, prodded by Department Head W Cottrell-Dormer, became involved in rice growing projects in the Mekeo, Madang and Sepik. This involvement was an attempt to build upon the initial enthusiasm of prominent indigenes for the crop and operated through Rural Progress Societies (see Chapters Two and Four).

During the early 1950s, agricultural extension officers were instrumental in the expansion of immediately consumed food production as well as marketed crops by smallholders. Most attention has focused upon the responsibilities of specific officers for the very rapid increases of cocoa and coffee production on the Gazelle Peninsula and in the Central Highlands.[148] However activities to extend export crops to other areas, and promote greater levels of food cropping were no less indicative of the comprehensive ambitions underlying intentional

143 Wright *State Practice* p. 408
144 Dick & McKillop *A Brief History* p. 14, see also pp. 17–18.
145 Dick & McKillop *A Brief History* p. 14
146 Dick & McKillop *A Brief History* p. 16
147 Dick & McKillop *A Brief History* pp. 20–22; Robin Hide *Pig Husbandry in New Guinea* pp. 8–9
148 Dick & McKillop *A Brief History* pp. 22–26, see also ch. 6.

development. Contrary to the claim that during this period agricultural policy focused upon 'plantation crops', and a few more advanced areas,[149] the promotion of village agriculture across the colony lay at the centre of ministerial and eventually departmental concerns. Although not opposed to export crop production, Hasluck's 'obstinacy' [his term: SM] was directed at giving primacy to locally consumed food production.[150]

Attention has been drawn previously to how in the early 1950s extension activities in Madang operated to successfully integrate export crop production with food growing for immediate consumption and local markets (see above). Here it is only necessary to point out that these efforts did not stop at the main population centres, or where agricultural conditions were especially favourable. The comprehensiveness required under uniform development meant a colony-wide focus. In July 1954, for instance, the Administration issued a press release noting the work being done on a coffee planting project near Lae, on the mainland, as well as on the Mortlock and Tasman Islands, 250 to 500 kilometres east of the main Bougainville Island. Having a total population of just 437 people, the atolls with a maximum height of 14 feet above sea level had little soil for growing crops. Shipping contact was rare prior to 1952 but within a year there were visits by three Administration patrols. Subsequently, under strict health requirements for ship crews, 'a trading vessel is now making periodic calls to buy copra and trochus shell'.[151]

A central feature of extension activities was distribution of improved seed and planting material, either from stations or when officers went on patrol. In 1952–53, to take just one example, smallholders were provided with cocoa and coffee seedlings, sweet potatoes, cowpeas, a range of vegetable seeds, rice, maize and sorghum seed, tree seeds and cinchona seedlings.[152] Expanding the planting of coconuts as a food crop and for copra production was a constant preoccupation of extension officers. The importance of what were termed native subsistence foods was also central to these activities, 'both to improve the quality and yield of existing food crops and to encourage the natives to grow new crops which will be of value to their diet'.[153] Peanuts, initially distributed for locally consumed food, increasingly filled this role as well as becoming a minor export crop. Administration support for local production and export of peanuts went

---

149   Dick & McKillop *A Brief History* p. 22–26

150   Hasluck *A Time for Building* pp. 133–136

151   NAA: A518/1 C2/1/1 *Advancement of Native Agriculture* 12/7/54 Administration Press Release 'Diversity in Native Economic Development'. See also AD Boag and RE Curtis 'Agriculture and Population in the Mortlock Islands' *Papua and New Guinea Agricultural Journal* 1959, vol. 12, no. 1, pp. 20–27.

152   NAA: A518/1 C2/1/1 *Advancement of Native Agriculture* REP Dwyer, Director, DASF 'Agricultural Extension and Native Production' A Report to the Administrator of Papua and New Guinea in August 1953 on the activities of the Division of Agricultural Extension in regard to Native Agricultural Production, p. 3.

153   NAA: A518/1 C2/1/1 *Advancement of Native Agriculture* Dwyer 'Agricultural Extension and Native Production' p. 5

against the opposition from Australian growers.[154] Unsuccessful efforts were made too to find markets in Australia for the expanding local production of betel nuts, used in powder form as a cleansing drug for intestinal worms in animals, in dyeing and tanning of hides and in the preparation of dentrifices (false teeth).[155]

In late 1953, extension service officers were located at 15 stations.[156] Patrolling to extend the reach of extension services beyond district and sub-district agricultural stations was a continuous feature of the division's work. Estimates of the amount of time spent patrolling varied from 90 per cent, for the officer-in-charge of the native cocoa project on the Gazelle and at Dagua, where there was no fixed station, down to 20 per cent where officers had to combine patrolling with running a one-man agricultural station.[157]

Such was the importance attached to extension work among indigenous households, that by 1954, a staffing level of 114 European officers had been approved for the Division, more than double the figure eight years earlier. However the international shortage of skilled agriculturalists was so great that filling these positions was estimated as likely to take a further six years. As the head of the Division noted in a memo to the Administrator: 'No matter how successful our recruiting programme is, it will be at least five years before agricultural services can be provided to natives in many areas of the Territory'.[158] Yet again, development goals for the colony came up against international conditions which were the principal determinant of the market for another commodity, skilled labour power.

As one means of trying to overcome the shortages, Minister Hasluck insisted on closer cooperation between staff from the Division of Agricultural Extension Services and the Department of District Services and Native Affairs. At the same time, Hasluck increased the work-load for DASF officials by insisting upon a six monthly report on progress in indigenous extension work and its relationship to annual district indigenous agricultural development plans. In March 1955,

---

154 NAA: A518/1 C2/1/1 *Advancement of Native Agriculture* Dwyer 'Agricultural Extension and Native Production' p. 4; NAA: A518/1 H927/4 *Economic Development of the Territories—Commodities—Peanuts 1950–1958*; NAA: A452/1 1957/3952 *Peanut Industry in Australia—Territories—Marketing in Australia 1951–1960*; NAA: A452/1 1959/647 *Visit of Queensland Peanut Marketing Board 1959–1959*; cf. Hasluck *A Time for Building* pp. 294–295
155 NAA: A518/1 GZ812/1/7 *Betel Nuts—Market for 1954–1956*
156 NAA: A518/1 C2/1/1 *Advancement of Native Agriculture* Dwyer 'Agricultural Extension and Native Production' p. 5. The stations were Maprik, Dagua, Bogia, Madang, Finschaffen, Kainantu, Goroka, Mt Hagen, Rabaul, Lorengau, Sohano, Samarai, Port Moresby, Inauaia and Beipa.
157 NAA: A518/1 C2/1/1 *Advancement of Native Agriculture* Dwyer 'Agricultural Extension and Native Production' p. 1
158 NAA: A518/1 C2/1/1 *Advancement of Native Agriculture* 29/3/54 FC Henderson to Administrator

the first six monthly report on extension activities was provided, covering the period July to December 1954. Subsequently the Minister was an avid reader of and commentator upon these reports.

Intensified extension efforts had to conform to what was acceptable internationally. The Minister and Department ensured that local policy recommendations did not stray from what would be approved under UN Trusteeship terms. Thus a proposal generated at the District Commissioners' Conference held at Lae in September–October 1953, and supported in principle by the Administrator, was quashed. Local extension officers and other officials wanted to reintroduce the pre-war policy of compulsory planting of crops by indigenes, but this could not be permitted.

As LGCs became less and less useful for area administration of smallholder agriculture, extension activities became more important. By mid-1959 there were 66 qualified expatriate extension officers and around 120 Papua New Guinean assistants.[159] In late 1959, the Minister announced a three year plan for a further substantial increase in agricultural extension personnel, to strengthen the Extension Division within the DASF. As well as the establishment of an additional 22 agricultural extension centres, an extra 74 European officers and 120 indigenous agricultural assistants were to be recruited. With the extra personnel and facilities, a further 1,000 indigenous farmers were to be trained annually in improved agricultural methods. The Minister anticipated a major increase in indigenous production of both food for immediate consumption and local sale, and export crops.[160] In 1962, there were 45 extension centres operating and since the 1959 announcement of Hasluck's three year plan, around 3,000 Papua New Guineans had received agricultural training at the centres.[161] By 1962, the Department of Territories was requiring preparation of a five year plan for further expansion of extension activities, and Hasluck was still urging the Department to keep a close watch on the Administration to see that extension work was a priority (cf. Map 5-2). In October 1962, the department released a Ministerial Press Statement announcing the approval of the five year plan:

> which would mean that the emphasis now being given to agricultural extension work among the indigenous people of Papua and New Guinea will be greatly intensified.[162]

159   Downs *The Australian Trusteeship* p. 132

160   Anon. 'Minister Announces Major Increase in Extension' *The Papua and New Guinea Agricultural Journal* September/December 1959, vol. 12, nos 2–3, p. 48. See also NAA: A452/1 1957/356 *Agricultural Extension Policy—Objectives and Administration Action—P and NG*, 1956–1960.

161   Downs *The Australian Trusteeship* p. 132. See also NAA: A452/1 1962/8276 *Agricultural Extension Work in Papua & New Guinea, 1961–1967*.

162   NAA: A452/1 1962/8276 *Agricultural Extension Work*

Conclusion

During the 1950s, the military significance of PNG for Australia's security waned, even though Australia's role in PNG's security remained part of the official conception of trusteeship for the colony.[163] Instead colonial development was given greater priority and a more precise definition. Through the policy of uniform development increases in production occurred. Despite substantial challenges to what was intended to happen, by the end of the decade the bulk of the population remained attached to smallholdings and probably had considerably higher living standards. The best indicators of improvements in welfare currently available are likely to be those which suggest declining mortality rates from 1949 onwards for adults and children in different areas, as colonial authority was extended to more and more of the indigenous population.[164]

The continuing tussles to raise revenues and improve the effectiveness of the colonial administration suggested that further increases in smallholder production would be difficult to achieve. International and domestic pressure for political and administrative reforms would only create more space in which the representatives of indigenous capital and its allies could challenge colonial policy. While recruiting more Papua New Guineans into state employment, especially managerial positions, and changing the Legislative Council's membership to include a significant number of elected indigenes would satisfy critics of Australian rule at the UN, the changes could also reduce the power of the Minister and his officials which had been crucial for uniform development.

However the 1950s and the early 1960s were marked by the efforts of the colonial Administration to improve indigenous living standards and raise the output of many crops for immediate consumption as well as for markets, local and overseas. The next chapter describes in some detail two particular success stories—coffee and cocoa—and one instance, rice production, where the outcome was not commensurate with the attention given and resources employed. Yet the case of rice, so widely perceived as demonstrating the failure of development intent, illustrates neatly an important point about colonial development policy and practice. Development is a unity of two processes, one spontaneous and the other intentional, both of which are always subject to the external authority of capital. Even if dry land rice production in PNG did not

---

163   Hasluck 'Present Tasks and Policies' in Wilkes (ed.) *New Guinea and Australia* pp. 78–79

164   RFR Scragg 'Historical epidemiology in Papua New Guinea' *Papua New Guinea Medical Journal* September 1977, vol. 20, no. 3, pp. 102–109; ESCAP/SPC *Population of Papua New Guinea Country* Monograph Series no. 7.2 (New York and Noumea: United Nations and South Pacific Commission, 1982) p. 167, Table 106 'Department of health field surveys of mortality, 1949–1952 to 1971–1976'. I am deeply indebted to Robin Hide for drawing my attention to these sources and for advice on the difficulties involved in providing conclusive evidence on population increases and health improvement during the 1950s.

attain sufficient levels to meet the desired objective of colonial self-sufficiency, the importation of rice produced in increasing quantities under irrigated, wet land, conditions in Australia made an important contribution to the broader goal of official policy, to improve living standards for rural and urban people.

4. Uniform Development in Practice

Introduction

The previous chapter concentrated upon the principal features of uniform development policy during the 1950s, and in particular what was intended to happen. Here emphasis is placed upon what occurred, as the intersection of spontaneous and intentional development. Several of the most substantial outcomes are shown through brief accounts of three particular crops, grown for international markets as well as immediate household consumption and local sale. However, as pointed out in the Introduction, this is not intended to be a comprehensive account of development in practice during the 1950s. Partly, this is because of the difficulty in showing the extent of the changes in household production of immediately consumed and locally marketed crops even if contemporary accounts referred to in the next chapter, including from the World Bank, suggest the output increases of these crops too was considerable. However coffee, cocoa and rice were such important pillars of the scheme of smallholder agriculture constructed through uniform development policy that selecting their growth and processing as key indicators of what occurred is warranted.

Some of the changes in the growth of these and other crops, including smallholder copra output, did not register immediately in output increases: bush and tree crops in particular take years between planting and reaching sufficient maturity before harvesting of cherries, pods and nuts can occur in worthwhile quantities (see Chapter Five, Tables 1 and 2). Although the Administration aimed for evenness among peoples and regions, uniform development did not imply simultaneous identical changes across the colony.

The most substantial indigenous plantings of coffee bushes by smallholders first began during the 1940s and 1950s in the Eastern Highlands and Chimbu, only reaching a faster rate of expansion during the next decade in the Western Highlands. The most important increases in smallholder cocoa followed a different, opposite trajectory, from 'west' during the 1940s and 1950s on the Gazelle Peninsula to 'east' during the 1960s and early 1970s on Bougainville. Although with much less by way of increased production, rice growing also became greater as the focus shifted from the south-west to the north-east of the mainland.

The chapter begins with coffee, the crop which during the late colonial period penetrated particularly deeply into the lives of rural Papua New Guineans in the Highlands and provided a major component for the scheme of smallholder agriculture. From the outset, coffee was a crop produced for international markets, with little domestic consumption. The first phase of coffee's expansion in the decade and a half after World War II owed much to the colonial administration's determination to find a means of securing village life at improved standards of living. High international prices and the region's geographic suitability for growing better quality Arabica assisted official policy to stem an initial postwar outflow of Highlanders to wage positions outside the region. By 1959, the area covered by smallholder plantings exceeded that on large holdings owned by expatriates. The former had begun the expansion from the initial base in the Eastern Highlands and Chimbu into the more spacious Western Highlands and was accompanied by continued international decline in coffee prices.

Cocoa provides the second pillar of the scheme of smallholder production considered here. While by far the most important increase of cocoa growing during the uniform development phase occurred on the Gazelle Peninsula in East New Britain, nevertheless official attention was directed to spreading the crop to many other parts of New Guinea and Papua where soil and other conditions were suitable. Of particular importance was the early adoption of cocoa on Bougainville. During the 1960s, a debilitating disease decimated yields in the major growing area. Separated and insulated by the Solomon Sea from East New Britain, plantings on Bougainville could be effectively quarantined against the spread of vascular streak dieback (VSD), at a time when a substantial smallholder expansion already had begun in the District.

Rice, briefly considered in the third section of the chapter, provides an appropriate counterpoint to the cases of coffee and cocoa. The failure to achieve a major increase in rice production might suggest that colonial efforts with the crop had little in common with the successful drive to extend coffee and cocoa outputs. Nevertheless the reasons for the lack of success with rice, as well as the amount of resources committed in attempting to attain a measure of colonial self-sufficiency, demonstrate much about the official desire to bring development through smallholder agriculture. While coffee and cocoa were encouraged as export crops, and for their contribution to domestic revenues, rice was seen as primarily for domestic consumption, marketed as well as non-marketed. However unlike the cases of coffee and cocoa, international availability and price provided conditions much more conducive for the importation rather than local production of rice.

Coffee's Beginnings and Initial Expansion

Of the crops which became central to the postwar scheme of smallholder production, coffee possibly had the most far-reaching consequences for indigenous households. Although coffee growing in the colony first occurred outside the Central Highlands region, mainly in what became Morobe and Madang districts, it attained greatest importance in the Eastern and Western Highland and Chimbu/Simbu districts. By the mid-1960s, smallholder output surpassed that from plantations. In the early 1970s, the area under crop was probably around 25,000 hectares planted with approximately 26 million bushes, most of them in the three Central Highlands districts, which later became provinces. Smallholders supplied more than 70 per cent of PNG's total yield of around 40,000 tonnes of the crop which displaced copra as the major agricultural export. One estimate suggests that more than a third of all the electors at the 1972 self-government poll, attached to about 200,000 holdings in the main growing areas, were from coffee producing households.[1]

Household production of this crop, as with cocoa, brought major changes to the lives of Papua New Guineans. The nature of these changes continues to be debated. On one side are those who see coffee as 'brown gold' grown on 'money trees', the basis for a major upward shift in living standards throughout the region. Opposition to this view is encapsulated by the Melanesian Pidgin (Tok Pisin) expression kopi kalabusim mipela, or 'coffee imprisons us/my people', responsible for reduced household self-sufficiency, impoverishment and a shift to 'undesirable' consumer goods, especially beer, which have further deleterious consequences.

Nearly all indigenous coffee growing occurred after World War II. The initial phase of smallholder plantings—the focus of this chapter—lasted until the early 1960s in the Central Highlands. During this period colonial administration officials tested the suitability of Arabica coffee, made seeds available, assisted with the selection of suitable sites, helped establish nurseries, and instructed on planting, mulching, shading and fertilising, harvesting and processing. Where there were no private buyers, especially in the less accessible areas to which coffee growing had moved before roads were constructed, Administration officers purchased and transported crop to major towns. The importance of the official activity for smallholder growing and processing runs directly counter to the mythology propagated by the relatively small number of European planters

---

1   LD Wilson and GBA Evans *Sample Survey of Smallholder Coffee Producers* (Port Moresby: Department of Agriculture, Stock and Fisheries, Rural Economics and Commodity Marketing Branch, February 1975) pp. 9–11, are suitably cautious about the accuracy of the survey, especially for the Western Highlands and Chimbu where they conclude the figures on plantings 'are serious underestimates' (p. 9), possibly because growers under-reported holdings due to a rumour that accurate reporting would have tax consequences.

and their supporters. This version gives an especially prominent, even primary role, in the establishment and subsequent growth of the coffee industry to the expatriate owner-occupiers of large holdings. One such account even refers to the period between World War II and Independence as 'the plantation era'.[2]

Instead and more accurately Ian Cartledge, official historian of the late colonial coffee industry and senior Department of Territories' officer,[3] stresses the importance of the multiplicity of roles performed by Administration officials. He credits 'advice, encouragement and agricultural education from officials' for the early success in coffee growing, particularly for the 'local people'.[4] US anthropologist Ben Finney too, despite his principal focus upon the 'partnership' between expatriate planters and emerging indigenous businessmen, most of whom straddled between coffee growing and other commercial activities, indicates the importance of Administration extension activities for the first phase of smallholder expansion in the Goroka area.[5]

So quickly did the crop attract smallholders and expatriate owner-occupier growers alike, that officers, especially in agricultural extension, were never really able to keep up with demand for their services. One consequence of this inability to provide sufficient assistance is that it subsequently became possible to underestimate the importance of the colonial administration's role from the outset of coffee growing in the region. While the Administration's presence is perhaps best documented for the Goroka, Kainantu and Henganofi sub-districts, this section shows how in the decade and a half after World War II ended, smallholders in Chimbu and the Western Highlands also were the focus of official efforts which were largely successful.

Goroka, Kainantu and Henganofi

Astute colonial officials early recognised that Highland climatic and soil conditions were favourable for Arabica coffee which grows best at altitudes above 1,000–1,500 metres. This coffee satisfied a niche market, in a similar

---

2   See Sinclair *The Money Tree*; David Anderson *An Economic Survey of Smallholder Coffee Producers—1976* (Port Moresby: Planning Economics Marketing Branch, Department of Primary Industry, September 1977) p. 4 is one among many who repeats the error of giving primacy to the role of expatriate planters in the origins of coffee growing in the region, claiming: 'In the Highlands, coffee was first grown by expatriates employing workers from neighbouring areas'.

3   Hasluck *A Time for Building* p. 437

4   Ian Cartledge *A History of the Coffee Industry in Papua New Guinea: from inception to the end of 1975* (Goroka: Papua New Guinea Coffee Industry Board 1978) p. 22. At the end of Chapter Four on the establishment of commercial production in the 1950s, Cartledge re-emphasises the point, stating: 'The conclusion is repeated that much of the credit must go to the Division of Extension and Marketing in D.A.S.F. for the rapid and large scale expansion of coffee growing by native communities in the highland areas'.

5   Ben Finney *Big-Men and Business: Entrepreneurship and Economic Growth in the New Guinea Highlands* (Honolulu: University Press of Hawaii, 1973) pp. 43, 53

manner to that occupied by Trinitario cocoa (see Chapter Two).[6] During 1936 early Highland coffee plantings were made by Department of Agriculture Inspector and Instructor Bill Brechin in nursery beds prepared at the Upper Ramu Police Post (now Kainantu).[7] The beds were planted with seed brought from the plantation owned by Karl Wilde at Wau, in what is now Morobe Province. The initial plantings flourished and in 1940 64 tons of Arabica coffee was produced.[8] Even more importantly, demands for coffee seed had begun to come from villagers who were showing considerable interest in growing the crop.[9]

While the wartime need for securing supplies of quinine made this crop more important for Aiyura, still Brechin's coffee plantings at the research station continued to flourish. The seed the bushes produced provided the basis for two deliberate efforts to expand smallholder plantings during and immediately after the war years. Michael Bourke notes that:

> The unpublished patrol reports indicate that between late 1944 and late 1945, village coffee plantings were promoted by ANGAU patrol officers in parts of the Goroka, Henganofi and Kainantu Districts of the Province. There were at least 12 coffee patrols and most ANGAU field officers were involved in coffee extension during this period.[10]

Foremost among the Aiyura staff who encouraged smallholder coffee was Agronomist-in-Charge of the Research Station, Aubrey Schindler who 'had been involved in the ANGAU-sponsored village coffee as early as 1944'.[11] From about 1950, Schindler began extension activities on smallholder coffee in the Kainantu area. This coffee had been grown as the result of distribution of seedlings from Aiyura to villages.

There was a further overlap between Aiyura and the ANGAU personnel which extended to smallholder coffee growing. Two especially important instances

---

6   Only a small proportion of PNG grown coffee is Robusta, which generally forms the base for cheaper blends and instant coffee. In the late colonial period Robusta came mainly from East Sepik District (see JP Munnull and DRJ Densley *Coffee Agriculture in the Economy A Series of Review Papers* (Konedobu: Department of Primary Industry, n.d., p. 3). For the earliest growing of Arabica and Robusta coffee, from the mid-1880s in PNG, see Sinclair *The Money Tree* chs 3, 4.

7   As discussed below, it seems likely that the Aiyura plantings were not the first in the Highlands but were preceded by at least two years with coffee grown for personal consumption at a Lutheran mission in Chimbu.

8   Sinclair *The Money Tree* p. 53, notes that when the Aiyura Research Station was established in May 1937, Brechin transferred the coffee plants, along with cinchona and tea plants to the station's nursery.

9   RM Bourke 'Village Coffee in the Eastern Highlands of Papua New Guinea' *Journal of Pacific History* 1986, vol. 21, nos 1 & 2, pp. 100–103 cites (p. 101) Brechin's May 1940 Aiyura monthly report: 'It is already clear from trials on this Station that high altitude [Arabica: SM] coffee is going to be an economic crop in this area. Local people are already asking why they can not start planting themselves'.

10   Bourke 'Village Coffee' pp. 101–102. See also Sinclair *The Money Tree* chs 6–7; cf. Randall Stewart *Coffee: The Political Economy of an Export Industry in Papua New Guinea* (San Francisco: Westview Press, 1992) p. 28. 'The first indigenous plantings of coffee in the Highlands in the Asaro Valley of the Eastern Highlands, was in 1952'

11   Bourke 'Village Coffee' p. 102

of this overlap were men who also became large holding pioneers, Jim Leahy and Jim Taylor. During the war Captain Leahy had his interest in coffee stimulated when he was farm manager at Aiyura. As Sinclair explains, Leahy 'had learned something of coffee culture during his time at Aiyura, and the ANGAU experiments [with smallholder coffee growing: SM] had proved that coffee could be grown in the Goroka valley'.[12] After toying with the idea of planting tea, from which he desisted because of the 'prohibitive cost of tea processing machinery',[13] Leahy used this knowledge of coffee cultivation to become an early expatriate large holding grower in the Highlands. In 1948, he used seed obtained from Schindler at Aiyura Research Station to plant on an approximately 150 acre lease, five miles west of Goroka, which became Erinvale plantation.[14] Following a path well worn by Europeans who owned coconut and cocoa large holdings in coastal and islands areas, Leahy subsequently mapped out a trajectory which was to be followed by some of the other European owner-occupiers who produced coffee in the Highlands. He moved from growing coffee into becoming one of the earliest purchasers of indigenous smallholder coffee, increasing volumes sold and improving cash-flow for his operations as coffee prices began to make a major upwards move.[15] In 1950, Leahy added labour recruiting for New Guinea Goldfields Ltd at Wau to his multiplex enterprise,[16] and subsequently began sawmilling of local timber. Two years later, when Leahy sold his first crop of 1,420 lbs, he received six shillings and ten pence per lb ex-Goroka.[17] The very high price received played an important role in encouraging expatriates to come to the Highlands and apply for large holding leases on which to grow coffee.

At least as important as Leahy for smallholder growing and the entire scheme of smallholder production was Jim Taylor. Until September 1944 Major Taylor was the ANGAU District Officer Ramu. While in this position, Taylor had delivered a paper at the February 1944 ANGAU District Officers' conference held in Port Moresby (see Chapter One).[18] The conference was chaired by Brigadier DM

---

12   Sinclair *The Money Tree* p. 75
13   Sinclair *The Money Tree* p. 75
14   Sinclair *The Money Tree* p. 75
15   Downs, district commissioner, planter and initial chairman of the Coffee Marketing Board established in 1964, emphasises the wider and continuing connection between the large holding owners and smallholder operations, noting that: 'Settlers established their own nurseries from selected seed and gave plants to their highland neighbours in order to establish the existence of coffee as a widespread planted crop and to lay the foundation for future coffee trading when village trees came into production' *The Australian Trusteeship* p. 180.
16   Sinclair *The Money Tree* p. 80
17   The New York spot price for washed Arabica was US$0.57 per lb in 1952 and had begun its post-war climb to the 1954 high. See Cartledge *A History of the Coffee Industry* p. 324, app. 30.
18   NAA: A9372 vols 1–3 *ANGAU*

Cleland, who subsequently became the long-serving Administrator of the colony. In his presentation, Taylor, known for his strong views on indigenous welfare, emphasised the importance of commercialisation through coffee growing.[19]

As Sinclair indicates, Taylor's proposal had an immediate follow-up. The ANGAU official who replaced him as District Officer Ramu, Major Tom Aitchison was 'like Taylor, genuinely interested in the welfare and development of the Highlands people', and 'actively began to push the extension of coffee planting'.[20] With the authority of the ANGAU behind them, police and the ANGAU personnel were able to exercise a degree of compulsion in pressing villagers to plant coffee. When international prices were still low following the 1930s period of oversupply on world markets, Sinclair's conclusion seems accurate: 'There is little doubt that many villagers planted coffee only because they were compelled to do so'.[21] Maintenance of bushes often ceased once the patrols moved on or the officers who had pushed smallholders into planting the crop left the area.

Nevertheless, by the end of the war considerable numbers of smallholders had experience with coffee especially in the area between Goroka and Kainantu townships. Even with prices still low, by comparison to what they were to become in the early to mid-1950s, these smallholders produced increasing quantities for export. Once again, as with shells and other consumables coming into the region, the availability of air transport—with favourable rates for back-loading planes which had limited cargoes to move out of the Highlands—provided a major means for linking households with international markets and global prices. Forming the commercial bridge between growers and these markets were Administration officials and a small number of private traders.

As Bourke indicates from his examination of unpublished records, 'some villagers had obtained modest returns from coffee between 1947 and 1954', that is even before the bushes planted under the impetus of the major DASF extension efforts of the early 1950s discussed below came into bearing.[22] These returns were obtained by selling coffee to the Administration, a practice earlier established for other local food crops, including a wide range of 'European' vegetables which were either locally consumed or flown out of the Highlands to Lae and Madang.[23]

---

19   Gammage *The Sky Travellers* ch. 18 provides a sense of the views Taylor and his close friend John Black held. See also Sinclair *The Money Tree* p. 62.

20   Sinclair *The Money Tree* p. 62. Aitchison, then Captain and District Officer South Markham, also attended the February 1944 Conference. For the list of attendees, as well as Taylor's presentation titled 'Native Welfare', see NAA: A9372 vols 1–3 *ANGAU*.

21   Sinclair *The Money Tree* p. 64

22   Bourke 'Village Coffee' p. 102

23   See also Sinclair *The Money Tree* p. 75.

An important contribution to smallholder coffee extension work was made by Robert Cottle, the first Goroka-based agricultural officer. Arriving during 1952, Cottle initially began to encourage passionfruit growing in order to supply a factory set up in the town by Cottees Passiona Ltd, an Australian firm. Cottle soon recognised that passionfruit was not an economic crop for smallholders beyond a certain radius around the factory. Instead, he decided to promote coffee growing, probably from mid to late-1952.

For coffee, where seed is best planted first in containers that make maintenance and plant selection most effective, the establishment of shaded nurseries using planting material obtained from the Aiyura Agricultural Research Station was one of the most important early stages for all coffee growing. Finney notes the warm reception Cottle received from indigenes, so that within a year there were coffee nurseries established from Bena Bena, east of Goroka into Chimbu to the west. Cottle was able to draw upon existing enthusiasm among local people to establish DASF-sponsored nurseries and coffee plots. Especially around central Goroka, many of the indigenous volunteers wanted to move beyond previous unsuccessful attempts at growing coffee. Thus:

> The many requests for his services from central Gorokans forced Cottle to offer these people advice and aid in coffee planting …. After the village nurseries were established, Cottle returned to each area and, with the help of Gorokan assistants, helped interested men select proper land, clear it, and then plant coffee seedlings and shade trees on it.[24]

The extension work continued even after Cottle left the District. The extent of demand for assistance produced endemic staff shortages. In 1955–56, '[p]rogress in the development of native owned coffee, now totalling approximately 450,000 and [sic] 700,000 nursery seedlings throughout the District, is most gratifying'.[25] Two years later: '197 new coffee nurseries [were] established by native peoples and it is estimated that these nurseries will provide seedlings for approximately 2,000 acres of coffee … the Administration is unable to meet the demand for assistance in coffee cultivation'.[26]

This demand soon spread to assistance in processing, where the techniques employed are especially important for the quality of coffee obtained. As the next year's Eastern Highlands Annual Report noted, at the same time as emphasising how the demand for assistance continued to outstrip capacity, attention had been extended to raising the standard of smallholder coffee sold to buyers.[27] The agriculture extension role continued to be central until the

---

24 Finney *Big-Men and Business* pp. 60–61
25 ToPNG Department of Native Affairs Eastern Highlands District [DNA-EHD] *Annual Report 1955–56* p. 6
26 DNA-EHD *Annual Report 1955–56* p. 4
27 DNA-EHD *Annual Report 1955–56* pp. 6–7

end of the 1950s, even as there began a temporary slow-down in the rate of new plantings coincident with falling international prices. Although the focus of official efforts was partly deflected from coffee to providing assistance with peanut growing, nevertheless there was consistent demand for advice on coffee production, especially processing.

As a consequence, with almost 2.5 million indigenous-owned trees in an area which at the time included Chuave and Chimbu sub-districts in the west of the Eastern Highands District, Administration officers were able to point to a continued improvement in the quality of smallholder produce. Increasing numbers of smallholders were purchasing hand hulling machines, which made it possible to speed up the process by which the outer skin was stripped from the coffee cherry. With the use of the machines which replaced manual removal of the outer skin, there were fewer damaged beans and fermentation prior to washing could occur under better controlled conditions. This elementary mechanisation accelerated the process so that drying to the parchment stage also could occur more quickly, with a consequent improvement in parchment quality.

Once given this initial treatment by growers, parchment coffee was then sold to either private buyers or brought to the coffee factory at Goroka for further processing into green bean, ready for export. As the 1959–60 Eastern Highlands Annual Report of the Department of Native Affairs noted (p. 3), the attention to improving processing standards had resulted in 'a native exhibitor in the Lae Show (winning) six of seven sections against all entries'.[28]

Chimbu

The importance of Administration efforts was seen even more clearly in Chimbu Sub-District, later District, where no expatriate plantations were permitted because of population density and shortages of suitable land. Despite the differing accounts of the introduction of the crop to the third most important coffee growing area, after Eastern and Western Highlands, there is no evidence that European planters initially played an important part, either as distributors of seed or as advisers on coffee growing and processing.

The first coffee in Chimbu was probably planted in 1934 or 1935 at the Lutheran Mission at Ega (subsequently the district/provincial capital Kundiawa).[29] Seed

---

28   Whether the 'native exhibitor' was a smallholder or one of the indigenous largeholders who were becoming prominent by the late 1950s is not known.
29   Hubert Stuerzenhofecker Letter from Ega (Lutheran Mission Station) to Adam Schuster at Neuendettelsauer (Neuendettelsauer Archives) 1 August 1935. Copied and translated by Christine Winter, Dec. 1994, note provided by Robin Hide. Stuerzenhofecker was in charge of the mission's gardens. Cf. Ian Hughes *Availability of Land and Other Factors Determining the Incidence and Scale of Cash Cropping in the Kere Tribe, Sina Sina, Chimbu District, New Guinea* BA (Hons) thesis, University of Sydney (1966) p. 112 who states that: 'The Lutheran mission at Kundiawa planted coffee for its own consumption in 1937'.

was soon made available for indigenous growing.[30] After the war, colonial officials played the primary role in the spread of coffee in the District, though indigenes returning to their own holdings after spells in wage employment outside the sub-district also were significant. Before the end of the 1940s, a nursery had been 'established at the Deri patrol post and a distribution of coffee plants and some crotolaria used for covering [shading bushes: SM] is being made available to these people'.[31]

However the most extensive plantings probably began in the early 1950s. As indicated above, Cottle's work in establishing nurseries from Bena Bena, east of Goroka, extended 'well into the Chimbu region'.[32] Substantial distribution of seedlings from the local nursery began in 1953–54.[33] In 1955 the nursery was enlarged when the first European Agricultural Officer was posted to Kundiawa. On his initial visits to parts of the District, this officer supervised plantings of seedlings and inspected existing plantings. In 1956, two further nurseries were established at Du in Sinasina by another DASF officer, travelling either on foot or by motorcycle. Away from the main road, being developed to join Kundiawa to Goroka through Chuave in eastern Chimbu, travel was slow and limited so that the Administration took on the extra role of coffee buying. Into the early 1960s, private buyers had a very limited role in Chimbu.

By the end of the 1950s, as colonial officials continued to oversee further plantings in Chimbu, concern was shifting to improving road access to more of the sub-district so that supervision of growing and processing could be increased as well as for easier marketing of the crop. Demand was starting to emerge for the introduction of central fermentaries to improve the quality of coffee produced and this extended to the formation of a cooperative organisation for purchasing and process smallholder coffee. The requests led to the establishment of a Rural Progress Society and were primarily to alleviate the cost of individual growers purchasing relatively expensive processing equipment.[34] For much of Chimbu,

30   Cf. RT Shand and W Straatmans *Transition from Subsistence: Cash Crop Development in Papua New Guinea* New Guinea Research Bulletin no. 54 (Port Moresby and Canberra: New Guinea Research Unit, ANU, 1974) p. 38; Harold Brookfield 'The Money that grows on Trees: the Consequences of an Innovation within a Man-Environment System' *Australian Geographical Studies* October 1968, vol. vi, no. 2, p. 100; Harold Brookfield 'Full Circle in Chimbu: A Study of Trends and Cycles' in Harold Brookfield (ed.) *The Pacific in Transition: Geographical Perspectives on Adaptation and Change* (Canberra: ANU Press, 1973) p. 137
31   I am indebted to Robin Hide for this reference, provided from his research notes taken from a patrol report compiled by JE Wakeford. CPR no. 2 of 1948/49. 25 Sept–9 Oct 1948 in the I-UI area [near Gumine: RH].
32   Finney *Big-Men and Business* p. 60; cf. Hughes *Availability of Land* p. 112. Robin Hide *Aspects of pig production and use in colonial Sinasina, Papua New Guinea* PhD thesis, Columbia Universty (1981) pp. 46–47 also dates the first promotion of coffee by the colonial administration in this part of eastern Chimbu as occurring in 1952–53. Shand & Straatmans *Transition from Subsistence* pp. 38–40
33   Michael Agiua Apa *Coffee Growing in Kupau Village, Simbu Province History of Agriculture* Working Paper no. 23 (Waigani: UPNG, Department of Primary Industry, December 1978) p. 2
34   Sinclair *The Money Tree* ch. 22

the rate of new plantings began to decline by the early 1960s, only to be lifted again with the 1964 formation of the Kundiawa Coffee Society, operating a central coffee fermentary and a string of local buyers.[35]

Western Highlands

In the Western Highlands, where the expatriate owner-occupiers established a substantial large holding presence later than occurred in the Eastern Highlands, the spread of coffee growing to smallholders initially occurred more slowly than in the Eastern Highlands and Chimbu. Although the first planting of coffee in the Western Highlands probably occurred before World War II, the major expansion commenced with the postwar price boom, from 1954 onwards.[36] Marie Reay, conducting research between 1953–55 among the Kuma/Nangamp, a population of about 25,000 who lived on the higher terraces and slopes of the middle Wahgi Valley but used the lower terraces for grazing pigs and planting extra gardens does not mention any coffee growing.[37]

In this District too it was the colonial administration which played a central role in the initial spread of coffee growing among indigenous smallholders. As Gordon Dick notes, Korn Farm near Mt Hagen was established before World War II as the first agricultural station operating in the Western Highlands. In 1944, the first block of coffee trees was planted at the Farm, a 535 acre site about seven miles from what was to become the District Headquarters at Mt Hagen. However this planting was probably preceded in the Western Highlands by mission and mission-encouraged indigenous growing of coffee.[38] Soon after the war, explorer, prospector and trader Dan Leahy also planted coffee on a more substantial scale at Korgua. Using seed obtained from Aiyura, Leahy established a large nursery and planted the seedlings out at Kuta. However this expensive experiment failed on thin soils with an impervious clay substratum, and Leahy moved his coffee plantings to nearby Korgua on valley floor land.[39]

During the 1950s, as expatriate planters began to plant coffee on large holdings of alienated land, generally larger than had been established in the Eastern Highlands, the administration extension role continued to be critical for household plantings. In 1953, now established as an agricultural extension station, Korn Farm's principal objectives were:

---

35   Sinclair *The Money Tree* pp. 299–300; Sumer Singh *Co-operatives in Papua New Guinea* New Guinea Research Bulletin, no. 58 (Port Moresby and Canberra: New Guinea Research Unit, ANU, 1974) ch. 8, pp. 128–145

36   Sinclair *The Money Tree* ch. 13, p. 144

37   M Reay 'Individual Ownership and Transfer of Land among the Kuma' *Man* 1959, vol. lix, pp. 78–82; M Reay *Freedom and Conformity in the New Guinea Highlands* (Melbourne University Press, 1959)

38   Gordon Dick *A History of Coffee Planting in the Mt. Hagen Area* History of Agriculture Working Paper no. 24 (Port Moresby: UPNG and Department of Primary Industry, December 1978) p. 1

39   John Fowke *Kundi Dan: Dan Leahy's life among the Highlanders of Papua New Guinea* (St Lucia: University of Queensland Press, 1995) ch. 14

extension work among the local people, with improved local and subsistence crops, Coffee, Passion-fruit, Peanuts and Maize .... It [was] also the distribution centre for vegetable and cover crop seeds, together with other types of seeds, and for the distribution of coffee seedlings among the local farmers of the district; the improvement of the economic position of the indigenous land-owners by the production of cash crops, and [in: SM] this regard half a ton of seed peanuts of Virginia bunch variety, has been procured for distribution.[40]

Over the next two years as Korn extended its coffee plantings, an experimental block was established to 'investigate the suitability of different varieties of coffee, shade trees, coffee spacing, pruning and fertilising'.[41]

With the Tolai experience in mind and in particular the legislation setting an official minimum of 500 cocoa trees in one block per registered grower (see below), the Korn Farm Coffee Project Manager:

[S]tarted a "Coffee Register" and he established gardens in each of the Census Divisions of Mt. Hagen Sub-district. He noted that the people were prepared to remove poorly established gardens and to replant them to approved standards with assistance from the Department's staff. Farmer trainees were taught all phases of coffee culture and in subsequent years are mentioned [in DASF Annual Reports: SM] accompanying patrols and assisting villagers.[42]

Again, as with the Eastern Highlands, staff shortages, especially of European agricultural specialists, pushed the Administration to emphasise the importance of training indigenes in coffee cultivation at Korn Farm. During 1955–56, there were 38 indigenes from the Mt Hagen Sub-District, and nine from Wabag in general training, plus a further 23, from Wabag, Minj and Sepik, receiving specialist coffee training in a six-month course, which also included experience with other crops. As well, extension staff from the station spent a further 210 days on patrol, providing agricultural advice, seed and encouragement.[43]

Coffee extension work continued from the Korn Farm base for the remainder of the decade. Dick is especially revealing, despite his criticism of the Administration's part in the increased smallholder plantings, when he notes along with official concern about the standard of smallholder plantings, that:

---

40   DNA-WHD *Annual Report 1955–56* p. 26
41   Dick *A History of Coffee Planting* p. 2
42   Dick *A History of Coffee Planting* p. 2
43   DNA-WHD *Annual Report 1955-56* pp. 26–27

Each annual [DASF: SM] report from Mt. Hagen from 1955 to 1960 mentioned the increasing amount of smallholder plantings and the fact that much of it was of poor standard.[44]

By 1956/57 there were at least 30,000 coffee bushes owned by smallholders in the District, including in the Nebilyer and Baiyer River valleys.[45] In 1958–59, 15 tons of smallholder coffee was produced in the Western Highlands,[46] and even '[w]ithout active encouragement from the Extension Division of the (DASF) coffee plantings have continued at a brisk rate, particularly in the Minj Sub-District'.[47]

Dick argues that from 1960 the overall Administration policy in the District of providing extension assistance when requested but not pushing further expansion of smallholder plantings changed substantially.[48] Two important factors, in addition to the growing indigenous interest in cash cropping, were at work. The first was a change in the top level of the District Administration. In 1960 a new District Commissioner, 'the dynamic, autocratic Tom Ellis' was appointed.[49] At a conference in October 1960, Ellis told his local officers that, in the face of indigenous planting which was occurring without official support:

> The policy towards coffee plantings by natives in this area is going to change and we will be actively encouraging native coffee planting and development.[50]

Secondly, and despite growing international and local concern about excess supply and falling prices, the behaviour of expatriate large holding owners had an unintended demonstration role for indigenous growers that is easily overlooked. Although the overseas marketing of the PNG crop was for the first time facing serious difficulties as prices declined to the 1962–63 low, senior Administration officials continued to encourage expatriate planters to extend their coffee plantings on already granted leases.[51] Accordingly:

44   Dick *A History of Coffee Planting* pp. 2–3

45   For an account of coffee's establishment in the latter area, see Peandui Koyati *Coffee growing in the Baiyer River Area of the Western Highlands Province* History of Agriculture Discussion Paper no. 14 (Waigani: UPNG and Department of Agriculture, June 1978).

46   Dick *A History of Coffee Planting* p. 3

47   DNA-WHD *Annual Report 1955-56* p. 3. The same Report noted with satisfaction (p. 11) that as demands for cash cropping and political representation increased, '[t]here is no evidence of detribalisation of labour throughout the District' even though there was a plentiful supply of unskilled, casual labour working mainly on coffee plantations proximate to villages and smallholdings.

48   By December 1960 there were over 400, 000 bushes, more than two thirds of them not yet bearing, in the District. Clearly there was increasing smallholder activity in coffee growing before the major Administration push of the early 1960s began, as discussed below. Department of District Affairs DNA-WHD *Annual Report 1960–61* p. 2

49   Dick *A History of Coffee Planting* p. 3; cf. Sinclair *The Money Tree* p. 267

50   Dick *A History of Coffee Planting* p. 4

51   In the first issue of the *Highlands Quarterly Bulletin*, official journal of the Highlands Farmers and Settlers Association published in January 1960, Director of Agriculture Frank Henderson drew attention to the 1957–58 decline in prices, well below the peak of five years earlier and noted that owners should increase the acreages planted to coffee on their large holdings for profitability reasons (p. 1).

There has been increased activity in the planting of coffee. Despite some doubt about the market for coffee, it was felt that the peoples [sic] desire to plant the crop should not be discouraged. The European farms around them were planting as fast as funds and labour permitted and it was most desirable that the native people be given the opportunity to plant if they desired.[52]

One consequence of this unintended demonstration, discussed in the next chapter, was that during the 1960s as the Administration changed direction by blocking continuing increases in bushes planted on expatriate large holdings, the pace of new smallholder plantings picked up. Even as official extension efforts to promote coffee declined, and attempts were made to shift attention to other crops, smallholder enthusiasm for coffee growing could not be switched on and off like a tap. During the 1960s and into the early 1970s Western Highlands' smallholder growers became the most important producers of coffee. The later emergence of household producers in the Western Highlands, after the initial dominance of Eastern Highlands and Chimbu growers, paralleled what occurred in cocoa growing.

Cocoa in the 1950s — Spontaneity Confronts Official Intent

In Chapter Two, it was explained how the colonial administration played an important part in the initial postwar rebuilding of cocoa production. This activity included checking efforts to increase areas of land available for large holding growing and encouraging PNG growers to plant and replant with Trinitario stock which was in demand for fine and flavour rather than Forastero for bulk chocolate. The initial drive by wealthy Tolai to grow cocoa on the Gazelle Peninsula was also described. These indigenous growers could provide a demonstration effect for nearby smallholders. By the early 1950s, the policy and practice of uniform development sustained a surge in smallholder enthusiasm for cocoa growing, particularly but no solely on the Gazelle Peninsula where plantations and other large holding forms were also embracing a wave of expansion.

While cocoa production among the Tolai of the Gazelle Peninsula provided the most prominent initial instance of the official development priority, Administration intentions were always that growing and processing the crop would also be carried out by smallholders in other coastal and islands areas. During the 1950s, in particular, the Administration made substantial attempts

---

52   DNA-WHD *Annual Report 1960-61* p. 2

to ensure that where climatic and soil conditions seemed suitable for cocoa growing, households were given what assistance was possible within existing resource constraints.

One specific measure undertaken during the 1950s by colonial officials, already noted, was especially fortuitous for the subsequent spread of cocoa beyond the Gazelle Peninsula. In 1954, a research program to improve cocoa stock had been established at Sohano in Bougainville. During the 1960s VSD disease attacked trees on plantations and smallholdings in East New Britain District, including the Gazelle Peninsula.[53] While the disease destroyed up to one-quarter of the trees on the Gazelle Peninsula, primarily but not solely upon plantations where there was a greater proportion of mature trees more susceptible to the virus, it did not spread to other areas where cocoa was grown. Because of the cocoa research being carried out on Bougainville, it was possible to prevent stock from outside the District being brought in and also to continue to upgrade plantings in other parts of the colony with improved VSD-free material.

At one time or other cocoa also has been grown in Gulf, Central, Milne Bay, Northern, Manus, Sepik, Madang, Morobe, and New Ireland districts, as well as in New Britain outside the Gazelle Peninsula.[54] At Independence, varying amounts of cocoa were still being produced by smallholders in most of these districts, with over 200 tonnes in each of Northern, Madang, East Sepik, New Ireland and West New Britain.[55] Nevertheless the two main areas where cocoa was grown at Independence were in East New Britain, particularly the Gazelle Peninsula, and Bougainville. The following account concentrates on the development in these areas during the 1950s. The former provides an especially sharp instance of how spontaneous development constantly undercut official intentions, forcing the latter to be reformed to meet the challenges posed. Bougainville, on the other hand, provides the exemplary case of how the initial spread of cocoa growing provided a base which subsequently became decisive. The very rapid spread of smallholder cocoa during the 1960s dampened the effects of a major threat to the scheme of smallholder agriculture in the form of commercialisation represented by the giant copper-gold mine at Panguna.

The immediate postwar international shortage of cocoa continued into the early 1950s and gave an impetus to the expansion of cocoa growing in PNG. Demand was further increased, with corresponding high prices, when in 1953–54

---

53   GAR Wood and RA Lass *Cocoa* 4th edn (Harlow, Essex: Longman, 1989) pp. 322–329 for a brief description of the disease, its characteristics and effects, as well as the outbreak and its treatment in PNG.

54   For an account of indigenous cocoa growing on Karkar Island, Madang District, see Shand & Straatmans *Transition from Subsistence* pp. 73–91, and for the formation of the Nalkul Cocoa Growers' Co-operative Limited within the southern Nalik villages of New Ireland, see Singh *Co-operatives in Papua New Guinea* pp. 59–61. Both descriptions emphasise the early attraction of the crop in the 1950s and the more substantial plantings of the 1960s.

55   Densley & Wheeler *Cocoa* p. 10, Table 5

rationing of chocolate consumption ended in Britain.[56] As explained in Chapter Two, selecting higher yielding Trinitario rather than Forastero had important benefits for household growers in PNG. In aiming smallholder production at the fine and flavour market the Administration was attempting to ensure demand for PNG cocoa would not be governed by the size of the relatively small Australian market. Officials in the colony were also trying to secure higher returns for households in this colony by comparison to smallholders elsewhere, especially in West Africa, where Forastero was grown and sold into global markets for cheaper bulk cocoa.

The tussle between Administration officials in PNG and Department of Territories' officers in Canberra over cocoa also extended to the extent of encouragement which should be given for increased production in the colony. Throughout the 1950s, while the former sought to encourage further expansion and recognised their limited capacity to check increased smallholder plantings, in Australia officials worried about the implications of producing more cocoa than could be utilised by manufacturers in the metropolitan country. An important concern was that should international prices decline but production increase PNG growers would be likely to demand financial support and a preferential arrangement into the Australian market from the colonial government.

This fear continued to manifest itself as the 1954–55 and 1958 Cocoa Action Plans were produced by the PNG Administration, under government advice transmitted from Canberra. Each time officers in the colony set production targets which aimed beyond the Australian market, in order to 'prevent the Australian manufacturer taking advantage of being the only outlet for New Guinea production',[57] Department of Territories' officials sought to restrain these ambitions. PNG-based officers did not want to confine production to the level of Australian demand for cocoa in either type or quantity. As Administrator Cleland noted in April 1955:

> Our aim should be to develop as rapidly as possible and, as we are producing a crop marketable throughout the world, there is no need only to consider Australia's requirements. In fact, it may be in the interests of Australia for the Territory to market its cocoa in hard currency areas and for Australia to buy its requirements in soft currency areas.[58]

---

56 F Helmut Weymar *The Dynamics of the World Cocoa Market* (Cambridge, Mass.: The M.I.T. Press, 1968) p. 13. Shand & Straatmans *Transition from Subsistence* p. 81, Table 4.11 provides an index of cocoa export prices (f.o.b.) from 1947–68. With a 1947–50 base of 100, prices were highest between 1952 and 1955, and again in 1958 and 1959. In 1955, the index reached 307.

57 NAA: A452/1 1957/3874 *Cocoa Action Plan* Undated Note Extract from Report by FC Henderson 'Future of Papua and New Guinea Cocoa Marketing.'

58 NAA: A452/1 1957/3874 *Cocoa* 14/4/1955 Administrator to Secretary, Department of Territories.

In other words, let manufacturers in Australia continue to buy lower priced 'Accra' bulk cocoa grown in Ghana and Nigeria, while producers in PNG tried to grow and sell as much higher priced fine and flavour as they could, including in markets outside the sterling area. Unsurprisingly, Canberra-based officials disagreed and continued over the next two years to restate their concerns that Australia would be pressed for subsidies when international prices declined. (As is shown in the next chapter, a parallel situation arose from the late 1950s with a major decline in coffee prices.) Only in 1958 did the Minister and Department capitulate, agreeing to an upper target of 25,000 tons of cocoa, well in excess of previously preferred limits.[59]

While keen to encourage a maximum rate of production increase, officials in the colony early recognised that they had limited capacity to restrain smallholder growers from planting more and more trees. It is clear that the local Administration was more attuned to the speed with which production was expanding, as well as the difficulty of limiting smallholder plantings once indigenous growers adopted the crop. The latter point had been central to the Administrator's memorandum to Canberra of April 1955, cited above, which was composed as very substantial increases started to occur in indigenous smallholder as well as large holding plantings. Short of adopting authoritarian measures to restrict production, such as banning further planting and tearing out trees, the most that could be done was cutting back on extension activities and limiting forms of price support. Through direct experience coordinating and supervising household plantings, including in the first important area of indigenous growing the Gazelle Peninsula, the political implications of any official practices were becoming more obvious to local officials.

The difficulty for Canberra-based officials in understanding the fast emerging problem of how to restrain production lay partly in the nature of the evidence they were using to measure the success of the postwar policy to expand cocoa production. Export tonnages constituted a limited, rear-vision mirror view of what was happening and only gave a measure indicating the successful lifting of production in line with overall policy. The export measure did not show the amount of new planting taking place, particularly among households, and which was yet to produce crops. The export measure thus obscured the important difference between a considerable ability to limit large holding expansion, primarily by preventing further alienation of land, and a negligible capacity to constrain smallholder increases, even if the latter had been intended. As the importance of the Australian market declined for PNG cocoa exports, so too did the expatriate owner-occupiers and Australian-based plantation firms become even less significant cocoa producers. The shift to smallholder predominance, however, took some time (see Chapter Five and Table 5-1).

---

59   NAA: A452/1 1957/3874 *Cocoa* Cocoa Action Plan Amended October 1958

While much of the smallholder expansion occurred with limited official capacity to restrain plantings, attempts were made in three directions to affect smallholder production. Measures were introduced which were intended to graft 'the advantage of plantation methods on to peasant production methods to give a quality product'.[60] DASF policy was based on three principles formulated in 1948–49, by comparison with what was believed to have occurred in the major cocoa growing areas of Ghana. The principles required minimum areas of trees planted by each grower, grower registration and centralised processing in fermentaries. Any tendency to laissez faire, which was understood to have applied during the infancy of the cocoa industry in Ghana, was not to guide the production and processing of cocoa in PNG.

The search for an official policy direction was accelerated by the rapid spontaneous increase of indigenous plantings. Colonial officials were forced to respond, particularly because of the political significance of the early prominence of indigenous large holdings and the need to have cocoa processed at internationally acceptable quality standards. The initial postwar cocoa growing and processing by ambitious Tolai on the Gazelle Peninsula noted in Chapter Two was important in stimulating the official response. However the first step in this response, the passing of legislation intended to set parameters for smallholding growing had a limited effect, as is now shown.

The Cocoa Ordinance's Limited Application

An early legal expression of the drive to shape household production away from what were seen as low productivity, low quality, unregulated peasant farming was the 1951 Cocoa Ordinance. Passed through the colony's Legislative Council, the Ordinance included two of the terms specified above by DASF official Henderson. That is, there were to be minimum areas planted by each grower, which given the proper spacing effectively meant a 500-tree minimum number per grower, and registration of growers to make supervision of conditions, including diseases, easier.[61]

The Ordinance provided a largely ineffectual legislative underpinning for the work of Administration officials trying to supervise new plantings. One official was Francis Xavier Ryan, the officer who in 1949 led the agricultural extension services introducing cocoa to Vunamami on the Gazelle Peninsula near Rabaul.[62] Ryan encountered considerable difficulty and criticism instructing growers, households and largeholders, on the spacing and other cultivation requirements demanded by the legislation. In an undated letter, probably written shortly after the Ordinance came into effect in 1952, Ryan gave some indication of the

---

60   PNGNA: AN12 16,497 F/N 1-4-99 *Report of the Cocoa Conference—Rabaul 16th to 18th April 1958* p. 15

61   Cf. Connell *Taim bilong mani* p. 143

62   Salisbury *Vunamami* p. 56

possibility for even more substantial opposition, if growers were unwilling to cooperate.[63] Ryan's letter also acknowledged the objection of the District Commissioner JK McCarthy to pulling out trees, and that concern over cultivation practices and standards was not confined to indigenous plantings. 'Bad plantations' were also 'cleaned up' and complaints from one expatriate planter against another acted upon.[64]

Most importantly of all, in listing the number of non-specific and unsubstantiated objections to his work, Ryan made clear just how difficult it would be to police the Cocoa Ordinance's regulations once planting of trees became widespread and extended beyond the growers of substantial numbers of trees. In Vunamami and nearby villages where large-scale planting was constrained by shortages of land and labour this was to be less of a problem: there a saturation level was reached in the early 1960s with somewhere around 20 per cent of the population growing cocoa.[65]

Even in parts of the District where the potential for widespread planting of cocoa trees was more substantial, the average number of trees planted per grower remained below the legal 500 tree minimum. A 1955 estimate was that 'the average Tolai grower cultivates less than half an acre of cocoa'.[66] In such circumstances, the tussle between an Administration determined to control cocoa growing and the possibilities of a crop which could be grown so easily from seed obtained either through official or unofficial channels soon became apparent.

Despite the legal requirement that all growers be registered, and registration be restricted to growers of 'not less than five hundred cocoa trees in continuous grove, planted as prescribed', by 1954/55 'an agricultural survey of cocoa listed 487,174 trees registered under the Cocoa Ordinance, and 697,285 additional trees reported', giving over 1.1 million trees in five Native Local Government Council areas populated by Tolai.[67] That is, the number of unregistered trees

---

63   PNGNA: AN12 16,706 F/N 23-3-1(C) *Cocoa Projects Other Than Tolai—New Britain District* F Ryan, DASF, Rabaul to Chief of Division, Plant Industry, Port Moresby p. 1, states that he had: 'pulled out trees in areas where they are neglected over a period, isolated trees, small areas which cannot be enlarged to 500 [trees minimum], areas planted since the Ordinance and not in accordance with the Ordinance. The position has been explained to each group before cutting out commences and we have had the approval of the owners before pulling out'.

64   PNGNA: AN12 16,706 F/N 23-3-1(C) *Cocoa Projects Other Than Tolai*, Ryan to Chief of Division p. 2, noting that: 'Steps are being taken to clean Mr Blake's plantation as a protection for Mrs Coote, who has made a verbal complaint through her daughter'.

65   The 20 per cent figure is my own 'guesstimate' drawn from the picture presented in Salisbury *Vunamami* p. 137, par. 1

66   Wright *State Practice* p. 354 cites DC JK McCarthy, DC Rabaul from a paper 'Managerial Staff for Native Economic Development Projects' 20 August 1955.

67   Epstein *Capitalism, Primitive and Modern* p. 115, citing KR Williamson 'The Tolai Cocoa Project' *South Pacific* 1958, vol. 9, no. 13, p. 595. For further consideration of why growers did not register plantings, see below.

already exceeded registered trees, around 35 trees per head. In 1960, an estimate suggested that a total Tolai population of 40,000 people had planted almost three million trees, or about 74 trees per head.[68]

Extensive pulling out of unregistered trees and fining unregistered growers AU£50 as specified by the Cocoa Ordinance was never a serious option for Administration personnel, even had official policy supported such action.[69] In any case, the small number of available agricultural extension and other officers who might have policed offences against the Cocoa Ordinance were at the same time struggling to deal with the growing demand for advice, information and improved seed stock from large and smallholders alike over many areas of the colony. Instead of fighting an unwinnable battle against smallholders planting relatively small numbers of trees among coconuts, vegetables and other crops, greater emphasis was placed on trying to maintain quality standards through centralising processing at a limited number of fermentaries.[70]

Processing Smallholder Cocoa

Cocoa pods can be left on trees for several weeks after they ripen but the risk that disease or pests will damage the ripe pods increases. A long delay in harvesting may also lead to beans starting to germinate inside the pod. Once cocoa pods are harvested, they need to be opened within a few days and the wet beans removed so that curing, which removes the mucilage surrounding the bean and much of the moisture content of the bean itself can take place. Curing involves two stages, the first when the beans ferment, as a consequence of chemical reactions in the bean pulp. During fermentation much of the pulp drains away. A further series of chemical reactions occurs within the bean, some continuing during the second, drying stage.

---

68   Epstein *Capitalism, Primitive and Modern* p. 115. As Epstein also shows (p. 131), as plantings continued to increase in the early 1960s, the proportion of registered trees continued to decline.

69   PNGNA: AN12 16,706, F/N 23-3-1(G) *Cocoa Projects Morobe District* 18/1/1963 Agricultural Officer, DASF Extension, Finschhafen to District Agricultural Officer, Lae notes: 'Cacao was established by the natives themselves before DASF became active in the area but these were subsequently cut out because of the incorrect methods which had been employed, so in 1953 two Finschhafen field workers were sent to Rabaul to gain some practical experience with the crop'. However, neither this experience nor the DASF presence stopped plantings on a small scale. The AO's survey attached to the January 1963 letter reported that more than 41,000 trees, many of them still immature, had been planted by 173 growers in 21 villages in the Mapi-Kotte area. Only 11 growers, or just over six per cent, owned more than 500 trees, while a twelfth had 499 trees.

70   A similar point is made by Epstein *Capitalism, Primitive and Modern* p. 117, who concludes, after noting the rapid increase in plantings, especially by growers with a few trees: 'Unless steps were taken to organise the native industry so that it had efficient processing and marketing procedures, there was the danger that it might become chaotic, which in turn might have had adverse effects on the overall development of the Territory's cocoa industry'. Cf. for another connection between cocoa and the idea of chaos, Gwendolyn Mikell *Cocoa and Chaos in Ghana* (New York: Paragon House, 1989).

Processing of wet beans, whether fermenting or drying, can be carried out with fairly rudimentary equipment. The equipment can include simple baskets and holes in the ground where fermenting beans are covered with leaves, and wood or tin trays on which beans can be spread for sun or indoor drying.[71] The certainty of fermentation understates the considerable potential for unsatisfactory processing to occur. Insufficient sun and continuous rain, as well as inadequate attention to the need to turn beans during fermentation and drying are among the conditions which reduce bean quality and affect flavour. Where beans are inherently uneven in size and shape, as is the case with beans from Trinitario trees, processing requirements include even more attention during the fermenting and drying stages. Increased attention is associated with the use of well-constructed fermenting boxes and extensive drying areas, plus driers propelling hot-air through the beans contained in rotating cylindrical drums. The extra labour and better equipment is necessary to produce superior quality bean which obtains the greatest price advantage from fine and flavour cocoa.

That is, inherent in the type of cocoa grown and the market being aimed at by Administration officials and marketing firms was the need for more sophisticated equipment and a standardised curing process. Neither the labour nor the equipment necessary for standardisation could be provided by a mass of smallholders individually processing the crop of a small number of trees. Where the total output from nearby households was below the amount judged necessary to make a central fermentary viable, about the yield of 50,000 trees or 1,000 growers under the Cocoa Ordinance's terms, colonial officials were willing to accept other trading and processing solutions. When the volume of cocoa produced by households was too small to warrant a centralised fermentary dedicated to their crop, Administration officials often sanctioned arrangements between indigenous growers and plantation owners, including churches.[72] While the ease of constructing small fermentaries made out of bush materials or selling to nearby plantations could be and was used where relatively small amounts of cocoa were produced by smallholders, neither practice met important requirements set by Administration policy and international markets. With small amounts of beans fermented poorly, quality standards of processing were hard to police. When smallholder wet beans were sold to plantations acting as

---

71   Wood & Lass *Cocoa* ch. 13 'From harvest to store' by GAR Wood, esp. pp. 446–451

72   See for instances from New Ireland and Madang, PNGNA: AN12 16,706 F/N 23-3-1(I) *Native Cocoa Projects—New Ireland District*. For the accepted processing and marketing of smallholder cocoa by and through plantations on Karkar Island, Madang District, as well as the close watch kept on prices received by growers and the future need for an indigenous-owned central fermentary, see PNGNA: AN12 16,706 F/N 23-3-1(L) *Part 1 Cocoa Projects—Madang District* 18/6/62 MJ White, Marketing Officer, DASF to Chief of Division, Extension and Marketing, DASF, Konedobu 'Report on the Marketing of Native Owned Cacao Kar Kar Island'. Shand & Straatmans *Transition from Subsistence* pp. 87–89 note how, at least until the early 1970s, indigenous smallholder cocoa on Karkar Island was processed in plantation fermentaries.

traders for processing in plantation fermentaries, a layer of merchant capital was interposed between the grower and exporter of beans, reducing the return to smallholders below what the Administration considered optimal.

In other cases, to encourage cocoa growing in more remote areas where there were no nearby plantations, joint ventures between Native Societies, the Department of Cooperatives and DASF operated fermentaries, pooled the profits accrued (between purchase price paid for wet beans and income received out of the sale of dry beans) for future use by the Native Societies.[73] Once more, the prices received by individual households for beans were not what the colonial administration intended as the optimum.

Administration policy was subsequently further reshaped to meet Henderson's third condition for 'grafting plantation methods' on to 'peasant methods'. Centralised fermentaries were established to improve quality and increase prices paid to smallholders. The Tolai Cocoa Project[74] on the Gazelle Peninsula provides the most substantial case of how colonial officials worked to establish and operate such fermentaries.

Export Standards, Households and the Tolai Cocoa Project

The connection between cocoa production and the construction of five Local Government Councils (LGCs) in the Gazelle Peninsula was particularly important for official efforts to coordinate and supervise smallholder cocoa. In 1950, Native Local Government Councils were proclaimed for the Rabaul, Reimber and Vunamami areas. Two years later, the Vunadidir-Toma-Nangananga Council was proclaimed and next year the Livuan LGC was proclaimed. These five LGCs were subsequently amalgamated into four councils, with Reimber-Livuan joining together, and in 1964 a further concentration produced one

---

73   For an instance where the colonial Administration initially encouraged indigenous producers to sell to plantations, while output of unfermented beans remained too small to warrant the construction of a central fermentary by growers, see PNGNA: AN12 16,706 F/N 23-3-1(C) *Cocoa Projects Other Than Tolai* 20/2/58 JC Lamrock, Senior Agricultural Officer, Regional Agricultural Office, to District Officer, District HQ, Rabaul re Native Cocoa Plantings—Bainings Coast.

74   There is as yet no comprehensive history of the Tolai Cocoa Project (hereafter the Project), despite the extensive documentation which is available. The brief summary presented here has been drawn from a large number of official files available in PNG and Australia, secondary sources, published as well as unpublished material and interviews with former colonial officials involved in administering the Project. See also: Williamson 'The Tolai Cocoa Project'; KR Gorringe 'The Tolai Cocoa Project, New Guinea' *Cocoa Grower's Bulletin* 1966, vol. 6, p. 27; Epstein *Capitalism, Primitive and Modern* ch. 6; Salisbury *Vunamami* ch. 7; Wright *State Practice* pp. 348–356; PNGNA: AN12 16,705 F/N 23-3-1(a) *Part 6 Cacao Fermentaries-Gazelle Peninsula (Tolai) Tolai Cocoa Project* 'A summary report prepared by the Department of the Administrator from material submitted by the Departments of Agriculture, Trade and Industry and District Administration and outlining developments up to March, 1966'; MB Allwood *A Report on the Tolai Cocoa Project* (Port Moresby: Department of Law, May 1971).

single Gazelle Peninsula Local Government Council. In 1969, the transformation of this Council into a multi-racial organisation which covered non-indigenous residents of the Peninsula as well as indigenes, with the former also eligible to vote and hold office, prompted widespread protests and gave further impetus to nationalist expression through the Mataungan Association (see Chapters Five and Six below). As noted in Chapter Three, the principal initial purpose of forming LGCs in the colony was to secure increases in the labour productivity of households. Where output of smallholder cocoa was an important measure of these increases, coupling the establishment of fermentaries to the development of LGCs in the most substantial area of cocoa production seemed to provide an especially significant opportunity to further the economic and administrative objectives of colonial rule.

Almost from the outset of cocoa growing on the Gazelle Peninsula, numbers of trees planted as well as anticipated output suggested the need for new fermentaries and drying facilities close to the areas of most rapid expansion. Conditions on the Gazelle Peninsula that give rise to a relatively brief period of the main cocoa flush when pods ripen, further strengthened this requirement.[75]

However centralisation of processing in factories could take a number of forms, including on plantations and separately constructed by private owners and operators. The form initially preferred by the Administration, some of the most influential and successful Tolais and many household growers resulted in the construction and operation of 18 LGC-affiliated fermentaries. These were operated under the Tolai Cocoa Project, which processed and then sold to exporters the largest proportion of the smallholder crop during the early period of cocoa growing. However as will also be shown, the Administration's commitment to individual property rights and competition meant that other Tolai as well as non-indigenous traders and fermentary operators were always able to build and operate private fermentaries. These continually attracted a share of the total smallholding output and threatened the viability of the TCP. That is, the constant tension between spontaneous and intentional development was manifested over cocoa processing. In the 1950s the tension was already obvious. However during the 1960s matters came to a head with the Administration forced to confront the demands of indigenous large holding growers more often (see Chapter Five).

---

75   Cocoa pods ripen over a fairly lengthy period, of anywhere between 165 and 200 days and on average about six months after fertilising the flower takes place. Because of weather and other factors, while some cocoa ripens over much of the year, there tends to be one or possibly two flush periods varying from a few weeks to around two months when most pods ripen. In the Gazelle, the main flush and thus the greatest need for fermentary capacity occurs each year over a short period, of six to eight weeks in May and June. Allwood *A Report on the Tolai Cocoa Project* pt 9 `Production and Marketing'. The main flush period occurs slightly earlier on the Gazelle Peninsula than it does in the other main cocoa producing areas of Bougainville and Madang. See DL Godyn *An Economic Survey of Cocoa in Papua New Guinea Part iii village cocoa* Port Moresby: DASF, June 1974, Table 2, p. 4

Wright, following and elaborating upon Scarlett Epstein, explains that the Project went through three phases.[76] The first phase began in 1951 when the Vunamami Council utilised revenues to build a cocoa fermentary. This construction followed a failure by individual growers to process their beans at Malekuna/Malakuna.[77] Salisbury notes a similar impetus for setting up a cocoa fermentary at Ngatur on a plot of land which had previously been planted to coconuts.[78]

The initial prestige of the Councils among many Tolai encouraged Administration officials, Councillors and leading cocoa growers alike to agree on the need for 'non-profit fermentaries' based upon elected LGCs which would 'process and market individual growers' beans'.[79] The Vunamami LGC provided AU£240 from revenues for the Ngatur fermentary, and AU£64 for the construction of sun drying facilities. Two years later, the Reimber/Livuan LGC allocated funds for a processing centre at Pelegir. Critically, at this stage, no growers individually provided funds. Each grower who decided to have wet beans processed and marketed to an exporter by a fermentary, was required to register with that fermentary. The fermentary subsequently marketed the beans under its own name, but ownership of the beans remained with individual growers. Until the late 1960s, growers were paid in two tranches, an initial advance or part-payment upon delivery of the wet beans and a final payment once the beans had been sold and operating costs of the fermentary deducted.

The early difficulties of the cooperative movement in the Gazelle, which was primarily involved with copra marketing and consumer goods retailing, ensured that in this area the cooperative model was not adopted for cocoa processing and marketing.[80] Instead the emphasis was placed upon the construction of LGC fermentaries which would maximise returns to growers who retained individual ownership of 'their beans' at all times. Even if subsequently the public utility appearance of the fermentaries and the maintenance of individual ownership of beans would undercut the Project, at the outset each made the Project more attractive to most growers as well as to the Administration.

---

76 Wright *State Practice* pp. 348–355

77 Williamson 'The Tolai Cocoa Project', p. 594 generalises the early experience with growing and processing, stating: 'Although marketing of beans did not reach substantial proportions, there was already evidence that processing of beans was haphazard and standards were generally low. Production was distributed among numerous growers on smallholdings acting independently and in consequence there was no strength in the marketing procedure from the producer's end'. Williamson then emphasises the consequences of inefficient processing and marketing procedures for the local and Territory economies, repeating points noted previously of the need to produce a uniformly high quality product to maximise prices on world markets and 'avoid at all costs the disasters which had occurred among peasant cocoa producers of Ghana'.

78 Salisbury *Vunamami* p. 256, states that: 'the Council had set up the fermentary on the same plot of land, ostensibly to provide for the active individual politicians and entrepreneurs who were privately growing cocoa'.

79 Allwood *A Report on the Tolai Cocoa Project* pt 1 'History of the Project' p. 2, citing Department of Agriculture 1965 *History of Tolai Cocoa Project*

80 Epstein *Capitalism, Primitive and Modern* p. 118

In the second phase of the TCP, the Administration provided loans, both low interest and non-interest bearing, to Reimber/Livuan, Vunamami and Vunadadir LGCs to further increase capacity and improve equipment. As well, some funds were provided by growers who relinquished final payments from a number of consignments that had been sold. These growers were subsequently repaid.[81]

However the rapid increases in output as more and more trees were planted and earlier plantings matured, soon exerted pressure for fermentaries with even greater processing capacity in all LGC areas. A serious overestimation of yield per trees, which amounted to almost doubling the actual yield of dry beans received, to 4 lbs per tree instead of 2.2 lb made the position appear even worse. A 1955 estimation of fermenting and drying capacity needed in the Gazelle concluded that 12 fermentaries would be required to process smallholder output, at a cost of approximately AU£80,000.

Funding the expansion was beyond the capacity of the LGCs and the Administration. The third phase, which effectively continued until the TCP was privatised in 1971, involved private capital underpinning the increase in the number of fermentaries built and the greater sophistication of the equipment employed to process wet and dry beans. Provided with the appropriate collateral of assets from the councils, which could not include titles to land and a guarantee by the Administration, the Bank of New South Wales (henceforth the Bank) agreed to lend up to AU£80,000 to the councils at 4.75 per cent interest per annum.[82] The first loan was made in 1956. Over the next four years, there were two further increases in borrowings. The peak of the loan commitment by the Bank reached AU£227,000 in 1960, while the maximum actual borrowing occurred in the following year at AU£177,930. In 1961 the balance in the redemption account, representing repayments from the levy of AU£35 per ton of dry bean sold, was AU£78,133. The net balance of indebtedness was less than AU£100,000. As a consequence of the prudent operation of the Project, the Bank agreed to a reduction in the redemption rate, from AU£35 per ton to AU£30 per ton.[83]

The Bank loan for plant and equipment was not the only money capital employed. In 1958, a Bank overdraft of AU£20,000 for other operating expenses was negotiated: three years later, the overdraft limit was raised to AU£30,000. With this support from the Bank, plus the continuing absorption by the colonial government of the salary and other costs of Administration personnel working on the TCP, the Project was able to expand the number of fermentaries. By 1964,

81 For two versions of how the growers were repaid, see Allwood *A Report on the Tolai Cocoa Project* pt 1 p. 4
82 Allwood *A Report on the Tolai Cocoa Project* pt 1 p. 5, gives January 1956, after the Administrator provided the guarantees to the Bank of New South Wales as the end of the development phase and the official commencement date of the Tolai Cocoa Project.
83 Allwood *A Report on the Tolai Cocoa Project* pt 1 pp. 5–6

at which time the four LGCs had been consolidated into a Gazelle Peninsula LGC, the TCP consisted of 18 fermentaries. At its peak, just a few years later, the annual output of these fermentaries was more than 1500 tons of dry bean. The Tolai Cocoa Project became the largest non-plantation exporter of cocoa, with the produce from some fermentaries obtaining premium prices on international markets.

As will be seen from the later account of the TCP, provided in Chapter Five, the 1950s and early 1960s represented the peak of official efforts to centralise processing in order to maximise returns to smallholder growers. It is now appropriate to outline the beginnings of cocoa growing in what was to become the largest producing area, and also the exemplar for what was intended by the scheme of smallholder agriculture. It was on Bougainville during the 1960s and early 1970s that the expansion of cocoa growing by households extended commercialisation of indigenous existence but without most of the population leaving their smallholdings to work for wages at the Panguna mine. Cocoa was important for sustaining rural existence on Bougainville during the most substantial industrial change experienced in late colonial PNG.

Cocoa on Bougainville During the 1940s and 1950s

While there is some disagreement over the date of the first indigenous cocoa plantings on Bougainville, it seems likely that the process was similar to that elsewhere in PNG, including on the Gazelle Peninsula. John Connell notes that:

> The first man to grow cocoa in south Bougainville was Widokuma of Mosigeta ... who planted a thousand cocoa trees in March 1953. He had previously worked on a Rabaul plantation, and possibly also at Keravat agriculture station where the cocoa seeds came from ....[84]

The similarity between this initial planting on Bougainville and by Scarlett Epstein's first Rapitok grower, also a migrant who had plantation experience and Administration support is striking. Connell also describes subsequent plantings in Buin, again involving former plantation workers, and in 1955 and 1956 in Siwai following Administration patrols.[85]

In Nasioi, eastern Bougainville, cocoa plantings began through a similar process. As Eugene Ogan explains:

---

84   Connell *Taim bilong mani* p. 108; cf. Donald D Mitchell II *Land and Agriculture in Nagovisi Papua New Guinea* Monograph no. 3 (Port Moresby: IASER, 1976) pp. 82–83, and Marion Ward *Road and Development in Southwest Bougainville* New Guinea Research Bulletin no. 62 (Port Moresby and Canberra: New Guinea Research Unit, ANU, 1975) p. 41, whose earlier conclusion was 'Cocoa was first introduced into the area [of southern Bougainville] about 1959 and was rapidly absorbed into the subsistence gardening economy'.

85   See also the case of Kepoama, whom Connell (*Taim bilong mani* pp. 147–148) describes as 'the first cocoa based Siwai businessman' who served with the ANGAU, was given encouragement by colonial policeman Barry Holloway, planted cocoa in the early 1950s, travelled to Rabaul to see cocoa growing there and became one of the first directors of the Siwai Rural Progress Society.

Villagers began to plant cocoa in the South Nasioi census division in 1952 with the encouragement of European plantations .... The 1959 DASF patrol report estimated that there were 22,600 cocoa plants in the South Nasioi census division .... Ownership of cocoa trees was generally associated with greater Europeanisation, as indicated by long-term contact with a European employer and/or fluency in Pidgin. All cocoa owners listed had coconut holdings above the mean, suggesting personal qualities of industriousness.[86]

Initially cocoa had a limited attraction for most smallholders, especially in areas where there were few roads and limited means of getting the crop to markets or stores where consumer goods were available. Not suitable for immediate household consumption, its attractiveness as a cash crop was for wealthy growers, particularly in Nasioi, near several plantations and the port at Kieta. For much of the 1950s, rice, peanuts and revitalised coconut plantings were more attractive crops for the bulk of households in southern Bougainville, where there was only one plantation, a limited market for wet beans and little fermentary capacity.

Connell describes the mid-1950s in southern Bougainville as:

> a period of uncertainty. External assistance was almost non-existent, markets were absent and the potential of crops such as cocoa was little known. Consequently enthusiasm for cash cropping was no longer as it had been in the first post-war period; migration to work in plantations restarted and there was a measure of disillusionment with the low cash returns that followed greater incorporation in the market economy.[87]

Donald Mitchell goes further, claiming that in Nagovisi the first plantings were opposed by colonial officials.[88] Whether there was opposition from officials, and if it was directed primarily at planting cocoa, the formation of an 'unofficial cooperative' or the ambitions of the planter as a member of the would-be bourgeois, is hard to resolve from this distance. However colonial officials throughout PNG had been alerted to the terms under which cocoa was to be grown and processed according to the 1951 Cocoa Ordinance (see above), which attempted to regulate spacing of trees, minimum numbers planted and encourage the establishment of central fermentaries. The 1954 opening of the Sohano experimental station at Buka Passage, where experiments on cocoa

---

86 Ogan *Business and Cargo* pp. 124–126

87 Connell *Taim bilong mani* p. 110

88 Mitchell *Land and Agriculture in Nagovisi* p. 82 where it is argued that: 'According to Nagovisi tradition, the first plantings were made at Mosigeta by a man named Widokoma, who had learned cultivation techniques while working on a plantation on the east coast [of Bougainville]. He had few imitators at first; in fact, the Administration actively opposed his efforts, which were also at that time connected with the formation of an '"unofficial cooperative", a type of organization which the Administration strongly discouraged. Nevertheless, he persisted, and over time other Nagovisi began to plant cacao also'.

growing under Bougainville conditions began,[89] aided the dissemination of information to agricultural officers and growers. Without processing centres to properly ferment and cure the crop, and adequate means for getting dry beans at a suitable quality to market, it is unlikely that at this early stage, colonial officials would have given much support to any grower producing a small quantity of beans at some distance from a plantation or other fermentary.

It was a different story within a few years. Even where Bougainvilleans from one district had worked for other indigenes in a nearby district, including Nagovisi employed by Siwais during the mid to late-1950s, this ended 'primarily because Nagovisis began to develop their own cocoa plantations'.[90]

Donald Mitchell extends and supports this description, stating:

> although planting did begin prior to 1960, I use the date 1960 to mark the beginning of intensive cacao plantings. The knowledge that money could be earned at home, on one's own land (more precisely, on one's wife's own land) was a powerful force in recalling Nagovisi from work elsewhere. During the first half of the decade 1960–70, nearly every married man returned to work on cacao. Young unmarried men who would not in any case be planting cacao were free to work elsewhere and many continued to do so, although not on plantations. Instead, they worked in Rabaul, in Kieta town or, in increasing numbers for the copper-mining company and its subcontractors.[91]

Fermenting and curing of beans, as well as marketing, also took a distinct route on Bougainville. The cooperative society model associated with processing and trading became predominant. Tussles subsequently occurred in these organisations over control of the processors and trading opportunities. The differences between Bougainville and East New Britain were striking, as 1973 figures for the different types of marketing and processing indicate. While in East New Britain:

> only 3% of smallholder production was sold through indigenously owned co-operatives and companies, 50% through traders and 20% was sold directly to exporters ... [in] the [N]orth Solomons [i.e. Bougainville] 67% was sold to indigenously owned co-operatives and companies, 32% to traders and only 1% was sold directly to exporters.[92]

---

89   Connell *Taim bilong mani* pp. 108–109
90   Connell *Taim bilong mani* p. 151. Ward *Road and Development* ch. 4, develops the point even further, noting possible variations in external employment patterns between areas in the southwest according to the periods when the most substantial cocoa plantings commenced and then were completed. Nevertheless, Ward indicates (p. 91) that except in two census divisions, 'the proportions of absent male workers [in the southwest] are ... at the lower end of the national range'.
91   Mitchell *Land and Agriculture in Nagovisi* p. 16
92   Densley & Wheeler *Cocoa* p. 18

With minimal buying and processing of smallholder cocoa by plantations and non-indigenous traders, the standard of processing in small bush fermentaries was generally low. To counter this, the colonial administration pushed for improved fermenting in the main south Bougainville growing area. Along with the setting up of an agricultural station at Konga in Siwai, to replace a station closed at Buin, in 1956 the first agricultural officer was permanently posted to the area. Kevin Tomlin played a major role in establishing the Siwai Rural Progress Society (later the Siwai Cooperative Society) to encourage and organise production and marketing in an area which he saw as having 'great potential'.[93]

Initially heavily involved with rice and copra production and marketing, the leadership of the Society was in the hands of the emerging bourgeoisie with work experience away from Siwai. These cooperative officials were already growing cash crops, including cocoa, and were not the old guard of traditional leaders. Tomlin, with knowledge of how Rural Progress Societies operated in the Sepik and Madang, arranged for the first seven directors to visit East New Britain 'to see the Native Cacao Scheme, Local Government Council organisation, Vudal Land Settlement Scheme and anything else of interest' as part of being '"well and truly indoctrinated on the subject of economic development and what is entailed in bringing it about"'.[94]

In the late 1950s, along with the general disinterest in cocoa growing in south Bougainville, the Society was little involved with the crop, and languished as an organisation.[95] Only from 1960, when the Siwai Local Government Council, with the Teop-Tinputz LGC, were set up as the first on Bougainville, did there occur the necessary political changes which were more favourable for increased agricultural activity by smallholders. A direct connection between administrative authority and household production was forged, with cocoa and to a lesser extent expanded production of other crops and marketed goods, embodying the link. As Connell indicates, by August 1960 at the seventh meeting of the Siwai LGC, the Council:

> were becoming more ambitious; they requested [of the Administration] an aircraft landing strip [to cut out carrying cocoa and coffee over the long road to Buin] but they were [also] beginning to evolve their own ideas on the organization of commercial agriculture.[96]

---

93 Connell *Taim bilong mani* p. 112

94 Connell *Taim bilong mani* p. 117. The latter phrase regarding indoctrination appears in a direct quote by Connell from a memo Tomlin wrote to the District Commissioner, ENB.

95 In nearby Nagovisi, the Rural Progress Society formed in 1957–58 had a brief existence, going into liquidation two years later. The 1966 formation of the BANA (BAitsi/NAgovisi) Local Government Council and the most substantial form taken by the BANA Society occurred simultaneous with the major increase of cocoa output in the area. See Mitchell *Land and Agriculture in Nagovisi* pp. 16, 82–84

96 Connell *Taim bilong mani* p. 126

These 'ideas' included opposing the 500 tree minimum required under the 1951 Cocoa Ordinance, in favour of allowing smaller plantings as the basis for subsequent expansion, and pushing for all households to be required to devote more labour time to growing cocoa.[97] The Council also appointed its own indigenous agricultural officer, a director who already had planted his own cocoa holding. In the early 1960s, the overlap between the LGC and the Society became considerable, with similar subjects and activities being discussed and proposed at meetings of each. Still, with few mature trees and cocoa bean to buy and sell to exporters, the Society developed little momentum. Standards of processing in small bush fermentaries continued to be so low that the first cocoa from local sellers taken by the Society to Rabaul was rejected by the Administration's cocoa inspectors.

Experience of the importance of fermenting and curing quality, combined with the rapid increase in trees planted and maturing, pushed the Society into constructing and owning fermentaries, as well as continuing to purchase beans. The expansion took the Society beyond Siwai into surrounding areas, including Nagovisi and Buin,[98] where there were either similar existing organisations or embryonic forms of cooperatives. Not only did the standard of Siwai Cooperative Society marketed cocoa improve dramatically during the late 1960s and 1970s, the Society itself became a model for other indigenous operations.[99]

However contrary to the Siwai direction of better quality cocoa processed at larger, centralised fermentaries, at the same time the increase of cocoa growing on widely dispersed smallholdings also made it possible for more small fermentaries to be constructed throughout Bougainville. These remained unregulated. Only cocoa inspection at major centres and the quality standards demanded by exporters imposed sufficient discipline on the processing which was occurring at these other fermentaries. The explosion of cocoa growing in the 1960s and the 1970s, discussed in Chapter Five, would increase the need for greater supervision of processing at the moment the ability of the colonial administration to coordinate and supervise smallholder growing and processing was declining.

Coffee and cocoa were intended to raise indigenous living standards through providing perhaps the most important means for commercialising consumption in areas where the crops could be grown. Cash income would make it possible

---

97   Ogan *Business and Cargo* p. 126, states the idea of expansion, to eventually reach a 15 acre, 3,000 tree holding, from the 2.5 acre, 500 tree minimum became a DASF guideline for a man and wife plus two adult male children household. Cited also in Connell *Taim bilong mani* p. 143.

98   Connell *Taim bilong mani* p. 153

99   Connell *Taim bilong mani* p. 153, states that: 'by 1965 the developments in Siwai were considered to be the best in Bougainville. Just as Siwais had gone to New Britain to see how cocoa was grown and societies operated, so, in its turn, the Siwai Society became a model of integrated development, based upon cocoa, and there were official visitors from Buin, Kieta and Buka, all areas which had hitherto been in advance of Siwai in terms of cash crop expansion'.

to purchase food and other products, some of them imported. However as noted previously, colonial policy also aimed to improve welfare through the increased production of foods which either entered directly, immediately into household consumption or were marketed locally. The latter could be exchanged for other locally produced foods or sold for cash, which in turn would allow increased purchases of a growing range of consumption goods.

Rice — Success or Failure of Colonial Development Practice?

As noted in Chapter Two, since the 1920s attaining rice self-sufficiency in the colony had been an objective of authorities in Papua, and this aim continued for 15 years after World War II. During the uniform development phase of the 1950s, considered in this and the previous chapters, Minister Hasluck repeatedly stressed the centrality of rice production to plans for bringing development.[100]

Despite the official attention and considerable commitment of resources, between 1946 and 1975 the gap between domestic production and consumption grew. In 1950/51, in the context of postwar international shortages and high prices, PNG consumption was approximately 13,100 tons, of which more than 12,700 tons was imported. While international supplies increased, and despite an intensified effort of the colonial administration guided by the 1954 Rice Action Plan, in 1956/57 total consumption had reached nearly 18,000 tons, of which almost 17,000 tons was imported.[101] Between 1966 and 1975 PNG production was often less and never more than 2.7 per cent of total consumption requirements. By Independence, about 55,000 tonnes were being consumed, with PNG production only providing about 1.5 per cent of this total.[102]

Such figures might suggest 'failure' of the intention to bring development, a sign of the relative impotence of state efforts in the face of more powerful markets, including the international rice market in which prices fell and availability rose after the wartime shortages. However any preference for simple, even simplistic conclusions regarding the power of markets versus the state should be held in abeyance in the face of the following. As pointed out throughout this account, development as officially conceived in postwar Australia and PNG always contained two united processes, one spontaneous the other intentional. Further these processes were always subject to the external authority of capital.

---

100   A more detailed consideration of rice production and consumption from the 1950s until 1975 is presented in MacWilliam *Development and Agriculture* ch. 5.

101   NAA: A452/1 1958/1327 *Rice Action Plan—Papua and New Guinea* 22/1/58 Folio 68 'Figures and Notes on Rice Requested by the Minister at Folio 57'

102   Hale *Rice* p. 47, Table 5

Rice growing and processing in PNG was not accompanied by barriers against the importation of rice from Australia, where production was increasing substantially beyond that country's domestic requirements. Even within PNG, the use of imported rice at Administration posts to provide rations for employees and indigenes incarcerated in local gaols, undercut local growing of foods, including rice. Official concern for raising living standards in the colony and thus the capacity to labour took priority over any particular means of feeding the local population. Where imported rice trumped domestically produced rice and other food in price, storage and other terms then colonial development policy supported the former over the latter.

It is within the above context that the very substantial attempts to grow rice in PNG during the 1950s should be considered. Personnel, mechanical and other resources were devoted to trying to expand production in the Mekeo where the first major postwar efforts began. In the Mekeo the tensions between dry and wet rice production, family labour processes and industrial processes with mechanisation first became pronounced. Even including rice grown at Epo Agricultural Research Station and on nearby expatriate-owned and operated farms, the total area planted probably reached a peak of around 800 acres in the 1953–54 season. Despite continuing efforts to improve the Project, initiated by senior local officials,[103] total plantings did not ever exceed 1,000 acres before the Project finally folded in 1959.[104]

Even as efforts in the Mekeo failed to produce desired results, colonial policy gave priority to dry rice growing as the focus changed to other areas and populations. Extension services continued to focus upon rice, including research efforts to find the most suitable varieties and growing conditions, but without providing the degree of mechanisation which had facilitated cultivation in the Mekeo. While there was greater long-term success, especially in the Sepik with smallholder production for immediate consumption and local markets increasing into the 1960s, the changed focus did not bring total production any nearer to meeting the objective of colonial self-sufficiency. Up until Independence there were sporadic efforts to increase production, including in a few cases by households using irrigation, which never became substantial.

A central feature of Hasluck's behaviour was a continuous willingness to respond to the empirical conditions which he encountered either directly or through advice received. During the second half of 1951, as the Minister

---

103   NAA: A452/1 1958/628 *Mekeo Rice* 'May 1954 Extract from Monthly Report of Territory of Papua and New Guinea'. For an enthusiastic and overly optimistic account of the future of the Project after some reforms to the Project had been initiated, see James McAuley 'Economic Development Among the Mekeo' *South Pacific* January/February 1956, pp. 217–220.

104   Jeffreys *Mekeo Rice* pp. 42–63 provides a more detailed account of the project's revitalisation in 1953–54, a brief period of increased production and then subsequent decline until finally terminated in 1959.

found his feet at the head of a department not noted for its vitality,[105] there was considerable concern in Canberra and Port Moresby at the failure to increase food production, including rice, in the Territory. Simultaneously, the first and most concentrated attempt to raise rice production in the colony, the Mekeo Project, was making only hesitant progress despite the devotion of substantial resources to mechanisation. Few pictures could have appealed less to the new Minister than the stagnation of indigenous production and the emphasis upon highly mechanised Administration-dependent production which had become dominant in the Mekeo.

In a press statement following his second trip to PNG, from 26 July to 8 August 1951, the Minister conceded that village rice production alone could not meet the Territory's domestic requirements. Thus he was: 'looking to the individual settler and to the big plantation companies for a substantial contribution of capital, enterprise and work to increase [rice] production'.[106] Nevertheless, the press release left no doubt that what had really caught Hasluck's attention was the expansion already underway in smallholder agriculture, as well as what seemed to be its potential for further growth including in rice production in native villages of the Sepik and Madang districts.[107] The Minister urged immediate attention by the Administration to a special project to expand village rice production 'to some thousands of tons' in these districts. Most importantly, Hasluck directed that the expansion occur through an increased Administration presence, including 'extension officers of the right type to work in conjunction with District Service officers in encouraging, instructing and supervising village rice production'.[108]

Hasluck was not alone in his enthusiasm for the agricultural potential of smallholders in the Sepik and Madang districts. Production increases already underway also fuelled the enthusiasm of important local officials, who proposed a modest project for the area.

As had happened in the Mekeo, the introduction of forms of mechanisation, which reduced the labour time necessary to perform elementary tasks, began to change attitudes in favour of rice production. In early 1951 rice was milled by powered equipment at Amele, under the supervision of a cadet agricultural

---

105   Hasluck *A Time for Building* pp. 7–10

106   NAA: M338/1 3 *Visit to New Guinea, April 1952* 29/4/52 'New Guinea—Ministerial Visit. Statement by the Minister for Territories, Mr. Paul Hasluck'. On 22 April, at the beginning of the visit, Hasluck had given an additional twist to the role he expected from increased large holding production of locally consumed food. He told three Europeans, members of the Madang Advisory Council, that he was most anxious to see mono-crop coconut plantations diversify by planting other crops. In particular, said the Minister: 'Plantation costs could be reduced by local production of rice and meat'. NAA: M338/1 3 *Visit to New Guinea* Report of 22/4/52 Meeting.

107   NAA: M338/1 3 *Visit to New Guinea* 29/4/52 'New Guinea-Ministerial Visit. Statement by the Minister for Territories, Mr. Paul Hasluck'. Nearly 25 years later, in his autobiographical *A Time for Building* pp. 133–134 Hasluck would again stress the effect upon him of this visit to Madang and the Sepik.

108   Hasluck *A Time for Building* pp. 133–134

officer of DASF.[109] This procedure was subsequently extended to Aitape and Bainyik agricultural stations. However the forms of mechanisation bore little resemblance to those utilised on the Mekeo Project, being primarily limited to providing elementary processing in villages where small five to fourteen horsepower engines were available. DASF officials were anxious to check the introduction of machinery for clearing, soil preparation and planting.[110]

Mechanisation was instead to be reserved for the lightly populated but extensive Sepik valley plains where future European development was being proposed. Here heavier tractors and ploughs, and possibly even managed irrigation could be considered. This possibility, of switching priorities from dry land to irrigated production, was exactly what the Minister did not want and he did not hesitate to make his priorities known.

In accepting departmental advice, to reject the PNG officer's suggestion that a research station be established at Marui, where trials could be conducted 'in the mechanised management of the Sepik Plain soils ... and [to] test the possibility of growing flooded rice under these conditions', Hasluck confirmed his predilections. The Minister emphasised that: 'This task [of expanding upland dry rice production] is mainly a task of agricultural extension and encouragement of native enterprise'.[111] The first Rice Action Plan, the forerunner of other crop Action Plans was approved on 30 June 1954, and then largely ignored.

For a year or so after the formulation of a proposal of late 1952 to commit further resources to rice growing in the Madang and Sepik districts, there were encouraging signs hinting at possible success. As the numbers of villages in the Madang and Sepik districts incorporated in official efforts to increase food production grew so too did rice production. In 1953 about 450 tons of milled rice was grown and processed, and the target for 1954 almost doubled.[112] In a few years the two districts came to dominate rice production in the colony, with households consuming locally grown crop and marketing produce as well.[113] European rice growers in the Markham Valley, Morobe District could not

109   NAA: A518/1 AM927/4 *Development of the Territories—Agricultural Village Rice Production 1952–1957* 21/10/52 REP Dwyer to Government Secretary, Port Moresby 'Native Agriculture-Village Rice Production. Madang and Sepik Districts.' p. 2
110   NAA: A518/1 AM927/4 *Development of the Territories* 21/10/52 REP Dwyer to Government Secretary p. 2
111   It needs to be re-emphasised that by native enterprise, Hasluck principally meant smallholders employing family labour processes to increase production rather than indigenous employers of wage labour. See also Wright *State Practice*.
112   NAA: A518/1 AM927/4 *Development of the Territories* 18/3/54 Press Statement 'Rice in New Guinea Villages. Statement by Minister for Territories—Mr. Paul Hasluck'
113   NAA: A452/1 1958/1327 *Rice* 3/11/55 DM Cleland, Administrator to Secretary, Department of Territories 'Rice Action Plan'

exceed output by smallholders in the two more northerly districts. Further, this primacy appeared to have arisen precisely because of the successful coupling of smallholder production and state supervision which the Minister advocated.[114]

However the ability of the Administration to provide more and more agricultural extension staff was limited.[115] While the programme outlined in October 1952 by DASF Director Dwyer estimated that about 20 agricultural extension officers would be needed, by June 1954 only two full-time and four part-time staff were employed. Less than two years later, eight DASF officers were working part-time on rice, supplemented by seven Department of Native Affairs staff. Other forms of cash cropping being taken up by smallholders demanded attention and drew support away from rice growing.[116] Rice no longer 'held pride of place in the area as a cash crop for village producers'.[117] As well, despite the Minister's continued emphasis upon the priority to be given to rice growing, field staff often encouraged planting of permanent bush/tree crops which provided higher returns instead of promoting rice growing.[118] For 1955/56, estimated production of marketed milled rice for the two districts was only 570 tons, from fewer than 5,000 families with small stocks of padi (unmilled rice), about 170 tons, held by 'various native societies'.[119]

In December 1957, due to the continuing dissatisfaction of the Minister and Department officials at the lack of progress, another adviser Mr CS Christian of the Australian Commonwealth Scientific and Industrial Research Organisation was employed to investigate and recommend means for increasing rice production. This time the terms of reference required finding a means of linking irrigated rice growing with family labour processes. A five volume Report was presented in November 1958, and was almost immediate described as 'long and not easy to follow'.[120] (The next month the Soviet Union's representative on the

---

114   NAA: A518/1 AM927/4 *Development of the Territories* 18/3/54 Press Statement 'Rice in New Guinea Villages. Statement by Minister for Territories-Mr. Paul Hasluck'

115   NAA: A452/1 1958/2847 *Native Village Rice Production—Madang and Sepik Districts* 3/5/55 EJ Wood Assistant Secretary, Industries and Commerce, Dept. of Territories to the Minister

116   NAA: A452/1 1958/2847 *Native Village Rice Production* 11/10/56 EJ Wood to the Minister

117   NAA: A452/1 1958/2847 *Native Village Rice Production* Report on Native Village Rice Production— Madang and Sepik Districts (n.d. covering period from 1 July 1955 to 30 June 1956) p. 1

118   In July–August 1957, EJ Wood from the Department of Territories went to PNG to discuss progress under the first Rice Action Plan. In addition to hearing senior local officials re-emphasise their commitment to smallholder production of dry upland rice rather than irrigated production, he was also informed that in Madang Co-operatives officers 'actually discouraged rice growing by the former Rural Progress Societies because (they) believe natives should go in for permanent tree crops, not annual crops'. NAA: A452/1 1958/1327 *Rice* 'Report on Visit to PNG'

119   NAA: A518/1 AM927/4 *Development of the Territories* 16/8/1955 A/Assistant Secretary, Department of Territories EJ Wood to First Assistant Secretary, copy of submission to Minister reporting on Village Rice project, with Minister's minute of 3/8/1955

120   For summaries of the Report, including the 'not easy' comment made by EJ Wood, Assistant Secretary, Industry and Commerce on 2 February 1958 and subsequent correspondence, see NAA: A452/1 1958/1327 *Rice*. Hale *Rice* p. 39 concludes that: 'The report is the most detailed done on rice in Papua New Guinea. After twenty years it is still relevant ... Unusually for such a report, there is great sensitivity to social values among the farming communities'.

Trusteeship Council of the United Nations made a wide ranging attack on the Australian Government for not making the colony independent of agricultural imports. Rice in particular was cited as a case of a crop which was neglected in the interests of Australian rice growers.)[121]

The Report resulted in the preparation of the second Rice Action Plan, approved in early 1960. The Christian Report presented an analysis of and recommendations on existing rice growing and proposal for a major resettlement project, utilising sparsely populated heavy tropical forest in Madang District. The two directions were joined, however, by a common premise adopted by Christian that existing efforts were too scattered. In order to increase the output of rice grown by smallholders, production should be centralised in a large irrigated rice project, with a further major commitment of funds to underpin this new direction.

The Report's suggestion that irrigated rice production could be adopted, either in a large holding form or by smallholders was dismissed.[122] Despite his continued efforts to increase smallholder production of dry, upland rice in PNG, Hasluck also became aware that departmental pressure forcing Australian producers to accept lower prices for their exports to PNG would reduce the incentive for rice production in the colony.[123] As efforts to substantially raise marketed production in PNG failed and domestic consumption of imported rice increased in conditions of greater international production and lower prices, the importance of rice growing diminished for the Minister and the colonial administration. Despite the international shortages and high prices, there were no indications that private firms would make the necessary investments in PNG to produce rice for export. In any case, alienating large areas of land which required substantial numbers of wage workers to grow irrigated rice was complete anathema to the colonial administration.

Conclusion

In Chapter Three, it w as indicated how by the mid to late 1950s, the Minister, the Department and the Administration began important policy shifts intended to further raise the rate of growth in smallholder production. Moving from a focus upon village level administration towards individual households buttressed by intensified extension services was central to a changed direction which still aimed to secure households upon smallholdings at improving standards of

---

121 NAA: A452/1 1958/1327 *Rice*; *South Pacific Post* 5 December 1958 'Russia Alone in Criticism of Agriculture'
122 NAA: A452/1 1958/2847 *Native Village Rice Production*; *South Pacific Post* 26 September 1958 'Rice Project Welcome'
123 Hasluck *A Time for Building* p. 135 notes how efforts by Secretary Lambert and himself 'lessened one of the arguments for replacing imports with home production'.

living. Accelerated development became the expression which, from the late 1950s into the 1960s, summarised the movement away from uniform or even development. The next chapter takes up the description of what occurred.

Accelerated development retained the primarily agrarian character, even in the face of important industrial changes which were to occur in the 1960s and 1970s. Most importantly, increasing the rate of growth was to occur first and foremost upon the base of expanded household production which had begun during postwar reconstruction and into the 1950s. As will be shown in the Chapter Five, accelerated development presumed the earlier plantings of bushes and trees which characterised even development. As these matured and provided enlarged harvests of cherries, pods and nuts, there was greater incentive to continue with further plantings even as international markets became less attractive. Both the production increases and the declining prices for agricultural produce required a more substantial, if changed, role for the colonial administration.

However increasing the rate of growth further also required the colonial government to recognise what was already apparent to local officials, that crops such as rice which furnished lower returns to households could not remain central for policy or practice. Further, if households were not to become trapped in over-reliance on a small number of crops, already in danger of oversupply on world markets, then diversification was necessary. Chapter Five details the continuing involvement of officials in trying to maintain returns to smallholding growers from crops already in production as output of these increased. Also shown are the attempts to maintain large holding output of existing crops, as an important revenue source, and to diversify crop production into forms which combined nucleus estates and smallholder production. The accelerated development phase was when important limits to growth based on smallholder agriculture became even more obvious.

5. Accelerated Development

Introduction

By the late 1950s it had become clear that the gradualism of uniform development could not satisfy international or internal PNG demands for rapid economic growth and major political reforms. However Minister Hasluck's 1958 acknowledgement, noted in Chapter Three, that the colonial administration had an increased role to perform in bringing development did not indicate anything but a desire to maintain the current priorities at an intensified level of application. It was uncertain just how the policy direction which gave primacy to smallholder agriculture as the basis for improved living standards could be further changed, while the colony moved toward trusteeship's ultimate objectives of self-government and a substantial degree of economic self-sufficiency.

This chapter initially shows how a further phase of development thought was shaped and then implemented as state policy. In the early to mid-1960s the need to obtain greater financial assistance to increase the developmental capacity of the colonial administration led to a change away from uniform to accelerated development. This change gave spontaneous development, in the form of increased investment and other commercial activities by private firms, a renewed importance.

Subsequently, as faster growth occurred during the mid to late-1960s and the colonial administration planned to lift the rate even further, accelerated development was subject to criticism. The second section of the chapter details the phase in which accelerated development was dominant as official policy, and the start of sustained opposition to it.

One irony of the growing objections to colonial rule and particularly accelerated development was that during the 1960s some of the most important consequences of the previous uniform development policy became apparent. The third section of this chapter outlines the extent of the change in smallholder agriculture's significance and how the colonial administration acted even more substantially to support households. This support was both local, including in Western Highlands and Bougainville where extensive planting of coffee and cocoa was occurring, and international. The case of coffee is particularly instructive in the latter regard.

Changing Development Priorities

Criticism of Australian colonial policy at the United Nations and from Australian Labor Party Federal MPs,[1] indicated growing unease about key aspects of the Federal Government's policies for the colony. Although Australian colonial policy became more definite about the timing of self-government, changing from anticipating that this might take decades to instead favouring 'sooner, not later',[2] there remained considerable uncertainty about how and when change might occur.

The Minister for Territories responded publicly to the increasing criticism.[3] Hasluck did so in terms which suggested that he remained attached to the premise that the rate of change could be lifted within existing policy parameters. Policy continued to focus on maintaining communities and improving standards of living, through increased production of immediately consumed and marketed crops by smallholders.

The Minister was supported by the views of academics at the ANU Research School of Pacific Studies, where the Australian Government funded a major expansion of research capacity. During the 1960s and 1970s, the university conducted a continuous research program on aspects of development in Southeast Asia and the South Pacific,[4] most prominently by economist EK Fisk and his associates.

According to the academics, the principal development problem remained how to increase the output of marketed production, while retaining the attachment of households to land. No radical break with past policies was required.[5] Instead an intensified program needed to be implemented which shifted the available 'surplus labour', especially of males, not currently engaged productively due to the existence of 'primitive' or 'subsistence' affluence, into productive activities. Household labour attached to smallholdings could be commercialised further

---

1   Downs *The Australian Trusteeship* pp. 232–234

2   See CoA *Minister for Territories Papua and New Guinea: Some Recent Statements of Australian Policy on Political Advancement* (Canberra: Government Printer, c. 1960).

3   See Address delivered on 20 October 1961 to the Economic Society of Australia and New Zealand, NSW Branch, subsequently published as Paul Hasluck 'The Economic Development of Papua and New Guinea' in *Australian Outlook* April 1962, vol. 16, no. 1, pp. 5–25.

4   Of particular importance for the research on PNG was the New Guinea Research Unit, established during 1961 in Port Moresby as part of the Research School of Pacific Studies. See Ron J May 'The New Guinea Research Unit: 1961–1975' in RJ May (ed.) *Research Needs and Priorities in Papua New Guinea* Monograph no. 1 (Port Moresby: Institute of Applied Social and Economic Research, 1976) pp. 7–14, which includes a list of the publications of the ANU Unit.

5   EK Fisk *Hardly ever a dull moment* History of Development Studies no. 5 (Canberra: NCDS, ANU, 1995) pp. 237–238

by raising the output of marketed crops. The income acquired from the sales of produce would make it possible for households to purchase more consumption items, and so raise standards of living.

Fisk's reasoning shows once again how development thought included anticipating problems and framing solutions. He foresaw that growth would have damaging consequences for village life, with a need to anticipate and counter these effects. He concluded that by abolishing warfare and improving health services to indigenes, there would soon be 'increase[d] population pressure on land resources' which would 'undermine the very basis of their present affluence'.[6] Development policies were required in advance of the population increases to prevent separation of the greater numbers of households from smallholdings and to improve living standards.

The World Bank and Accelerating Development

With the Administration's role central to increasing household production, any program to speed up economic growth required a major injection of state funds. Throughout the 1950s the political difficulties associated with substantially lifting the amounts provided from Australian revenues had been apparent to the Minister and his Department. Fortuitously, there was a source of authoritative advice available which was prepared to accept the primacy of smallholder agriculture and aid the Minister's cause. That this advice would also encourage the end of the policy of uniform development was unanticipated.

By the late 1950s the Minister and the Administration had just fought the bruising, if ultimately successful, battle to introduce direct, mainly income, tax in PNG. Under the 1955 Cabinet directive the share of total revenues levied in the colony as a proportion of all revenues was to increase as the latter rose. However even this shift was insufficient for a major increase in the colonial administration's role in making development happen. During 1959, the Minister and the Department began to consider requesting a World Bank study of PNG.[7] While the final Report of the mission to PNG did not arrive in Australia until 1964, after Hasluck ceased to be Minister, the process of commissioning the study was completed while he held office. Hasluck denies that a 1962 United Nations visiting mission, led by British diplomat Sir Hugh Foot (later Lord Caradon), was responsible for initiating the move to involve the Bank.[8]

Ian Downs provides an additional reason why the discussions within the Department of Territories led to a detailed proposal for Bank assistance. In order

---

6   Fisk *Hardly ever a dull moment* p. 233
7   Subsequently published as IBRD/WB *The Economic Development of the Territory of Papua and New Guinea* (Baltimore: The Johns Hopkins Press for the IBRD, 1965), hereafter the *Report*.
8   Hasluck *A Time for Building* pp. 302–303

to obtain agreement from a reluctant Cabinet and Treasury for major increases in funding for the colony, Hasluck needed the support of a more prestigious and powerful agency than his own Department and the Administration in PNG.[9]

While the Australian Government announced in its 1961–62 annual report to the United Nations that arrangements had been made for a World Bank Survey, it was not until mid-1963 that the survey team reached Australia, and then subsequently worked in PNG. The Australian Government received a draft report in mid-1964, and the final report was eventually tabled in the first PNG House of Assembly on 18 May 1965. In the meantime, the 1962 UN Mission, headed by Foot visited PNG prior to preparing a highly critical report of the pace of development, political and economic. While the UN Mission seems to have played little, if any part in the Australian Government's decision to look to the World Bank, Downs' assessment that the 'effect of the [mission's] report was to accelerate change and persuade the bureaucracy that the time factor was now working against them' probably also is valid.[10]

Downs' explanation for why the Minister and Department involved the World Bank might have been strengthened further by noting that in 1961 the importance of gaining external support for PNG became even greater. There was a brief credit squeeze induced recession in Australia. On 9 December 1961 the Menzies' coalition government was narrowly returned at a national election. In such circumstances, demands for a major increase in grants for PNG were even less likely to receive Coalition Government and Treasury support.[11]

Before examining what became colonial government policy, a detailed look at the Report is necessary. The purpose of the analysis is to show how although the Report seems to support a view of development in which smallholder production has primacy nevertheless there was sufficient ambiguity to permit the formulation of another policy direction, which could retain the Bank's authority for the shift. As Downs recognised: 'Like the Bible, the report of the IBRD survey team was capable of more than one interpretation'.[12]

---

9 Downs *The Australian Trusteeship* p. 253. A line of inquiry that I have not yet been able to pursue is that Treasury, which provided the direct administrative link between the Australian government and the Bank, also favoured the Bank's involvement as a means of obtaining IBRD loans because this would reduce pressure on the Australian budget, at least in the short term.

10 Downs *The Australian Trusteeship* p. 241. In December 1963 Hasluck ceased to be the Minister responsible for the Department of Territories, prior to the Bank's Report being received. Downs' assessment of the significance of the UN visiting mission includes that it assisted in obtaining Cabinet support for political reforms for which Hasluck had been unable to obtain Government backing in August 1960. See Hasluck *A Time for Building* pp. 396–398 for Hasluck's account.

11 Hasluck *A Time for Building* pp. 302–303, does not mention the domestic circumstances of 1960–62.

12 Downs *The Australian Trusteeship* p. 241. For a contrary view on how the *Report* was received by the Administrator Donald Cleland, see Rachel Cleland *Pathways to Independence* pp. 325–326.

One obvious alternate interpretation of the Report, in which expatriate plantation and other commercial operations became the principal focus for development efforts, was subsequently used to support the preferred direction of the colonial administration under a new minister. Contemporary and subsequent attacks on the new policy direction have tended to conflate the World Bank survey team's views with what became the principal thrust of colonial policy from 1964 to the early 1970s.[13] The politics surrounding the conversion of the Report into policy for the late colonial administration of PNG disappears in the conflation.

The first chapter of the Report sets out the dilemma of how to raise revenues for an expanded development program in a colony which the mission construed as 'truly underdeveloped'.[14] Chapter Two 'A Program for Economic Development' makes clear why in addition to paying 'special attention to the rapid expansion of production by native planters', the survey team recommended a further increase in large holding production and other areas of expatriate enterprise. This was because:

> The continuing participation by the European, both in the private sector and in the Administration, is vital for the objectives of the advancement of the indigenes and economic development to be realized.[15]

Where agricultural growth was a central target, the Report proposed moving indigenes:

> away from purely subsistence agriculture into the production of commercial crops, largely on a smallholder basis, at as fast a rate as the availability of the staff needed to direct and guide the program will permit. It proposes to make the maximum practical use of European producers to aid the Territory toward a more viable economy.[16]

Furthermore:

> The comparative need for the European in other sectors of the economy [than agriculture] is even greater .... In commerce, industry, banking and the professions, the European must continue to supply his skills and capital if further development is to be achieved.[17]

---

13   See Mark Turner *Papua New Guinea: The Challenge of Independence a nation in turmoil* (Ringwood, Vic.: Penguin Books, 1990) p. 13 where it is claimed that the *Report* advocated 'continued advantage for the whites', and John Connell *Papua New Guinea: The Struggle for Development* (London: Routledge, 1997) p. 22 who asserts that the *Report* 'assumed that economic development would follow expatriate initiatives and increased government services'.

14   IBRD/WB *The Economic Development of the Territory* pp. 1, 23

15   IBRD/WB *The Economic Development of the Territory* p. 40. While indicating the strong emphasis the *Report* gave to indigenous economic development, Downs *The Australian Trusteeship* p. 253 notes: 'The private sector in Papua and New Guinea gained comfort from World Bank endorsement of the role of the European as the essential provider of capital, technical skills, training and marketing'.

16   IBRD/WB *The Economic Development of the Territory* p. 47

17   IBRD/WB *The Economic Development of the Territory* p. 40

By this reading, the Report provides a primarily instrumental purpose for expatriate plantation agriculture and other commercial activities. At a time when the colonial administration required increased revenues to expand administrative support for smallholder agriculture, these businesses would also provide more taxes.

It was possible to reduce the previous policy emphasis upon households producing for immediate consumption and shift priorities to increasing production of marketed food because 'the peoples of the Territory are not short of food'.[18] That is, postwar reconstruction and the emphasis under uniform development of food produced for immediate consumption had provided the necessary groundwork to make a further change possible. With no substantial land shortages, existing land-use methods of households are generally 'conservative rather than destructive in character'.[19] The Report also noted that: 'the rapid expansion in production of cash crops by the indigenes has brought a fivefold increase in income from this source since 1950/51, a growth rate much above that in the non-indigenous sector'.[20]

Presenting evidence on less impressive growth in some plantation production,[21] the language used to describe the change from the pre-war situation, where indigenes contributed little to commercial farming is striking.

> Since the war and particularly since 1956, the change has been phenomenal .... With peace, the Administration engaged in a progressive policy of encouragement of native farming for cash .... By 1962, native participation in commercial production reached impressive levels. They held nearly 50% of the area in coconuts and produced about 25% of the copra production. They controlled 60% of the land in coffee and produced over 40% of the coffee output. They farmed 17% of the cocoa areas and produced some-what less than 25% of all cocoa.[22]

Furthermore, the change was expected to continue, including in new plantings of export crops. The ten-year planting program of new trees envisaged by the Mission makes it clear that in the main crops of coconuts and cocoa where further planting was readily acceptable internationally (see below), indigenous plantings were anticipated to increase at a greater rate than non-indigenous.[23]

---

18 IBRD/WB *The Economic Development of the Territory* pp. 68–69
19 IBRD/WB *The Economic Development of the Territory* pp. 77–78
20 IBRD/WB *The Economic Development of the Territory* ch. 1, p. 27
21 The description of expatriate coconut plantation operations acknowledges that these do not utilise all available unplanted land on large holdings and have adopted a 'stand-still' attitude toward replanting where palms were senile or near-senile. IBRD/WB *The Economic Development of the Territory* p. 89
22 IBRD/WB *The Economic Development of the Territory* pp. 82–83
23 IBRD/WB *The Economic Development of the Territory* p. 47, Table 1

Indigenous farmers were the sole producers of what the Report terms 'dual-purpose crops', that is those produced for immediate consumption as well as for markets, including coconuts, peanuts, rice and vegetables. The Report concluded that the quantity of dual-purpose crops exchanged through what it terms barter was unknown.[24] The Report provides no evidence of stagnation in household production and claims that the opposite had occurred. However existing production was not regarded as sufficient to meet the principal economic goal for the colony of 'standing on its own feet' or future national self-sufficiency required to accompany the political objective of self-government.

In order to achieve increased output, the Report proposed a break with one of the central components of uniform development policy. It urged redirection of effort toward the most advanced areas of the colony, where marketed crop production was especially substantial. For the Bank's team, accelerated development in these areas could occur without other areas and peoples sliding into poverty given the achievements made under uniform development. The Report proposed three 'broad principles or policies' to further expand production and advance 'the indigenous people [emphasis added: SM]'.[25]

The first principle advocated was that '[government] expenditures and manpower should be concentrated in areas and on activities where the prospective return is highest'.[26] Acknowledging that 'political factors' might impinge upon this redirection, the Bank Mission nevertheless 'strongly recommends against an across-the-board policy which distributes scarce manpower and finance throughout the Territory without due regard to the benefits to be derived in comparison with those realiseble elsewhere'.[27] What Hasluck had specifically rejected was now to be encouraged and this could be done because of the major changes which had already occurred under postwar reconstruction efforts and uniform development policy.

Secondly, the 'standards of Administration services and facilities should be related to Territory conditions, if the maximum numbers of people are to benefit from the money spent on the program'.[28] In other words, instead of applying standards which had become established in industrial, developed countries, colonial officials were instead to utilise appropriate local measures for

---

24   IBRD/WB *The Economic Development of the Territory* p. 83

25   IBRD/WB *The Economic Development of the Territory* p. 35

26   IBRD/WB *The Economic Development of the Territory* p. 35

27   IBRD/WB *The Economic Development of the Territory* p. 35. This principle, of concentrated effort to maximise resources and produce faster growth, was readily adopted by some government officials. For a strong defence of the direction proposed in the *Report* from a senior official of the Department of Territories, though with the usual disclaimer that he was not giving the official view, see GO Gutman 'Aspects of Economic Development in Papua and New Guinea' *The Australian Journal of Agricultural Economics* 1966, vol. 10, no. 2, pp. 128–141.

28   IBRD/WB *The Economic Development of the Territory* p. 36

the provision of services. As will be seen below, this direction jarred with the ambitions of the indigenes who increasingly filled many public service positions and fuelled the anti-colonial nationalism which gathered pace from the mid-1960s. Once again, the change in direction was to be possible because of the previous attention to improving health, which drew upon the 1947 Nutrition Survey that had used international standards drawn from industrial cities in the USA and Australia (see Chapter Two). Thirdly, if 'benevolent paternalism' was the appropriate description of previous Administration efforts, the future required 'a shift in emphasis toward policies giving greater responsibilities to the people'.[29]

The Report was presented to the Australian Government at a significant moment. The departure between 1963 and 1966 of the three most important colonial officials, Hasluck, Cleland and Lambert, who had been central for uniform development, was critical for how the Report was subsequently interpreted to provide the basis for a major break in colonial development thought and policies.

The Politics of Introducing Accelerated Development

As emphasised above, the Bank Report gave large holdings and other commercial enterprises a largely instrumental role in what was intended to be a faster rate of commercialisation of smallholder agriculture. The change was to be underpinned by a major expansion of the colonial administration's place in coordinating and supervising the growth. While smallholder production of marketed, particularly exported, crops continued to be supported, greater attention also was to be given to revitalising largely expatriate-owned and operated plantations.[30] The colonial administration promoted the establishment of the new crops of oil palm and tea based on nucleus estates,[31] and the copper-gold mine at Panguna on Bougainville.[32]

---

29 IBRD/WB *The Economic Development of the Territory* p. 37
30 As the IBRD/WB *The Economic Development of the Territory* p. 74 notes, of the more than one million acres alienated for expatriate large holdings, in 1962 approximately 70 per cent of the land was undeveloped. Also cited in Robin Hide 'A most just cause of Warre: A lesson to be learned at Merani...' *New Guinea* 1968, vol. 3, no. 1, pp. 25–42, who provides an instance of an attempt by one expatriate rubber plantation owner to settle indigenes on smallholdings sub-divided out of his undeveloped land at Cape Rodney in Papua.
31 See DRJ Densley *Agriculture in the Papua New Guinea Economy* (Konedobu: Department of Primary Industry, n.d.) p. 15; WA Arthur *Tea: Agriculture in the Economy A Series of Review Papers* (Konedobu: Department of Primary Industry, n.d.) pp. 2–3; J Christensen and DRJ Densley *Oil Palm* (Konedobu: Department of Primary Industry, n.d.) pp. 3–10; Bob Densley 'Rural Policies: Planning and Programmes, 1945 to 1977' in Denoon & Snowden *A time to plant* pp. 285–286; Downs *The Australian Trusteeship* pp. 293–294
32 Downs *The Australian Trusteeship* p. 340; FF Espie 'Bougainville Copper: difficult development decisions' in May (ed.) *Priorities in Melanesian Development* Papers delivered at the 6th Waigani Seminar (Canberra and Port Moresby: RSPAS, ANU and UPNG, 1973) pp. 335–342; Don Vernon 'The Panguna Mine' in Regan & Griffin (eds) *Bougainville before the conflict* pp. 258–273; James Griffin 'Movements Towards Secession' pp. 291–299; Donald Denoon *Getting under the skin: the Bougainville copper agreement and the creation of the Panguna mine* (Melbourne University Press, 2000)

In December 1963, Hasluck departed and a Country Party MP Charles Barnes became Minister for what was once more the Department of External Territories, with the domestic responsibilities removed. Soon after Barnes' appointment, long-serving Department Secretary Lambert, who had been another of the important advocates of uniform development, retired. Lambert was replaced by George Warwick Smith, previously Deputy Secretary of the Department of Trade and Industry.[33] Both changes increased the chance that colonial policy would move in favour of Australian plantation and other commercial interests, and give these more than an instrumental role for lifting smallholder output.

Barnes was less inclined than Hasluck to exercise tight control over the colonial administration, except where overseas investment was involved, such as in the negotiations with Conzinc Rio Tinto Australia (CRA) regarding the Panguna mine exploration and operations.[34] The loosening left greater room for the colonial administration to follow the swing toward rapid economic growth with restrained political advance favoured by the Minister. Prime Minister Menzies also became personally involved, urging Australian businessmen and fellow politicians to be more commercially active in the colony.[35]

There were other propitious circumstances for the shift to accelerated development within the colony as well. These included the absence of a vociferous and strong indigenous nationalism expressed in representative institutions.[36] Although the fifth Council elected in 1961 had more indigenous members, six instead of three chosen by a substantial indigenous electorate through a complex indirect process, there was little change in the nature of their political participation, with only one, John Guise, becoming 'a major figure in Council business'.[37]

Further constitutional reform leading to the establishment of the House of Assembly in 1964 nevertheless raised the possibility that indigenous representative politics would become more focused upon central institutions

33 Downs *The Australian Trusteeship* p. 274 notes how Smith's appointment was arranged between the Deputy Prime Minister (Sir) John McEwen, also Minister for Trade and Industry and leader of the Country Party (CP) in the Menzies Liberal-CP coalition government, and his colleague Barnes.

34 Downs *The Australian Trusteeship* p. 349; also cited in Griffin 'Movements towards Secession' p. 292

35 For a specific instance of investment propelled by Menzies' exhortations, see the case of ANG Holdings and its affiliated companies, owning and operating coffee and tea plantations in the Estern and Western Highlands, timber milling, road and house construction in Papua, and Port Moresby commercial property. Apart from Registrar of Companies files, I am indebted to Mr John Millett for advice on the firm established in 1963–64.

36 Colin A Hughes 'The Development of the Legislature: The Legislative Councils' in David G Bettison, Colin A Hughes and Paul W van der Veur (eds) *The Papua-New Guinea Elections 1964* (Canberra: ANU, 1965) p. 10. For the fragmented and nationally marginal forms of indigenous politics prior to the 1960s, see the essays in Ronald M Berndt and Peter Lawrence (eds) *Politics in New Guinea Traditional and in the Context of Change Some Anthropological Perspectives* (Nedlands: University of Western Australia Press, 1971).

37 Hughes 'The Development of the Legislature' p. 22. Guise was subsequently knighted and in September 1975 became independent PNG's first governor-general.

rather than at the margins, on LGCs. The 1964 House of Assembly had 44 members from Open electorates and ten from Special (expatriate only) electorates, with adult suffrage and a common roll for the former constituencies. The House now had more elected than nominated and official members. However the official political education program for voters, the election campaign, and the voting by an overwhelmingly rural smallholder electorate reinforced what has been described as a '"certain timidity" among the indigenous population about political activism'.[38]

On occasion dissenting MPs were able to defeat the Administration. Nevertheless colonial officials continued to dominate most proceedings. Domination of the legislature as well as control of the executive, the Administrator's Council, later Administrator's Executive Council, combined with ministerial and departmental authority exercised from Canberra. For most of the 1960s, this strong hold on state power ensured that the overall shift to an intensive program of economic growth was able to proceed largely unchallenged.

However the change to focusing upon some areas and peoples while down-grading the resources provided to others opened the colonial administration to two possible charges. Firstly, that its trusteeship obligations were no longer being met equally for all the indigenous population. Instead of trying to provide extension services as widely as possible, by late 1965 the earlier five year plan was being 'recast entirely taking account of the new approach involved in the agricultural and livestock development plans'.[39] By encouraging immigration of Europeans as investors and skilled workers, the Administration was exposed to a second objection, that it was further down-grading trusteeship obligations to the indigenous population.[40] Both of these criticisms plus others were to become stronger and louder by the end of the 1960s.

---

38 RS Parker and Edward P Wolfers 'The Context of Political Change' in AL Epstein, RS Parker and Marie Reay (eds.) *The Politics of Dependence Papua New Guinea 1968* (Canberra: ANU, 1971), p. 19. Downs *The Australian Trusteeship* p. 487, charts the changes between 1951 and 1972 in the balance between official members, appointed members and elected members in the Legislative Council and House of Assembly. In the first House, elected in 1964, there were ten official members and 54 elected, with 37 of the latter indigenous.
39 See NAA: A452/1 1967/5758 *Agricultural Extension Work in Papua & New Guinea, 1964–1970* 9/12/1965 EJ Wood, Assistant Secretary, Industry and Commerce Section, Department of External Territories, 'Notes on Discussions with Messrs [Frank] Henderson and [Bill] Conroy [Department of Agriculture, Stock and Fisheries, PNG: SM]'. This meeting followed a July instruction from Department Secretary, G. Warwick Smith to the Administrator (contained in the same file) that 'extension officers should be concentrated in areas with promising combinations of developmental resources, both physical and human, with proper attention to accessibility and markets' while dispersing 'extension effort' to the Western District 'is unnecessary'.
40 Downs *The Australian Trusteeship* p. 277

Faster Economic Growth

During the 1960s, and particularly the second half of the decade, there was a major boost in public revenues and overseas investment, as well as a rapid inflow of expatriates taking up skilled and semi-skilled managerial and wage positions. Between 1964 and 1968, the rise in the Administration's receipts was especially pronounced. While the Commonwealth grant increased from AU$56 million to AU$78 million, locally levied revenue jumped from AU$28 to AU$50 million, so that the share of total receipts raised within the colony went from 31 to almost 37 per cent. In the four years from 1964–65 to 1967–68, total receipts rose by almost 50 per cent.[41] Direct expenditure by Commonwealth departments operating in PNG, which was not included in grants, increased considerably.[42] In 1970–71 locally raised revenue exceeded the Australian grant for the first time. By 1972, with self-government imminent, the Commonwealth grant had increased to almost AU$70 million, while locally raised revenue reached AU$95 million.[43]

Loans by trading banks, branches of banks based in Australia, to fund commercial expansion also rose substantially. From AU$7 million dollars in January 1964, the amount advanced for term loans, overdrafts, farm development loans and personal instalment loans reached AU$18 million four years later. By July 1971, total advances were over AU$100 million.[44] Indigenous savings also increased, as Downs notes:

> By 1968 (Papuans and New Guineans) were also investing in savings and loans societies and savings clubs organised by the Reserve Bank. In the case of the savings and loans societies and savings clubs, membership rose to 24,042 and savings increased to $994,000 in 1966–67. As at June 1967, indigenous savings bank deposits amounted to $11.1 million out of a total of $29.8 million.[45]

This increase in indigenous savings deposited with banks based overseas gave rise to criticism, including that these funded an expanded loan program for expatriate commercial activities and private consumption.

In 1967, the Papua and New Guinea Development Bank was established in order to further boost investment. Over the first four years funding of AU$11 million was provided out of Territory budgets and direct supplementary grants from the Australian Treasury. This amount reached in excess of AU$25 million by

---

41 Downs *The Australian Trusteeship* p. 320, Table 10.3
42 Downs *The Australian Trusteeship* p. 289
43 Downs *The Australian Trusteeship* p. 397
44 Downs *The Australian Trusteeship* p. 321, Table 10.4
45 Downs *The Australian Trusteeship* p. 290

Independence.[46] While the Bank was insufficiently capitalised to attract requests for large loans from international firms, it became the centre of a tussle between expatriates and indigenes seeking funding for small enterprises.[47]

The Development Bank also facilitated the expansion of indigenous agriculture, including providing credit for the first palm oil project which commenced in 1967. A nucleus estate and oil mill was established at Hoskins, West New Britain, through a 50/50 joint venture between the colonial administration and Harrisons and Crosfield (ANZ), a subsidiary of the major international agriculture firm based in the UK. Between 1967 and 1972, nearly 1,600 loans for approximately AU$3.2 million were made to smallholders growing oil palm trees.[48] The oil palm project and smallholder cattle projects were allocated more than half of all agricultural loans up until Independence. Between 1965 and 1973, tea was also established on a nucleus estate basis in the Western Highlands, with approximately 450 indigenous households settled on about 2,000 hectares.[49]

There was a major influx of immigrants into the colony, for the employment and commercial opportunities opened up by the shift to accelerated development. Between 1963 and 1971, the non-indigenous population doubled to 53,000, out of a total PNG population of 2.1 million people.[50] The reaction produced by this sudden increase became part of the opposition to colonial rule and the changed development policies.

From the mid-1960s, the establishment and early operations of the enormous copper-gold mine at Panguna in Bougainville District dwarfed all other activities during a period noted for rapid growth.[51] The company outlaid expenditure of AU$40 million to prove the viability of the project, and AU$400 million to AU$500 million to make the mine operational. While the company which began the project

46   GoPNG *Development Bank Annual Reports and Financial Statements* (Port Moresby: Government Printer, 1967–1975); MacWilliam 'International capital, indigenous accumulation and the state in Papua New Guinea: the case of the Development Bank' *Capital and Class* Summer 1986, no. 29, pp. 150–181

47   For conflicting accounts of the Bank's activities before and immediately after Independence, see M Donaldson and D Turner *The Foreign Control of the Papua New Guinea Economy and the Reaction of the Independent State* Political Economy Occasional Paper no. 1 (Waigani: UPNG, December 1978); and MacWilliam 'International capital'.

48   For planting and production estimates from 1967 until 1975 for oil palm and cattle, see Downs *The Australian Trusteeship* p. 324, Table 10.7 and p. 326, Table 10.9 and 10.10.

49   MacWilliam 'International capital'; J Longayroux *Hoskins Development: The Role of Oil Palm and Timber* New Guinea Research Bulletin no. 49 (Port Moresby and Canberra: New Guinea Research Unit, ANU, 1972); PF Philipp, LL Langness, F von Fleckenstein and M Evans *Four Papers on the Papua New Guinea Cattle Industry* New Guinea Research Bulletin no. 63 (Port Moresby and Canberra: New Guinea Research Unit, ANU, 1975). For an objection to the 'rural elite', or 'wealthy farmer' bias in 'the cattle boom' from 1962 until 1972, see RF McKillop *Problems of Access: Agricultural Extension in the Eastern Highlands of New Guinea* Presented at a Seminar, UPNG November 1974; Dick & McKillop *A Brief History* pp. 30–35. On tea, see Arthur *Tea* pp. 2–5; and Marie Reay 'But Whose Estates? The Wahgi smallholders' *New Guinea* 1969, vol. 4, no. 3, pp. 64–68.

50   Downs *The Australian Trusteeship* pp. 319–320, Table 10.2

51   According to one official estimate, between 1960 and 1966, the cash economy grew by 12.5 per cent per annum in current prices, with a decline in the predominance of primary production and a 'very steep increase in private capital formation' since 1963–64. ToPNG *Programmes and Policies for the Economic Development of Papua and New Guinea* (Port Moresby: Government Printer, 1968) p. 8

was a joint venture between the Australian subsidiary of multinational Conzinc Riotinto, CRA Ltd, and New Broken Hill Consolidated Ltd, another Australian-based firm, over the next ten years major changes took place in the corporate form which owned and operated the mine as Bougainville Mining Ltd (BML).

In 1967, Bougainville Copper Pty Ltd was established as a partnership between the colonial administration and the joint venture partners. In 1970, equity shareholding in Bougainville Copper was set at 80 per cent owned by BML, with two-thirds of these shares owned by CRA, and 20 per cent by the colonial administration. During the next year, BML made a public offer of shares in PNG and Australia, which resulted in one million shares being taken up 'by indigenous organizations and individuals', totaling 9,000 Papua New Guineans. In 1973, BML was replaced by Bougainville Copper Limited (BCL) as the public company owning and operating the project. With issued capital of AU$133,687,500 and 267,375,000 50 cent shares in 1973, the firm was by far the largest operating in PNG. Twenty per cent of the shares were held by the PNG Government-owned Investment Corporation, over 26 per cent by individual and organisational shareholders, and the balance by CRA. The bulk of the operating capital was borrowed internationally, making the firm and the colonial administration extremely wary of the effects of any political unrest.[52]

As Downs notes:

> The project was so big that it would compromise the use of Papua and New Guinea manpower for years to come and influence all wage rates. Bougainville would absorb commodities and equipment like a giant sponge and require services of every kind beyond the capacity of all local sources to produce.[53]

The mine also shifted the focus of development toward the Bougainville District, which had not been given priority in previous administration efforts. Gaining access to sufficient land for the mine, residential land for housing of mine workers and associated commercial enterprises, as well as for transportation of semi-processed minerals and waste disposal, threatened many aspects of earlier colonial policy, especially regarding labour and land. While the Minister Barnes insisted on sticking to mineral ownership principles with which other officials and he were familiar,[54] demands from indigenous owners for compensation threatened to move land prices substantially upwards throughout the colony.

---

52   Downs *The Australian Trusteeship* pp. 340–362; Denoon *Getting under the skin*; Espie 'Bougainville Copper'; Vernon 'The Panguna mine'
53   Downs *The Australian Trusteeship* p. 341
54   These principles were that while ownership of the land was secured under various forms of private title (eg leasehold, customary title), ownership of minerals extracted from underneath the surface belonged to the (colonial) state. The assertion of state ownership caused not only confusion but also became the source of dispute and grievances, not satisfactorily resolved by the provision of compensation to individuals, lineages and associated organisations.

However, projections which showed the scale of the expected exports, revenue in the form of royalties and taxes and employment dwarfed all contemporary considerations of difficulties to be faced. Downs has calculated that:

> the projected value of copper and gold to be exported would far exceed the value of all other Territory exports. The average annual profit of the company would become equal to half the Territorial revenue. Before that profit was declared the royalties and taxes paid to future Papua New Guinea governments would equal or exceed the declared profit.[55]

As the sharp end of the program of accelerated development, planning and early construction at Panguna went ahead despite continuous local opposition, which struck a chord with those raising wider objections to late colonial policy. As James Griffin noted:

> Under Warwick Smith, Canberra assumed detailed day-to-day control by telephone and telex where experienced, delegated authority should have been exercised. Even psychologists were sent in to analyse the putative mental ills of people who would not understand why they did not own the sub-surface of their land.[56]

Objections to the change in development policy had begun to appear as soon as the World Bank's Report was presented locally, in mid-1965, and became more prevalent over the next three years as official plans that drew upon the Report were prepared and presented in the colony. The most important subsequent documents were the 1967 Economic Development of Papua and New Guinea and the 1968 Programmes and Policies for the Economic Development of Papua and New Guinea.[57]

The Programmes and Policies document was the colony's first comprehensive development plan. Covering 1968 to 1973, the plan continued the emphasis on rapid growth. Both documents drew upon the World Bank Report for their founding premises, including the need to improve the colony's domestic revenue base in order to hasten the move to self-government. Increasing indigenous agricultural production and accelerating 'the movement of indigenes from subsistence to commercial production' was to be a major objective of the revised agriculture, livestock and fisheries programme. But the 1968 Programmes and Policies plan went even further than the Report, stating that:

---

55 Downs *The Australian Trusteeship* p. 341

56 See Griffin 'Movements Towards Secession' p. 292, citing Downs *The Australian Trusteeship* pp. 346–349.

57 ToPNG *Economic Development of Papua and New Guinea* (Port Moresby: Government Printer, 1967), prepared by direction of the Administrator and Tabled in the House of Assembly 1 June 1967; ToPNG *Programmes and Policies*

For many crops, the proposals advanced in this paper place proportionally more stress on development by the indigenous people than did the 1964 Bank Mission's programme. About half the land under commercial agriculture is already cultivated by indigenes, and indigenous holdings contribute about 40 per cent of the total value of crop production. These proportions will be substantially increased under the proposed development programme. At the same time the trend towards larger holdings in indigenous hands is expected to continue [Emphasis: SM].[58]

Accelerated Development Under Fire

While the criticism of accelerated development did not become very politically important until later in the 1960s, an initial indication of the direction that objections would take appeared at a 1965 seminar held in Goroka in the Eastern Highlands. This first public forum at which the 1964 World Bank Report was discussed in PNG produced controversy. University of Sussex academic Bernard Schaffer outlined objections which he subsequently developed in a lengthy journal article.[59] Schaffer asserted that indicative of the 'general attitude' underpinning the Report were three major conclusions and recommendations. These could be summarised as: a need to increase the immigration of skilled labour from Australia; a focus upon increasing cash crop production, primarily from 'Australian plantations in copra, coffee, cocoa, and rubber'; and indigenous advance through 'more participation in production and education'.[60]

Schaffer drew attention to what he regarded as an opposition between the increased levels of skilled immigration and plantation production on one hand, and indigenous advance. The crux of Schaffer's criticism was that the former were long-term strategies for growth whereas rapid short-term change was needed to satisfy indigenous ambitions.[61] The Governor of the Reserve Bank, Dr HC Coombs, and the Deputy Labor Leader of the Federal Opposition in Australia, Gough Whitlam also attended the seminar. While Whitlam gained most public

---

58   ToPNG *Programmes and Policies* p. 19, for this statement and the previous shorter quote.
59   Bernard Schaffer 'Thoughts at Goroka, Sins of the World Bank team' *New Guinea* 1965, vol. 1, no. 2, pp. 72–79; Bernard Schaffer 'Advising about Development: The Example of the World Bank Report on Papua and New Guinea' *Journal of Commonwealth Political Studies* March 1966, vol. iv, no. 1, pp. 30–46. See also Downs *The Australian Trusteeship* pp. 276–277. As Ron May notes, the Goroka seminar and one held in Melbourne with the same purpose, to discuss the *Report*, were organised by the Council on New Guinea Affairs, for which the Reserve Bank of Australia provided funding. RJ May *Nugget, Pike, et al. The Role of the Reserve Bank of Australia in Papua New Guinea's Decolonisation* Discussion Paper no. 8 (Canberra: ANU, North Australia Research Unit, 1998) p. 10
60   Schaffer 'Advising about Development' p. 30
61   Schaffer 'Advising about Development' p. 36

attention by asserting that PNG should be independent by 1970,[62] Coombs presented a paper which 'expressed dissatisfaction with the [Report's] "lack of precision in dealing with the task of stimulating indigenous enterprise"'.[63]

The Report had distinguished between the positions occupied by expatriates and indigenes, and recognised the presence of indigenes as owners and operators of large holdings.[64] However the Bank Mission did not foresee the economic or political consequences of encouraging further the emerging class of 'native capitalists', which the colonial administration had long tried to contain. Urging that 'greater responsibilities [should be given] to the [indigenous] people', where 'the people' were largely seen as an undifferentiated mass, the Bank Report did not envisage that the ambitions of indigenes to substantially increase their presence in large holding agriculture could threaten the scheme of smallholder production. In the early 1970s, during the transition to Independence, and subsequently this threat became central to the PNG political economy (see Chapter Six).

The public exchanges about the Report, the two subsequent planning documents of 1967 and 1968, and accelerated development in general tended initially to be dominated by expatriate officials and academics. The critics included several from ANU who had been involved in the preparation of the colonial administration's plans.[65] Their criticism was fuelled in part by the growing numbers of expatriates in local employment and commerce as well

---

62   See Downs *The Australian Trusteeship* p. 279. As May notes, in early 1964 (ie. before Whitlam's provocative statement) at Coombs' direction the Reserve Bank had prepared a 'Plan of Work for TPNG' which assumed self-government within the next few years and how this would affect the Reserve Bank's structure and operations. Apart from playing a role in the establishment of a comparable banking institution in PNG, the Reserve Bank emphasised the importance of indigenisation in employment and commerce. May *Nugget, Pike et al.* p. 11

63   May *Nugget, Pike et al.* p. 10. See also the assessment by the Reserve Bank's most influential official in PNG which foresaw a conflict between economic growth in general and that which specifically placed the indigenous presence foremost: PWE Curtin 'The World Bank report. A review' *New Guinea* 1965, vol. 1, no. 1, pp. 52–58, and a paper by Henry Roberts, an economics student at the University of Sydney, who subsequently as Henry ToRobert became Governor of the Bank of Papua New Guinea and later knighted. The latter pointed to the growing importance of an 'educated elite leadership' which was poised to displace 'most of the present indigenous parliamentarians,' representative of 'traditional leadership'. See H Roberts 'New Guinea's Leadership: Problems of the Prestige Period' *New Guinea* 1965, vol. 1, no. 3, pp. 12–16; also cited in Downs *The Australian Trusteeship* p. 280.

64   IBRD/WB *The Economic Development of the Territory* p. 80

65   The principal expatriate contributors to the public debate included: PWE Curtin 'But Whose Development? How to be inconsistent' *New Guinea* 1968, vol. 3, no. 1, pp. 19–24; RG Crocombe 'That Five Year Plan: For New Guineans-token development' *New Guinea* 1968–69, vol. 3, no. 3, pp. 57–70; Heinz Arndt 'An Answer to Crocombe—I: Too many invidious and invalid comparisons?' *New Guinea* 1969, vol. 4, no. 2, pp. 54–59; Ric Shand 'An Answer to Crocombe—II: In defence of nucleus estates' *New Guinea* 1969, vol. 4, no. 2, pp. 60–63; EK Fisk 'An Answer to Crocombe—III: How fast do you go?' *New Guinea* 1969, vol. 4, no. 2, pp. 64–71; Crocombe 'Crocombe to His Critics: The debate goes on...' *New Guinea* 1969, vol. 4, no. 3, pp. 49–58; Crocombe 'Australian Planning in the New Guinea Economy' in FS Stevens and EP Wolfers (eds) *Racism: The Australian Experience vol. 3 Colonialism and After* (Sydney: ANZ Book Co., 1977) pp. 148–162; T Scarlett Epstein 'The Plan and its assumptions...' *New Guinea* 1969, vol. 4, no. 3, pp. 59–63; Reay 'But Whose Estates?'.

as overseas ownership of the largest enterprises.[66] Crocombe pointed to the substantial presence of expatriates in small commercial operations, taxis, shops, hairdressing and the like.[67]

Anti-colonial nationalism from expatriate academics, indigenous would-be bourgeois and their political allies gained greater traction as popular dissatisfaction increased, particularly over access to land by a growing population. The establishment of the Panguna mine provided further ammunition for the wider opposition to the colonial regime and the drive to accelerate development.[68] In the late 1960s and early 1970s, the politics of opposition shifted, so that the local protest against specific circumstances was joined to national and international arenas where anti-colonial politics was especially powerful.

Younger educated indigenes, with commercial as well as representative political aspirations, also injected an increasingly strident note into the criticism of colonial policy.[69] Kaputin flagged the growing ambition by indigenes to acquire large holdings utilising more accessible bank loans.[70] (This direction mirrored Kaputin's personal commercial trajectory on the Gazelle Peninsula—see below and Chapter Six.) The case of John Kasapwailova is illustrative of how local experiences were joined with international currents. In 1969 as a university student Kasapwailova 'participated so deeply in the New Left Movement at the University of Queensland that he failed to receive a scholarship to continue as a student. He returned home fired with ideas for radical change in the Trobriands'.[71] Kaputin, who had also studied overseas, was a particular influence on Kasapwailova's commercial and political ambitions, according to Leach.

Central to the shift in PNG was the transformation of indigenous leadership, subject both to domestic pressures and the growing Australian determination to hasten the transition to self-government. Under the banner of anti-colonialism, this leadership began to challenge components of the colonial power's development policy. They also worked to displace the stratum of indigenous chiefs and others who held power and remained supporters of colonial authority. Attention now turns to the politics of their challenge and its implications for development policy.

---

66   Downs *The Australia Trusteeship* p. 288, notes the significance of relative disadvantage in fuelling indigenous objections. He states: 'In the course of [the 1968 program] many nationals made money and became as profit conscious as expatriates. Others, less fortunate, did not have the land assets to take part and they became embittered. Economic plans were prepared without politics being in mind, but they became the basic cause of unrest and disorder'.

67   Crocombe 'Crocombe to His Critics' pp. 52–53

68   Downs *The Australian Trusteeship* pp. 340–362; Griffin 'Movements Towards Secession'

69   John Kaputin 'Australia's Carpetbaggers: After the apple—a miserable core?' *New Guinea* 1969, vol. 4, no. 1, pp. 35–42

70   Kaputin 'Australia's Carpetbaggers' p. 40

71   Jerry W Leach 'Socio-historical conflict and the Kabisawali Movement in the Trobriand Islands' in RJ May (ed.) *Micro-nationalist movements in Papua New Guinea* pp. 249–289, esp. p. 264

Anti-Colonial Politics

The initial reforms of the Legislative Council and then the first House of Assembly did not immediately produce a major shift in indigenous representative politics, as was noted above.[72] Instead it was outside the legislature that a more aggressive anti-colonial opposition appeared.

As anticipated and intended by both the colonial government and the World Bank, accelerated development was pursued through a considerably enlarged colonial administration. The World Bank Report contained two distinct recommendations regarding public employment. Firstly, in anticipation of the need to staff an administration for a self-governing country, the Report urged that standards of services and facilities should be related to Territory conditions. Secondly, for the short-term needs of accelerated development, the Report encouraged substantial overseas recruitment of skilled personnel.

This recruitment came on top of a major change which had occurred in the number of Papua New Guineans in state employment. As a direct consequence of the rapid expansion in state positions, and increased employment of Papua New Guineans, there were substantial numbers of indigenous employees. By 1968 'upwards of 12,000 [indigenes] had found … employment in government service' but 'only a handful were yet in positions of any seniority'.[73] The higher levels were filled with either long-serving or newly recruited expatriates. The increased availability of secondary, then tertiary education for indigenes with the establishment of the Administrative College of Papua New Guinea and subsequently the University of Papua New Guinea contrasted with the barriers to their advance in the colonial administration.

The most important early clash between indigenous aspirations and existing public service employment came in a colony where most waged and salaried positions were some distance from rural homes, and required employees to rent or purchase housing. With regard to wages and conditions for public employees, the World Bank Report recommended that there be a difference between expatriates and indigenes. This was already practised, with the difference in wages and salaries being paid as an expatriate allowance, and expatriates engaged in an auxiliary division, outside the Territorial service. However in August 1964, following the direction favoured by Hasluck the Administration decided that in a re-organised integrated public service, there would be different pay rates for overseas and local employees. But all would be employed as part of the same colonial service.

---

72   Parker & Wolfers 'The Context of Political Change' pp. 20–30
73   Parker & Wolfers 'The Context of Political Change' p. 14

Less than a fortnight after this decision, the Public Service Commissioner made a statement on his wage and salary determination for a dual salary classification system to the House of Assembly. Anger was immediate.[74] Outside the legislature, Papua New Guineans active in the Public Service Association (PSA) and other representative bodies were provoked into action. Michael Somare, an office-holder in the PSA and the Workers' Association branches in Wewak, later claimed:

> There was probably no other single issue that made Papua New Guineans more aware of the injustices of colonialism.[75]

The battle over the terms of employment for indigenous public employees spurred legal action. In April 1966, the advocate for the Australian Council of Trade Unions, RJL (Bob) Hawke, later Australian Labor Party Prime Minister, appeared for the PSA in an arbitration case over improved wages and salaries. In May 1967, the arbitrator granted small increases which provoked a large demonstration in Port Moresby.[76]

Opposition to existing public service conditions was soon extended to a wider criticism of colonialism. Educated Papua New Guineans and sympathetic expatriates formed the Bully Beef Club in Port Moresby which brought leading opponents of colonial rule together on a regular basis. Also in April 1966, a group based at the Administrative College in Port Moresby startled the Administration and local conservatives by calling for a major reform of the colonial executive and limited self-government within two years. A more extensive submission to the previously established Select Committee on Constitutional Development called for a rapid program through which expatriates would be replaced by indigenes in public employment, and promotion of indigenes to senior positions within the Administration. The submission and the reaction to the demands of what were popularly dubbed the 'Thirteen angry men' led directly to the formation of the Pangu—Papua and New Guinea Union—Pati, which included MHAs dissatisfied with colonial rule.

---

74   As Downs, himself an MHA, notes: 'Expatriate and local members were shocked by the low basic level for local officers in the classification and disturbed by the delayed announcement which had the appearance of being deliberately arranged to trick them'. *The Australian Trusteeship* p. 315. See also Cleland *Pathways to Independence* pp. 303–322, esp. p. 315, 319.

75   Somare *Sana*. Cf. Downs *The Australian Trusteeship* p. 317, who asserts that 'the dissatisfaction was confined to the Port Moresby '"elite" without real following in the villages'. Downs also concedes that the grievance lingered and had subsequent consequences. Cf. Cleland *Pathways to Independence* p. 319, on Downs' response to the political actions taken by Papua New Guinean state employees.

76   Downs *The Australian Trusteeship* p. 317. See also Somare *Sana* p. 43 where Somare extends the objection beyond public employment conditions. 'I knew that some expatriates were making a lot of money in our country. But they paid their employees poorly. In all towns Europeans reserved the best land for themselves in so-called "high covenant" areas. Papua New Guineans were isolated in their poorly built compounds. With the new salary scheme it became practically impossible for any Papua New Guinean to move into one of the more comfortable houses.'

The 1968 Elections and the Triumph of Parliamentarism

The 1968 election campaign suggested that the dissatisfaction with colonial authority among some of the formally educated urban Papua New Guineans did not have a national reach in a country where the bulk of the population remained attached to smallholdings. The 1968 House of Assembly election for an enlarged legislature in which the expatriate presence was reduced even further, reinforced the weight of rural electorates and local demands. While the first 1964 House had 54 elected members (44 Open, and ten Special electorates), the second had 84 elected members (from 69 Open and 15 Regional electorates). In both there were ten appointed official members. From 100 per cent of the three elected members in the first Legislative Council, formed in 1951, the expatriate proportion declined to 20 per cent in 1968, and 8.6 per cent of a further expanded House of Assembly in the 1972 election which preceded self-government.[77]

By and large conservative in terms of any pronounced drive for self-government and national independence, most candidates and elected MHAs were closely tied to the concerns of rural electorates for state facilities and economic growth.[78] Even in rural areas where some opposition to colonial authority was longstanding, enlarging the legislature for the 1968 election channelled many of the most important critics into electoral politics. This effect was especially noticeable on the Gazelle Peninsula. In the area popular dissatisfaction had begun in the early 1950s, then continued and strengthened during the 1960s. Discontent was being fuelled by a rapid population increase and growing land shortages, where the pre-World War II alienation of land for plantations had been especially substantial.[79] Large areas of undeveloped and partly planted land on these large holdings invited organised as well as spontaneous occupation by squatters.

The demands for land from the landless were easily joined politically to claims for more large holding areas by Tolai bourgeois and would-be bourgeois. Members of the indigenous capitalist class had become wealthy through cocoa growing, processing and trading, as well as other commercial activities. However their ambitions were restricted in one of the colony's most economically advanced

---

77 Downs *The Australian Trusteeship* p. 487
78 Cf. Edward Wolfers 'The 1968 Elections' *New Guinea* 1968, vol. 3, no. 3, pp. 50–61, who concluded (p. 53): 'For many Papuans and New Guineans the quadrennial House of Assembly elections are no more than a device, or the occasions, for the expression of traditional rivalries in their areas'. However, as Parker indicates, there was some difference between attitudes of electors and candidates towards the Administration and expatriates, with further variation in different parts of the country. See Parker 'From Dependence To Autonomy?' in Epstein, Parker & Reay (eds) *The Politics of Dependence* p. 324. Also TG Harding and P Lawrence 'Cash Crops or Cargo?' in Epstein, Parker & Reay (eds) *The Politics of Dependence* pp. 162–207.
79 T Scarlett Epstein 'The Mataungan Affair' *New Guinea* 1969/70, vol. 4, no. 4, pp. 9–14, claims (p. 9): 'About 30% of all the Gazelle Peninsula land is in non-indigenous hands'. See also Ann Chowning, AL Epstein, TS Epstein, Jane Goodale and Ian Grosart 'Under the Volcano' in Epstein, Parker & Reay (eds) *The Politics of Dependence* p. 52.

and land scarce areas. The nationalist anti-colonial appeals, directed against 'foreigners' helped to cover the inherent opposition between the two forms of claims for land by indigenes, as smallholdings or plantations, on the Peninsula. Nationalism became important in the transformation of direct action, squatting, unauthorised planting of vacant land and other measures, into electoral politics.

Longstanding grievances united generations of Tolai. The Varzin claim regarding the ownership of a plantation by an expatriate planter which ran from 1952 until rejected in 1964 by a decision of the High Court of Australia was seminal in this respect.[80] From the mid-1960s, 'more and more plantation boundaries came into dispute and unoccupied portions of European plantations were invaded by Tolais'.[81] By 1966 there were over 150 appeals by indigenes waiting to be heard by the Supreme Court against Land Titles Commission decisions. Most appeals concerned land on the Peninsula.[82]

When in September 1967 squatters occupied and planted a portion of Raniola, a WR Carpenter and Co. plantation, the Administration was forced to act in support of the firm. Previously instructed by the Department of External Territories' Secretary Smith to take police action in support of the legal owners, the Administrator passed on this advice to the DC, East New Britain. The ejection of squatters from Raniola, conducted by unarmed police, pushed the land claimants into electoral politics. One of the squatters' leaders, Oscar Tammur won the electorate of Kokopo Open at the 1968 House of Assembly elections.[83] Educated at a Roman Catholic seminary, he was a schoolteacher, 'the son of a prosperous cash cropper and former luluai [administration appointed village headman]'.[84] At 26 Tammur became the youngest MHA. His success and that of Matthias To Liman, the sitting Member for Gazelle Open seat, who campaigned on the need to settle Tolai land claims, took local grievances to the House of Assembly. The Rabaul Open seat too was taken by a regular government critic, Epineri Titimur.[85]

On Bougainville, the 1968 election also had the effect of further channelling opposition to planning and initial construction of the Panguna mine into

---

80   Downs *The Australian Trusteeship* pp. 170–174
81   Downs *The Australian Trusteeship* p. 335
82   Downs *The Australian Trusteeship* p. 335. Downs also notes: 'Patrol officers were overburdened with investigations and surveys in response to Tolai incursions. Sometimes survey pegs were moved, gardens planted within plantations or palms cut down. The people invaded estates to stage mass protests by simply squatting on the ground. The properties of Coconut Products Limited, a subsidiary of the island colossus WR Carpenter (Holdings) Ltd, were a major target'.
83   Epstein 'The Mataungan Affair' pp. 9–10
84   Chowning et al. 'Under the Volcano' p. 63
85   Chowning et al. 'Under the Volcano' caution (p. 72) against any simple explanation of the outcome. They point to a reduced voter turnout from the previous 1964 election, evidence that voters did not necessarily connect selecting an MHA with solving their immediate concerns, as well as an ambiguity in attitudes towards the Administration. Nevertheless, they also note (p. 76) that in Gazelle and Kokopo, 'land was pre-eminently what many people had on their minds'.

parliamentary politics. Paul Lapun, who in 1964 had been elected to the House of Assembly for the South Bougainville Open electorate, strengthened his position between the two elections by successfully pushing for an amendment to the Mining Ordinance which increased the royalty paid to local landowners at the mine site. Appointed as Under-Secretary for Forests, Lapun's 'superior education and articulateness enabled him to take a much greater role [in the House] than less sophisticated members from the Highlands'.[86] While separatist sentiments had already begun to appear among Bougainvilleans, Lapun was easily re-elected, despite associating himself with the mainland-dominated Pangu Pati.[87]

Prior to the 1968 election, the ten Special electorates reserved for non-indigenous members were abolished, replaced by 15 Regional electorates. An educational qualification, the Territory Intermediate Certificate or equivalent, applied instead of the racial qualification which had been in place for the Special electorates. No qualification was required for Open seats. The election campaigns for the Regional and Open seats largely mirrored the manner in which a generational and educational shift was tied to local demands in most of the colony's electorates.[88] The shift in the educational attainments of some elected MPs would soon have implications for national politics.[89] The distance was rapidly widening between the earlier 'traditional' holders of authority and the people who would take power within a few years, even while the bulk of the electorate continued to reside on smallholdings.

The parochialism of electoral contests among rural populations was reflected in the fragmentation of parties and the predominance of unaffiliated and/or only loosely allied candidates.[90] Expatriates too, representing concerns about the prospect of self-government and the rise of indigenous nationalism, were unable to form more than loose personal alliances. Where parties were formed these tended to be locally based. The seven parties, including Pangu, which had candidates who identified even loosely with their titles and programs were established in just four out of the colony's 18 administrative districts, East Sepik, Central, Madang and East New Britain.[91] Only the Pangu Pati 'proved

86   Eugene Ogan 'Charisma and Race' in Epstein, Parker & Reay (eds) *The Politics of Dependence* p. 143
87   Ron Crocombe 'Bougainville! Copper, C.R.A. and secessionism' *New Guinea* 1968, vol. 3, no. 3, pp. 39–47, notes that Bougainvilleans and (British) Solomon Islanders discussed the possibilities of uniting, instead of the former remaining in Papua New Guinea, at a South Pacific Conference held in 1965 at Lae. This meeting was held well before the full significance of the mine's economic scale was understood.
88   Wolfers 'The 1968 Elections' p. 58
89   Wolfers 'The 1968 Elections' p. 58; Parker 'From Dependence To Autonomy?' pp. 320–321
90   On the beginnings of parties, see Edward P Wolfers 'The Political Parties' *New Guinea* 1967, vol. 2, no. 3, pp. 10–31; Wolfers 'The Emergence of Political Parties in Papua and New Guinea' *Journal of Pacific History* 1968, no. 3, pp. 155–159; Parker & Wolfers 'The Context of Political Change' pp. 30–35; David Stephen *A History of Political Parties in Papua New Guinea* (Melbourne: Lansdowne Press, 1972); Downs *The Australian Trusteeship* pp. 381–391; Somare *Sana* p. 47.
91   Parker & Wolfers 'The Context of Political Change' p. 34

able to field candidates—officially or informally—in most regions of the Territory at the 1968 elections'.[92] Yet Pangu also was like other parties largely 'irrelevant at the popular level'.[93]

In part, the absence of parties reflected the limited role of the legislature, where colonial officials still dominated. According to Parker, 'except over very restricted areas no political voice had yet been heard which could rival that of the Administration'.[94] It was not until after 1968 when the incorporation of PNG as a state within the Australian federation was formally rejected, and July 1970, when during a visit to PNG Australian Prime Minister John Gorton insisted upon a greater measure of indigenous responsibility for the government of the country, that approaching self-government consolidated representative blocs into more substantial organisations.

The loosely organised blocs, faced with the increasing determination of the Australian Government to hasten the transition to self-government, were split over the speed and terms of this move. Although subjected to increasing criticism, accelerated development remained influential in colonial policy during and immediately after the 1968 election. The initial brushing aside of opposition on Bougainville and the Gazelle Peninsula from 1969 and into the early 1970s showed the continuing power of this variant of development, and its effects on colonial officialdom. Subsequently the push to bring about self-government was associated with a reaction against some aspects of accelerated development. The next chapter shows that while the certainty of national independence was joined with a continuing attachment to the idea of agrarian development, there was less certainty about what this meant and how it could be implemented.

Before the immediate pre-Independence period uncertainty about development policy can be considered however, it is necessary to examine what was happening to the scheme of smallholder agriculture during the shift at the most senior official levels to accelerated development. What can be shown is that while policy change occurred at certain levels of the colonial administration, especially those close to the Australian Government and Canberra-based department, domestic and international changes forced support for continuity. Smallholder agriculture, particularly in the Highlands and Islands, continued to be underpinned including by action at the international level to support prices. Such action could involve maintaining barriers against the further expansion of large holdings, even as the official policy turned toward the latter.

92   Parker & Wolfers 'The Context of Political Change' p. 33
93   Wolfers 'The Elections' New Guinea 1967, vol. 2, no. 4, p. 68
94   Parker 'From Dependence to Autonomy?' p. 340

Continuity Within Change

The extent and timing of the expansion of smallholder production during the late colonial period was deceptive, and continues to be misunderstood.[95] Initially the total acreage under cocoa trees, on plantations and smallholdings, increased from less than 4,000 hectares in 1950 to over 30,000 hectares in 1959 and almost 50,000 hectares in 1965/66.[96] During this decade and a half household output remained negligible as a proportion of the total. In 1966, smallholder production was still less than 1,000 tonnes while large holding output had reached 14,658 tonnes.[97] That is, after a lengthy period in which colonial policy had given primacy to indigenous smallholder production, in cocoa the superficial appearance was that policy had little effect.

However while output remained low, by 1965 indigenous growers had planted about eight million cocoa trees, with the majority not yet mature.[98] By 1970/71, before the most substantial takeover of plantations occurred after Independence, the real extent of the earlier smallholder expansion of plantings became obvious. With over 8,000 tonnes, households were now producing almost a third of total PNG output of 26,000 tonnes. As well, the full effect of a major wave of new household plantings on Bougainville was yet to become apparent. That is, what appeared as an effect of accelerated development was instead primarily a consequence of its policy predecessor, as explained further below.

As Tables 5-1 and 5-2 indicate, and Map 5-1 shows, for the three most important agricultural exports, coffee, cocoa and coconuts the postwar increases of smallholder growing and processing were spectacular. However the widespread adoption of cocoa and coffee by household growers is entirely a postwar phenomenon.[99] From the early 1950s until 1975 total production for each of the three crops rose and household output became proportionately more significant. In each case, though at varying rates, households became the most important producers, relegating plantation production to second position. By the late 1950s the acreage planted to coffee on smallholdings exceeded that on plantations, and within a few years output from these bushes surpassed the

---

95   See David Guest 'Enhancing PNG smallholder cocoa production through greater adoption of disease control practices' ACIAR Research that works for developing countries and Australia, retrieved 12 September 2012 at <http://www.aciar.gov.au/project/ASEM/2003/015> where it is claimed that households emerged as substantial producers upon the break-up of the 'plantation sector', presumably after the early 1970s.

96   NAA: A452/1 1958/4219 *Cocoa—Marketing of—Papua & New Guinea* c. March 1960 Note on PNG Cocoa for Department of Trade Mission to Latin America; Densley & Wheeler *Cocoa* p. 2

97   Densley & Wheeler *Cocoa* p. 3, Table 2

98   Densley & Wheeler *Cocoa* p. 2

99   The experience on Karkar Island, Madang District is probably typical of indigenous cocoa growing during the inter-war years. Shand & Straatmans *Transition from Subsistence* pp. 65–66 note that: 'Three islanders developed sizeable plantations (coconuts, or coconuts with cacao); one (Gaum) under the guidance of a European planter, another with assistance from the Lutheran mission'.

crop harvested from large holdings. Cocoa production on smallholdings did not exceed that from plantations until after Independence, but it was during the 1950s that the first important increase in plantings and processing began.

Table 5-1: Total cocoa and coffee production (selected years 1950–1975).

	Cocoa		Coffee	
	Total (tons)	Smallholder (%)	Total (tons)	Smallholder (%)
1951	485*	n/a	33	n/a
1966	15,561	6	10,665	64
1971	26,077	31	26,536	72
1975	38,580	36	35,042	67

Note: Yearly totals include plantions and smallholder production.

* refers to export total only.

Source: Adapted from Munnell & Densley *Coffee* p. 28, Table 4 and Densley & Wheeler *Cocoa* p. 3, Table 1.

Coconuts had been grown in substantial quantities for local consumption and made into copra by smallholders for many years prior to World War II. As well, smallholders had often sold unprocessed nuts to nearby plantations for processing, thus blurring the lines between smallholder and plantation produce. Figures on smallholder coconut growing and copra production remained distorted due to both immediate consumption by households and the sales of nuts to nearby plantations.

Table 5-2: Total copra production (selected years 1954–1975).

	Copra	
	Total (000 tons)	Smallholder (%)
1954–55	99.2	20
1969–70	129.4	34
1974–75	131.9	42

Note: The copra production data includes that from plantations and smallholders.

Source: Adapted from Wheeler, Sackett & Densley *Coconuts* p. 5, Table 2.

As already noted, accelerated development as a changed policy priority was made possible, in large part, because of the achievements of uniform development. Further, and of importance for the remainder of the chapter, even as the central premises of policy changed the colonial administration had to act along previously established lines, including through DASF Agricultural and Extension Centres (see Map 5-2) to support smallholder agriculture.

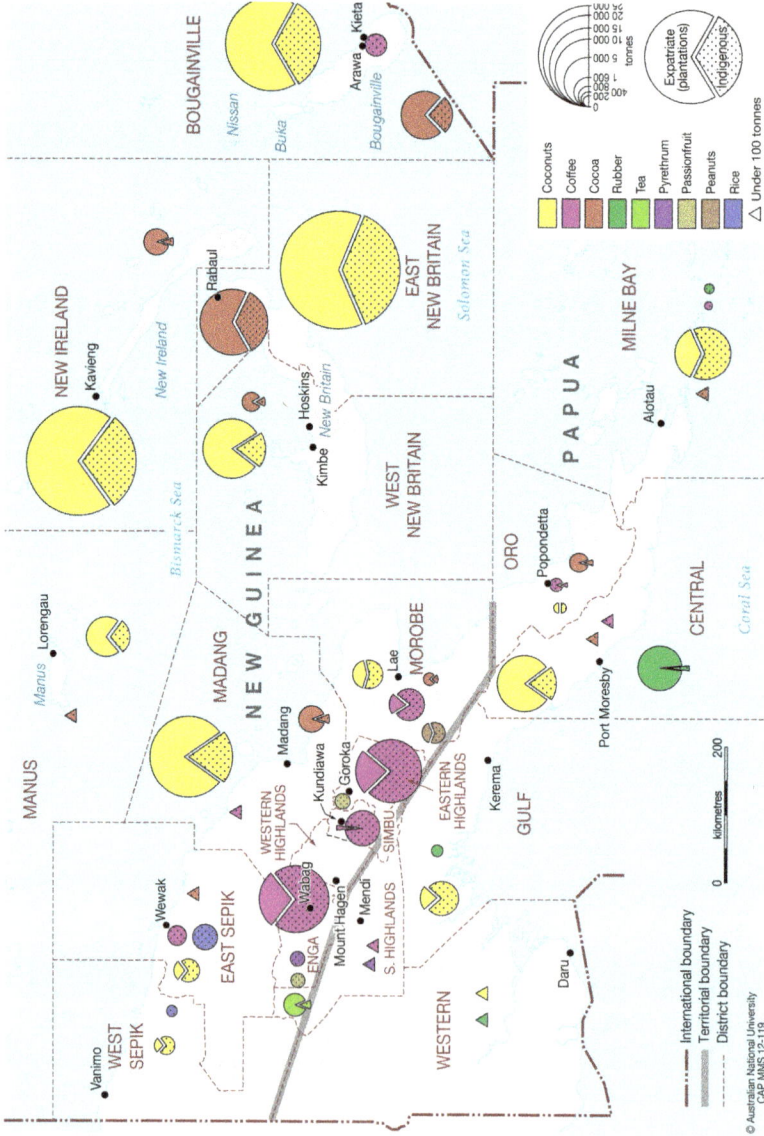

Map 5-1: Selected crop production by district (1969–1970)

Source: Adapted from R Gerard Ward and David A M Lea (eds.) *An Atlas of Papua and New Guinea* Glasgow, Harlow Essex and Port Moresby: Collins and Longman, Department of Geography, University of Papua New Guinea, 1970 by Multimedia Services, CAP, ANU.

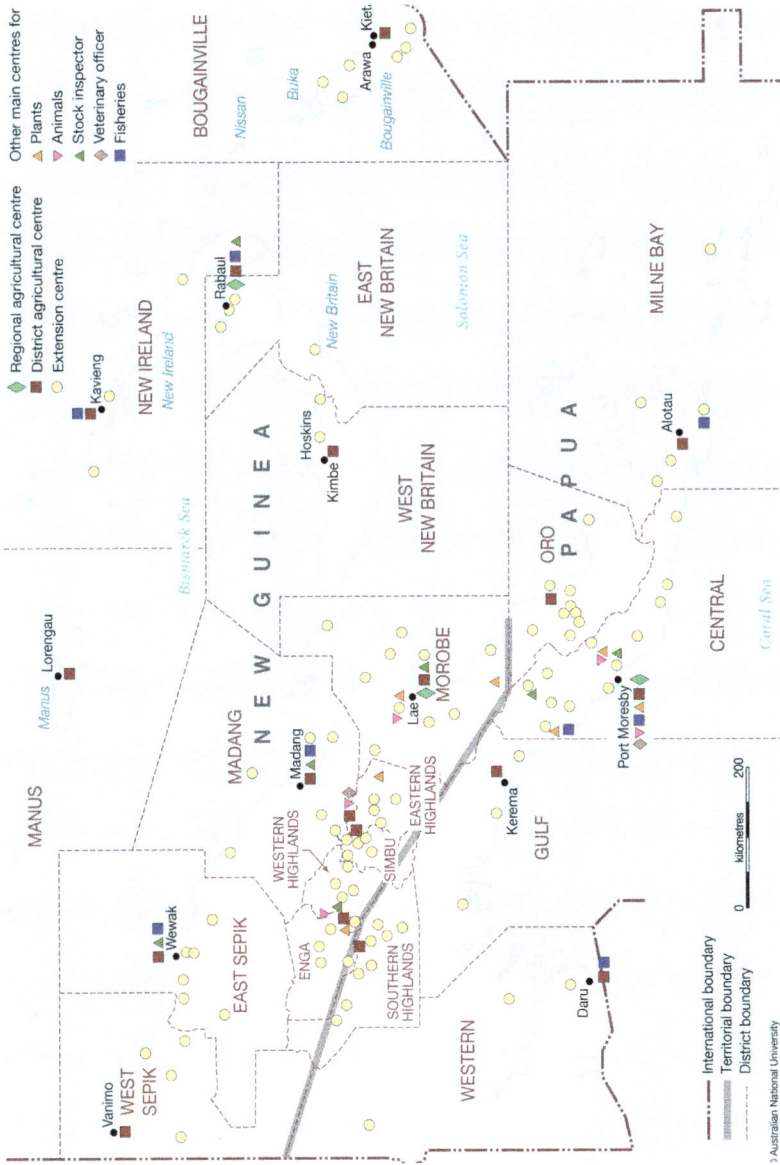

Map 5-2: Agricultural and Extension Centres (1969–1970)

Source: Adapted from R Gerard Ward and David A M Lea (eds.) *An Atlas of Papua and New Guinea* Glasgow, Harlow Essex and Port Moresby: Collins and Longman, Department of Geography, University of Papua New Guinea, 1970 by Multimedia Services, CAP, ANU.

That this support sometimes operated against what would seem to have been central and necessary for the new direction further illustrates the tensions between spontaneous and intentional development which lie at the centre of the idea of development itself. These tensions are now illustrated with further descriptions of cocoa and coffee production during the 1960s and early 1970s in PNG. The account commences where it left off in Chapter Four, with a necessarily shortened examination of official support for smallholder growing and processing of cocoa in Bougainville and East New Britain.[100]

Cocoa on Bougainville

An explosion of cocoa plantings occurred in Bougainville during the 1960s, so that by the early 1970s, cocoa had a dominant position in many parts of the District. Marion Ward calculated that between 1965 and 1972, there was a growth rate of plantings of 18 per cent per annum in southwest Bougainville. By 1972 there were nearly three million trees and production of 1,288 tons of dry cocoa bean in the area.[101] Although smallholders still only produced about one-fifth of plantation-produced cocoa in Bougainville, the extent of immature plantings soon to come into production in this District suggested the potential for household dominance of PNG's total output which occurred soon after Independence.

The expansion was encouraged and supervised by the colonial administration, although it was not until the 1960s that much in the way of agricultural extension work was carried out, as the postwar shortage of agricultural and other skilled workers began to be overcome. So successful was the emphasis upon planting and processing standards, that by the late 1960s, the percentage of smallholder cocoa marketed by Buin and Kieta cooperative societies and rejected at cocoa inspections was approaching the low levels attained by plantations. Connell gives a more specific indicator of the change in the standard of smallholder cocoa, noting that: 'In 1965 Rowntrees, ultimately the main purchaser of New Guinea cocoa, refused to give a grade to Siwai production because of its taste. (Ten years later good Siwai cocoa was the best in Bougainville and ranked with any in the world)'.[102]

The primary basis of the Bougainville expansion, as the colonial government and local Administration intended, was smallholders utilising family labour processes to grow and harvest wet beans. While there were some substantial

---

100   A more detailed and longer account can be found in MacWilliam *Development and Agriculture* ch. 6.

101   Ward *Road and Development* pp. 36–37, 42

102   PNGNA: AN12 16,706, F/N 23-3-1(H) 23/3/70 *Native Cocoa Projects Bougainville District* Bob Moreland 'South Bougainville Cocoa Production' Table 1; cf. Connell *Taim bilong mani* p. 153

indigenous growers with thousands of trees in all cocoa growing areas of the District,[103] most growers had a few hundred trees inter-planted with coconuts and other food crops. A survey of 55 growers carried out during the early 1970s in the East New Britain, Bougainville and Madang districts, suggested that growers in the first district had more trees and more mature trees per household (786) than growers in Bougainville (549) and Madang (489). Bougainvilleans had more immature trees (292), than either East New Britain (175) or Madang (138) growers, with all growers considerably below DASF recommendations for the average number of trees per hectare.[104]

The consequences of fitting cocoa into the place of permanent tree crops in household gardens were twofold. A previously 'flexible system of garden land use and re-use [had] been crystallized' by permanent tree crop plantings. Secondly, 'the normal fallowing cycle [had] been permanently disrupted [so that] practically no gardens planted during 1960–70 were allowed to fallow'.[105] That is, household labour processes and land use were intensified as a result of growing cocoa on smallholdings.

On Bougainville matrilineal inheritance seems to have been strengthened by cocoa growing which led to more fights over inheritance, as the scarcity of good cocoa land became pronounced. There is, at least as yet, no basis for suggesting that the strategies for avoiding inheritance claims adopted by Tolai growers, and particularly those with the most extensive plantings, discussed below, were widespread on Bougainville. Instead the large growers were initially less restricted in their ability to acquire land, especially in southern Bougainville where plantations hardly existed, but they faced labour shortages because so many households grew their own cocoa. Instead ambitious Bougainvilleans moved into private trading and fermentary operations. However as already noted in Chapter Four, processing and marketing took a different route on Bougainville by comparison to the Gazelle Peninsula. In the former the cooperative movement model was more influential for processing and trading.

By the end of the 1960s and early 1970s the increase of cocoa growing on widely dispersed smallholdings also made it possible for more small fermentaries to be constructed throughout Bougainville. These remained unregulated and the standards of cocoa produced varied considerably. Only cocoa inspection at major centres and the quality standards imposed by exporters imposed sufficient discipline on the processing which was occurring at these other fermentaries.

In 1974, under the recently introduced Cocoa Industry Act, the newly formed Cocoa Industry Board was given wide powers, including the power to register

---

103   Connell *Taim bilong mani* pp. 153–154
104   Godyn *An Economic Survey of Cocoa* p. 10
105   Mitchell *Land and Agriculture in Nagovisi* p. 81

fermentaries. Soon after Independence registration became obligatory but this remained little more than a revenue raising procedure. No action was taken to limit the number of fermentaries or impose other than minimum requirements on fermenting equipment as a condition of registration. The colonial administration's efforts to ensure that smallholders produced high quality fine and flavour cocoa became a fading memory.

If smallholder production on Bougainville was particularly significant for its part in pressing households to land and reducing the pull of wage labour, development in East New Britain, and particularly on the Gazelle Peninsula, showed the process of continuity within change in another direction. Here official efforts to sustain smallholder production against attempts to expand large holdings and the growing prominence of 'native capitalists' were particularly pronounced. These efforts continued into the 1960s even as accelerated development with its pronounced bias toward indigenous enterprises, more large holdings and international investment became policy. The on-going struggles between colonial officials and among Tolai over the main processing operations on the Gazelle provide another instance of how the tensions inherent in the idea of development appeared in practice.

Tussles in the Tolai Cocoa Project

In Chapter Four, the establishment and early years of the operation of the Tolai Cocoa Project were described. It was noted that during the mid-1960s the Project became the largest non-plantation exporter of cocoa, some of very high quality obtaining premium prices on international markets. However at the same time the TCP was under increasing pressure. Much of the pressure arose from the major expansion of smallholder production which stimulated the formation of other competing enterprises trading in and processing household grown cocoa.

Between 1961 and 1965 smallholder production on the Peninsula increased to over 4000 tons of dry beans, from more than four million mature trees, with 3.6 million of those registered. However at the same time as the total output of wet beans increased, the TCP share of beans processed declined to little over one-third. In 1967, the management of the Project was changed and the Project was vested entirely in the newly formed Gazelle Peninsula LGC. Changes undertaken by the new management appeared to breathe life into the TCP. While smallholder production remained below the 1965 peak, the Project increased production by gaining a greater share of smallholder wet beans, which in 1968 reached 63 per cent of the beans grown. A (short-lived) price stabilization fund was introduced and in February 1968, a conference decided on a policy of centralising TCP fermentaries. It was determined that the number of operating fermentaries would be reduced to three, with former fermentaries continuing as buying points for wet bean. This bean was transported to the three surviving processing centres.

By mid-1968, the initial bank loan for building and equipping fermentaries was repaid. However the Project was forced to increase its overdraft limit to AU$300,000 to accommodate increased operating costs.[106] In 1968, responding to demands from growers, the Project also began purchasing coconuts. These were processed into copra in a recently constructed copra dryer.

The improvement in the Project's trading position was brief, however. Over just nine months, between May 1969 and January 1970, its share of smallholder cocoa declined to 32 per cent as other processors gained the ascendancy. What had become a profitable operation soon changed so that it appeared unlikely the Project could repay a sizable bank loan obtained to construct the ultra-modern central fermentary opened in 1969 at Volavola.[107] The Administration again turned to a Sydney adviser who repeated his earlier recommendation for privatisation of the TCP. On 15 July 1970 a special meeting of the Gazelle Peninsula LGC adopted this recommendation, as did the Director of Agriculture. Over the next year, a conversion program was put into effect. Why the TCP, an organisation affiliated to and supported by the Administration, LGCs and many growers, was wound-up is now explained.

TCP's Management—A Contested Realm

Since the 1950s, the dominance of the Administration in determining the operations of the TCP had prompted much local criticism which reflected the tensions inherent in the structure of a public utility. While 'the establishment of the Project was due entirely to the efforts of the Administration who wished to avoid some of the problems [with] which West Africa had had to deal over the years',[108] there was also, as noted previously, the initial objective of restraining 'the wealthy' in an area of PNG where these were especially advanced.[109]

The structure of the TCP's administration and management up until 1967, when the Project was effectively passed to/taken over by the Gazelle Peninsula LGC, ensured the Administration's continued authority and tied this to the provision of loans. On the Gazelle Peninsula, four Council Cocoa Committees were

---

106   In February 1966, the Australian currency was changed from AU£ to AU$, with the latter legal tender in PNG until April 1975, when the national currency, kina and toea, was introduced.

107   Allwood *A Report on the Tolai Cocoa Project* pt 1, pp. 7–11

108   Allwood *A Report on the Tolai Cocoa Project* pt 5 'Administration Involvement' p. 1

109   TS Epstein *Capitalism, Primitive and Modern* chs 1–4; Salisbury *Vunamami* pts 1–2; AL Epstein *Matupit: Land, Politics and Change among the Tolai of New Britain* (Canberra: Australian National University Press, 1969) ch. 1

established to run the fermentaries. Committee duties included overseeing the disbursement of loan funds for fermentary construction, the control of policy and the operations of each fermentary in the appropriate council area. These Council Committees were dominated by a General Manager, from the Department of District Affairs, a Field Manager from the DASF and an Accountant—all employed and paid for by the Administration.[110]

Little changed with the 1958 formation of a Board of Management for the Project that included a representative from each fermentary, by then 18, as well as a representative from each Council. Control was still exercised through five Administration officers on the Board. The District Officer was Chairman, and there were an Executive Officer, a Field Manager, an Accounts Officer and the District Agricultural Officer. '[A]t the fermentary level the "didiman" [agricultural officer] and "kiap" [district officer] supervised operations'.[111]

The selection of the local representatives for the Board of Management showed the extent of the Administration's authority, but also the continuing push by the most substantial growers to dominate the TCP. This push was conveyed directly to the most senior levels of the colonial administration. In August 1957 WL Conroy, Chief, Division of Agricultural Extension wrote to the Senior Agricultural Officer, Rabaul supporting their demands and proposing that the five heaviest deliverers of wet bean from the last harvest should be the grower representatives on each fermentary committee.[112]

The next month JC Lamrock, the Senior Agricultural Officer (SAO) to whom Conroy had written, showed a clearer understanding of the implications for a public utility of letting the biggest producers dominate the management of fermentaries. For the drive by wealthy Tolai to have more influence on the TCP's operations came at the same time as Councils and local district agricultural officers were in agreement on the need to stop the erection of 'bush material' fermentaries. These were privately owned by Tolai individuals for the processing of their own and purchased wet bean. The central Administration was opposed to any restraints on such operations, and could block Native Local Government Council rules 'as restrictive in principle' and thus invalid. That is, the spontaneous in development was to have the reins in this commercial arena at least.[113] However SAO Lamrock was not prepared to let the large producers have complete dominance of indigenous representation on the Project's Board of Management.

110   Williamson 'The Tolai Cocoa Project'
111   Allwood *A Report on the Tolai Cocoa Project* pt 5, p. 2
112   PNGNA: AN12 16,704, F/N 23-3-1(a) *Part 1 Production and Marketing—Native Projects Cacao Fermentaries—Gazelle Peninsula* 7/8/1957 WL Conroy to Senior Agricultural Officer (SAO), Rabaul
113   PNGNA: AN12 16,704, F/N 23-3-1(a) *Part 1 Production and Marketing* See correspondence of early 1958 on Rule 9 of NLGCs.

He proposed a compromise to be applied to each Council Cocoa Committee, where the five paid Administration personnel held near-complete authority. In a letter sent above Conroy's head to the Director of DASF, Lamrock recommended that five grower representatives, three large and two small growers be appointed.[114] That is, the large grower push could be contained within a form which protected small growers, assuming the local Administration personnel were of like mind or willing to accept instruction from the SAO. As long as the Administration continued to provide substantial assistance, none of it costed or charged out,[115] protection of smallholders against the drive by indigenous accumulators could to an extent continue within the Project.

Since encouraging competition between enterprises was also a central component of colonial policy, the protection afforded the TCP was nevertheless limited. As trees matured and production increased, the competition among traders and between fermentaries intensified further. In the competition, the continuing Administration dominance of the TCP's management could be used against the Project by indigenous as well as non-indigenous commercial concerns. The privatisation of the TCP, referred to above, showed to what extent the Project, having initially provided space in which household production could be expanded, had lost support commercially as well as politically among the most powerful Tolai. The second major arena of tussle, linked with management, concerned ownership of the Project.

Fermentary Ownership

Tying the fermentaries to the LGCs as a public utility could 'overcome any difficulty there might be in collecting share capital from growers'.[116] Collecting share capital from individual growers would open ownership of fermentaries to different forms and amounts of share ownership. Trading in shares would make the ownership of fermentaries subject to the process of accumulation. This process could also undercut a major objective of colonial policy, that all growers' incomes would be optimised by continued ownership of 'their' crop until sold to international trading firms. Such optimisation was central to making household production of crops, including cocoa, preferable to wage employment. Privately owned fermentaries, on the other hand, purchased wet bean, at which point the growers lost all proprietorial rights and possibilities of further income increases in the produce as a consequence of processing.

---

114 PNGNA: AN12 16,704, F/N 23-3-1(a) *Part 1 Production and Marketing* 2/9/1957 JC Lamrock, SAO, Rabaul to Director, DASF

115 Allwood *A Report on the Tolai Cocoa Project* pt 5. See in particular a December 1968 memo to the Assistant Administrator (Economic Affairs), which takes up almost a foolscap page of paper, listing all the forms of assistance provided free of charge to the TCP.

116 Allwood *A Report on the Tolai Cocoa Project* pt 4 'Nature of the Project' p. 2

From January 1956 onwards, TCP growers were levied on a tonnage basis for the repayment of the loans provided by the Bank of New South Wales. Growers, particularly those who produced more cocoa and therefore per person paid more of the levy, increasingly conceived of this as a payment which acquired equity in the fermentaries constructed and operated with the borrowings. Regularly aired at meetings, the grievances of larger producers became most significant when in 1971 no shares were given to TCP growers in the privatised New Guinea Islands Produce, and this firm obtained the assets of the TCP at a bargain-basement price (see Chapter Six).

Although it was the Councils and the colonial administration which provided collateral for and ultimately guaranteed repayment of the loans, the fact that repayments in full were always made, easily gave the impression that such backing, however necessary from the Bank's perspective, was rather meaningless. Growers' efforts repaid the borrowings which made the building and equipping of fermentaries possible: therefore, went the reasoning, growers, and especially the more substantial growers, owned—or at least had substantial equity in—the fermentaries. These growers expected to be beneficiaries if and when the Project was wound-up and its assets privatised. That this did not occur only intensified the dissatisfaction with colonial development policy from the wealthiest Tolais who had continued to have their cocoa processed at Project fermentaries.

Competition from Processors and Traders

Even before the formal inception of the TCP in 1956, a substantial amount of smallholder cocoa had been sold to traders and nearby plantations for processing in non-TCP fermentaries. Before and after 1956, this activity continually led to public criticism by Project supporters and to demands for action to make these sales illegal. In the late 1950s several LGCs passed regulations prohibiting the activity and imposed fines upon some Tolai. However the Administration, through the Crown Law Department, ruled that council legislation prohibiting the sales and imposing fines for transgressors was ultra vires. The legislation had to be rescinded but the criticism did not cease.[117] Although changes in payment policy and in operations improved the TCP fermentaries' position in obtaining a greater share of an increased total smallholder output in the late 1960s, as already

---

117   As Epstein notes, in support of the Tolai Cocoa Board's aim to secure a monopsony over Tolai cocoa processing, there was 'a motion proposed by a leading Tolai and passed by a large majority' at a January 1961 meeting of the Board of the TCP which requested that the Administration 'bring in legislation to compel all Tolai people within council areas to take their wet beans to council fermentaries'. *Capitalism, Primitive and Modern* p. 121

noted the Project never held unchallenged dominance.[118] The decision to close down many TCP fermentaries and centralise production in just three fermentaries also reduced the amount of bean processed.[119]

In the late 1960s, some of the loss of grower support for the Project can also be explained by mounting opposition from the nationalist Mataungan Association (MA).[120] However that the growing nationalist sentiment on the Gazelle Peninsula of the 1960s and early 1970s did not turn indigenous growers even more towards the TCP and away from non-indigenous traders and fermentary owners suggests the need to find another possible explanation for Tolai sales to non-TCP fermentaries and traders. This explanation needs to encompass the tussle that had been central to indigenous cocoa production throughout and which continued in the 1970s.

The Clash: Indigenous Capital Against Household Production

It has been argued that the most important explanation for the attractiveness of selling cocoa to traders rather than having wet bean processed and sold by the TCP lay not in the immediate realm of financial return but in the growing clash between 'tradition', represented by matrilineal inheritance patterns, and 'modernity'. The latter described the desire of cocoa-growing males to hide the extent of their holdings so that these could be passed on to their sons according to rules of patrilineal descent.[121] In short, the requirement that producers register with the Project as a condition of accepting wet bean for fermenting and curing laid male producers open to scrutiny by members of the matrilineage upon whose land the cocoa was grown, as well as their own kin. The latter could easily find the extent of tree ownership and output from the register.

Such scrutiny would eventually preclude plantings from being passed on to sons, as the senior males desired and instead subject the plantings to disputes about ownership between the land-owning matrilineage and the kin-group of the trees' owners. In this dispute, the intentions of the owner-producers—for the trees to be inherited by their son(s)—would only rank as one determinant among many of the outcomes.[122]

---

118 Epstein *Capitalism, Primitive and Modern* Table 19, p. 16; Allwood *A Report on the Tolai Cocoa Project* apps A, B

119 Allwood *A Report on the Tolai Cocoa Project* pt 2 'Management Structure' p. 9 cites Mr K Gorringe, Manager of the Project, as claiming 'that it was due to the endeavour to centralize that the present [late 1960s and 1970: SM] downward trend in input can be attributed'.

120 Allwood *A Report on the Tolai Cocoa Project* pt 1, p. 10

121 Allwood *A Report on the Tolai Cocoa Project* pt 6 'Drift away from Fermentaries' provides a lengthy discussion of the competition with traders and other fermentaries. The discussion includes a summary of Epstein's 'rules of inheritance' explanation, discussed below.

122 Epstein *Capitalism, Primitive and Modern* p. 126 states that: 'A considerable number of Rapitok men, who have had their own matrilineage lands planted with cocoa by their sons, wish to conceal this fact from their fellow parishioners', estimating that over 80% of 'the house-holders in the Rapitok area sold some cocoa

When land boundaries had not been formally surveyed and registered, and disputes were settled by leading elders, inheritance became even more uncertain. Cash which could be 'hidden' became especially attractive. While there were some means of circumventing the difficulty, such as by registering a son or sons as the owner of trees on matrilineage lands, none of these was without its own possible problems. Instead by not selling a substantial portion of cocoa to the TCP, a grower-producer—especially one cultivating many trees on lands obtained through several distinct arrangements—could accumulate the funds, deposit the money in bank accounts or engage in other commercial activities with less scrutiny and greater certainty. At worst, the trees themselves would be lost during squabbles over inheritance. But at least the grower-producer could deploy the proceeds received during his lifetime as he intended and improve the chances that his intentions would be satisfied after his death. This anthropological explanation, it is suggested, based upon conflicting inheritance customs best explains the practice of growers selling such a substantial amount of cocoa to traders rather than the TCP, even if there appeared to be no immediate financial incentive to do so.[123]

A major difficulty with this explanation, and the ultimate failure of the TCP which lead to privatisation, is that it does not take the next, necessary step. The anthropological explanation does not distinguish between the drive to accumulate by Tolai who formed the local indigenous class of capital, and the possibility that for other, most, Tolai, cocoa provided the means for acquiring consumption goods.[124]

For members of the emerging capitalist class any principal of inheritance which dispersed assets, either as welfare or by passing them into the hands of a commercial rival, would have been anathema. Being able to determine the present as well as future ownership of assets is critical for accumulation. In this case a 'new' principal of inheritance, individual determination by the current owner(s) was chosen. However for the members of households for whom cocoa income provided the basis for immediate, possibly enlarged consumption, the hiding of assets by the class of accumulators was an attempt to reduce their welfare. Unsurprisingly, the tussle between accumulation and welfare was a constant feature in all cocoa growing areas. Where land to expand plantings was least plentiful, including on parts of Peninsula, the conflict was especially sharp.

---

to the traders in 1959/60 as a means of providing for their sons'.

123   Allwood *A Report on the Tolai Cocoa Project* pt 6, which provides an extensive list of possible financial and other reasons why Tolai sold to traders rather than to the Project.

124   Salisbury *Vunamami* p. 237, hints at the distinction, referring to two types of activities practised by Tolais, between *bisnis* (Melanesian Pidgin tok pisin: business) and 'not-*bisnis*' (food) as with 'land purchase and cultivation for subsistence'.

The distinction between accumulation and welfare is critical for understanding central features of the late colonial establishment of cocoa growing, marketing and processing among the indigenous population of the Gazelle Peninsula. As noted previously (Chapter Three), wealthy Tolai who had been involved in the pre-war increases in copra production and trade were among the first to plant cocoa, not always successfully. Indigenous growers with substantial numbers of cocoa trees as well as other commercial activities were also involved in the first efforts to construct a fermentary utilising Council resources at Ngatur. The same people were leaders of the LGCs, established in the early 1950s, who joined commercial activities with forms of political power. Their progress occurred despite the best efforts of the colonial administration which hoped to restrain any advance of the class, which as with international and expatriate capital might increase landlessness and proletarianisation.

Despite this intention to limit indigenous capital in cocoa growing, a small number of growers owning thousands of trees—often spread over a number of landholdings owned and operated under different arrangements—emerged. By 1974, 15 per cent of all indigenous-owned cocoa in East New Britain and Bougainville was grown using wage labour.[125] The extent of other labour-forms employed by the most substantial indigenous growers is unknown.[126]

Initially the format of the TCP assisted in concealing the opposition between growers engaged in accumulation and those reproducing consumption at varying levels of need. Central to the disguise was the previously noted condition that all cocoa processed and sold through the Project remained the private property of each grower who registered with and sold to one or more of the Project's fermentaries. That is, distinct ownership conditions—for accumulation and consumption—could appear as the same private property rights. At the same time as the processed cocoa was secured as the private property of growers, Administration objectives regarding land usage—that the crop be grown on 'native land' which could not be bought and sold—and product quality could be met as well. That is 'better control of the product through all stages of production from land usage to final processing can be exercised' if the 'economic unit' is tied to the 'existing administrative organisation [Council]'.[127]

125   Densley & Wheeler *Cocoa* p. 18, citing Godyn *An Economic Survey of Cocoa* p. 21. By the early 1970s there were labour shortages, so substantial was the drive to plant more cocoa in south Bougainville where there were competing demands for labour from the newly opened mine and what John Connell describes as 'the lure of a new cattle industry'. 'At the February 1970 Busiba Society directors' meeting a motion was passed that Busiba should find labour from outside Bougainville ("Highland labour") since local labour was in short supply. The Society were also willing to construct houses for such labourers....' Connell *Taim bilong mani* p. 175

126   In the context of labour exchange in rural Africa, Harold White has pointed to the limits of confining analysis of hired labour to wage employment. See Harold White 'Combining Quantitative and Qualitative Approaches in Poverty Analysis' *World Development* 2002, vol. 30, no. 3, pp. 511–522. There is no reason to believe that the point is any less relevant for rural PNG, and the means by which indigenous capitalists obtained labour to work their large holdings.

127   Allwood *A Report on the Tolai Cocoa Project* pt 4, p. 1

However the TCP format also constrained the capacity of the indigenous bourgeoisie to accumulate in a potentially important area of commercial activity, processing smallholder cocoa. While individual Tolai could establish smaller fermentaries, compete with expatriate-owned plantation processors and Chinese operations, the centralised production operations of the TCP offered a superior alternative. Gaining control of the TCP's assets became especially important, and privatisation of its operations added to the intensity of political tussles as self-government approached.

While the colonial administration was driven by uniform development, the restraints on accumulation were especially powerful on the Gazelle as elsewhere in the colony. Although some barriers remained in place during the accelerated development phase of colonial policy, nevertheless by the late 1960s these had weakened. During the drive for self-government the tussles between smallholders, indigenous capitalists and their respective allies would become more obvious, including on the Gazelle. In the early 1970s, shaping the political and ideological forms of resolution would occupy national politicians and administrators, academics and advisers alike.

In production and processing of coffee in the Highlands similar tensions and tussles emerged as colonial policy changed to accelerated development. However coffee is sufficiently distinct from cocoa to warrant separate treatment, including because for the former the international dimension of the colonial administration's efforts to secure huseholds was much more pronounced. The account now turns to the continued expansion of smallholder coffee production during the late 1950s and 1960s.

Coffee's Expansion Sustained

From the late 1950s coffee production and consumption worldwide entered a new phase of sustained oversupply and declining prices. This change occurred just as PNG smallholder production was becoming significant. The Australian Government and colonial administration responded in several ways to further encourage household producers. Three of the most important aspects of the support will be briefly outlined here. They were the continuing extension, marketing and other local assistance for smallholders, the provision of price subsidies for PNG coffee sold into the Australian market and the successful efforts of Australian officials who obtained favourable treatment for PNG exports to other markets in International Coffee Agreement (ICA) negotiations. While these and other measures were largely successful in terms of the aims of uniform development, households remaining attached to land at higher standards of living, they also undercut one of the stated objectives of accelerated development policy. The more household plantings of coffee expanded, utilising fertile land suitable for the crop, the prospects for increasing the large holding presence were reduced.

Checking Plantations While Bolstering Smallholders

After a frantic rush by ambitious owner-occupiers to acquire and establish large holdings in the early to mid-1950s price boom, by the end of the decade forms of industrial agricultural capital had begun to takeover and consolidate existing operations. During the 1960s, this change continued. Without increased prices and the inability to extend planting areas, discussed below, only a small number of owner-occupiers survived. But even as large plantation and trading firms displaced the expatriate settlers they came up against planting restrictions. Once the ICA and the overseeing International Coffee Organisation were in place, the colonial authorities were required to limit new plantings by explicit and implicit processes. New plantings were not permitted even on existing vacant plantation land, and extension services for coffee reduced. Within a few years, the early 1960s local official support for large holding plantings was stopped.[128]

However as was well understood in Canberra and the colony, even if it had been desired that the policy also applied to smallholder plantings—which it was not—nothing could be done to put such barriers in place. The lesson from cocoa on the Gazelle had been well learned. In the Western Highlands in particular, the 1960s directive from DC Ellis noted in the last chapter that households be encouraged to plant continued to be implemented. The third phase of smallholder expansion, beyond the initial period of limited plantings during the 1940s and early 1950s, and the more substantial increases with sustained official assistance in the 1950s, occurred during the 1960s and early 1970s.

Western Highlands' smallholders began a decade long expansion which by the early 1970s would surpass the previously preponderant Eastern Highlands household growers in area and output. The precise degree of this preponderance is harder to document but the best available estimates suggest that although in 1972 there were more growers in the Eastern Highlands, Western Highlands smallholders owned more trees (12.2 million as against 8.5 million), planted on a greater area (10,775 hectares compared to 7,992 hectares in the Eastern Highlands), with an output of 11,804 tonnes by comparison with 8,157 tonnes.[129] While the rate of new plantings slowed during the late 1960s and early 1970s, as prices paid to growers either stagnated or fell, the expansion continued. Anderson suggests that for all Central Highlands households, in 'the eight years

---

128   Cartledge *A History of the Coffee Industry* p. 135
129   Wilson & Evans *Sample Survey of Smallholder Coffee Producers* pp. 2, 8, 11–12

to 1974/75 the rate of increase in production was 11 per cent per annum',[130] which was almost certainly considerably greater for the later starting Western Highlands. By the early 1970s the limits to land suitable for growing coffee also were being reached in the Highlands and tussles increased, producing an outbreak of what was invariably dubbed 'tribal fighting' (see Chapter Six).[131]

The Coffee Marketing Board

As noted in the previous chapter, once smallholder plantings became substantial, Administration attention turned to the need to ensure that processing occurred at the highest possible standard. While some smallholders could sell cherry and/ or parchment to nearby plantations, during the 1950s processing facilities at many expatriate large holdings were rudimentary also, in line with the general state of these operations. As well, the planters were often far from knowledgeable about the best processing methods. Early smallholder parchment coffee was often of poor, even unusable quality. If initially processed by smallholder methods, parchment was then either sold to buyers or transported by individual producers to central factories for further drying, polishing and grading before being bagged for export.[132]

By the late 1950s and early 1960s, once transportation improved in the principal smallholder growing areas, the presence of buyers—many of them attached to the principal processing factories and most important exporting firms— made it more possible for households to sell their coffee as either cherry or parchment. Accordingly cherry sales to the larger central processing factories became central to smallholder production and marketing. This accelerated in the late 1960s when the Coffee Marketing Board began to restrict the ability of expatriate-owned plantations to purchase and process smallholder coffee from proximate plantings in their factories.[133]

With the production increases and growing difficulties selling PNG's crop overseas, there was more pressure to establish a supervisory body within the country to oversee local standards and represent the industry internationally. In July 1963 legislation to establish a Coffee Marketing Board was passed. In March 1964 a Board was appointed comprising five grower representatives and one public servant, the Director of DASF. There were three expatriate growers and

---

130   Anderson *An Economic Survey* p. 5

131   For claims of increasing threats received by expatriate plantation owners from indigenes seeking to takeover plantations, Coffee Marketing Board Archives (CMBA): F/N 217 February 1974–June 22 1978 *Localizing* 2/74 RBE Smith 'Proposal for District Investment Authority.'

132   FW von Fleckenstein 'Observations on Coffee Marketing in the Eastern Highlands' *Yagl-Ambu* 1975, vol. 2, no. 2, pp. 116–132

133   CMBA: F/N 158 *Registration of Processing Facilities 17/11/67–3/9/72; 11/11/72–30/9/74; 1/10/74–13/7/77*

two indigenes.[134] In the CMB Ordinance the possibility for a future centralised marketing role for the Board was retained. But initially the Board had other roles associated with the existing private buying, processing and export marketing structure of the industry in PNG. The most important of these roles included allocating to exporters the quotas determined under the ICA so as to maximise 'market accommodation for the increasing coffee production of the Territory'.[135] This allocation included balancing exports between the Australian and other overseas markets, and issuing licences or registering exporters, buyers and processors.

The Board did not have an inspectorial role but became involved in trying to maintain standards as coffee quality concerns attained greater significance in the late 1960s and early 1970s.[136] Checking coffee processing quality was a mixture of DASF inspection, primarily for smallholders using small local fermentaries to turn cherry into parchment before selling, and exporter testing to ensure that coffee sold overseas was of the grade and quality attested to in sales documents. But the Board also had an important role through its capacity to refuse registration of processors, primarily on the grounds that the equipment and facilities being used were inadequate to ensure processing reached a satisfactory standard.

Without substantial price incentives, in the late 1960s it became even more difficult to maintain the quality of smallholder coffee. It also became harder to police cherry sales, to ensure that sellers actually grew the coffee offered for sale. The possibility that produce sold had been stolen from growers in turn produced a major political controversy, with a subsequent albeit short-lived ban against the purchase of cherry in Chimbu District.[137]

Except at a relatively small number of plantations which produced at a similar level, in the PNG Highlands the standards generally attained were lower than in Kenya but still as high if not higher than from other countries producing what are described as 'Other Milds'. There was no pressure from exporters for state supervised and administered centralised processing—from cherry to

---

134   Cartledge *A History of the Coffee Industry* p. 79 notes that: 'The two local people were substantial coffee growers, accepted leaders and influential in their own coffee growing communities'.

135   Cartledge *A History of the Coffee Industry* p. 94

136   On 10 February 1972, the Executive Officer to the Board sent a circular letter to all processors drawing attention to recent complaints from American buyers of New Guinea coffee. The buyers indicated that during late 1971 they had noticed a decline in the quality of 'Y' grade, generally smallholder coffee. The US had become an increasingly important market, so the Board advised processors if the complaints continued it may be necessary to request the Administration 'to impose stringent export inspections'. CMBA: F/N 158 *Registration of Processing Facilities 17/11/67–3/9/72*

137   Cartledge *A History of the Coffee Industry* p. 161; Sinclair *The Money Tree* ch. 22, esp. pp. 307–308

parchment—of smallholder coffee because there was no difficulty selling PNG coffee at the existing quality, which was often superior to the best Colombian coffee.[138]

An important component of quality control was the development of factories which further processed, graded and bagged coffee purchased from plantations and smallholders. The first two central factories not on plantations were Goroka Coffee Producers, established in 1958, and Wahgi Valley Coffee Company mill built soon after at Banz. Goroka Coffee Producers did not handle coffee cherry but only engaged in dry processing of parchment.[139]

As smallholders produced increasing amounts of coffee and expanded their consumption of purchased goods (see Chapter Six), the proportion of household grown coffee sold as cherry increased. By the late 1960s and early 1970s, the competition among buyers attached to factories and export companies had become ferocious,[140] and there was a noticeable decline in the quality of coffee being offered for export.[141] The early 1970s tussles over localisation of coffee buying and processing which absorbed governments and all government agencies, including the Coffee Marketing Board acted to undercut quality even further as more and more small coffee dealers scoured the Highlands for supplies.[142]

The Coffee Marketing Board in PNG also supervised the export quota arrangements required under the ICA. The CMB in concert with the colonial administration provided financial support to make possible a stock withholding program which became especially important during the 1971–72 marketing crisis.[143] With exports dominated by four firms,[144] overseeing the prices paid to growers by processors and merchant firms was a further important role of the CMB.

---

138   Notes of Interview with Bob Oatley, founder of ANGCO, dated 20/4/90. For a brief biography of Oatley and description of the operations of Angco, the most important exporting firm of the late colonial and early post-colonial periods, see Sinclair *The Money Tree* ch. 18. Downs *The Last Mountain* p. 264 also notes how produce from Kenya, Colombia and Costa Rica was established as the benchmark for PNG coffee, stating that: 'As a new and comparatively small producer, New Guinea would have to aim for the high quality market [which these countries' coffee represented: SM]'.
139   Sinclair *The Money Tree* p. 289
140   For the establishment and operation of another dry factory, associated with expatriate planting interests in the Western Highlands which folded under the competition, see Roger Southern '"Hagenkofi"—an episode of enterprise in the New Guinea Highland coffee industry' *Yagl-Ambu* 1974, vol. 1, pp. 39–53; Files of Ulya Plantation courtesy of Edith Watts.
141   CMBA: F/N 138 *Board Minutes 10/9/71–5/9/74; 22/6/72 Minutes of Board Meeting*—discussion with Highland Coffee Dealers' Association; *28/9/72 Minutes of Board Meeting*—discussion on quality control in response to reply from Highland Coffee Dealers' Association.
142   CMBA: F/N 138 10/9/71-5/9/74 *Board Minutes 6/12/73* Discussion of Proposed Changes to Coffee Marketing Board Ordinance at the direction of the Minister for Agriculture, Stock and Fisheries, Mr Iambakey Okuk.
143   Cartledge *A History of the Coffee Industry* ch. 30
144   For the number of exporters, and the per cent of total exports each handled in selected years from 1965/66 until 1990/91, see MacWilliam 'The Politics of Privatization' p. 484, Table 1. From the CMB's beginnings in 1964 until Independence in 1975, concentration of exports in the four main trading firms was invariably around 90 per cent of the total.

Price Support for Sales to Australia

In 1954, prices attained a postwar high, reaching US$0.80 per lb for washed Mams/Colombian mild Arabica, the yardstick for PNG exports. However from the late 1950s until early 1970, the price regularly fell below US$0.50 per lb and in 1963 fell to below 50 per cent of the postwar peak.[145] Because of rapidly increasing production at a rate well in excess of the growth in consumption, prices would have fallen even further had not governments in producing and consuming countries embarked upon important measures to halt a major decline, then place a floor under prices.

Two especially important changes occurred in 1958 which were to affect coffee prices for PNG growers. Attacks on US Vice-President Richard Nixon during an official visit to Venezuela were important for shifting the official US position on international commodity agreements. It was also the year during which the Australian Government and its colonial officials began to develop a policy for price support to PNG growers faced with falling prices. While the campaign for price support most prominently featured expatriate large holding owners and officials of their representative organisation, the Highlands Farmers' and Settlers' Association, once again it was Administration officials and colonial government officers based in Canberra who were most important in shaping the response.[146] Their action was driven first and foremost by the policy of uniform development, for which the increasing significance of smallholder coffee growers was critical.

Preferred access to the Australian market was seen as integral to development in the colony. Further it would not be 'tape recordings of the anguished squeals of Territory planters' which would decide the extent of Australian support but 'the efficiency of Territory industries'.[147] Well aware that efficiency would be assessed through a process involving the Department of Trade, as well as the Tariff Board and Treasury, which might tend to scrutinise applications for assistance by formal economic criteria, Hasluck was effectively shifting the ground so that any claim for support would be biased towards smallholder production whose efficiency was not so easily ascertained.

While the 1958 Goroka coffee conference was not attended by either Hasluck or some of the main Australia-based manufacturers, the seriousness of the situation

---

145 Cartledge *A History of the Coffee Industry* p. 324, app. 30

146 Hasluck *A Time for Building* p. 295, citing a 15 April 1958 Minute responding to a memorandum from the Administrator in Port Moresby.

147 The 'anguished squeals' expression is Hasluck's, taken from his 15 April Minute. In November 1957 a delegation from the HFSA had visited Canberra regarding the looming difficulties of marketing PNG coffee, at this time still primarily from large holdings. Subsequent to this meeting, Minister Hasluck announced 'that the marketing of all PNG primary products was "under review"' (Sinclair *The Money Tree* p. 232). Similar appeals had come from large holding cocoa producers, which resulted in the April 1958 Cocoa Conference in Rabaul. See also Cartledge *A History of the Coffee Industry* p. 29

was given extended consideration by a large gathering. At the conference, the difficulties, as well as the proposed solution, were primarily couched in terms of selling PNG's output of mainly plantation-produced coffee in the Australian market.[148] During 1959, as the international problem of excess coffee beyond demand deepened the Department of Territories was directed by the Minister to facilitate further talks between growers and coffee buyers in Australia.

The Administration and the Department of Territories conducted research into the availability of markets overseas, and the Australian Trade Commissioner Service plus other Australian agencies were asked for assistance in the international search. A Commonwealth Bureau of Agricultural Economics survey was proposed, while it was recognised that little suitable information would be available on smallholder production. The Survey, conducted in 1960 and reported in 1961, was therefore primarily concerned with large holding production and extremely limited in scope given how few plantations had either substantial numbers of bearing bushes or adequate records of operations.[149]

The Survey readily took up what was to become the official Administration and Australian Government position which emphasised the significance of coffee for indigenous advance,[150] and led to a reference to the Tariff Board emphasising the need to assist PNG growers. The terms of reference emphasised the developmental objective of the request, citing 'the Commonwealth's responsibility for the Territory of Papua and New Guinea' as the primary matter to be considered in deliberations about a request for renewed protection.[151]

While the Tariff Board deliberated, in August 1961 the Coalition Government announced a temporary by-law arrangement which was designed to encourage manufacturers to source green bean from PNG rather than from other producing countries, including East Africa. The by-law remitted duty to importers of raw and kiln-dried coffee from the latter if 28 per cent of their requirements were sourced from PNG.

---

148 ToPNG *Report of the Coffee Conference held in Goroka from 19th to 22nd January 1959* (Port Moresby: Unpublished paper, February 1959); Cartledge *A History of the Coffee Industry* pp. 28–32; Sinclair *The Money Tree* p. 233

149 Cartledge *A History of the Coffee Industry* p. 46; Bureau of Agricultural Economics *The Coffee Industry in Papua New Guinea* (Canberra: Government Printer, 1961) Summary

150 Bureau of Agricultural Economics *The Coffee Industry* p. 10

151 As Sinclair *The Money Tree* p. 237 notes, there were important personal ties between senior Administration personnel and top officials in the Department of Trade. Bill Conroy, chief of the Division of Extension and Marketing in DASF had been a student of John Crawford, formerly lecturer in economics at the University of Sydney and head of the Department of Trade when the request was made for a Tariff Board Report. Conroy had another important contact in the Department, whom he persuaded to visit PNG and see the difficulties of 'buying this native coffee'. Conroy became one of three colonial officials to give evidence before the Tariff Board.

The 1962 Tariff Board Report made clear that it also took the developmental role seriously.[152] In the Board's summary of the arguments advanced for 'increased protection', two of the eight emphasised the importance for economic development of coffee growing 'in certain areas'. Argument five repeated the line which also was stressed in ICA negotiations being conducted almost simultaneously (see below).[153]

> Economic development is lagging behind political, social and administrative advancement in the Highland areas of New Guinea. If coffee production can be put on a reasonably sound basis, this imbalance in development can be overcome.[154]

The Report's conclusion left no doubt as to which directions the Board's recommendations would take, drawing particular attention to the Trusteeship clauses of the UN Charter which:

> commit Australia … to the "political, economic, social and educational advancement" of the inhabitants of Papua and New Guinea. The ultimate aim of such advancement is the independence and self-government of the Territory.

> The full contribution of any one activity, such as coffee growing, towards "advancement" cannot be exactly measured because this advancement has many intangible elements. The Board considers, however, that the coffee industry materially aids advancement. It augments the Territory's export earnings, provides employment for its inhabitants, and, with the capital it attracts, stimulates the development of many native communities.[155]

At a time when indigenous smallholder production still lagged behind that of large holdings, it is unsurprising that the Report did not place more emphasis

---

152   CoA *Tariff Revision: Tariff Board's Report on Coffee* (Canberra: Government Printer, 27th April 1962). Subsequent accounts of the Board, written by insiders and academics alike, have entirely missed the significance of either the 1962 or subsequent 1966 Inquiries into PNG coffee production and marketing. The developmental underpinnings of Board deliberations and decisions either for Australia or PNG do not figure in these accounts. See: Leon Glezer *Tariff Politics Australian Policy-Making 1960–1980* (Melbourne University Press, 1982); Alf Rattigan *Industry Assistance the Inside story* (Melbourne University Press, 1986); Kym Anderson and Ross Garnaut *Australian Protectionism Extent, Causes and Effects* (Sydney: Allen and Unwin, 1987) esp. chs 2–4. Perhaps surprisingly given Garnaut's long association with PNG as a government adviser, in a section headed 'Australia's trade with developing countries' (pp. 17–27) *Australian Protectionism* does not mention either Tariff Board hearing or the Reports. Nor does the subject appear in Chapter Four on 'Protection to the 1970s'.
153   See also the Commonwealth's Submission to the July 1962 United Nations Coffee Conference which stressed the relationship between encouraging the indigenous growing of coffee to the terms of the UN Trusteeship Agreement. Cartledge *A History of the Coffee Industry* p. 291
154   CoA *Tariff Revision* p. 5
155   CoA *Tariff Revision* p. 13

upon household output of coffee. Nevertheless the Report noted that coffee was not only a significant cash crop for smallholding growers, but also important in extending the consumption of purchased goods (see Chapter Six).

To the global support given to coffee prices worldwide by the 1962–63 ICA, the Commonwealth Tariff Board recommended continuing duty free access to Australia. The Board also recommended retaining the by-law conditionality for importers sourcing coffee from other countries, which provided for the remission of import duty to any importer who sourced 25 per cent or more (but less than 30 per cent) of total requirements from PNG. Sourcing 30 per cent or more of coffee from PNG would be rewarded with a remission of five pence per lb, or the entire amount dutiable on green bean from other countries. The Board also recommended increased duties on roasted coffee, thus encouraging greater import of green bean by roasters operating in Australia.[156]

In rejecting a bounty scheme for PNG coffee exported to Australia, the Tariff Board drew attention to the difficulty of administering such an arrangement in the absence of any marketing authority in the colony. (The former Secretary of the Department of Trade [Sir] John Crawford had earlier provided his opinion on the need for a marketing board to the HFSA.)[157] While the Tariff Board's recommendation that a marketing board might be established with a sole-seller role was not taken up, over the next year discussions took place in Australia and PNG about the formation of such a body (see above).[158]

The 1962 Tariff Board Report suggested that the operation of its recommendations should be reviewed in two years, so in November 1964 this was done, under identical terms as had been used for the 1961 reference and subsequent Report. With an ICA in place holding up prices internationally there was reduced opposition to the measures adopted in 1962. The Tariff Board concluded that over the period since the 1961 examination had been conducted, the coffee industry had become of even greater importance in helping the Commonwealth meet its trusteeship obligations for PNG. In particular, the Board noted that in addition to the employment and self-employment role for indigenes on large holdings and their own smallholdings, coffee had an even wider effect.

> The industry has also made a profound social and economic impact on numerous highland communities, by introducing cash cropping to many primitive groups and by serving as a medium for extension of the Administration's influence.[159]

156   CoA *Tariff Revision* p. 15
157   Cartledge *A History of the Coffee Industry* p. 72
158   Cartledge *A History of the Coffee Industry* chs 10, 11
159   CoA *Revision Tariff Board's Report on Coffee* (Canberra: Commonwealth Government Printer, 15th July 1966)

The positive effects of the present tariff arrangement, according to the Tariff Board, were to increase the proportion of PNG coffee consumed in Australia, and influence (ie raise) the prices paid for exports to Australia. Accordingly the Board recommended only a minor change in duty payable as well as a change which would simplify and expedite payment, and speed of receiving refunds. The change in duty brought down to 30 per cent the total coffee imported from PNG by any firm before it received a full remission of duty on coffee from other countries.

Although total exports of PNG green bean to Australia continued to increase over the next decade at the same time the proportion exported to the metropolitan country declined. The price benefit of Australian tariffs became less and less important while by comparison the importance of prices obtained on exports under the ICA agreement countries increased.

In addition to the support given to PNG growers for exports to the Australian market, the metropolitan government and colonial administration also joined the international drive for price support. PNG producers benefited from the prices which flowed from action taken at an international level and for imports into Australia, without suffering the most important of the production constraints forced upon growers in other countries. Smallholder growers in particular were sheltered by the actions of colonial officials which made continuous expansion of household plantings and output increases more likely.

The International Coffee Agreements

The first ICA[160] was reached in 1962–63, then renegotiated in 1967/68 with further measures taken to deal with the surplus stocks crisis of 1971/72.[161] During the initial negotiations, the renegotiations and surrounding circumstances Australian government and colonial officials as representatives of the coffee industry in PNG constantly constructed their role as trustees, acting on behalf of the majority of growers who were smallholders.[162]

Under the ICA, price support occurred through the provision of official and unofficial subsidies, in the forms of development aid and higher prices paid by consumers in the industrial countries. The higher prices were secured from 1964 until 1972 through an export quota arrangement specified under the ICA, and overseen by the ICO, whose operations were in turn closely watched

160 The following description is a necessarily abbreviated version of a more detailed account. See my forthcoming 'The International Coffee Organisation: Cartel or Development Agency?'.

161 Cartledge *A History of the Coffee Industry* chs 18–29 provides the most substantial account of this period from the perspective of a colonial official who considered himself as acting on behalf of PNG.

162 Cf. Stewart *Coffee* ch. 13 where the ICA is given a central role in the 'underdevelopment' of the PNG coffee industry.

by exporting and importing member countries. The principal purpose of the subsidies to coffee prices, for governments in both producing and consuming countries, was to promote economic and political development when there was general concern about political instability and impoverishment. The particular, specific concern was that either or both of the last conditions would provide favourable circumstances for the advance of socialism, specifically of the Soviet Union-backed variety of 'Communism'.[163] In addition to the internationally constructed means of lifting prices, further efforts were also taken by governments in producing countries, as with the tariff subsidies for PNG coffee exported to Australia just discussed.[164]

As had been the case for several hundred years, coffee consumption after World War II remained primarily centred in the industrial countries, although in a small number of producing countries, including Brazil, coffee drinking absorbed a substantial proportion of the local crop.[165] This condition, where production and consumption took place in distinct countries and regions of the world, increased the volatility of the global coffee market by making it harder to construct political conditions for matching supply with demand. Climatic conditions, especially frosts and droughts in the main growing regions of the world's largest producer, Brazil, also regularly exacerbate supply and price movements. Most importantly, the twentieth century predominance of smallholder production and the limited desire as well as capacity of governments in producing countries to check further plantings and thus control output introduced an additional, new element of instability into the international coffee market, as well as the global political economy.[166]

Re-opening of European and other markets after World War II boosted global demand, while at the same time colonial as well as other governments embraced expanded coffee production, mainly by smallholders, as an important component of postwar development objectives. Two severe frosts during 1953 and 1955 in Brazil, then producing at least 80 per cent of total world supply, plus an increased demand while new plantings came into production resulted in

---

163   For the regular use of the capitalised expression during the period, see Richard M Nixon *Six Crises* (London: WH Allen, 1962) pp. 183–234.

164   One version of these efforts is provided by Robert Bates *Open-Economy Politics: The Political Economy of the World Coffee Trade* (Princeton University Press, 1997).

165   As Mauricio A Font stresses, coffee production and consumption also was important in the political economy of Brazil's industrialisation. *Coffee, Contention and Change in the Making of Modern Brazil* (Cambridge, Mass.: Basil Blackwell, 1990)

166   By way of illustrating the difficulties of reducing total coffee output when smallholder production predominates, Mark Pendergrast *Uncommon Grounds: The History of Coffee and How It Transformed Our World* (New York: Basic Books, 1999) pp. 275–276 cites a British coffee exporter writing from Kenya in 1960: 'To millions in this Continent [ie. Africa: SM], coffee means the difference between too little to eat or enough .... To any smallholder having three acres ... it would take a great deal of filtered economics, plus a gun, to begin to persuade him to cut production'.

the price boom which as shown in Chapter Four was so important in stimulating coffee growing in the Central Highlands of PNG. However by the late 1950s, oversupply once again dominated global markets.

The price fall was especially significant for policy makers in the USA, by far the largest market for coffee.[167] Falls in coffee prices, which were central to the living standards of millions in Latin America limited the capacity of people in the region to consume US goods.[168] This in turn increased pressure for local manufacturing industries to be supported, along the lines of ideas promoted by the Economic Commission for Latin America, in particular Argentinian economist Raúl Prebisch.[169] Out of the US recognition of the developmental role of coffee came the policy shift toward Latin America and commodity agreements noted above.

In 1961 the Kennedy Administration publicly reversed the previous government's opposition to international commodity agreements, with the result that years of producer efforts to regulate exports were suddenly supplanted.[170] In 1962, predicted coffee surpluses over the next five years were expected to drive prices to the lowest point since the late 1940s. By September of that year, 54 exporting and consuming countries signed the ICA, to come into effect on 1 October 1963 and last for five years.

Between 1963 and 1972, the 'principle effect of the Agreement was to raise and stabilize prices',[171] ie prices were generally steadier at a higher price, which also made it possible for producing countries to further expand output even as stocks continued to increase. While there remain arguments about the wisdom of such commodity agreements, assessments closer to events have concluded

167   In addition to the ICO *History of Recent International Coffee Agreements*, the following section draws heavily upon Nixon *Six Crises* esp. ch. 4 'Caracas'; SK Krasner *The Politics of Primary Commodities: A Study of Coffee 1900–1970* PhD thesis Harvard University (1971); Bart Fisher *The International Coffee Agreements: A Study in Coffee Diplomacy* (New York: Praeger, 1972); World Coffee Information Center (WCIC) *Thirty-Four Years of US Coffee History* (Washington, D.C.: Samuel E Stavisky and Associates, 21 April 1974); Jos de Vries *International Commodity Agreements: A Losing Proposition* Unpublished Paper, November 1979, Annex 1 'The History of International Action in Individual Commodity Markets' pp. 3–6 'Coffee'; Stephen G Rabe *Eisenhower and Latin America: The Foreign Policy of Anticommunism* (Chapel Hill: The University of North Carolina Press, 1988).
168   WCIC *Thirty-Four Years* pp. 26–27; Pan-American Coffee Bureau *Impact of Coffee on the U.S. Economy* (New York: Pan-American Coffee Bureau, c.1963); WCIC *Economic Impact of Coffee: How the International Coffee Agreement contributes to the progress of developing countries and the United States* (Washington, D.C.: Pan-American Coffee Bureau, c.1968)
169   Rabe *Eisenhower and Latin America* pp. 74–75
170   ICO *History of Recent International Coffee Agreements* pp. 6–38; WCIC *Thirty-Four Years* pp. 14–18
171   Stephen D Krasner 'Business Government Relations: The Case of the International Coffee Agreement' *International Organization* September 1973, vol. 27, Issue 4, p. 501. Subsequently, from the late 1970s and in different global conditions, the effect of the ICA and other commodity agreements have been subject to a plethora of examinations. See de Vries *International Commodity Agreements*; Takamasa Akiyama and Ronald C Duncan *Analysis of the World Coffee Market* (Washington: World Bank, 1984); United Nations Conference on Trade and Development *Studies in the processing, marketing and distribution of commodities: The processing and marketing of coffee: Areas for international co-operation* (New York: United Nations, 1984); Bates *Open–Economy Politics*.

that not only did the ICA dampen price variability, it prevented a major price fall and in so doing benefited producing countries and coffee producers. In more specific terms, the US Government also saw economic pay-offs as a device for securing Latin American diplomatic support, particularly for action against Cuba.[172]

During the late 1950s and early 1960s the Australian Government too had concerns about prices for coffee prevailing on international markets, noted above. One long-term consequence of the marketing shortfall was to push the most adventurous trading firms, including Colyer Watson that held a pre-eminent position among exporters,[173] to search for long-term international markets for PNG coffee. By the mid-1960s more than half of PNG exports went to northern hemisphere markets, and the proportion of coffee marketed in Australia had begun a permanent decline.[174] International price support became proportionally more important than Australian subsidies.

While PNG was still a very small exporter, there was concern in the colony and in Canberra about the possible implications of an ICA.[175] With the fear that an ICA could limit further, particularly smallholder, increases Australian officials became heavily involved in ICA negotiations. The constantly repeated theme of the involvement was that PNG was an exceptional case of not just 'a developing country' but a UN Trust Territory. In particular, with limits already in place on further expatriate land alienation, assistance to the industry was vital when 'coffee is the only proven economic crop available for development activity on any worthwhile scale' in 'the isolated highlands'.[176]

The Australian negotiators ultimately succeeded in having PNG exports given favourable treatment under the first ICA. The delegation obtained US support for a position which became known as netting. Under this formula, Australian consumption and PNG production were to be calculated together, with PNG exports only being subject to quota once they exceeded Australian imports. Because of the limited Australian market for the type of coffee produced in PNG, the formula would permit exports to other countries while Australia continued

---

172   Krasner 'Business Government Relations' p. 502. The connection between economic and political development was, of course, a broader concern of US government officials, academic advisers and others due to events in Europe and Asia, especially Vietnam. See SP Huntington 'Political Order and Political Decay' *World Politics* 1965, vol. 17, no. 3, pp. 386–430; Huntington *Political Order in Changing Societies* (New Haven: Yale University Press, 1968); Robert A Packenham 'Political–Development Doctrines in the American Foreign Aid Program' *World Politics* January 1966, vol. 18, no. 2, pp. 194–235

173   Sinclair *The Money Tree* ch. 18; Interview Bob Oatley 20/4/90

174   Cartledge *A History of the Coffee Industry* p. 318, app. 25. The shift away from Australia as the principal market for PNG coffee was unanticipated just five years earlier when the Commonwealth Bureau of Agricultural Economics claimed: 'For several reasons the Australian market appears likely to continue as the principal outlet' (*The Coffee Industry in Papua New Guinea* p. 107).

175   Cartledge *A History of the Coffee Industry* p. 86

176   Cartledge *A History of the Coffee Industry* p. 88

to import Robusta and Arabica coffee from other sources. The ICA was ratified in late 1963, with Australia and PNG joining the ICA as a single importing member.

While the quota system had at its centre commitments by members to restrict further increases in production, it was easily concluded by Australian officials that 'this was most difficult under local conditions'.[177] Thus commitments made under this provision of the ICA, however well intended, could never be applied, especially to the continuing smallholder expansion described above. Banning any further leasing of large holding land was easier to effect, with the result that there was continued criticism within the colony, particularly from expatriate planters of the ICA and the Administration's acceptance of its terms. [178]

For PNG growers, especially smallholders, the best subsequent assessments suggest that the ICA prevented further substantial falls in prices throughout the 1960s.[179] As was also demonstrated in the early 1970s overproduction crisis, quantities sold and prices obtained in non-member markets (Annex B countries under the terms of the ICA) were 'meagre and unprofitable'.[180]

Perhaps the best test of the consequences of the ICA, at least for the rest of the colonial period, was the continuing increase in PNG exports to consuming member countries other than Australia.[181] In each case, these were primarily ICA member country (Annex A) markets. By 1965/66, total exports were not only almost double what they had been during the earlier ICA negotiations, more coffee was sold to other countries than to Australia. By 1969/70 exports to the USA alone were greater than to Australia.[182]

However even as the proportion of PNG coffee sold to Australian manufacturers declined, the volume grew as the metropolitan market increased in size. Exports from the colony to Australia almost doubled between 1963 and 1968, as exports

---

177   Cartledge *A History of the Coffee Industry* p. 100

178   Sinclair *The Money Tree* pp. 240–241 details the opposition from planters to the ban on new acreages being leased for plantations, while the Administration claimed it could do little more than reduce further extension work 'designed to increase village coffee growing'.

179   Cf. Ian Downs' 1994 statement in Sinclair *The Money Tree* p. 240, regarding the outcome which was 'to cut a long story short, we won in the beginning, and we went on winning' with the more cautious but nevertheless similar assessment made by officials in Australia and PNG when ratification of the terms of the 1962–63 ICA was being considered in Cartledge *A History of the Coffee Industry* pp. 107–110, and Stewart *Coffee* chs 11–13. Cartledge also reports (p. 189), that during discussions regarding ratification of the 1968 ICA, official calculations in Australia and PNG were that the ICA had produced price levels 20–30 per cent higher than they would have been without an ICA.

180   Cartledge *A History of the Coffee Industry* p. 108. The principal Annex B importing countries were Japan, Poland, USSR and South Africa.

181   Sinclair *The Money Tree* ch. 18, Downs *The Last Mountain* ch. 16

182   Cartledge *A History of the Coffee Industry* p. 318, app. 25

to the USA exploded, from 20 tons to 5,000 tons.[183] The enlarged volume sold to Australia was secured partly as an effect of the price advantage given to PNG coffee under reformed tariff arrangements (discussed above).

However the 1968 ICA extension provided no major improvement in PNG's quota position, despite the continuing growth in production. Nevertheless despite the original misgivings Australia eventually ratified the extension to the ICA as an importer with its position extended to PNG. PNG was to be allowed to export up to the amount of total Australian imports, even as these increased. That is, unlike countries where there were to be actual reductions in production, breathing space was retained for PNG to continue increases, albeit under even greater international scrutiny. It was anticipated that the crunch would come in 1972 or 1973, when PNG exports would surpass Australian imports. Once again, as with the initial joining of the ICO, the official assessment was that PNG would benefit by Australia's membership.[184] Nevertheless a major crisis did envelope the coffee industry from late 1971 into 1972.

Conclusion

During the 1960s there was an important change in the overarching development policy for PNG. A faster pace of economic growth was encouraged with the exploration and proving process for a massive copper and gold mine at the forefront of means by which development would occur. Encouragement was given to large holding owners, especially indigenes who produced copra and cocoa to further increase production. Overall the rate of economic growth became substantial.

However two main features of the changes relied upon the effectiveness of the earlier uniform or even development policy phase. Firstly, what had occurred by way of improvements in health and household production for immediate consumption from the late 1940s onward provided a substantial platform for accelerated development. Secondly, even as accelerated development became the central policy position, the colonial administration continued to provide support in key areas along the lines required by uniform development. Household producers expanded production of the crops which had been at the centre of the earlier policy position, including coffee and cocoa discussed here. As the next chapter shows, the domestically marketed production of other crops also continued to increase, to such an extent that from the 1950s there was a major growth in local markets as well as in the consumption of imported food including rice.

---

183   Cartledge *A History of the Coffee Industry* p. 318, app. 25
184   Cartledge *A History of the Coffee Industry* p. 193

However by the end of the 1960s and into the self-government period prior to Independence in 1975, there were signs that the scheme of smallholder production had begun to reach important limits, including of land. As well, growth began to produce its inevitable corollaries of unemployment and disorder in urban and rural areas. With a major change in ideas about development affecting domestic politics and public policy, the transition to self-government and then Independence was fraught with uncertainty about what should occur. Development policy became a contested terrain, at the centre of which was the opposition between households in occupation of smallholdings, producing for immediate consumption as well as markets, and the ambitions of the indigenous capitalist class to extend its reach. The next chapter considers the main features of a period when all the contestants wanted development, even if they were divided on what it might mean.

6. Uncertain Development and Independence

Introduction

Once it was settled in the mid to late 1960s that self-government and then Independence would occur within a decade, uncertainty reigned in PNG. The condition extended from electoral politics to the composition of the first indigenous government formed at the 1972 elections and to the structure of the new nation-state as outlined in the yet-to-be finalised constitution. While these and related matters, including the extent of the Australian commitment to provide financial and other support captured most attention, a more important struggle was taking place among indigenes. Screened by the emotional power of nationalism, primarily now indigenous but continuing to be bolstered by expatriate anti-colonialism, the division between indigenous capital and households was becoming increasingly important for the country's future political economy.

The indigenous attachment to development as an idea and objective of state policy remained powerful, even as there was uncertainty about what forms this would take and how development could be made to happen. The first section of this chapter notes the continuing power of the idea, and details how domestic conditions challenged attempts by the first indigenous coalition government led by Michael Somare to shape development policy.

These local circumstances made the task of shaping policy to bring development difficult. The differences between the late colonial policy heritage and newly prominent internationally fashionable ideas added to the uncertainty. The second section details the contest which took place prior to Independence over the direction of development policy, including the tussles among leading PNG politicians.

The third and final section of this chapter discusses how underneath the apparent uncertainty over development policy a major struggle was taking place which affected the legal and political shape of the future nation-state. As the colonial authority was being removed, state power was defined in terms which strengthened the hold of the indigenous bourgeois and would-be bourgeois. An especially important feature of the structure of the National Constitution became how it presented increased opportunities for members of the class to press claims for preferential treatment. The establishment of provincial governments provides a telling instance of how separatist and secessionist demands pushed to the limits of representative politics opened space at the centre of independence constitutional arrangements. The case of Bougainville and the coupling of an aggressive separatist politics with commercial ambitions is examined here to illustrate the argument.

The Continuing Attraction of Development

A commitment to intentional development and the agrarian focus of thought about development passed easily from the Australian authorities to the Papua New Guineans who gained power during the late 1960s and early 1970s. Speaking in the House of Assembly on 3 March 1969, two of the most important indigenous politicians signalled the importance of 'bringing development' as the appropriate objective for a representative holding state power. Moving a condolence motion on the death of Kaura Duba, newly elected Member for the Jimi Open Electorate, Tei Abal, Ministerial Member for Agriculture, Stock and Fisheries, said:

> He wanted to develop his own electorate and he also worked for national development....

Opposition party leader Somare, Member for East Sepik Regional, reiterated Abal's description in seconding the motion:

> He was the elected representative of his people; he came here both to bring development to this country and to his people ....[1]

Further, for indigenous representatives as well as for colonial officials and expatriate advisers, the preferred direction of development efforts remained the rural areas, as the primary base for the productive endeavours of the majority of the people as well as the most desirable means for dealing with rising unemployment and disorder.

Urban Growth and Impoverishment

The urban dimension to the problems facing policy makers, especially the newly empowered politicians, was sharpened as for the first time these areas too contained greater numbers of indigenes, with impoverishment apparent in major towns. In August 1969 a motion was passed in the House of Assembly:

---

1 See PNG *House of Assembly Debates* Second House vol. 2, nos 4–5, 3 March to 27 June 1969, p. 825, for both statements.

indicating that a majority of its members saw urbanisation as a threat to village life and as a cause of unemployment, and requested the Administration to reintroduce restrictions on movements to towns except where employment was assured or for short visits.[2]

In October 1970, when visiting Washington DC, Pangu Pati leader and MHA Somare compared children at play in slum conditions in the US capital with those 'to be seen at home in the slums that have started to grow on the periphery of our larger towns'. In his autobiography, PNG's first prime minister asked rhetorically:

> Will we at home have to go through the same experience [as evidenced by impoverishment in US cities: SM]? I hoped that we would be able to get rid of our slums and help our people live better.[3]

The Prime Minister's concern continued. In September 1975 shortly after Independence, PM Somare visited China to explore the possibilities of diversifying foreign aid sources away from Australia, and finding ways to reverse the increasing drift of the population from the countryside to towns.[4] Somare's visit had been preceded in January 1975 by Sir Albert Maori Kiki, Deputy PM and Minister for Foreign Affairs and Trade who went to China with the announced aims of promoting PNG, looking for a market for coffee and cocoa, and 'to study Chinese programs especially in village development and small-scale industries'.[5]

During the 1940s and 1950s colonial officials shaped development policy for PNG *in anticipation of as well as with* the initial signs that increases in urban populations and wage employment could also lead to the related effects of unemployment, impoverishment and disorder.[6] However indigenous policy makers were not concerned about a possible future condition but having to deal immediately with the effects of a major change which had begun in the mid-1960s, concomitant with rapid economic growth. Population increases in the most important centres were especially striking, and changed completely the character of the main towns. They had previously been primarily expatriate enclaves, with the indigenous presence confined to the perimeters in peri-urban settlements, except during daylight working hours. Between the first census

---

2   Marion Ward 'Urbanisation—Threat or Promise?' *New Guinea* 1970, vol. 5, no. 1, pp. 57–62. Reprinted in Ron May (ed.) *Change and Movement: Readings on Internal Migration in Papua New Guinea* (Canberra: PNG Institute of Applied Social and Economic Research in association with ANU Press, 1977) pp. 52–57. Ward's thesis, that 'urbanisation should be regarded far more positively than appears to be the case in Papua New Guinea at present' was exceptional in the circumstances. See also JD Conroy 'Urbanisation in Papua New Guinea: A Development Constraint' in May (ed.) *Change and Movement* pp. 59–70.

3   Somare *Sana* p. 82

4   Ralph Premdas 'Papua New Guinea in 1976: Dangers of a China Connection' *Asian Survey* January 1977, vol. 17, no. 1, pp. 55–60

5   James Griffin 'Papua New Guinea' *Australian Journal of Politics and History* 1975, vol. 21, no. 3, p. 129

6   See NAA: A452/1 1963/8164 *Native Unemployment in Urban Areas in Papua and New Guinea 1958–1967*

in 1966 and second in 1971, there was a rapid indigenisation of most urban residential areas, with a population increase probably in the order of 17 per cent per annum, compound. The outcome was that towns now held about ten per cent of the total indigenous population, with growth exceeding that in other areas of the country.[7]

As a consequence of the overall movement to urban centres, the main political-administrative town, soon-to-be national capital contained a reduced proportion of the country's total urban population. Nevertheless, between 1966 and 1971 Port Moresby's indigenous population almost doubled to 60,000. Lae, the main manufacturing centre with 32,000 indigenes resident, was the second largest town.[8] This rapid growth in urban populations, without substantial improvements in the availability of housing and urban services was linked initially with a major expansion of various forms of wage employment.

Between 1962 and 1964 there had been a 40 per cent increase in indigenous workers in public administration, and growth continued at a rapid rate into the 1970s. Later, especially after the beginning of construction work at Bougainville, private employment also expanded sharply. That work, primarily in urban jobs associated with tourism, commerce and manufacturing, as well as mining and construction, involved fewer employment agreements. Unlike the earlier widespread use of formal agreements for many plantation workers, throughout the 1960s private employment was increasingly accompanied by casualisation. By the early 1970s, a substantial majority of workers outside the public administration had little employment security.[9] A downturn in the rate of growth of wage employment of the early 1970s coincided with weak commodity prices for farm crops, which in turn 'reduced rural incomes and demand for urban goods and services'.[10] Urban unemployment increased, although more sharply for work-age males than females, and especially in Port Moresby.[11] National politicians were concerned about this change.

---

7   Ross Garnaut 'Urban Growth: An Interpretation of Trends and Choices' in May (ed.) *Change and Movement* p. 74. See also Ross Garnaut, Michael Wright and Richard Curtain *Employment, Incomes and Migration in Papua New Guinea Towns* Monograph no. 6 (Boroko: IASER, 1977) pp. 3–5, including qualifications regarding the data.

8   Garnaut 'Urban Growth' pp. 75–79

9   Garnaut 'Urban Growth' pp. 72–74. Contra the concerns of national politicians for the effects of urbanisation, Garnaut (p. 72) describes the 'marked decline in the relative importance of formal employment agreements' and the increase in casual employment as indicating 'growing self-confidence and mobility in the workforce' which 'paved the way for the migration of family groups, which became increasingly important through the 1960s'.

10   Garnaut 'Urban Growth' p. 87

11   Garnaut 'Urban Growth' pp. 75–81. Garnaut also argues (p. 72), against criticism of the first years of the Michael Somare-led government, that between mid-1971 and 1977 there was no increase in the proportion of men in Port Moresby who did not have wage or salaried employment: see also Ross Garnaut 'The Neo-Marxist Paradigm in Papua New Guinea' in RJ May (ed.) *Social Stratification in Papua New Guinea* Working Paper no. 5 (Canberra: Department of Political and Social Change, RSPAS, ANU, August 1984) pp. 63–81. However

Although the bulk of the urban population increases had occurred through people from peri-urban settlements and proximate rural areas moving into the towns, substantial migration from the heavily populated Highlands also began to make a significant contribution to urban populations. While in 1971 a majority of the indigenous population in towns were migrants, and the proportion of migrants born nearby remained greatest, an important change was underway. In Port Moresby, Lae, Madang and Wewak 'the most notable development in the origins of migrants to these towns was the greatly increased flow from the highlands provinces'.[12] By 1972, one estimate suggested that for a Port Moresby population of around 75,000, there were approximately 10,000 migrants, or just under ten per cent, from the Highlands.[13] As the proportion of coastal (i.e. not including the Southern Highlands) Papuans in the main highlands towns of Goroka and Mt Hagen fell, Highlanders also began to migrate in substantial numbers to urban centres outside the region. A key component of uniform development, keeping smallholders on land in the Highlands to grow coffee and other crops, had begun to unravel. Out-migration was one consequence.

Rural Tensions

To make matters more difficult for the incoming indigenous government, rising unemployment and underemployment was also occurring in the rural areas. Squatting continued on Gazelle plantations,[14] and separatist even secessionist demands were being pressed in Bougainville and among Papuans.[15] There was a major re-appearance of 'tribal fighting' in the Highlands. On the smallholdings where coffee was grown, a substantial generation gap was beginning to emerge, with most growers older, less well educated, dependent on extension services. The next generation was being squeezed off the land.[16]

Coffee from the Highlands had become the country's most important agricultural export. Fighting threatened both smallholder production, which yielded around 70 per cent of the national output with up to 80 per cent of households growing the crop, and plantations. The Committee set up in 1973 by the first

between 1971 and 73/74, at least, the proportion of all people in wage employment fell, as more and more women and children moved into Port Moresby, Lae, Rabaul, Madang and urban centres on Bougainville. See Garnaut, Wright & Curtain *Employment, Incomes and Migration* pp. 23–25

12   Garnaut 'Urban Growth' p. 81

13   See James Griffin 'Movements for Separation and Secession' in A Clunies Ross and J Langmore (eds) *Alternative Strategies for Papua New Guinea* (Melbourne: Oxford University Press, 1973) p. 109. This was not a census year and the figure was supplied to Griffin by Councillor ND Oram.

14   Downs *The Australian Trusteeship* pp. 424–437 and pp. 510–525 details the continuing revolt on the Gazelle Peninsula.

15   James Griffin 'Movements for Separation' pp. 99–130; A Clunies Ross 'Secession without Tears' in Clunies Ross & Langmore (eds) *Alternative Strategies* pp. 131–138 provides some justification for as well as mechanisms appropriate for achieving secession. See Downs *The Australian Trusteeship* pp. 525–529 on Papua Besena.

16   David Anderson *An Economic Survey* p. 9

Somare Government rejected a mono-causal explanation for the increase in the scale and degree of violence associated with the fighting. Nevertheless it concluded that 'most of the fights are connected with disputes over land'. New cash crops had made land more valuable, and impending self-government had encouraged claimants of disputed land to try to obtain possession in the belief that 'possession at that date [that is, of self-government: SM] will be the basis of future legal ownership'.[17]

Opposition to self-government was especially powerful in the Highlands by comparison with other regions of the colony. There were increasing tussles among smallholders, as well as between these and the indigenous capitalist class over the large holdings being vacated by expatriate owner-occupiers and firms. During 1974 'the apparently rising incidence of unsavoury and openly hostile attitudes towards plantation owners and expatriate workers [was] prompting a number of owners to place their properties on the market' in the Western Highlands.[18] There was also concern among Highland leaders and university students from the region that a too-rapid departure of the colonial administration would result in coastal and island politicians dominating the national government. Hasluck's concern, noted in Chapter Three, that the country's government might pass into the hands of 'smart boys' and 'shrewd heads' from Port Moresby and Rabaul resonated in the pre-Independence jostling for power.[19]

The Downside of Commercialised Production and Consumption

Beneath the surface of urban and rural life, a further major change had taken place which heightened uncertainty. As was intended by colonial development policy, the increases in production of immediately consumed as well as locally and internationally marketed crops had become tied through commercialisation to changes in household consumption. As Shand and Straatmans note, during the 1960s 'virtually all growers [they interviewed in several areas, including

---

17   GoPNG *Report of the Committee Investigating Tribal Fighting in the Highlands* (Port Moresby: Government Printer, May 1973) pp. 2–5

18   MacWilliam 'Smallholder Production, the State and Land Tenure' in Peter Larmour (ed.) *Customary Land Tenure: Registration and Decentralisation in Papua New Guinea* (Boroko: IASER, 1992) pp. 25–26. These incidents were not, of course, confined to the Highlands: see more generally Jim Fingleton 'Policy-Making on Lands' p. 237, who notes that in 1974 a Division of District Administration list showed 'that around the country some sixty properties were illegally occupied, either totally or partly, and anther forty properties were threatened with occupation'.

19   Bill Standish 'Elite Communalism: The Highlands Liberation Front' in May (ed.) *Micronationalist movements in Papua New Guinea and Social Change* Monograph no. 1 (Canberra: Research School of Pacific Studies, ANU, 1982) pp. 359–392

where coffee and cocoa were produced: SM] indicated that a desire to purchase European goods had strongly influenced their decision to introduce cash crops'.[20]

But the change from consuming food and other items domestically produced to marketed produce went much deeper than adding imported items to some household needs. From the mid-1950s, coincident with the major increase in household production of coffee in the Highlands, markets were established in the main urban centres. During 1955, the Goroka market was created when coffee prices were at a postwar peak. Four years later, while prices for the crop declined, a similar situation arose in Mt Hagen as villagers harvested from their later plantings. Two reasons for the early establishment of official administration sanctioned markets in these centres may have been for health control and for the distribution of crop seeds by extension officers.[21] Nevertheless the markets in these and other locations also indicated an important change in the relationship between household production and consumption, with both increasingly commercialised. However, the shift was not only occurring through the growing of export crops.

By the early 1970s a trend away from once or twice a week to daily markets was accompanied by a major change in the commodities exchanged. To cite only the instance of the Mt Hagen market set in one of PNG's fastest growing districts with a high population density, demand was no longer dominated by Europeans but by indigenes resident in and near the town. The goods traded at this market had become, in Jackson's terms, 'dominated by basic foodstuffs'. With major retail stores the source of imported manufactured goods, markets sold agricultural produce from nearby as well as from other areas of PNG, especially the coast. Even within the area proximate to Mt Hagen, between 1967 and 1973 motor transport made it possible to increase the distance from which produce came from 11.3 kms to 17.5kms. For the Goroka market in 1973, approximately 85 per cent of the sellers travelled via motorised transportation.[22]

Of the change Jackson concludes:

> What started as a small weekly operation dominated by male sellers catering for mainly European demand has become a very big, almost daily event dominated by women selling their surpluses of basic foodstuffs to meet urban Melanesian demand.[23]

Two points arise from the description of the items sold as 'surpluses of basic foodstuffs', distinct from the possibility that such items were no longer 'basic' in

---

20   Shand & Straatmans *Transition from Subsistence* p. 138
21   Richard Jackson 'The Impact of the Introduction of Markets: A Case Study from the Highlands of Papua New Guinea' *Savanna* December 1976, vol. 5, no. 2, p. 175
22   Jackson 'The Impact of the Introduction of Markets' pp. 178–179
23   Jackson 'The Impact of the Introduction of Markets' p. 180

the consumption of the sellers' households. Taste preferences may have changed so that imported foods, tinned fish and rice to name just two possibilities, were now common in these households leaving space for 'surplus' domestically grown vegetables to be sold at the Mt Hagen market.

Firstly, the increased availability of local produce for sale and purchase in markets was a central aim of colonial development policy, as noted previously. Against the proposition that the official concern was solely or overly directed at increasing export, even plantation, crop production the growth of markets from the 1950s where 'surpluses' of 'basic foodstuffs' were bought and sold suggested a development success in another direction altogether. Where possible, households increased production of crops for domestic, marketed and non-marketed consumption *as well as* production of export crops.

Secondly, this apparent success needs to be qualified, as events soon after Independence were to show in the Highlands. Commercialised production and consumption does not necessarily always lead in a direction which 'preserves' either previous forms of household existence or result in continuous improvements in living standards. Households may become vulnerable to detrimental changes in terms of trade, including even on occasions when a short-term favourable shift occurs.

During 1975 a severe frost in Brazil, the main producing country, drove coffee prices sharply higher. With this windfall, producers, now predominantly smallholders sought to take maximum advantage of the advantageous price change. If possible, more cherry was picked from existing bushes and sold. An especially obvious effect of the upward shift in prices was the transformed consumption of purchased items. (In central Kenya, that country's major coffee-growing region, stone replaced previously used materials in house construction.) In the PNG Highlands, as well as purchasing motor vehicles, store-bought food, clothing and durable items for domestic use, indigenes—primarily but not solely younger males—dramatically increased their consumption of alcohol, mainly beer.[24]

One effect of the rapid increase in commercialised consumption was to reveal to what extent households had become reliant upon coffee and other incomes, while at the same time reducing the production of immediately consumed foods. Even if the area planted to permanent crops, including coffee did not substantially reduce the availability of suitable fertile land for growing immediately consumed vegetables and other crops, and food for pigs, the allocation of labour time was transformed. When household incomes rose dramatically, as during the coffee boom, increased leisure and alcohol consumption became an attractive

---

24   Mac Marshall (ed.) *Through a Glass Darkly: Beer and Modernization in Papua New Guinea* Monograph 18 (Boroko: IASER, 1982)

possibility. So too did reducing the effort involved in maintaining food gardens, with purchased food a preferred and available option. However once prices fell, as they did from 1977, living standards which had undergone a major upward shift were threatened. The decline had even greater immediate consequences where production for immediate household consumption, so-called subsistence production, had been 'radically undermined by the commercial economy'.[25]

Where permanent tree and bush crops now occupied substantial areas, including land previously employed for growing immediately consumed food, smallholders had a reduced capacity to absorb the effect of export price falls by increasing plantings of either export crops or gardens to meet immediate consumption needs. Increased commercialisation of food crops, evidenced by the late colonial spread of markets in which buying and selling of food dominated, did signal the possibility of rising living standards. However the increasing vulnerability of households to rapid fluctuations in export prices suggested another possibility, impoverishment across wide swathes of the countryside.

During the early 1970s, academics debated whether there was indeed unemployment, with some urging measures to encourage further expansion of smallholder agricultural production to reduce underemployment.[26] However important politicians had no doubt about the seriousness of conditions being faced in towns and rural areas by substantial numbers of indigenes. But indigenous politicians were not the only ones concerned with the rapidly developing inequalities among indigenes. Australian Minister for External Territories Andrew Peacock was also aware 'of the dangers of developing an unstable society with an unhealthy gap between impoverished peasants and a prosperous isolated elite'.[27] An urgent problem facing the colonial administration and then the self-government coalition was what policies were most suitable for a national government directing an independent nation-state.[28] Before Independence, three important reports provided advice on post-colonial development policy. The 1973 Faber report and the 1973 report of the *Commission of Inquiry into Land Matters,* followed in 1974 by the *Constitutional Planning Commission* report, pointed away from the colonial administration's favoured accelerated development policy.

---

25 Grossman *Peasants, Subsistence Ecology and Development* p. xvii. See also Larry Grossman 'Beer Drinking and Subsistence Production in a Highland Village' in Mac Marshall (ed.) *Through a Glass Darkly* pp. 59–72

26 For one summary of the positions taken regarding unemployment and underemployment, see Garnaut, Wright & Curtain *Employment, Incomes and Migration* pp. 7–13.

27 Downs *The Australian Trusteeship* p. 537. See the Minister's Opening address to the Sixth Waigani Seminar at UPNG, held from 30 April to 5 May, which begins with the sentence: 'Development will clearly be one of the main interests of the new government and the House of Assembly'. The address appears in May (ed.) *Priorities in Melanesian Development* pp. 3–6. See also Garnaut 'Problems of Inequality' pp. 52–62

28 Some indication of the intellectual ferment and uncertainty of the period can be gained from other papers presented to the 6th Waigani Seminar. See May (ed.) *Priorities in Melanesian Development*; Ivan Illich 'Design for a Convivial Society?' *New Guinea* 1972, vol. 7, no. 2, pp. 2–7; Oskar Spate 'Problems and Priorities: Summing up the Sixth Waigani' *New Guinea* 1972, vol. 7, no. 2, pp. 50–62

The Search for a New Direction

The Faber Report

In the turmoil and uncertainty of the early 1970s, during which the 1972 election produced an unexpected outcome with the victory of the Somare-led coalition government, the reaction against colonial authority and policies became particularly powerful. The strength of the reaction became obvious in June 1972 when one of the first acts of the newly formed Somare Government was to present a white paper, intended to provide the basis for a sequel to the 1968–73 five year plan *Programmes and Policies for the Economic Development of Papua and New Guinea*. Prepared by the Office of Programming and Coordination (OPC) within the Administration but introduced into the parliament by the new government, the proposed program supported a continuation of accelerated development policies. This direction was rejected by the parliament as unsuited to the economic and political circumstances.

These circumstances included alternate advice which had begun to flow to the incoming government from a number of international and domestic sources.[29] The rejection of the five year plan was couched in terms which showed the influence of ideas promulgated by an advisory group which from March to May 1972 had visited PNG. This group conducted a study arranged by the Australian Government through the World Bank as executive agent for the United Nations Development Program (UNDP). The Bank commissioned consultants from the University of East Anglia to provide advice on development strategies for the five years from 1973.[30] Over the next few months the group began to circulate their draft report, before its final submission in September to the World Bank and the Australian Government.[31]

---

29 John Ballard 'Policy-Making as Trauma: The Provincial Government Issue' in Ballard (ed.) *Policy-Making in a New State* pp. 95–132, notes (p. 131) how influential non-Australian consultants, including Canadians, were especially important 'in any kind of radical administrative reform' such as decentralisation (on which more below).

30 For one assessment of the members of the Overseas Development Group from East Anglia who conducted the study and the international shifts underway in thinking about development see Peter Fitzpatrick, who was a government adviser during the transition: 'The Making and Unmaking of the Eight Aims' in Peter King, Wendy Lee and Vincent Warakai (eds.) *From Rhetoric to Reality? Papua New Guinea's Eight Point Plan and National Goals After a Decade* (Waigani: UPNG, 1985) pp. 22–31. Other important documents charting the shift, listed by Fitzpatrick, include ILO *Employment, Incomes and Equality: A Strategy for Increasing Productive Employment in Kenya* (Geneva: International Labour Organisation, 1972) and H Chenery, MS Ahluwalia, CLG Bell, JH Duloy and R Jolly *Redistribution with Growth* (London: Oxford University Press, 1974). For a later account of the shifting ideas about development, see Martha Finnemore 'Redefining Development at the World Bank' in Frederick Cooper and Randall Packard (eds) *International Development and the Social Sciences: Essays on the History and Politics of Knowledge* (Berkley: University of California Press, 1997) pp. 203–227. See also Downs *The Australian Trusteeship* pp. 537–538.

31 Fitzpatrick 'The Eight Aims' p. 24, suggests that the administration-prepared plan was 'an effort to outflank Faberism which offered lots of principles and lots of choices but, in the end, there remained one

Although not finally published until February 1973, the Faber Report was highly influential well before publication.[32] The views of the Mission's members influenced the December 1972 announcement by Chief Minister Somare of the government's economic plans and the establishment of a small planning secretariat answerable to a Cabinet Committee of the governing Coalition parties' leaders. As a result of Finance Minister Julius Chan's resistance to the term 'Development Programme', the plans were initially described as an 'Improvement Programme'.[33] The Programme would become better known as the Eight Aims, foremost of which were indigenisation of the control of the economy, equalisation of economic benefits, and decentralisation of economic activity. Over the next three years, the Eight Aims were at the centre of intense political tussles among indigenous leaders and government critics. The debates over design and implementation continued after Independence.[34]

Just as the colonial administration transferred authority, changes to the manner in which policy was designed and asserted by the newly elected government fuelled domestic opposition. As the Faber report's recommendations were being considered, the government deliberately abolished the previous administration's OPC and later established a Central Planning Office (CPO).[35] The government kept a tight rein on the formulation of the Eight Aims, including by relying on sympathetic and thus reliable expatriate advisers.[36] While this was done in part to pre-empt anticipated opposition from the remaining colonial officials, objections were also expected from some ministers and other members of parliament.[37] Subsequently the Eight Aims were further shaped by a number

---

priority: maximum growth in the formal economy fuelled by foreign investment'. The importance of other international sources of ideas should not be underestimated: the 6th Waigani Seminar in April–May 1972 had not only heard Peacock's cautionary words, noted above, but also from René Dumont, French agronomist and Ivan Illich, educationist. R Dumont 'Some reflections on priorities in Melanesian development' in May (ed.) *Priorities in Melanesian Development* pp. 7–19, emphasised (p. 7) 'that it is imperative at the beginning to foster a more rapid growth of agriculture', citing a phrase 'Agriculture is the base of the economy, industry the engine of development' which he claimed was the basic formula of Chinese development since 1960. See also Illich 'Design for a Convivial Society?'

32 IBRD/WB *A Report on Development Strategies for Papua New Guinea* Report prepared for the IBRD/World Bank by a Mission from the Overseas Development Group, University of East Anglia, February 1973.

33 Fitzpatrick 'The Eight Aims' p. 24

34 For the second Somare government's sensitivity to criticism over the effectiveness of government programs to implement the Aims during the first seven years after Independence, see Deputy Prime Minister and Minister for National Planning Paias Wingti 'Standing By Our Principles in Tough Times' in King, Lee & Warakai (eds) *From Rhetoric to Reality* pp. 15–21.

35 Garnaut 'The Framework of Economic Policy-Making' pp. 157–211 discusses the formation and subsequent operation of the CPO. Garnaut was a research fellow at the New Guinea Research Unit from 1972 to 1975, during which time he acted as consultant and adviser to the government, including to the Finance Minister. See Ballard 'Contributors' in Ballard (ed.) *Policy-Making in a New State* p. xiv, for an extended statement on Garnaut's official roles during and immediately after self-government.

36 Garnaut 'The Framework of Economic Policy-Making' pp. 157–211

37 See Tony Voutas 'Policy Initiative and the Pursuit of Control' in Ballard (ed.) *Policy-Making in a New State* pp. 33–47 for an insider's view of the 'development of a broad policy framework'.

of committees, and specific programs submitted to the CPO. Tony Voutas, MHA from 1966 and 1972, founding member of Pangu Pati, and principal research officer in PM Somare's office from 1972 to late 1974, explains that:

> The powerful Constitutional Planning Committee boosted the process of commitment to agreed national aims even further by developing the Eight Aims and having them incorporated in Papua New Guinea's Constitution as a bipartisan statement of the philosophy behind the new state.[38]

Voutas may well be correct that the lineage of the National Goals and Directive Principles included in the preamble to PNG's Constitution leads from the Eight Aims through the Constitutional Planning Committee (CPC) to the Constitution.[39] But the phrase 'bipartisan statement of philosophy' avoids more fundamental questions about what was the 'philosophy behind the new state'. Major disputes surrounding 'philosophy' were becoming apparent, especially over two matters, land and the structure of the new nation-state's governing institutions.

The Commission of Inquiry into Land Matters

As noted previously, since the late 1950s the need to change land tenure arrangements in order to lift smallholder productivity began to affect policy deliberations. The complexity and difficulty of making the desired changes was also recognised. In the last days of the colonial administration an attempt was made to introduce legislation which would make it possible to substantially extend adjudication and systematic registration of land held under customary title in selected areas. Encumbrances on registered titles, including those which limited the powers of mortgagees, were to be removed and control of dealings in land decentralised to land control boards, where local landowners would exercise authority.

One result of this late colonial attempt at legal and institutional reform was the formation of a powerful coalition, which included indigenous politicians, expatriate academics and lawyers, opposed to the proposed legislation. The growing squatter revolt and generalised lawlessness underpinned a nationalist opposition to any such late expression of colonial authority. The fear that the moves promoted by the legislation would accelerate what one critic termed 'an agrarian revolution' which increased landlessness strengthened the opposition.[40]

---

38 Voutas 'Policy Initiative and the Pursuit of Control' pp. 36–37
39 For the Constitution and the source of specific sections, see: Brian Brunton and Duncan Colquhoun-Kerr *The Annotated Constitution of Papua New Guinea* (Waigani: University of Papua New Guinea Press, 1984).
40 AD Ward 'Agrarian Revolution: Handle with care' *New Guinea* January 1972, vol. 6, no. 4, pp. 25–34. For an exchange between Ward and Ron Crocombe over Ward's article, see: 'Letters' *New Guinea* vol. 7, no. 1, 1972, pp. 63–64.

The proposed legislation was withdrawn and in February 1973, the same month that the Faber report was published, the Administrator appointed the Commission of Inquiry into Land Matters (CILM). Its report was submitted in October 1973.

There is no need to revisit here the CILM's composition, its activities or report: the literature on each subject is extensive and comprehensive, some of it by committed participants and some by subsequent commentators.[41] One of the former, Jim Fingleton has assessed the CILM report as a threat not only to the 'privileges of dominant commercial entities in the country' but also to the aspirations 'of the emerging Papua New Guinean class of entrepreneurs'.[42] For this account, it is sufficient to note that as a consequence of the CILM report and the political tussles surrounding land reform, four Acts were passed in 1974 and a fifth, the *Land Disputes Settlement Act*, in the following year.[43]

The fourth piece of legislation which followed the direction proposed by the CILM report, the *Land Trespass Act*, blocked the movement by squatters on to large holdings. In their entirety the five Acts meant that takeover could only be sanctioned by the state and made illegal any other forms of occupation and ownership. The legislation also provided the basis for an important compromise between two distinct forms of contestants for the land. The takeover of large holdings provided for the continued operation of some as plantations but the Acts also opened the door for some break-up of large holdings to meet smallholder demands. The legal compromise was crafted by a committee, whose official members were Papua New Guineans with supporting staff 'entirely expatriate'.[44] Under the legislation a short-term resolution of the tussle between indigenes, for plantations and smallholdings, was made possible by the departure of European settlers who had been the owner-occupiers of estates, the surrender of unplanted acreages by major plantation companies, and the release of large areas held as government land.[45]

As a further effect of the legislation, the ownership and occupation rights of large and smallholders alike were now dependent upon post-colonial state

---

41   Alan Ward and Jim Fingleton were supporting staff for the CILM: see Fingleton 'Policy-Making on Lands' pp. 212–237; Fingleton 'Plantation Redistribution among the Tolai' *Melanesian Law Journal* 1983, vol. 11, pp. 99–123; AD Ward 'Customary Land, Land Registration and Social Equality' in Denoon & Snowden *A time to plant* pp. 249–264; AD Ward 'The Commission of Inquiry into Land Matters 1973: Choices, Constraints and Assumptions' *Melanesian Law Journal* 1983, vol. 11, pp. 1–13; Larmour *Land Policy and Decolonisation*; AD Ward 'Time to Make a New Start' in Larmour (ed.) *Customary Land Tenure* pp. 177–194; Larmour 'Registration of Customary Land: 1952–1987' in Larmour (ed.) *Customary Land Tenure* pp. 51–72.

42   Fingleton 'Policy-Making on Lands' p. 216

43   The 1974 legislation consisted of the *Lands Acquisition Act*, *Land Redistribution Act*, *Land Groups Act* and *Land Trespass Act*. Fingleton 'Policy-Making on Lands' p. 231 concludes these acts 'furnish(ed) the government with the legislative basis for its plantation redistribution policy'.

44   Fingleton 'Policy-Making on Lands' p. 215

45   MacWilliam 'Smallholder Production' p. 20

power and made subject to the holders of this power, the indigenes who held national executive and administrative authority. With regard to Voutas' proposition regarding the development of a 'philosophy behind the new state', the compromise over transferring land ownership from expatriates to indigenes was critical in the process of establishing a central element of the philosophy. Indigenous governments wielding post-colonial state power would enshrine and defend private property rights, whether of large holding or smallholding owners, and would not provide support for squatting or any other forms of illegal occupation.

As much as this compromise dealt with ownership and occupation, it often left unresolved the more important matter of how to make productive what had become or threatened to become unproductive, land and labour. After Independence, as the compromises over land ownership were worked out in different areas of the country,[46] the critical question became 'What Do We Do About Plantations?'[47] As one contributor to a 1981 conference devoted to this question asked, regarding plantations which were subject to redistribution to indigenes as large holdings 'Who wants to be the Labourer?'[48] Clearly, household ambitions to avoid wage labour remained powerful.

If reformed land legislation provided the basis for an initial solution to the tussles between owners and would-be owners of large holdings and households, a more serious matter was still to be settled which could not be done by mere legislative reform. This was because while planning was proceeding for the new nation-state, a struggle was taking place which in its most serious form raised important questions about development as national development. What would be the territorial parameters of PNG and what would be the governing institutions that reflected these boundaries? When including or excluding particular areas of the country had important implications for government revenues, and in turn the capacity of the state to bring development, attempts to remove or separate particular districts from the new nation-state were critical. The third section of the chapter takes up the account of how these matters were determined.

Such fundamental questions were the concern of the CPC, the most important of the numerous bodies established in the early 1970s to chart the direction of the independent nation-state. The CPC's deliberations as well as its final report presented in August 1974 to Chief Minister Somare were pivotal for future institutional arrangements and development policy.

---

46   See, for instance, Fingleton 'Plantation redistribution among the Tolai'
47   Michael AHB Walter (ed.) *What Do We Do About Plantations?* Monograph no. 15 (Boroko: IASER, 1981). Minister for Finance, former Mataungan Association leader Kaputin, opened the conference, stating: 'Sadly, results of localization of plantations have in many cases proved disappointing. Productivity has greatly declined....'
48   Bob McKillop 'Managing Plantations in Papua New Guinea Today: Who Wants to be the Labourer?' in Walter (ed.) *What Do We Do About Plantations?* pp. 25–32

Structure and Power

The Constitutional Planning Committee

The 1972 elections which preceded the formation of the self-government coalition had ensured that the opposition to accelerated development would have substantial parliamentary representation. During 1969 the Mataungan Association and Napidakoe Navitu had been formed to coordinate and represent opposition to important aspects of the accelerated development program on the Gazelle Peninsula and in Bougainville respectively. Both organisations were electorally successful, and the most important anti-colonial indigenes were elected. Of the prominent critics of Australian colonialism, only the radical Bougainvillean student leader Leo Hannett failed to win endorsement to stand for a seat.[49] Once elected, however, the MA's leaders began to play a mediatory role, between plantation owners and squatters.[50] The successful Bougainvilleans concentrated initially upon improving compensation for land taken by the mine and acquiring a larger share of lease monies for landowners. For the colony overall, the generational change noted above at the 1968 elections continued, if in a form mediated by 'tradition'.[51]

A conservative coalition headed by the United Party had been expected to win the 1972 self-government election and take power. However the surprise victory and formation of a coalition government led by Pangu Pati and Somare advanced the co-optation of the anti-colonial nationalists. This coalition brought the strongest critics of the Administration's plans to continue with accelerated development into positions of influence. Although the Mataungan leaders Tammur and Kaputin did not initially accept ministries, they supported the Pangu Pati-led coalition. The senior Bougainvillean MHA Paul Lapun became Minister for Mines, while Father John Momis became deputy speaker of the House and then effectively *de facto* chair of the CPC. A third Bougainvillean, Donatus Mola as Minister for Business Development was one of four People's

---

49   See Ian Grosart and Christine F McColl 'East New Britain' in David Stone (ed.) *Prelude to Self-Government: Electoral Politics in Papua New Guinea 1972* (Canberra: RSPAS, ANU and UPNG, 1976) pp. 373–399 and Thomas Anis, Ephraim Makis, Theodore Miriung and Eugene Ogan 'Toward a New Politics?—The Elections in Bougainville' in David Stone (ed.) *Prelude to Self-Government* pp. 442–468; James Griffin 'Napidakoe Navitu' in May (ed.) *Micronationalist movements* pp. 113–138 and Ian Grosart 'Nationalism and micronationalism: the Tolai case' in May (ed.) *Micronationalist movements* pp. 139–176

50   See MacWilliam 'International Companies and Nationalist Politics in Papua New Guinea' *Journal of Contemporary Asia* vol. 17, no. 1, p. 19, where a May 1973 statement from Burns, Philp's general manager plantation division based in Rabaul is cited, noting that: 'Matanguans [sic] have become a reformed capitalist organization, and have been of very great assistance to me in settling land disputes'.

51   Cf. Bill Standish 'New Men for an Old Society: the Chimbu Regional Campaign' and Leo Kuabaal 'Sinasina Open Electorate' in Stone (ed.) *Prelude to Self-Government* pp. 308–349, 350–370

Progress Party MPs, including Julius Chan as Finance Minister, who took senior economic ministries.[52] The most important Bougainvillean politicians had a strong grip on power at the centre of the soon-to-be independent state.

The inclusion in the government coalition of most of the strongest critics of colonial rule and policy also meant that the government was to an extent dependent upon their support to maintain a parliamentary majority. The radical nationalists, represented especially by Momis and Kaputin, pushed this dependence, particularly in the formation and operation of the CPC. To balance their presence, and aided by the June 1972 parliamentary endorsement, Somare ensured that the CPC included what he termed 'the most skilled backbenchers', to formulate 'a home-grown constitution'.[53] If the composition of the CPC was an attempt to be inclusive, locking major radical nationalists into the process of devising a constitution, it also gave the same critics an institution through which they could exert political leverage. The result was especially important for the structure and operations of the National Government, as well as in settling that all areas of the colony would remain within the new nation.

Although Somare was the formal *ex officio* chair, much of the direction taken by the CPC was determined by Momis and Kaputin—who first joined the government as Justice Minister in August 1973 and then was dismissed in October 1974, two months after the final CPC report was presented. Utilising a number of permanent and visiting consultants, between May and August 1973 members of the CPC travelled widely within PNG. Visiting 'almost every sub-district' and 'holding over one hundred public meetings attended by an estimated 60,000 people' the Committee also called for and accepted 'well over 2,000' submissions.[54]

For this study three features of the CPC's activities and final report are significant. Firstly, the very public process through which the CPC operated gave full vent to the radical nationalist position, in nearly all its aspects. This position sometimes caused concern and discomfort for the Australian and PNG governments, even to the extent that the date for Independence was delayed from 1974 to 1975. However with support from the opposition parties, especially the United Party, the government was able to defeat the radicals in parliament and strengthen its authority. Chief Minister Somare and his close ally John Guise tabled a minority CPC report 'Government Paper on Constitutional Proposals', which skilfully captured majority parliamentary support. Forcing conservative

---

52   Downs *The Australian Trusteeship* pp. 488–490, and Somare *Sana* p. 93 provides a list of the ministry, while Somare *Sana* pp. 83–94, Griffin, Nelson & Firth *Papua New Guinea* pp. 178–186, and David Stone 'The Political Turning Point: The Birth of the National Coalition Government' in Stone (ed.) *Prelude to Self-Government* pp. 529–538, discuss the unexpected formation of the governing coalition.

53   Somare *Sana* p. 98

54   GoPNG *Final Report of the Constitutional Planning Committee 1974 Part 1* (Port Moresby: Government Printer, 1974) p. 1/1

nationalists, cautious about self-government and strengthening the central government machinery, to back the Chief Minister against the radicals provided room for manoeuvre when the more substantial challenges appeared. As had been the case for most of the late colonial expatriate officials, including Hasluck, development continued to have national development through a strengthened state machinery, nation-building at its centre.[55]

What remained to be resolved was the structure and operation of this machinery. Indigenisation of the public service, especially at the senior levels, was a critical component of strengthening. Before Independence the expatriate presence both in the permanent positions and as advisers to ministers was considerably reduced. Some of this reduction was in response to government actions taken to deal with criticisms by CPC members. The departure of Voutas from the PM's office in late 1974 was a striking example of the power of the CPC radicals and the importance of indigenisation within the idea of indigenous development.

Secondly, the CPC re-enforced the move against accelerated development, when this was conceived primarily as increases in gross domestic product regardless of the consequences for land occupation and impoverishment. Instead the Committee emphasised three 'ideas', equality, self-reliance and rural development. The National Goals which it recommended to follow from the Eight Aims were subsequently incorporated into the Constitution. The first goal, of the five recommended for inclusion, was 'Integral Human Development-Liberation and Fulfilment':

> All activities of the state should be directed towards the personal liberation and fulfilment of every citizen, so that each man and woman will have the opportunity of improving himself or herself as a whole person and achieving integral human development.[56]

Further, the CPC's members did not take:

> development to be synonymous with material progress. For us the only authentic development is integral human development. This means that we use the term development to mean nothing less than the unending process of improvement of every man and woman as a whole person ... integral human development must reach out and enrich Papua New Guineans in every part of the country.[57]

---

55   See Somare *Sana* pp. 95–108, especially p. 99 for Somare's summary of his relations with Momis; Diana Conyers *The Provincial Government Debate: Central Control Versus Local Participation In Papua New Guinea* Monograph no. 2 (Boroko: IASER, 1976) pp. 40–50; Downs *The Australian Trusteeship* pp. 491–495, 499–510.
56   GoPNG *Final Report* vol. 1, p. 2/3
57   GoPNG *Final Report* vol. 1, p. 2/3

The third outcome of particular relevance, alongside strengthening the government and cementing the ideological shift against accelerated development, was the Committee's role in checking separatism. This claim may appear to be at variance with the politics of key CPC members. The CPC's most important members Momis and Kaputin continued to be associated with movements on the Gazelle Peninsula and Bougainville which variously espoused separatist and in the latter case secessionist sentiments.[58] However through widespread consultation, and the dominant nationalist views of the CPC's membership, the Committee's deliberations kept attention focused upon how the national state could be constructed to include—rather than exclude—representatives from all areas which had been part of the colonial territory. As Somare noted, despite his radicalism, CPC ideological leader Momis was above all a (PNG) nationalist.[59]

The national state and the Somare Government were strengthened by other means as well. A substantial rise in international copper prices, and the determination of government officials to renegotiate the agreement with RTZ/CRA/BCL, secured a major increase in revenues at an especially critical moment.[60] The accession to power of the ALP in Australia and the willingness of the new PM Gough Whitlam to make a three year commitment on aid from 1974–75 further assisted planning.[61] Soon after Independence, the extensive frost in the main coffee growing areas of Brazil noted above resulted in a very substantial price increase for PNG's major agricultural export which further boosted government revenues, commercial activity and grower incomes.

The CPC's linking of state activities, nationwide comprehensive development and individuality may seem, at first sight, to have much in common with the earlier uniform development pushed so determinedly in the 1950s by the Hasluck-led colonial administration.[62] However beneath the change in the racial and national identities of those who held state power, from Australians to Papua New Guineans, a more fundamental shift was under way.

The shift expressed major changes in the character of state and class power. These changes ensured that beneath the superficial similarities there was little

---

58   Griffin 'Movements for Separation' distinguishes between the sentiments of separatism and secessionism, as well as the forms of opposition to the national government on the Gazelle Peninsula, Bougainville and Papua.

59   See Somare *Sana* p. 99 for Somare's description of the CPC leader as a 'true nationalist'.

60   Somare *Sana* pp. 121–122; Garnaut 'The Framework of Economic Policy Making' pp. 193–195; see also Griffin 'Movements Towards Secession' pp. 295–296; Downs *The Australian Trusteeship* pp. 540–545.

61   Somare *Sana* p. 97; G Whitlam *The Whitlam Government 1972–1975* (Ringwood, Vic.: Penguin Books, 1985) pp. 98–99. This commitment turned out to be less important when in November 1975 the Labor Government was dismissed by the Governor-General and the aid program had to be renegotiated with the incoming Malcolm Fraser-led Coalition Government.

62   See, for one more instance, the GoPNG *Report* statement (p. 2/3) 'No particular area or grouping of people should be developed at the expense of another, materially or in other ways. There should always be an equitable distribution and balanced sharing of all the benefits and opportunities the nation has to offer.'

in common between uniform development and the development policy which characterised the first Somare government. This was largely because instead of being marginalised, as was a central objective of the initial postwar development policy, during the transition to independence the indigenous capitalist class gained a substantial hold on state power. This hold was utilised for commercial advantage and also to shape the post-colonial state, most notably in the establishment of provincial governments which could be engaged to open up further arenas for commercial operations. Political power exercised by and on behalf of indigenous capital became a major feature of representative politics. In turn, it became less possible for those who represented the leading commercial figures to claim that they were also acting on behalf of smallholders and other indigenes. The possibility that the government of the newly independent state could exercise trusteeship was diminished. Consideration of the political advance of indigenous capital and its allies shows in an especially clear manner how the political economy of the pre-Independence phase differed from that of the late 1940s and 1950s.

Indigenous Capital—Class and State Power

For most of the late colonial period Australian officials, who were not themselves members of the capitalist class either in the metropole or the colony acted as trustees for the particular form(s) of development detailed here. Their ability to do so was enhanced by regulations which prevented straddling between state employment and private accumulation. Public officials were specifically barred from engaging in commercial activities, including farming and trading. There were expatriate state officials who, prevented from straddling, left senior positions to start or join existing commercial enterprises in PNG. George Greathead and Ian Downs were just two.[63]

Australian public service regulations precluded officials from also engaging in commercial enterprises, although by the late 1960s and early 1970s means of surmounting this barrier were regularly employed. In one case, that of a Port Moresby steel furniture manufacturing business, of the five expatriates who floated the firm, several were public servants. In order to take up shares in the firm, the public servants were required to obtain the permission of the Administrator. Approval 'was granted only in view of the intention to foster indigenous participation'. In 1969, the leading expatriate promoter of the firm

---

63   Hasluck *A Time for Building* pp. 119–120

financed a 75 per cent buyout by a Papua New Guinean, with the Development Bank taking a one-quarter ownership share. Other expatriate state employees used spouses, relatives and friends to run private enterprises.[64]

None of the Australian Ministers with responsibility for policy had any commercial interests in the colony, and only Barnes—Minister in the accelerated development period—could be regarded as having close ties with private businessmen who had operations in PNG. Ward and Hasluck were committed to the means and goals of late colonial trusteeship, particularly securing smallholder attachment to land. As explained in Chapter Three, especially during the 1950s the Australian Government's hold on state power had been highly centralised which ensured that international firms, expatriate owner-occupiers and the emerging indigenous bourgeois could not exercise unacceptable leverage against the colonial administration. Whether or not the colonial state of the Ward-Hasluck period conforms to the descriptions of a bureaucratic state or Administrative Colonialism is not important here.[65] What needs to be recognised is that neither of these characterisations adequately capture the principal objective of colonial rule which was to bring development as the basis for self-government. This direction required the deliberate marginalising of particular forms of accumulation.

During the 1960s, while power was still exerted in a form of colonial trusteeship, accelerated development opened space for not only the well known and obvious forms of international enterprise, including the Panguna mine, but other forms of commerce as well. While some of these commercial activities were a focus for the anti-colonial nationalist criticisms raised by Crocombe, Kaputin and others (see Chapter Five), important moves by indigenous capitalists and would-be capitalists were also occurring. The critics' attention to the clash between expatriates and indigenes over petty commerce (taxis, shops, hairdressing salons etc.) often indicated thwarted ambitions. At the same time, there was also a substantial shift of 'big men into major businessmen' to extend Ben Finney's description of what was occurring in the Eastern Highlands, around Goroka, to other parts of PNG.[66] As indigenisation of colonial administration employment occurred, legal and other barriers to straddling between state positions and private commercial activities were lowered.

---

64   Cf. Lesley Andrews *Business and Bureaucracy: A Study of Papua New Guinean Businessmen and the Policies of Business Development in Port Moresby* New Guinea Research Bulletin no. 59 (Port Moresby and Canberra: New Guinea Research Unit, ANU, 1975) p. 55

65   Hawksley *Administrative Colonialism*

66   The academic literature of the 1970s and 1980s is replete with studies which documented the growing presence from the 1960s at least of indigenous entrepreneurs. See, for example, Finney *Big-Men and Business* and works listed in Finney's Bibliography pp. 189–199. See also Andrews *Business and Bureaucracy* for the establishment since the early 1960s of indigenous enterprises in the largest urban centre. In this literature, the pre-Independence presence of Papua New Guineans in commerce was widely acknowledged but in the confused descriptions of the period, including 'new elite', 'big peasants', 'rich peasants', 'middle peasants',

Much of the political running against colonial rule was made by disgruntled civil servants, academics and would-be businessmen, including Mataungan leader Kaputin, who hoped to become owners of large holdings and other commercial enterprises.[67] As expatriates in small and more substantial businesses departed, many indigenous politicians extended their commercial holdings. By the early 1970s, political leaders, as well as the main parties, Pangu, United Party and Peoples' Progress Party, represented indigenous commercial ambitions in a range of individual and corporate forms. These ambitions had quickly out-grown their local origins. Papuan separatist leader Josephine Abaijah claimed 'New Guineans were taking over the indigenous business affairs of Port Moresby'.[68]

Two observations from the period will suffice to illustrate the conjunction of electoral-parliamentary politics and commerce. David Hegarty notes regarding the number of candidates who contested the February–March 1972 election, that:

> The heaviest concentration of candidates occurred in the Highlands which may still reflect the persistent solidarity of the traditional clan-based political units in the region. It may also reflect, however, the emergence of a new entrepreneurial type or group in the Highlands which sees its economic success as being a basis for political support.

He also states (p. 297) that :

> close to 40 per cent of (the elected) MHAs are classified as businessmen (planters, traders, farmers, store-owners, etc), about 30 per cent as government officials (interpreters, clerks, senior officials) and about 17 per cent as school teachers'.[69]

The second instance, identified by James Griffin and Donald Denoon, occurred in late 1975 when 'the business arms of Pangu party (the leading party of the national coalition [government]) and of the United Party (the only

---

'(educated) petty bourgeoisie', 'national bourgeoisie', 'rural capitalists' and 'rich rural classes'. For a lengthy list of the accounts which employ one or more of these characterisations, see Herb M Thompson and Scott MacWilliam *The Political Economy of Papua New Guinea: Critical Essays* (Manila and Wollongong: *Journal of Contemporary Asia Publishers*, 1992) pp. 85–119, ch. 3 'From Acquisition to Accumulation: The Formation of an Indigenous Class of Capital', esp. p. 87, fn. 4.

67   Finney's mid-1986 follow-up study *Business Development in the Highlands of Papua New Guinea* Research Report Series no. 6 (Honolulu: Pacific Islands Development Program, East-West Center, 1987) p. 1 notes the rapidity of the pre and post-Independence advance of indigenes in Goroka commerce. See also Paula Brown 'New Men and Big Men: Emerging Social Stratification in the Third World, A Case Study from the New Guinea Highlands' *Ethnology* April 1987, vol. 26, no. 2, pp. 87–106; John Finch 'From proletarian to entrepreneur to big man: The story of Noya' *Oceania* December 1997, vol. 68, no. 2, pp. 123–133.

68   David Hegarty 'Papua New Guinea' *Australian Journal of Politics and History* December 1973, vol. 19, no. 3, p. 441

69   David Hegarty 'The Territory of Papua and New Guinea' *Australian Journal of Politics and History* August 1972, vol. 18, no. 2, pp. 295–296

party on the opposition side) were jointly proposing to enter the lucrative field of motor car sales [a field dominated by subsidiaries of the major Australian South Pacific firms Burns, Philp and WR Carpenter]'.[70]

The principal arena for the initial advance of indigenous capital, however, was the countryside, in agriculture. The Tolai movement into large holding cocoa growing, processing and trading, which began in the late 1940s, is documented in Chapters Two and Five. A parallel advance also occurred in the Central Highlands, where Papua New Guineans had extensive coffee plantings, and other enterprises. As a result of the major expansion of smallholder coffee production from the 1950s, processing and trading smallholder produce and household consumption goods, as well as growing other marketed crops provided a starting point for indigenous commercial operations. As a consequence of their earlier expansion, members of the indigenous bourgeoisie and would-be bourgeoisie were anxious to acquire plantations being vacated by departing expatriate owner-occupiers and international firms. However the smallholder agricultural increases of the 1950s and 1960s also contributed to the land shortages and triggered clashes over the former expatriate-owned large holdings (see above).

If the unplanted land on many large holdings attracted squatters and other indigenous households seeking to extend their holdings, by the 1960s and 1970s the existence of under and unutilised land often signalled that the expatriate owners and operators of the plantations were uncertain about their future. In 1974, during an especially torrid political battle over the need for legislation and action on compulsory acquisition of 'foreign-owned' plantations, Burns, Philp packaged a substantial area of its landholdings as a political offering to the Somare Government in exchange for a guarantee of continued ownership and operation of its profitable holdings.[71] Other large holding owners were not in as strong a position as Burns, Philp and were forced to adopt different strategies to sell entire properties as plantations. During 1974 an expatriate coffee plantation owner proposed that a District Investment Authority be established to fund the takeover and continued operation of large holdings in the Highlands.[72]

An especially prominent form of indigenous business organisation established to facilitate the takeover of large holdings was rural development corporations. Their formation had two principal purposes. The first was to ensure that previously expatriate-owned and operated businesses continued as forms of centralised and concentrated property. This meant blocking the ambitions of

70   James Griffin 'Papua New Guinea' *Australian Journal of Politics and History* 1976, vol. 22, no. 1, pp. 126–127 and Donald Denoon 'Papua New Guinea' *Australian Journal of Politics and History* 1976, vol. 22, no. 3, p. 437

71   MacWilliam 'International companies'

72   See MacWilliam 'Smallholder Production' pp. 25–26. Andrews *Business and Bureaucracy* documents the beginnings of the takeover of expatriate businesses during the early 1970s in Port Moresby and the provision of PNG Development Bank finance for the indigenous businessmen.

smallholders and other indigenes for a form of redistribution which would have divided the assets of the departing settlers and small businessmen. The second purpose was to include households in the ownership of the plantations and other enterprises as shareholders. Instead of acquiring separate parcels of assets, including small blocks of land carved out of the plantation, shareholders were offered the prospect of increased consumption out of share dividends, if and when these eventuated. Including indigenous smallholders as shareholders assisted in raising money for purchases, and made it easier to obtain loan funds. The development corporations also dampened smallholder dissent, holding out the possibility of higher levels of consumption funded by share dividends. Central to the formation and operation of many of these enterprises were powerful politicians, who could attract investors from among local populations and facilitate access to state resources.[73]

While the development corporations were critical for fulfilling the ambitions of Papua New Guineans aiming to take over and maintain plantations, agricultural operations did not represent the extent of the indigenous bourgeoisie's ambitions. Members of this class moved into crop processing and export, transportation, trade, urban real estate and other areas of commerce. These moves were invariably made possible by representatives of the class and its small business allies gaining political power. While some of the political advance took place through gaining representation on boards, state agencies which allocate licenses and finance, a more substantial basis involved restructuring the post-colonial state itself. An especially significant instance of major changes was the establishment of provincial governments, which in the most advanced provinces were quickly captured by leading indigenous businessmen and their political representatives.

Provincial Governments and Indigenous Capital

The end of colonial rule was accompanied by moves to decentralise administration at the district and local government levels.[74] The CPC provided an important

---

73   For some of the extensive literature on firms which employed the development corporation and related templates, see Rolf Gerritsen *Aspects of the Political Evolution of Rural Papua New Guinea: Towards a Political Economy of the Terminal Peasantry* Canberra Marxist Discussion Group Seminar, 26th October 1975; Gerritsen *Groups, Classes and Peasant Politics*; Mike Donaldson *Class Formation in Papua New Guinea: The National Bourgeoisie* Paper presented at the Sociological Association of Australia and New Zealand Conference, Canberra, July 1979, esp. pp. 26–29; Mike Donaldson and Kenneth Good *Class and Politics in the Eastern Highlands of Papua New Guinea History of Agriculture* Discussion Paper no. 9 (Waigani and Konedobu: UPNG and Department of Primary Industry, March 1978); Donaldson & Good 'The Eastern Highlands: Coffee and Class' in Denoon & Snowden *A time to plant* pp. 143–169, esp. pp. 167–168; Good & Donaldson *The Development of Rural Capitalism in PNG: Coffee Production in the Eastern Highlands* (Boroko: Institute of Papua New Guinea Studies, n.d.); Donaldson & Good *Articulated Agricultural Development: Traditional and Capitalist Agricultures—Papua New Guinea* (Avebury, Aldershot: Gower, 1998) esp. pp. 127–146, ch. 6 'Coffee Consolidation, the Development Corporations and the Rich Rural Classes'.
74   See Conyers *The Provincial Government Debate* chs 1–3; Ghai & Regan *The Law, Politics and Administration* ch. 1

policy direction for decentralisation. The CPC recommended a reduction in the power of the central administration through the establishment of political means by which citizens could participate in decision-making. According to Ghai and Regan, this was an attempt by the CPC to formulate a new 'paradigm of development', which was heavily influenced by '(e)vents in and demands for autonomy or secession by leaders from Bougainville ... since the 1960s'.[75] While Ghai and Regan, and Conyers correctly identify the 'centrality of the Bougainville experience' for the decentralisation push and formation of provincial governments, neither of these accounts adequately explains what was critical about that 'experience' for late colonial and post-Independence development policy in PNG.

Decentralisation and the formation of provincial governments extended the means by which indigenous capitalists were able to combine class and state power to enlarge their opportunities for accumulation. The case of Bougainville was central because the establishment and operation of the Panguna mine, after and in addition to the well-established commercial agricultural base in the district, created more room for the local bourgeoisie. The willingness of the Bougainville bourgeoisie to play separatism in an aggressive secessionist form showed how rapidly the class was advancing and the extent of their ambitions. The creation of provincial governments became a seminal moment during which policy was pushed away from agrarian smallholder development as state revenues were captured to support the ambitions of indigenous capital.

Once provincial governments were established, local businessmen-politicians campaigned for the formation of business arms formally connected to these institutions. While sometimes justified as a means for securing revenues which would permit the provision of public services, these businesses also made the takeover of plantations and other enterprises from departing expatriates possible. Subsequently, after Independence, this form of public enterprise became a shell as the assets were transferred to private ownership.

In the process of constitutional transformation, the establishment of the Bougainville Provincial Government was distinct. This was because of the very substantial and exceptional commercial development which had already taken place around the Panguna mine, and the popular opposition to its establishment which could be mobilised into a political movement. The reaction was further driven by the immediate effects of the mine's establishment, including land alienation and rapid migration into the area from other parts of PNG. Bougainvilleans who had previously eschewed working as plantation labourers found themselves in competition with, and in the presence of considerable numbers of people from other parts of PNG seeking wage employment in 'their

---

75   Ghai & Regan *The Law, Politics and Administration* p. 16

district'. Specific events, including the 1974 deaths of two Bougainvilleans in a pay-back killing in the Highlands added to popular disaffection. The physical difference between black-skinned Bougainvilleans and 'red-skinned' Papua New Guineans, the distance of the district from the rest of PNG, especially Port Moresby, its proximity to Solomon Islands 'kin', and the failure of the colonial administration to 'bring development' to the district were used to provide further support for secessionist demands as a particularly aggressive form of separatism.[76]

Secessionism became the means by which a section of indigenous capital gained a hold on and played a part in reconstructing national state power to advance their accumulation. In particular, key members of the indigenous bourgeoisie held managerial positions in the Bougainville Development Corporation (BDC) while also occupying the most important elected and managerial offices in the Provincial Government. This linking of private and public office was used to strengthen their commercial position.

Officially registered in 1975, the Development Corporation was established to carry out a business strategy framed the previous year.[77] The firm had the Provincial Government and the local diocese of the Roman Catholic Church holding 75 per cent of the issued share capital. The Provincial Government's shares were held in the form of a royalty trust, indicating that the source of the funds was royalties from the mine. Over the next ten years BDC became the most important indigenous commercial entity on Bougainville. Until 1984, Hannett and his group also controlled the Provincial Government. Hannett was both company chairman and provincial premier. This close connection between political and economic power in what had become the most prosperous province in the country, provided a template for developments in other provinces, where provincial governments established business arms.[78]

Phase 1 of the BDC's business strategy was to own and operate service industries around the Panguna mine. These included investing copper royalties in transport and commerce as well as acquiring a nearby tourist resort frequented by highly paid mine workers.[79] BDC acquired the wet canteens at the mine. With a largely migratory male workforce, the outlets were very profitable. In the 1980s, the

---

76   A detailed account of the formation of provincial governments, and the importance of Bougainvillean secessionist politics is provided in Conyers *The Provincial Government Debate*. For the Prime Minister's personal involvement, see Somare *Sana* esp. pp. 114–122. See also Thompson & MacWilliam 'The Bougainville Rebellion' in *The Political Economy of Papua New Guinea* pp. 14–48, ch. 2

77   Thompson & MacWilliam 'From acquisition to accumulation' p. 104, notes how in 1979, BDC's management pin-pointed 1974 as the year the strategy of the firm was first set.

78   Thomson & MacWilliam 'From Acquisition to Accumulation' p. 118, fn. 80 provides a specific instance of the importance of the coupling of political and economic power in the personae of Hannett.

79   James Griffin 'Papua New Guinea' *Australian Journal of Politics and History* 1975, vol. 21, no. 3, p. 124; Donald Denoon, 'Papua New Guinea' *Australian Journal of Politics and History*, 1976, vol. 22, no. 3, p. 442

closure of the canteens in response to the changing drinking habits of a more permanent workforce reduced BDC's income and pushed it into other activities. These included forcing BCL to use lime from the BDC-owned mine, rather than CRA/RTZ's cheaper international sources.

Phase 2 involved utilising this commercial base to move into plantation agriculture, smallholder cocoa marketing and exporting. In the third phase the firm extended operations beyond the North Solomons in shipping and manufacturing. In 1985–86, while still espousing the firm's role in providing funds which could be utilised by the Provincial Government to provide services, directors privatised BDC by increasing its share capital and themselves acquiring the issued shares.[80]

The firm's formation and activities became an important indicator of just how extensive were the commercial ambitions of indigenous capital. BDC's operations were also an acknowledgement that commercial advance in post-Independence PNG required holding considerably more political power than had been permitted under colonial rule. By playing the politics of separatism to the limit, leading Bougainvilleans won substantial commercial benefits for the Development Corporation. The commercial opportunities provided by the enormous mine were critical for the ambitions of this section of the Bougainville bourgeoisie. But without political power there was no guarantee that the opportunities could be taken and rivals from other parts of PNG kept out, for the honey-pot of the giant mine had excited the ambitions of indigenous labour and capital alike across the country. The route taken by Bougainvilleans with commercial ambitions but politically marginal to remedy the latter changed the structure of the state.

As noted previously, at the 1972 national elections, radical student leader Leo Hannett had failed to win endorsement to run for a seat. Subsequently, his political marginalisation and the co-optation of leading Bougainvillean politicians Lapun, Momis and Mola into the central political and administrative machinery of the new government gave the impetus for the secessionist politics which were to be so important in reshaping late colonial and post-Independence state power. While co-optation of the most out-spoken of the younger generation who were using separatism as a political tactic became one of the important achievements of the first Somare Government, this strategy was less successful in dealing with the ambitious Bougainvilleans, including Hannett, who had been marginalised.

In February 1973, Hannett had been appointed special adviser to PM Somare on Bougainville affairs. Dissatisfied with the pace of the move to district/provincial government, Hannett subsequently launched a public attack on

---

80   BDC's post-Independence advance and subsequent decline following the 1988 revolt on Bougainville are charted in Thompson & MacWilliam *The Political Economy of Papua New Guinea* pp. 103–109.

the two Bougainvillean ministers in Somare's Government, Lapun and Mola. Somare dismissed Hannett from the adviser's position. The latter proceeded to further develop his political base on Bougainville, with a continuous escalation of demands and threats. In January 1974, the first meeting of the Bougainville Constituent Assembly was held, with an appointed, not elected, membership. Five months later, Bougainville was provided with a special financial allocation by the national government in lieu of royalties from the mine. Hannett and another critic of the central government, Moses Havini became Planner and Executive Officer of the newly established Provincial Government, with considerable power over the province's finances.

The government's handling of the CPC and its report included measures to reduce the powers of the proposed provincial governments. Specifically, the Somare Government was concerned that 'the CPC proposals could result in an undue concentration of power at the provincial centre'.[81] After a prolonged and often bitter tussle over the powers of provincial governments and their constitutional standing, a compromise was reached. Provincial governments gained power to make laws including on agriculture and rural development, business, rural and urban land use, and transport, providing these did not contravene national laws. However in giving constitutional and administrative effect to the compromise, through which provincial governments were removed from the Constitution but included under a special organic law, negotiations between the new Bougainvillean political leadership and the central government broke down.

At different times, both Somare and Hannett agreed that decentralisation provided the best prospects for national unity.[82] However by May 1975 Bougainvillean officials, including Hannett, were threatening that the province would secede from PNG. Demands for increased royalties and capital works funds continued to escalate, particularly after a renegotiation between BCL and the PNG government substantially lifted the royalties paid by the firm. On 1 September 1975, two weeks before PNG's Independence Day, the Bougainvilleans led by Hannett declared their independence. However this action did not prevent Bougainville being included in the territory of the nation which came into being at Independence.[83] Instead the demands and threats secured an important and potentially powerful political and administrative structure in the new nation-state. While the North Solomons Provincial Government was the most developed initial form of this structure, similar arrangements followed for PNG's other remaining districts. These became 18 provinces and a nineteenth

---

81   Conyers *The Provincial Government Debate* p. 45, citing PNG Government Government paper: 'Proposals on constitutional principles and explanatory notes' Port Moresby, August 1974.
82   Conyers *The Provincial Government Debate* p. 55; Somare *Sana* p. 122
83   Conyers *The Provincial Government Debate* pp. 55–64

administrative unit, the National Capital District, which was created based on Port Moresby and its immediate surrounds. After Independence, indigenous businessmen-politicians held office in several provinces, particularly those most commercially advanced, including the Eastern Highlands.

Conclusion

The period between the formation of the Michael Somare-led coalition government in April 1972 and formal Independence in September 1975 was notable for the unresolved political conflicts among indigenes. These conflicts often centred on what redistribution was to mean, especially for land being vacated by departing expatriate plantation owners. Development thought in and for PNG during the transition retained the emphasis upon the primacy of 'village life', even as securing smallholders upon land at increasing levels of marketed production had become a less certain component of state policy. One important dimension of the conflict which gave rise to the uncertainty about development policy was the growing political and economic ascendancy of indigenous capital. The political and economic power of this class made it unlikely that independent PNG governments would design policies which gave smallholder agriculture primacy. By Independence, the phrase which had captured the essence of postwar colonial policy, 'the paramountcy of native interests' had acquired a distinctive meaning, becoming synonymous with indigenisation and local ownership of commercial properties.

Smallholder production of export crops had either become dominant or was gaining the ascendancy and would soon surpass large holding production. Major changes had also occurred in indigenous consumption, of domestically produced items, some locally manufactured commodities and imported goods, including rice and other foods. The indigenous population had probably doubled, from about 1.25 million in 1949 to around 2.5 million at Independence, which suggested successful rehabilitation after the war and a subsequent improvement in living standards for many.[84] An indigenous government had come to power in a newly independent nation-state, fulfilling one of the central terms of Australia's trusteeship obligations.

The population increase, improved living standards, and the continued attachment of the majority of the population to smallholdings occurred under policies

---

84   From 1949 until 1970, the population figure increased in part simply by the extension of colonial authority to more areas and peoples. While the 1949 figure does not include people in the 'restricted areas', not completely under colonial rule, from the 1966 census a more comprehensive count begins to emerge. In 1966, the colony had a population of 2.12 million, which five years later had risen to 2.43 million. See M Bathgate 'Basic composition of the population' in ESCAP/SPC (ed.) *Population of Papua New Guinea* Country Monograph Series no. 7.2 (New York and Noumea, United Nations and South Pacific Commission, 1982) pp. 13–47.

constructed in the name of agrarian development. The outcome described in this study appears to confirm not only the power of the idea of development but the capacity of the colonial administration to implement what was intended. Even if there were signs that the terms of the household occupation of smallholdings were shifting, with a rapid increase in some urban populations and unrest in the rural areas, 'village life' retained much that was attractive. Unsurprisingly, perhaps, conditions suggested considerable optimism was warranted about the government's capacity to continue to make development happen.[85]

However, with the coming to power of Papua New Guineans who were major beneficiaries of the production increases and political reforms to hasten self-government, state power had taken on a schizophrenic character. Official planning and key government officials continued to applaud, and to try to strengthen means of maintaining the centrality of household production and village life.[86] Pushed by international advice and domestic aspirations, the national government was still intent upon keeping development centred upon rural areas, in accord with the National Aims.[87]

In 1974, under the direction of the National Planning Committee of Cabinet, the CPO prepared two documents. Under the general heading *Strategies for Nationhood* the documents *Programmes & Performances* and *Policies & Issues* were intended to give effect to the Eight Aims. This was to be done by relating items of departmental and other government expenditure specifically to the Aims. Both documents are testament to the continuing pull of these Aims and the idea of development, with its indigenous and rural focus, contained in the Aims. Thus: 'Development of a Papua New Guinean society also means increasing the capacity of village communities to improve their own lives'.

However accelerated development and the political reforms leading to self-government and Independence had given a major boost to the position of indigenous capital. This class' representatives sought to use their new found political power to reshape state power to extend accumulation. While a series of political and commercial compromises made some temporary solutions possible during the prelude to Independence nationalist euphoria only partly concealed the contradictory ambitions of indigenous capital to accumulate and demands from other indigenes for increases in consumption. Major changes, particularly

---

85   Ron May 'From Promise to Crisis: a Political Economy of Papua New Guinea' <http://epress.anu.edu.au/sspng/mobile_devices/ch.15.html> captures the sense of optimism which pervaded governing and administrative circles at Independence.

86   HK Colebatch 'Policy-Making for Rural Development' in Ballard (ed.) *Policy-Making in a New State* p. 257–279 documents one 'field of governmental activity—the Rural Improvement Programme (RIP)—whose proclaimed aim was to link central financial resources with local initiative in order to improve the way of life of rural people …. The National Coalition government placed great stress on this programme, particularly in its early years in office, as a means of translating into action its concern for improving the lives of rural people [as opposed to what it saw as a narrow concern for economic growth]'.

87   GoPNG *Strategies for Nationhood Policies and Issues* (Port Moresby: Government Printer, December 1974) p. 14

in rural PNG, which were stimulated by colonial development policy made the task of post-Independence policy makers seeking to satisfy both the ambitions and the demands monumental.

7. Conclusion

Papua New Guinea remains a country in which more than 80 per cent of the population live in the countryside on smallholdings. However with a rapidly increasing population of more than seven million, it is not a place where the bulk of the population exists at rising standards of welfare. A recent Australian Agency for International Development (AusAID) report claims that:

> The Pacific as a whole is significantly off track to meet the MDGs [Millenium Development Goals] by 2015 .... Of greatest concern are [PNG] and Timor-Leste, two significant countries which are both off track on almost all MDGs.[1]

Other accounts have portrayed a people divided into two nations, comprising 'a wealthy elite' with the bulk of the population living in rural 'villages ... and shanty township settlements', with 'fair nutrition' but little else, 'among the poorest people in the world'.[2] At best, PNG is a country which struggles to 'come back from the brink' of even greater decline, relative to other countries.[3]

In such circumstances a prescription for an aid program appears which would not have been out of place in policy documents of the 1950s. A 2005 report prepared for a White Paper on Australia's aid program emphasised that:

> It is important to the overall stability of PNG to recognise the on-going importance of village agriculture, and to ensure that the aid program does not undermine its role by inflating expectations that are illusory. It is clear that, even on the most favourable assumptions about growth, village agriculture will continue to sustain the overwhelming majority of Papua New Guineans for the foreseeable future.[4]

In this book I have argued that at least until Independence in 1975, the attachment to land of most of the country's people was to a considerable extent the effect of late colonial policy and practices. This policy direction was carried

---

1   AusAID *Tracking development and governance in the Pacific* (Canberra: AusAID, August 2009) p. 1. For a more recent, slightly more optimistic assessment regarding several of the seven Goals, see: United Nations Papua New Guinea 'PNG Progress: MDGs Status at a glance: PNG's progress towards achieving the MDGs' retrieved 12 September 2012 at <http://www.un.org.pg/index.php?option=com_content&view=article&id=58&Itemid=24>

2   Helen Hughes and Susan Windybank 'Papua New Guinea's Choice A Tale of Two Nations' *Issue Analysis* 31 May 2008, no. 58, p. 1

3   Helen Hughes 'Can Papua New Guinea Come Back from the Brink?' *Issue Analysis* 13 July 2004, no. 49, following Susan Windybank and Mike Manning 'Papua New Guinea on the Brink' *Issue Analysis* 12 March 2003, no. 30, which began with the assertion that: '(PNG) shows every sign of following its Melanesian neighbour, the Solomon Islands, down the path to economic paralysis, government collapse and social despair'.

4   Alan Morris and Rob Stewart *Papua New Guinea Analytical Report for the White Paper on Australia's aid program* (Canberra: AusAID, September 2005) pp. 9–18

out in the name of development. While before World War II and during the military conflict rural households were under threat of being separated from land, until at least the mid-1960s the position was reversed. After the war, and particularly from the 1950s until the mid-1960s, the Australian colonial administration aimed to secure households on smallholdings at increased levels of production and with higher living standards.

As noted here, the modern idea of development was invented in the early nineteenth century to deal with conditions of unemployment and disorder in rapidly industrialising Western Europe. The idea subsequently travelled widely, including to Australia in the twentieth century. There it was further reformed, for dealing with conditions in postwar Australia and for the colony of Papua as well as for the UN Trust Territory of New Guinea. In what became after 1949 a unified territory for administration purposes, development meant securing 'the paramountcy of native interests' through colonial trusteeship, or guardianship. The 'natives' whose 'interests' were to be given primacy occupied smallholdings and applied family labour processes to reproduce consumption.

However much colonial development policy appeared driven by a desire to conserve, maintaining what might be regarded as a peasant way of life, this is a misunderstanding of what was intended. Particularly during the 1950s under uniform development policy, the colonial administration aimed to shift households into increased production of immediately consumed, as well as locally and internationally marketed crops. The change was regarded as a rejection of the static character of production in peasant agriculture. With intensified coordination and supervision by the colonial administration smallholders throughout PNG were to raise production of a range of crops, including cocoa, coffee and copra. Increased production was to be joined with increased consumption and improved welfare, transcending what were also seen as the relatively static living standards of peasant households.

In order to secure households at higher living standards with increased output of agricultural products, colonial development policy also included measures to restrain, even block, forms of capitalist enterprise which might have deleterious effects for the scheme of smallholder production. While maintaining competition among firms that traded in smallholder produce and consumption goods, as well as in processing of crops, colonial officials erected barriers against other forms of enterprise. These barriers were especially pronounced over the acquisition of land for large holdings or plantations. There was nothing socialist about the measures but a largely successful effort by liberal developers to prevent the centralised and concentrated forms of capitalist production that could threaten household occupation of land.

By the late 1950s and early 1960s, the successes of colonial policy were apparent. Increased smallholder production was acknowledged by Australian and World Bank officials. However important limits had been reached which reduced the possibilities of further growth. With the departure of the Minister, Hasluck, and others who had been central for uniform development policy, a major change could take place to raise growth rates. This change was characterised as accelerated development. Built upon what had already been achieved in terms of economic growth and improved living standards, the new direction meant encouraging further increases in areas where smallholder production was already most advanced. A major mineral deposit was explored, proven, approved for operation and established at Panguna, on Bougainville. Oil palm and tea plantings were made on nucleus estates. Indigenous capitalists were encouraged, especially in large holding agriculture and also in urban enterprises.

Political institutions, particularly the parliament, executive and administration were reformed, with a substantial expansion of the electoral process which tied rural households into the reformed state. A new generation of indigenous leaders came to the fore, characterised not merely by age differences with the previous incumbents but also because they linked political and commercial ambitions to further their accumulation. An increasingly prominent indigenous bourgeoisie acquired a substantial hold upon state power just as the state was being reformed to accommodate self-government and national independence. The growing struggle over land among households as well as between these and other indigenes with large holding ambitions became especially prominent as expatriates and international firms relinquished ownership of substantial areas of the most fertile soil.

With this struggle dominating in the countryside, plus growing unemployment and impoverishment in urban and rural areas as the political transition to independence was being negotiated, development as official policy and practice became especially uncertain. While development remained the principal desired objective of the departing colonial officials and the ascending indigenous leadership, distinct and different views emerged as to what this might mean in the independent nation-state.

One source of views was the international advice received and which appeared during 1973 in the influential Faber Report. More important, however, for shaping future policy was the tussle between indigenous leaders over electoral and parliamentary power, the institutional structure of the new state and state policy directions generally. This tussle included separatist and secessionist demands which culminated in the new nation state having a unitary constitution but with substantial powers for provincial governments inscribed at the centre of this state. Independence arrived with the prospect that provincial level officeholders could play a major role determining national policy regarding mining, agriculture and other industries. After 1975, the consequences of the newly adopted constitutional arrangements by way of a reduced state capacity to coordinate and supervise smallholder agriculture became apparent.

Among the questions raised by the argument advanced here is if and to what extent the effects of colonialism over the 30 postwar years in PNG are better described in comparative terms that include more than just this country. The question which was posed in the Introduction (Did colonialism bring development?) as well as the claims made by Hughes and others invite an answer. The conclusion constructed here suggests that colonialism did bring development, even as what was intended and occurred had distinct phases across the postwar years.

If this conclusion is accepted then a major comparative question arises. How should this late colonial state be considered? Should the colonial state from at least 1945 until Independence be categorised as belonging to the lineage of what has become known as the developmental state?

The Developmental State Debate and PNG

In its contemporary form, this debate commenced in the early 1980s regarding Japan and was subsequently extended to other countries undergoing manufacturing industrialisation.[5] As the originator of the description, academic Chalmers Johnson subsequently emphasised:

> I invoked the concept of "developmental state" to characterize the role the Japanese state played in Japan's extraordinary and unexpected post-war enrichment. I never said or implied that the state was *solely* [emphasis in original: SM] responsible for Japan's economic achievements or that it behaved like the state in command economies in assigning tasks and duties to the Japanese people.[6]

Or as Johnson also stated: 'The essence of the argument is that credit for the postwar Japanese economic "miracle" should go primarily to conscious and consistent governmental policies dating from at least the 1920s'.[7] The

---

5   For some of the extensive literature, see: Chalmers Johnson *MITI and the Japanese Miracle: The Growth of Industrial Policy, 1925–1975* (Stanford University Press, 1982); Alice H Amsden *Asia's Next Giant: South Korea and Late Industrialization* (New York: Oxford University Press, 1989); Robert Wade *Governing the Market: Economic Theory and the Role of Government in East Asian Industrialization* (Princeton: Princeton University Press, 1990); Jung-en Woo *Race to the Swift: State and Finance in Korean Industrialization* (New York: Columbia University Press, 1991); Yu-Shan Wu *Comparative Economic Transformations: Mainland China, Hungary, the Soviet Union, and Taiwan* (Stanford: Stanford University Press, 1994); Chalmers Johnson *Japan, Who Governs? The Rise of the Developmental State* (New York: Norton, 1995).
6   Johnson 'The Developmental State' pp. 33–34
7   Johnson 'The Developmental State' p. 37

developmental state is a description of one form of the capitalist state, distinct from other forms, including what Johnson termed the regulatory state of the USA. The main point of his distinction was to 'go beyond the contrast between the American and Soviet economies' which 'had become a feature of virtually all the canonical works [mainly by economists: SM] of the American side during the cold war'.[8] He made the deliberate distinction between forms of the capitalist state and socialist states, with the developmental state a particular instance of the former. In other words, the developmental state as conceived by Chalmers Johnson is subject to the authority of capital.[9]

So too, as has been pointed out repeatedly in this study, was the late colonial state in PNG. From the postwar re-establishment of capital's authority worldwide, through international commodity markets, financial and political institutions, this subjection was never in doubt. A principal objective of colonial authority was to ensure that households produced for markets as well as for immediate non-marketed consumption and also to purchase goods including those produced by industrial processes elsewhere. To repeat a conclusion explained previously, and for more than PNG, rural household labour was subsumed by capital *without* separation from occupation and ownership of land. Along the lines of arguments developed earlier by Jairus Banaji and Michael Cowen, there is no:

> essential form of the subjection of labour to capital, since there is only the necessity of the production of surplus value where capital prevails. The centralised large holdings and factories so important in the European experience which appears in the formulation by Marx of the abstractions capital and labour are not essential to the abstractions.[10]

One effect of Johnson's purpose, to counter the arguments of the economists with whom he disagreed, is that he too took on board the preoccupation with growth, having to explain why growth occurred in the Japanese 'miracle'. Economic growth and economic development tended to be elided in his account, and that of most others who have followed.[11]

However in the description presented here I have been at pains to point out that for late colonial policy and practice development was more than growth

---

8   Johnson 'The Developmental State' p. 32

9   Cowen & Shenton *Doctrines* p. xv

10   Thompson & MacWilliam 'Introduction' in Thompson & MacWilliam *The Political Economy of Papua New Guinea* p. 6 and ch. 4 'Household Production in the Countryside' pp. 120–155; Banaji *Theory as History* esp. ch. 2 'Modes of Production in a Materialist Conception of History'. For Cowen's extensive list of publications on households in Kenya, see Bob Shenton 'Obituary' *The Journal of Peasant Studies* July 2000, vol. 27, no. 4, pp. 163–166.

11   For another instance, see Atul Kohli 'Where Do High-Growth Political Economies Come From? The Japanese Lineage of Korea's Developmental State' in Woo-Cumings (ed.) *The Developmental State* pp. 93–136.

and more than economic. As Territories Minister Hasluck stated in 1956, 'the problems that may be set up by the early creation of a landless, urban proletariat' had to be anticipated, not by intention which was repressive but by paying:

> regard to the risks [to] which the individual and the group will be exposed in the course of the transition. We have to be careful that they do not lose their social anchorage in the village before we can be sure that they find an equally safe social anchorage … as wage-earners in the town.[12]

The growth with which Johnson and others have been primarily concerned was manufacturing industrialisation in countries with substantial urban populations and extensive wage labour employees. The developmental state debate has so far focused upon the capitalist firms, *zaibatsu* and *chaebol* in the Japanese and South Korean cases, which owned and organised production and trade to increase output and consumption of manufactured commodities. In PNG, as documented here, an agrarian rather than a manufacturing doctrine of development was predominant instead. This doctrine emphasised increased smallholder production of crops for local consumption and for exports.

At least until the late 1960s, when forms of industrialisation were encouraged in mining, agriculture and some limited import substituting manufacturing, manufacturing development was not the direction followed in PNG. Nor was Australian policy for the colony neo-mercantilist, discouraging imports and subsidising exports as characterised the 'miracle' developmental states of East Asia. Even where expanded production was for local consumption, as in the case of initial attempts to promote colonial self-sufficiency in rice, increased imports of the same product were also encouraged.

Further, the colonial state in PNG was not constructed in competition with, even in opposition to other national states and their economies, as has been emphasised for the initial exemplars of the developmental state. The state of this particular colony was not, as Woo-Cumings has described the origins of East Asian developmental states, an 'idiosyncratic response to a world dominated by the West' where 'state policies continue to be justified by the need to hone the region's economic competitiveness and by a residual nationalism'.[13] Even if anti-colonial nationalism, expressed by Australian officials including Minister Hasluck, by expatriates in PNG and by indigenes, was a continuing theme

---

12 Hasluck 'Australian Policy in Papua and New Guinea' George Judah Cohen Memorial Lecture presented at University of Sydney 4 October 1956.
13 Woo-Cumings 'Introduction: Chalmers Johnson and the Politics of Nationalism and Development' in Woo-Cumings (ed.) *The Developmental State* p. 1

affecting development policy for the colony it was never as strong or influential as in the independent nation-states of the debate either in East Asia or Central and South America.[14]

Finally, last but not least in this brief introduction to what hopefully will lead to further consideration of whether and in what circumstances the colonial state should be considered as belonging to the lineage of developmental states, there is the matter of agency. As Meredith Woo-Cumings explained: '"Developmental state" is a shorthand for the seamless web of political, bureaucratic, and moneyed influences that structures economic life in capitalist Northeast Asia'.[15] For Chalmers Johnson there are two central dimensions to why and how the Japanese state was developmental. Firstly, as Johnson's initial study emphasised, there was a pilot organisation, the Ministry of International Trade and Industry (MITI), at the centre of the Japanese bureaucracy which planned, coordinated and arranged in concert with the most important firms the direction of postwar recovery and subsequent expansion. With staff recruited from the top Japanese universities and a budget substantially quarantined from the vagaries of electoral and parliamentary politics, MITI was in an especially powerful position in a bureaucracy that had been strengthened by the Allied occupation. In particular the Supreme Commander for the Allied Powers (SCAP) had reduced the political power of the Japanese military and the commercial importance of the *zaibatsu* over government economic decisions.

Secondly, as Johnson summarised his earlier argument, there was: 'A political system in which the bureaucracy is given sufficient scope to take initiative and operate effectively. This means ... that the legislative and judicial branches of government must be restricted to "safety valve" functions'.[16]

While there is as yet no comparable history for the Department of Territories, its consistent budgetary increases and the eventual shift to raising more taxes within the colony placed this department in a powerful position. Staff shortages in the metropole and the colony, as well as the limited role played by the small Australian university system in producing graduates for colonial service constrained the Department and the Administration's effectiveness. Nevertheless and particularly with Hasluck at its head, Territories exerted centralised control, marginalised political opposition and was able to allocate a mainly instrumental purpose to private firms. As in Japan, South Korea and other developmental states, the Department and the colonial administration were not restrained by popular democratic forces. In the national Australian parliament, while Hasluck was Minister, there was continuing parliamentary support from the

---

14   Ben Ross Schneider 'The Desarrollista State in Brazil and Mexico' in Woo-Cummings (ed.) *The Developmental State* ch. 9, pp. 276–305
15   Woo-Cumings 'Introduction' p. 1
16   Johnson 'The Developmental State' p. 38

ALP opposition for the policy direction being followed.[17] Colonial trusteeship or Hasluck's preferred guardianship was based in legal authority. The direction received strong international support as well as continuing approval in the metropolitan country.

Conclusion

A more detailed consideration of the colonial state in PNG can not appear here. Perhaps these remarks will encourage others to consider whether during at least a major part of the postwar years in and for PNG the appellation developmental state is appropriate. In so doing, Bruce Cumings' advice, to recall the European origins of developmental state practice should be taken seriously. He correctly concludes that 'whatever we might say about Japan's state-directed development, it is or ought to be understood as a variant of the European continental tradition and not something *sui generis*'.[18] That is, the policies and practices described as the developmental state have a lineage and there is no worthwhile reason why this lineage should be confined either territorially or in time as long as capitalism's association with development continues.

Cumings' point should also be extended to recall that the idea of development itself which now has such a global reach was invented in the circumstances of early nineteenth century Europe. When scholars and others speak and write about the uniqueness of the country or area of which they are specialists, this is almost always done with ideas which contain their origins. So too with government policies carried out in the name of development. Hopefully understanding development's history will be enriched by extending its consideration to this South Pacific country during the 30 years after World War II.

---

17 A point dealt with in some detail in my forthcoming 'Conservative Hero or Liberal Developer: Locating Paul Hasluck'.

18 Bruce Cumings 'Webs with No Spiders, Spiders with No Webs: The Genealogy of the Developmental State' in Woo-Cumings (ed.) *The Developmental State* p. 62

Appendix on Data

Constructing any argument about the process(es) of change in late colonial PNG faces a number of substantial challenges. The almost complete absence of time series data, or data adequate enough to construct into such a series is one especially formidable difficulty. This absence continues as is regularly documented in studies. One recent account describes 'rural development' and utilises data collected over just six years, from 1990 to 1995 inclusive.[1]

However it is not an adequate defence of the more controversial aspects of this study to note that previous accounts which have made sweeping generalisations about colonial rule and its effects have often done so without reference to even the material utilised here or in the PhD which preceded it.[2] The sources of information consulted for the argument mounted here are cited in this Appendix, the longer Bibliography of this book and the even more extensive Bibliography in my PhD thesis.

The best information available, including on population and health, is limited in part because of the terms of colonial rule. Important areas of PNG were not 'open' for the collection of population information until after 1965: the first colony-wide census occurred in 1966. Even today the conduct of elections is plagued by the inaccuracy of census data and the difficulties associated with matching names, places of residence and electorates, as well as physical and other dangers for census officers.

As the official website for the National Statistical Office, that oversees PNG censuses, notes:

> The conduct of the population censuses has a short history in PNG. The first census for the country was held in 1966 and since then censuses were conducted in 1971, 1980, 1990 and the recent one in 2000. Every censuses conducted thus far have used different enumeration strategies. The important aspect of doing trend analysis is therefore lost due to lack of uniformity in enumeration methods and questionnaire contents.[3]

However even the first two 'national' censuses, of 1966 and 1971, were not full enumerations, with complete coverage of the urban and rural non-village sectors, plus stratified samples of approximately 10 per cent of rural village populations.

---

1   LW Hanson, BJ Allen, RM Bourke and TJ McCarthy *Papua New Guinea Rural Development Handbook* (Canberra: Department of Human Geography, RSPAS, ANU, 2001) p. 20
2   Cf. the entirely unsubstantiated assertions about the effects of colonial rule made by Hughes 'Aid has failed the Pacific'; MacWilliam *Development and Agriculture*.
3   National Statistical Office of Papua New Guinea '2000 National Census' retrieved 21 September 2012 at <http://www.spc.int/prism/country/pg/stats/2000_Census/census.htm>

Only in 1980, five years after Independence, did the first comprehensive coverage of the country's population take place. The next censuses are generally regarded as less reliable than the 1980 census.[4]

The data on changes in birth-weights, life expectancy and related matters is limited but, as the study suggests, the best available for deducing the improvements in living standards which were the effect of increased smallholder production and the importation of food, including rice.

Some of the reasons why there is, for example, no colony-wide time series evidence on the expansion of smallholder agriculture from 1945 to 1975, which might provide visual images such as maps, have to do with aspects of colonial administration outlined in this study.[5] While there was no doubt about the strength of development intent expressed by senior colonial officials, the resources available in terms of skilled personnel to collect and process information for at least the two decades after World War II ended were very limited. Not until the mid-1960s with the establishment of the New Guinea Research Unit as part of ANU did academics start to collect some of the data which has been utilised in this study. Even in these studies, there appeared very little data which permitted the measurement of change over long periods.

As two academics noted while compiling their contribution on agricultural crops for a late 1960s atlas: 'The reliability of the data on which this map is based is not high and therefore the map should only be considered as a first approximation'.[6] The colonial administration had reached a similar conclusion on the validity of the data collected by the first postwar colony-wide 'census of native agriculture' carried out between 1947 and 1954 and never tabulated the results or printed them in any form.[7]

Only in the 1960s and early 1970s, as self-government and Independence approached, did the most systematic and detailed work suggesting changes commence on particular locations, populations and crops. However even these studies invariably relied on interviews and data collected at one point in time when trying to infer longer change processes. Louise Morauta, for instance, in her study of villages in Madang compares 'the traditional Madang economy and that of today', as well as describes what are termed 'the political aspects of

---

4   Hanson et al. *Papua New Guinea Rural Development Handbook* p. 20

5   For early attempts to map changes, see David AM Lea and R Gerard Ward 'Crop Combinations' in Ward & Lea *An Atlas of Papua and New Guinea* (Glasgow: Collins and Longman, 1970); D Vasey 'Subsistence Crop Systems' in David King and Stephen Ranck (eds) *Papua New Guinea Atlas: A Nation in Transition* (Port Moresby: Robert Brown and Associates (Australia) P/L in conjunction with the Geography Department, UPNG, n.d. c. 1980) pp. 50–51; David King and Nancy Burge 'Cash Crops' in King & Ranck (eds) *Papua New Guinea Atlas* pp. 52–53.

6   Lea & Ward 'Crop Combinations' p. 56

7   Robin Hide and Scott MacWilliam 'Early National Surveys of Agriculture in Papua New Guinea' (forthcoming)

traditional life'. It is clear from the account that the sources of genealogies and clan histories, along with other material on 'the traditional way of life' are primarily local informants relying upon memories, legends etc. While supplemented with surveys she carried out in the late 1960s, the only aggregate data of a time series nature utilised in the study is that of populations in 17 villages taken from post-World War II censuses between 1944/1945 and 1967. These villages are from an area of the country which had been visited, subsequently settled in and ruled over by missionaries, European planters and colonial officials since the end of the nineteenth century. The conduct of surveys in this and similar areas was easier and more likely to be reliable than in remote, less accessible and less secure areas.[8]

During the late colonial period, research was further handicapped by official restrictions on the use of many of the most detailed sources of information collected by the colonial administration. Patrol and other Reports, including by agricultural officers, were only available through a lengthy process of accreditation by the Administration. Many other Australian Government documents dealing with late colonial PNG were unavailable due to the 30-year rule prohibiting access. Ian Cartledge's history of the coffee industry and Ian Downs' substantial account of the 30 years of the postwar trusteeship are exceptional for the amount of access to government files and documents granted to the authors.[9]

While this study had the advantage that the access rule prohibition did not apply for most of the period referred to here, there were other barriers—including the sheer size of the task—which prevented a systematic study of Patrol Reports. These remain a largely unexplored lode for future researchers of late colonial PNG, although as is shown here some researchers have made specific and geographically limited, albeit important, use of reports from some areas.

The lode is likely to be especially useful for two of the main themes of this account. The spread of locally marketed produce grown by smallholders is often documented in the Patrol Reports consulted for this study, and should in the future provide the basis for more detailed and reliable accounts than exist. Here the aggregate data compiled by marketing boards and the DASF is utilised, as well as that from particular files on specific topics. There is, however, much more on the process of expansion which could become available through detailed examination of the Patrol Reports, especially for the first two decades after World War II.

---

8   Louise Morauta *Beyond the Village: Local Politics in Madang, Papua New Guinea* (London: University of London Athlone Press and Humanities Press, 1974)
9   Cartledge *A History of the Coffee Industry*; Downs *The Australian Trusteeship*

Secondly, for reasons outlined in the study, patrol officers were especially alert to the increasing prominence of the indigenous bourgeoisie. The economic and political activities of the wealthiest Papua New Guineans were recognised and recorded, especially where representatives of this class sought particular advantages from the colonial administration. The study documents one especially prominent instance in the tussle over the activities of the Tolai Cocoa Board, between the most important Tolai cocoa growers and colonial officials determined to guard the interests of the smaller growers. Any substantial history of the late colonial expansion of indigenous capital should benefit from a more systematic study of official records, including Patrol Reports, than has been possible for this study.

There is a further source which, in the not too distant future, should shed more detailed and systematic light on the emergence and growing prominence of indigenous commerce during the 30 years before Independence. Administration records of company activities prior to World War II were destroyed during the military conflict, and the only ones which survived were in the archives of companies which had head offices overseas, mainly in Australia. However postwar companies were required to register with the colonial administration. I have an extensive data base taken from these official records and intend to publish the results of the study which utilises this material as soon as possible.

Bibliography

Official Documents

National Archives of Australia

Department of (External) Territories

National Archives of Australia (NAA):

Series 452/1 Item 1957/356 *Agricultural Extension Policy—Objectives and Administration Action—P and NG, 1956–1960*

———— 1957/2748 *Native Labour from Highlands. Employment of (On Lowlands & Coastal Regions) Papua & New Guinea*

———— 1957/3874 *Cocoa Action Plan*

———— 1957/3952 *Peanut Industry in Australia—Territories—Marketing in Australia 1951–1960*

———— 1958/628 *Mekeo Rice Project P & NG*

———— 1958/1327 *Rice Action Plan—Papua and New Guinea 1954–1960*

———— 1958/2847 *Native Village Rice Production—Madang and Sepik Districts*

———— 1958/4219 *Cocoa—Marketing of—Papua & New Guinea*

———— 1959/647 *Visit of Queensland Peanut Marketing Board 1959–1959*

———— 1959/1969 *Wages Policy—Papua & New Guinea*

———— 1962/8276 *Agricultural Extension Work in Papua & New Guinea, 1961–1967*

———— 1963/8164 *Native Unemployment in Urban Areas in Papua and New Guinea 1958–1967*

———— 1967/5758 *Agricultural Extension Work in Papua & New Guinea, 1964–1970*

Series A518/1 Item A1927/2, 30/7/1958 *P Hasluck to Department Secretary Lambert*

———— A58/3/1 *Cocoa—Papua and New Guinea, Research General*

———— A58/3/3 *Commodities—Cocoa Papua and New Guinea Proposals for Development*

———— AJ822/1/6 *Provisional Administration. Financial. Financial Assistance to Planters 1946–1952*

———— AL800/1/7 *Part 1, Papua & New Guinea Administration—Policy for the Administration of PNG*

———— AM927/4, *Development of the Territories—Agricultural Village Rice Production 1952–1957*

———— AQ800/1/1 *Part 1, Administration—Territory of Papua-New Guinea, Coordination of Plans for Development. Inter-Departmental Committee. 1947*

———— AQ800/1/1 *Part 2, Administration—Territory of Papua-New Guinea, Coordination of Plans for Development. Inter-Departmental Committee. 1947*

———— AQ927/4 *Development. Papua & New Guinea. Rice Production—W Poggendorff—Printing of*

———— AR927/4 *Development. Papua & New Guinea. Rice—Research*

———— AU800/1/1 *Administration general. Subjects to be dealt with by Inter-Departmental Committee on co-ordination of plans for development of the Territory of Papua-New Guinea*

———— AY927/4 *Rice in British Colonial Territories*

———— B58/3/3 *Commodities—Cocoa. Papua and New Guinea. Proposals for Development, Commonwealth Chocolate and Confectionery Manufacturers Association*

———— B822/1/6 *Papua & New Guinea Finance. Establishment of Banking Facilities 1945–1956*

———— BB822/1/6 *Taxation—Policy—Papua & New Guinea 1950–1960*

———— BY822/1/6 *Part 1, Revenue—General Revenue. Papua and New Guinea 1953–1958*

———— C2/1/1 *Advancement of Native Agriculture—Papua & New Guinea 1954–1956*

———— C58/3/3 *Commodities—Cocoa. Papua and New Guinea. Proposals for Development. British Overseas Food Corporation*

———— C927/9 *Rice Mechanisation—Papua and New Guinea*

———— CR800/1/1 *Summary of Government Achievements During Each Year 'The Record of the Menzies Government 1950–1955'*

———— DG840/1/4 *Alleged Exploitation of New Guinea Natives by European Traders*

———— G927/4 *Economic Development of the Territories—Commodities—Rice*

———— GZ812/1/7 *Betel Nuts—Market for 1954–1956*

———— H927/1 and Attachment, *Development of the Territories. Organisational. Report on Present Conditions in Papua & New Guinea (February 1950)*

———— H927/4 *Economic Development of the Territories—Commodities—Peanuts 1950–1958*

———— I927/1 *Development of the Territories. Organisational. Minister's Policy Speech, June 1950*

———— J927/1 *Development of the Territories. Organisational. Development Programme*

———— K927/1 *Development Papua and New Guinea. Administration's Seven Year Plan for Development*

———— L927/1 *Financial methods of encouraging development—Territories—General*

———— P927/2 *Part 1, Dollar Loan*

Series A1422 Item 12/2/11 Part 1, *New Guinea and Papua—Cocoa 1938–52*

———— Item 12/2/11 Part 2, *New Guinea and Papua. Cocoa 1957–66*

Series A1838/283 Item 301/1 *8/9/1947 J.K. Murray Memorandum on the Policy of the Administration*

Series A9372 Volumes 1–3, *ANGAU [Australian New Guinea Administration Unit] Conference of Officers of Headquarters and Officers of District Staff. Port Moresby 7–12 Feb. 1944. Papers and Discussions*

Series CP637/1/1 Item 65 *The Situation of Australian Colonies as at January 1944*

Series M331/1 Item 2 *Discussions with Administrator in Canberra February 1956*

———— 35 *D. Fienberg—Correspondence*

———— 58 *Lands Policy (Papua and New Guinea)*

———— 74 *Native Labour Ordinance Papua and New Guinea*

Series M335/1 Item 2 *Australia in New Guinea. The Post-War Task. A Paper prepared in the Department of Territories During the Term of Office of the Hon. P. Spender*

———— 3 *Departmental Brief on Agriculture and Land. January 1954* 'Papua and New Guinea. Agricultural Production and Marketing'

Series M336/1 Item 2 *Notes on New Guinea October–November 1951*

Series M338/1 Item 1 *Visit Papua and New Guinea 26th July to 8th August, 1951*

———— 3 *Visit to New Guinea, April 1952*

———— 17 *Notes for Minister's Visit to Papua and New Guinea May–June 1958*

Series M1775/1 Item 6 *Spate-Belshaw-Swan—Report on economic structure of Papua and New Guinea*

Series M1776/1 Vol. 1 *Minister for Territories Instructions to Department 4/6/1951 to 30/6/1952*

———— Vol. 2 *Minister for Territories Instructions to Department 1/7/1952 to 31/12/1952*

———— Vol. 5 *Minister for Territories Instructions to Department 1/1/1954 to 30/6/1954*

———— Vol. 8 *Minister for Territories Instructions to Department 1/7/55 to 31/12/55*

National Library of Australia

National Library of Australia (NLA): E.J. Ward Papers MS2396, Series 12, Folder 557–624 *Statement by the Hon. E.J. Ward, MP, Minister for Territories December 6, 1946* 'External Territories of the Commonwealth'

Papua New Guinea National Archives (PNGNA)

Department of Primary Industry (DPI)

Accession Number (AN) 12 Box 3,875, F/N 1-1-4 *Plans for Native Welfare, Social Development and Economic Development, 1947–1951*

———— 3,880 F/N 1-1-12 *Administration and Organisation General British Overseas Food Corporation, 1947–1949*

———— 3,883 F/N 1-1-26 *Conversation Director General Agriculture, 1947*

———— 3,891 F/N 1-1-42 *Administration and Organisation General Five Year Plan—Central Highlands: Committee Inter-Departmental*

———— 3,893 F/N 1-1-84 *Planning and Development Part 1, 1949–1952*

———— 3,895 F/N 1-1-122 *Submission on Suggested Development of Agriculture in Territory of Papua-New Guinea by REP Dwyer, 1951*

———— 3,896 F/N 1-1-150 *Administration and Organisation General. Development Corporation—J Pollard*

———— 3,896 F/N 1-1-176 *Comments on the Standing Committee on Agriculture following their visit to P and NG 1955*

———— 3,901 F/N 1-2-6(D) *Mekeo Rice Project*

———— 3,902 F/N 1-2-6(G) *Administration and Organisation—Madang Project*

———— 3,902 F/N 1-2-6(P) *Administration and Organisation. Divisional Rice Project—Buin*

———— 3,902 F/N 1-2-6(Q) *Administration and Organisation Divisional Native Rice Project Kieta Sub-District*

———— 3,902 F/N 1-2-6(R) *Administration Organization. Divisional Report by Treasury Inspector Duncan on Mekeo Rice Project*

———— 3,925 F/N 1-4-65(A) *Administration and Organisation—Conferences— Agricultural Conference of Extension Officers at Goroka 1956*

———— 3,934 F/N 7-1-6 *Part 1 Education Native Agriculture—General 1952– 1959*

———— 3,934 F/N 7-1-6(A) *Education—Native Copra, 1956–1960*

———— 4,102 F/N 19-1-9 *Part 1 Native Affairs—District Native Agriculture Development Policies—6 Monthly Report to the Minister 1/7/56–31/12/56*

———— 16,382 F/N 1-1-26© *Personal Correspondence Mr Tei Abal—Ministerial Member for Department of Agriculture Stock and Fisheries*

———— 16,491 F/N 1-4-65 *Administration and Organisation Conferences— Agricultural Conference of Extension Officers—Madang 1955*

———— 16,497 F/N 1-4-99 *Report of the Cocoa Conference—Rabaul 16th to 18th April 1958*

———— 16,664 F/N 19-1-12 *Native Affairs—Native Economic Development Land Use and Tenure Policy, September 1953–October 1958*

———— 16,704 F/N 23-3-1 (a) *Part 1 Production and Marketing—Native Projects Cacao Fermentaries—Gazelle Peninsula*

———— 16,705 F/N 23-3-1(a) *Part 6 Cacao Fermentaries—Gazelle Peninsula (Tolai) Tolai Cocoa Project*

———— 16,706 F/N 23-3-1(C) *Cocoa Projects Other Than Tolai—New Britain District*

———— 16,706 F/N 23-3-1(G) *Cocoa Projects Morobe District*

———— 16,706 F/N 23-3-1(H) *Native Cocoa Projects Bougainville District*

———— 16,706 F/N 23-3-1(I) *Native Cocoa Projects—New Ireland District*

———— 16,706 F/N 23-3-1(J) *Native Projects—Manus District*

———— 16,706 F/N 23-3-1(K) *Native Projects—Sepik District*

———— 16,706 F/N 23-3-1(L) *Part 1 and Part 3 Cocoa Projects—Madang District*

———— 16,706 F/N 23-3-1(M) *Higaturu Native Cocoa Project Local Government Area—Northern District*

———— 16,706 F/N 23-3-1(N) *Cocoa Projects Milne Bay District*

———— 16,706 F/N 23-3-1(0) *Cocoa Projects Central District*

———— 16,706 F/N 23-3-1(P) *Cocoa Projects Gulf District*

———— 18,509 F/N Z/12-1/51 *Highlands Land Policy, 1963–1968*

Papua New Guinea Registrar of Companies (PNGRoC)

File No. C3193 *New Guinea Islands Produce Company Ltd*

———— C3868 *New Guinea Development Corporation Ltd*

———— C4313 *Angco Holdings P/L*

North Solomons Provincial Government Archives

(These archives were held in the North Solomons Provincial Government Offices, but subsequently destroyed.)

North Solomons Provincial Government Archives (NSPGA): Buin Patrol Reports *Report No. 4, 1952/53Patrol to Kono Paramountcy*

———— Buin Patrol Reports *Report No. 10, 1959/60Patrol to Eastern Paramountcy of Buin Sub-District*

Papua New Guinea Coffee Marketing Board Archives (CMBA)

File No. 138 *Board Minutes 10/9/71–5/9/74*; *22/6/72 Minutes of Board Meeting*

———— F/N 158 *Registration of Processing Facilities 17/11/67–3/9/72; 11/11/72–30/9/74; 1/10/74–13/7/77*

———— F/N 217 *February 1974–June 22 1978 Localizing 2/74*

Other Official Documents and Reports

Allwood, M.B. 1971 *A Report on the Tolai Cocoa Project* Port Moresby: Department of Law, May

Australian Agency for International Development (AusAID) 2003 *Papua New Guinea and the Pacific—A Development Perspective* Canberra: AusAID, September

———— 2009 *Tracking development and governance in the Pacific* Canberra: AusAID, August

Australian School of Pacific Administration 1963 *Indigenous Economic Development and Its Relationship to Social and Political Change* no. 7 Course for Senior Officers of the Territory of Papua and New Guinea, Mosman: Sydney 1st April–26th April

Commonwealth Bureau of Agricultural Economics 1961 *The Coffee Industry in Papua New Guinea* Canberra: Government Printer, February

Commonwealth of Australia (CoA) 1949 *Report to the General Assembly of the United Nations on the Administration of the Territory of New Guinea—From 1st July 1947 to 30th June*, 1948 Canberra: Government Printer

———— Department of External Territories 1950 *Report of the New Guinea Nutrition Survey Expedition 1947* Sydney: Government Printer

———— Department of Territories, Minister for Territories c.1960 *Papua and New Guinea: Some Recent Statements of Australian Policy on Political Advancement* Canberra: Government Printer

———— 1962 *Tariff Revision: Tariff Board's Report on Coffee* Canberra: Government Printer, 27th April

———— 1966 *Revision Tariff Board's Report on Coffee* Canberra: Commonwealth Government Printer, 15th July

Dwyer, R.E.P. 1948 *Cocoa Production Territory of Papua-New Guinea The Economics of Cocoa Production* Port Moresby: Department of Agriculture, Stock and Fisheries, 3 July

Eastern Highlands District Advisory Council Committee Report 1965 *The Economic Development of the Eastern Highlands District of the Territory of New Guinea: Comment on the International Bank for Reconstruction and Development Report of September, 1964* No publication details available

Economic and Social Commission for Asia and the Pacific, and South Pacific Commission (ESCAP/SPC) 1982 *Population of Papua New Guinea*. Country Monograph Series no. 7.2, New York and Noumea: United Nations and South Pacific Commission

Government of Papua New Guinea (GoPNG) 1967–1975 *Development Bank Annual Reports and Financial Statements* Port Moresby: Government Printer

———— 1973 *Report of the Committee Investigating Tribal Fighting in the Highlands* Port Moresby: Government Printer, May

———— 1974 *Final Report of the Constitutional Planning Committee*. Parts 1 and 2, Port Moresby: Government Printer

———— 1974 *Strategies for Nationhood: Policies & Issues*. Port Moresby: Central Planning Office, December

———— 1974 *Strategies for Nationhood: Programmes & Performance*. Port Moresby: Central Planning Office, September

International Bank for Reconstruction and Development/World Bank (IBRD/WB) 1965 *The Economic Development of the Territory of Papua and New Guinea* Baltimore: The Johns Hopkins Press for the IBRD

———— 1973 *A Report on Development Strategies for Papua New Guinea* Prepared by a Mission from the Overseas Development Group, University of East Anglia, February (Popularly known as the Faber Report)

International Coffee Organisation (ICO) 1963 *History of Recent International Coffee Agreements: Their Background, provisions, Operations and Related Developments, 1954–63* International Coffee Council 1st Session 28/6/63 Washington, D.C.: ICO

International Labour Organisation (ILO) 1972 *Employment, Incomes and Equality: A Strategy for Increasing Productive Employment in Kenya* Geneva: International Labour Organisation

Poggendorff, W. 1953 *Rice Production in Papua and New Guinea* Canberra: Department of Territories

Territory of Papua and New Guinea (ToPNG) 1948 *Report of the Economic Development Committee of the Provisional Administration* Port Moresby: TPNG, September

———— 1959 *Report of the Coffee Conference held in Goroka from 19th to 22nd January 1959* (Port Moresby: Unpublished paper, February)

———— 1967 *Economic Development of Papua and New Guinea* Port Moresby: Government Printer, Prepared by direction of The Administrator and Tabled in the House of Assembly 1 June

———— 1968 *Programmes and Policies for the Economic Development of Papua and New Guinea* Port Moresby: Government Printer, September

ToPNG Department of Native Affairs Eastern Highlands District [DNA-EHD] *Annual Report 1955–56* (Unpublished)

———— *Annual Report 1959–60* (Unpublished)

———— *Annual Report 1955–56* (Unpublished)

———— *Annual Report 1960–61* (Unpublished)

United Nations Conference on Trade and Development 1984 *Studies in the processing, marketing and distribution of commodities: The processing and marketing of coffee: Areas for international co-operation* New York: United Nations

Urquhart, D.H. and R.E.P. Dwyer 1951 *Report on the Prospects of Extending the Growing of Cacao in the Territory of Papua and New Guinea* Bournville, UK: Prepared for and Published by Cadbury Brothers Ltd

Theses and Other Unpublished Material

Badu, Nao 1982 'Papua Besena: Case Study of a Separatist Movement' MA thesis Sydney: University of Sydney

Bourke, R. Michael 1988 'Taim Hangre: Variation in Subsistence Food Supply in the Papua New Guinea Highlands' PhD thesis Canberra: The Australian National University

Cowen, Michael P. 1979 'Capital and Household Production: the Case of Wattle in Kenya's Central province 1903–64' PhD thesis Cambridge, UK: University of Cambridge

de Vries, Jos 1979 'International Commodity Agreements: A Losing Proposition' Unpublished Paper, November

Dick, Gordon 1977 'Knowledge and Performance in Village Coffee Production: A Study from the Western Highlands of Papua New Guinea' MA thesis (Education) Port Moresby: University of Papua New Guinea

Fingleton, James S. 1980 'Land, Law and Development: A Case Study of Tenure Conversion in Papua New Guinea' MA thesis (Law) Port Moresby: University of Papua New Guinea, July

———— 1985 'Changing Land Tenure in Melanesia' PhD thesis Canberra: The Australian National University

Fingleton, Jim (ed.) 2005 'Privatising Land in the Pacific' Discussion Paper no. 80, Canberra: The Australia Institute

Gerritsen, Rolf 1979 'Groups, Classes and Peasant Politics in Ghana and Papua New Guinea' PhD thesis Canberra: The Australian National University

Harris, Geoffrey T. 1973 'The Determinants of Internal Migration in Papua New Guinea; An Examination of Economic Rationality in a Less Developed Country' MA thesis (Economics) La Trobe University

Hawksley, Charles M. 2001 'Administrative Colonialism: District Administration and Colonial "Middle Management" in Kelantan 1909–1919 and the Eastern Highlands of Papua New Guinea 1947–1957' PhD thesis Wollongong: University of Wollongong

Hide, Robin L. 1981 'Aspects of Pig Production and Use in Colonial Sinasina, Papua New Guinea' PhD thesis New York: Columbia University

Howlett, Diana R. 1962 'A Decade of Change in the Goroka Valley, New Guinea: Land Use and Development in the 1950s' PhD thesis Canberra: The Australian National University

Hughes, Ian 1966 'Availability of Land and Other Factors Determining the Incidence and Scale of Cash Cropping in the Kere Tribe, Sina Sina, Chimbu District, New Guinea' BA (Hons) thesis Sydney: University of Sydney

Jeffreys, F.J. 1974 'The Mekeo Rice Project' MA thesis Port Moresby: Economics Department, University of Papua New Guinea

Jinks, Brian 1975 'Policy, Planning and Administration in Papua New Guinea, 1942–1952 with Special Reference to the Role of J.K. Murray' PhD thesis Sydney: University of Sydney

Krasner SK 1971 'The Politics of Primary Commodities: A Study of Coffee 1900–1970' Phd thesis Harvard University

Larmour, Peter 1987 'Land Policy and Decolonisation in Melanesia: A Comparative Study of Land Policymaking and Implementation before and after Independence in Papua New Guinea, Solomon Islands and Vanuatu' PhD thesis Sydney: Macquarie University

Lowe, Michael 2006 'Smallholder agrarian change: the experience in two Tolai communities' PhD thesis Canberra: The Australian National University

MacWilliam, Scott 2009 'Development and Agriculture in Late Colonial Papua New Guinea' PhD thesis Canberra: The Australian National University

Reynolds, W. 1985 'H.V. Evatt: The imperial connection and the quest for Australian security, 1941–1945' PhD thesis Newcastle: University of Newcastle

Standish, William A. 1991 'Simbu Paths to Power: Political Change and Cultural Continuity in the Papua New Guinea Highlands' PhD thesis Canberra: The Australian National University

Stanner, W.E. 1947 'Reconstruction in the South Pacific Islands A Preliminary Report Part One' 'The Territory of Papua and the Trustee Territory of New Guinea' Section I 'The Pre-war Situation' Unpublished Paper

Stewart, Randall G. 1986 'Dialectic of Underdevelopment: Imperialism, Class and State in the Coffee Industry of Papua New Guinea' PhD thesis Canberra: The Australian National University

Timms, Wendy 1996 'The Post World War Two Colonial Project and Australian Planters in Papua New Guinea: The search for relevance in the colonial twilight' PhD thesis Canberra: The Australian National University

Wehner, H.G. Jr 1963 'The Cocoa Marketing Board and Economic Development in Ghana: A Case Study' PhD Ann Arbor: University of Michigan

Wright, Huntley L.R. 1999 'State Practice and Rural Smallholder Production: Late-Colonialism and the Agrarian Doctrine in Papua New Guinea 1942–1969' PhD thesis Palmerston North: Massey University

Published Material

Books, Chapters, Articles, Book Reviews and Reports

Ackland, Michael 2001 *Damaged Men: The precarious lives of James McAuley and Harold Stewart* Crows Nest, NSW: Allen and Unwin

Akiyama, Takamasa and Ronald C. Duncan 1984 *Analysis of the World Coffee Market* Washington: World Bank

Allen, Bryant J. 1981 'The North Coast Region' in Donald Denoon and Catherine Snowden (eds) *A time to plant and a time to uproot: a History of Agriculture in Papua New Guinea* Port Moresby: Papua New Guinea Institute of Applied Social and Economic Research Institute of Papua New Guinea Studies for the Department of Primary Industry, pp. 105–141

———— 1984 'The Importance of Being Equal: the Colonial and Post-Colonial Experience in the Torricelli Foothills' Paper prepared for the Wenner-Gren Foundation for Anthropological Research Symposium no. 95, *Sepik Research Today: the Study of Sepik Cultures in and for Modern Papua New Guinea*, held in Basel, Switzerland 19–26 August

Altvater, Elmar 2001 'The Growth Obsession' in Leo Panitch and Colin Leys (eds) *A World of Contradictions Socialist Register 2002* London: Merlin, pp. 73–92

Amarshi, Azeem, Good, Kenneth and Rex Mortimer 1979 *Development and Dependency: The political economy of Papua New Guinea* Melbourne: Oxford University Press

Amsden, Alice H. 1989 *Asia's Next Giant: South Korea and late industrialization* New York: Oxford University Press

———— 2007 *Escape from Empire: the Developing World's Journey through Heaven and Hell* Boston, Mass.: MIT Press

Anderson, David 1977 *An Economic Survey of Smallholder Coffee Producers—1976* Port Moresby: Department of Primary Industry, Planning Economics Marketing Branch, September

Anderson, David and Valmai Trainor 1978 'Fresh and Frozen Meat Consumption in the Eastern Highlands Province, 1975–1976' *Yagl-Ambu* vol. 5, no. 3, pp. 65–68

Anderson, D 2005 *Histories of the Hanged: The Dirty War in Kenya and the End of Empire* New York: W.W. Norton

Anderson, Ian 2003 *Globalization, Trade and Development: What is left for aid to do?* Canberra: AusAID, December

Anderson, Kym and Ross Garnaut 1987 *Australian Protectionism Extent, Causes and Effects* Sydney: Allen and Unwin

Andrews, C. Lesley 1975 *Business and Bureaucracy: A Study of Papua New Guinean Businessmen and the Policies of Business Development in Port Moresby* New Guinea Research Bulletin no. 59, Port Moresby and Canberra: New Guinea Research Unit, The Australian National University

Anis, Thomas, Makis, Ephraim, Miriung, Theodore and Eugene Ogan 1976 'Toward a New Politics—The Elections in Bougainville' in D. Stone (ed.) *Prelude to self-Government: Electoral Politics in Papua New Guinea 1972* Canberra: Research School of Pacific and Asian Studies, The Australian National University and University of Papua New Guinea, pp. 442–468

Anon. 1939 '"A Second Kenya" in Central New Guinea: Return of Hagen—Sepik Exploring Party' *Pacific Islands Monthly* 15 August, vol. 10, no. 1, pp. 19–20

———— 1955 'Land Systems Come Under Fire in NG: E. Highlands' Plain Talk to Official' *Pacific Islands Monthly* January, vol. 25, no. 6, pp. 19, 138–139

———— 1978 *Lowlands Agricultural Experiment Station Keravat, Papua New Guinea 1928–1978* Rabaul: Trinity Press

Apa, Michael Agiua 1978 *Coffee Growing in Kupau Village, Simbu Province History of Agriculture* Working Paper no. 23, Waigani: UPNG and Department of Primary Industry, December

Arndt, Heinz W. 1969 'An Answer to Crocombe—I: Too many invidious and invalid comparisons' *New Guinea* vol. 4, no. 2, pp. 54–59

———— 1985 *A Course through Life: Memoirs of an Australian Economist* History of Development Studies 1 Canberra: National Centre for Development Studies, The Australian National University

———— 1985 *Sir John Crawford* Pacific Economic Papers no. 128 Canberra: Australia-Japan Research Centre, Research School of Pacific and Asian Studies, The Australian National University, November

———— 1987 *Economic Development: The History of an Idea* University of Chicago Press

Arthur, W.A. n.d. *Tea: Agriculture in the Economy A Series of Review Papers* Konedobu: Department of Primary Industry

Ballard, John 1981 'Policy-Making as Trauma: the Provincial Government Issue' in J. Ballard (ed.) *Policy-Making in a New State Papua New Guinea 1972–77* St Lucia: University of Queensland Press, pp. 95–132

Banaji, Jairus 2011 *Theory as History: Essays on Modes of Production and Exploitation* Chicago: Haymarket Books

Bates, Robert 1997 *Open-Economy Politics: The Political Economy of the World Coffee Trade* Princeton University Press

Berndt, Ronald W. and Lawrence Peter (eds) 1971 *Politics in New Guinea Traditional and in the Context of Change Some Anthropological Perspectives* Nedlands: University of Western Australia Press

Blackburn, Sir Richard, Coombs, H.C. et. al. 1986 *Sir John Crawford* Canberra: The Australian National University

Boag, A.D. and R.E. Curtis 1959 'Agriculture and Population in the Mortlock Islands' *Papua and New Guinea Agricultural Journal* vol. 12, no. 1, pp. 20–27

Bourke, R.M. 1982 *Agronomic field trials on food crops in Papua New Guinea 1928 to 1978* Technical Report 82/3 Port Moresby: Department of Primary Industry

———— 1986 'Village Coffee in the Eastern Highlands of Papua New Guinea' *Journal of Pacific History* vol. 21, no. 1/2, pp. 100–103

Bredmeyer, Theo 1975 'The registration of customary land in Papua New Guinea' *Melanesian Law Journal* vol. iii, no. 2, p. 269

Brookfield, Harold C. 1961 'Native Employment within the New Guinea Highlands' *Journal of the Polynesian Society.* vol. lxx, pp. 300–313

———— 1968 '"The Money that grows on Trees": the Consequences of Innovation within a Man-Environment System' *Australian Geographical Studies* October, vol. vi, no. 2, pp. 7–119

———— 1973 'Full Circle in Chimbu: A Study of Trends and Cycles' in Harold Brookfield (ed.) *The Pacific in Transition: Geographical Perspectives on Adaptation and Change* London: Edward Arnold pp. 127–160

Brookfield, Harold C with D. Hart 1971 *Melanesia: a geographical interpretation of an island world* London: Methuen

Brown, Ed 1996 'Deconstructing development: Alternative perspectives on the history of an idea' *Journal of Historical Geography* vol. 22, no. 3, pp. 333–339

Brown, Paula 1973 *The Chimbu: a study in change in the New Guinea Highlands* London: Routledge and Kegan Paul

———— 1987 'New Men and Big Men: Emerging Stratification in the Third World, A Case Study from the New Guinea Highlands' *Ethnology* April, vol. 26, no. 2, pp. 87–105

Brown, Nicholas 1999 '"It's a Case of Using Any Stick to Beat a Dog": R.I. Downing, the Keynesian revolution and reconstruction' *History of Economics Review* Summer, no. 30, pp. 90–107

Brunton, Brian and Duncan Colquhoun-Kerr 1984 *The Annotated Constitution of Papua New Guinea* Waigani: University of Papua New Guinea Press

Bryan, Dick 1985 'Monopoly in Marxist Method' *Capital and Class* Summer, no. 26, pp. 72–92

Buckley, K., Dale, B. and W. Reynolds 1994 *Doc Evatt: Patriot, Internationalist, Fighter and Scholar* Melbourne: Longman Cheshire

Buckley, K. and K. Klugman 1983 *"The Australian Presence in the Pacific": Burns, Philp 1914–1946* Sydney: George Allen and Unwin

Campbell, Ian C. 2000 'The ASOPA Controversy: A Pivot of Australian Policy in Papua and New Guinea, 1945–49' *The Journal of Pacific History* vol. 35, no. 1, pp. 83–99

Cartledge, Ian 1978 *A History of the Coffee Industry in Papua New Guinea: from inception to the end of 1975* Goroka: Papua New Guinea Coffee Industry Board

Cheetham, R.J. 1962–1963 'The Development of Indigenous Agriculture, Land Settlement, and Rural Credit Facilities in Papua and New Guinea' *The Papua and New Guinea Agricultural Journal* December–March, vol. 15, nos 3–4, pp. 67–78

Chenery, H., Ahluwalia, M.S., Bell, C.L.G., Duloy, J.H. and R. Jolly 1974 *Redistribution with Growth* London: Oxford University Press

Chowning, A, Epstein, A.L., Epstein, T.S., Goodale, J. and I. Grosart 1971 'Under the volcano' in A.L. Epstein, R.S. Parker, R.S. and M. Reay (eds) *The Politics of Dependence: Papua New Guinea 1968* Canberra: ANU Press, pp. 48–90

Christensen, J. and D.R.J. Densley n.d. *Oil Palm: Agriculture in the Economy A Series of Review Papers* Konedobu: Department of Primary Industry

Cleland, Sir Donald 1971 'An Administrator Reflects' in K.S. Inglis (ed.) *The History of Melanesia* Canberra and Port Moresby: Research School of Pacific and Asian Studies The Australian National University and University of Papua New Guinea, pp. 209–228

Cleland, Dame Rachel 1985 *Pathways to Independence; Stories of Official & Family Life in Papua New Guinea from 1951–1975* Cottesloe: self-published

Clunies Ross, A. 1973 'Secession without Tears' in A. Clunies Ross and J. Langmore (eds) *Alternative Strategies for Papua New Guinea* Melbourne: Oxford University Press, pp. 131–138

Colebatch, H.K. 1981 'Policy-Making for Rural Development' in J. Ballard (ed.) *Policy-Making in a New State Papua New Guinea 1972–77* St. Lucia: University of Queensland Press, pp. 257–279

Coleman, William, Cornish, Selwyn and Alf Haggar 2006 *Giblin's Platoon: The Trials and Triumph of the Economist in Australian Public Life* Canberra: ANU E Press

Connell, John 1978 *Taim bilong mani: The evolution of agriculture in a Solomon Island society* Development Studies Centre Monograph no. 12, Canberra: Australia National University

——— 1979 'The emergence of a peasantry in Papua New Guinea' *History of Agriculture* Working Paper no. 27, Waigani and Port Moresby: University of Papua New Guinea and Department of Primary Industry, March

——— 1997 *Papua New Guinea: The Struggle for Development* London: Routledge

Connolly, Bob and Robin Anderson 1987 *First Contact: New Guinea's Highlanders Encounter the Outside World* New York: Viking Penguin

Conroy, John D. 1977 'Urbanisation in Papua New Guinea: A Development Constraint' in R.J. May (ed.) *Change and Movement: Readings on Internal Migration in Papua New Guinea* Canberra: Papua New Guinea Institute of Applied Social and Economic Research in association with ANU Press, pp. 59–70

——— 1982 *Essays on the Development Experience in Papua New Guinea* Monograph no. 17, Boroko: Papua New Guinea Institute of Applied Social and Economic Research

Conroy, W.R. and L.A. Bridgland 1947 'Native Agriculture in Papua-New Guinea' in Commonwealth of Australia, Department of External Territories *1950 Report of the New Guinea Nutrition Survey Expedition 1947* Sydney: Government Printer pt 3, pp. 72–91

Conyers, Diana 1976 *The Provincial Government Debate: Central Control Versus Local Participation In Papua New Guinea* Monograph no. 2, Boroko: Papua New Guinea Institute of Applied Social and Economic Research

Coombs, H.C. 1971 *Other People's Money* Canberra; ANU Press

———— 1981 *Trial Balance* South Melbourne: Macmillan

Cornish, Selwyn 1999 'Sir Leslie Melville Keynesian or Pragmatist?' *History of Economics Review* Summer, no. 30, pp. 126–150

Cowen, Michael 1984 'Traditions of Populism' *Economy and Society* vol. 13, no. 1, pp. 72–88

———— 1984 'The Early Years of the Colonial Development Corporation: British State Enterprise Overseas during Late Colonialism' *African Affairs* January, vol. 83, no. 330, pp. 63–75

———— 1986 'Change in State Power, International Conditions and Peasant Producers: The Case of Kenya' *The Journal of Development Studies* vol. 22, no. 2, pp. 355–384

Cowen, M.P. and Shenton, R.W. 1992 *The Roots of Trusteeship: The Moral Basis of Fabian Colonialism; Development and Agrarian Bias* pt 1: *The Original Theory of Development: Development and Agrarian Bias* pt 2: *Agrarian Bias; Development and Agrarian Bias* pt 3: *Land Nationalisation* Working Papers 18–21, Department of Economics, Faculty of Business, City of London Polytechnic

———— 1996 *Doctrines of Development*. London: Routledge

Crawford, Max 1987 'My Brother Jack: Background and Early Years' in L.T. Evans and J.D.B. Millar (eds) *Politics and Practice Essays in Honour of Sir John Crawford* Sydney: ANU Press and Pergamon Press

Creech Jones, Arthur (ed.) 1959 *New Fabian Colonial Essays* London: Hogarth Press

———— 1959 'The Labour Party and colonial policy, 1946–51' in Arthur Creech Jones (ed.) *New Fabian Colonial Essays* London: Hogarth Press, pp. 19–37

Crockett, Peter 1993 *Evatt A Life* Melbourne: Oxford University Press

Crocombe, R.G. 1964 *Communal Cash Cropping Among the Orokaiva* New Guinea Research Bulletin no. 4, Canberra and Port Moresby: New Guinea Research Unit, The Australian National University

———— 1968 'Bougainville! Copper, C.R.A. and secessionism' *New Guinea* vol. 3, no. 3, pp. 39–47

———— 1968/69 'That Five Year Plan: For New Guineans—Token Development' *New Guinea* vol. 3, no. 3, pp. 57–70

———— 1969 'Crocombe to His Critics: The Debate Goes On …' *New Guinea* vol. 4, no. 3, pp. 49–58

———— 1977 'Australian Planning in the New Guinea Economy' in F.S. Stevens and E.P. Wolfers (eds) *Racism: The Australian Experience* vol. 3 *Colonialism and After* Sydney: ANZ Book Co., pp. 148–162

Crocombe, R.G. and G.R. Hogbin 1963 *The Erap Mechanical Farming Project* New Guinea Research Bulletin no. 1, reprinted July, Canberra and Port Moresby: New Guinea Research Unit, The Australian National University

Cumings, Bruce 1999 'Webs with No Spiders, Spiders with No Webs: The Genealogy of the Developmental State' in Meredith Woo-Cumings (ed.) *The Developmental State* Ithaca: Cornell University Press, pp. 61–92

Curtin, P.W.E. 1965 'The World Bank Report: A Review' *New Guinea* vol. 1, no. 1, pp. 52–58

———— 1968 'But Whose Development? How to be Inconsistent' *New Guinea* vol. 3, no. 1, pp. 19–24

Dalziell, Allan 1967 *Evatt The Enigma* Melbourne: Lansdowne Press

Dand, Robin 1993 *The International Cocoa Trade* Cambridge, UK: Woodhead Publishing Ltd

Dennis, Maxine n.d. 'Plantations' in Donald Denoon and Catherine Snowden (eds) *A time to Plant and a time to uproot A History of Agriculture in Papua New Guinea* Port Moresby: Institute of Papua New Guinea Studies for the Department of Primary Industry, pp. 219–245

Denoon, Donald 1976 'Papua New Guinea' *Australian Journal of Politics and History* vol. 22, no. 3, pp. 435–443

———— 1985 'Capitalism in Papua New Guinea; Development or Underdevelopment' *Journal of Pacific History* vol. xi, no. 3, pp. 119–134

———— 2000 *Getting Under the Skin: The Bougainville Copper Agreement and the Creation of the Panguna Mine* Melbourne: Melbourne University Press

Denoon, Donald and Catherine Snowden (eds) 1981 *A time to plant and a time to uproot: A History of Agriculture in Papua New Guinea* Port Moresby: Institute of Papua New Guinea Studies for the Department of Primary Industry

Denoon, D., Dugan, K. and L. Marshall 1989 *Public Health in Papua New Guinea. Medical possibility and social constraint 1884–1984* Cambridge: Cambridge University Press

Densley, D.R.J. n.d. *Agriculture in the Papua New Guinea Economy* Konedobu: Department of Primary Industry

———— n.d. 'Rural Policies: Planning and Programmes, 1945 to 1977' in Donald Denoon and Catherine Snowden (eds) *A time to plant and a time to uproot: A History of Agriculture in Papua New Guinea* Port Moresby: Institute of Papua New Guinea Studies for the Department of Primary Industry, pp. 285–286

Densley, D.R.J. and M.A. Wheeler n.d. *Cocoa: Agriculture in the Economy A Series of Review Papers* Konedobu: PNG Department of Primary Industry

Dick, Gordon 1978 *A History of Coffee Planting in the Mt. Hagen Area History of Agriculture* Working Paper no. 24, Port Moresby: University of Papua New Guinea and Department of Primary Industry

Dick, Gordon and Bob McKillop 1976 *A Brief History of Agricultural Extension and Education in Papua New Guinea* Extension Bulletin no. 10, Port Moresby: Department of Primary Industry

Dixon, Robert 2001 *Prosthetic Gods: travel, representation and colonial governance* St Lucia: University of Queensland Press

Donaldson, M. 1979 *Class Formation in Papua New Guinea: The National Bourgeoisie* Paper presented at the Sociological Association of Australia and New Zealand Conference, Canberra, July

Donaldson, M. and Good, K. 1978 *Class and Politics in the Eastern Highlands of Papua New Guinea History of Agriculture* Discussion Paper no. 9, Waigani and Konedobu: University of Papua New Guinea and Department of Primary Industry, March

———— n.d. 'The Eastern Highlands: Coffee and Class' in Donald Denoon and Catherine Snowden (eds) *A time to plant and a time to uproot: A History of Agriculture in Papua New Guinea* Port Moresby: Institute of Papua New Guinea Studies for the Department of Primary Industry, pp. 143–169

———— 1998 *Articulated Agricultural Development: Traditional and Capitalist Agricultures in Papua New Guinea* Avebury, Aldershot: Gower

Donaldson, M and Turner, D. 1978 *The Foreign Control of the Papua New Guinea Economy and the Reaction of the Independent State* Political Economy Occasional Paper no. 1, Waigani: University of Papua New Guinea, December

Downs, Ian F.G. 1978 'Kiap, Planter and Politician: a Self-Portrait' in James Griffin (ed.) *Papua New Guinea Portraits: The Expatriate Experience* Canberra: ANU Press, pp. 225–251

———— 1980 *The Australian Trusteeship Papua New Guinea 1945–75* Canberra: Australian Government Publishing Service

———— 1986 *The Last Mountain: A Life in Papua New Guinea* St Lucia: University of Queensland Press

Dumont, R. 1973 'Some reflections on priorities in Melanesian development' in R.J. May (ed.) *Priorities in Melanesian Development* Canberra and Port Moresby: Research School of Pacific Studies, The Australian National University and University of Papua New Guinea, pp. 7–19

Easterly, William 2006 *The White Man's Burden: Why The West's Efforts To Aid The Rest Have Done So Much Harm And So Little Good*. New York: Penguin

Edwards, Peter G. 1983 *Prime Ministers and Diplomats: The Making of Australian Foreign Policy 1901–1949* Melbourne: Oxford University Press

Eggleston, F.W. 1953 *Reflections of an Australian Liberal* 2nd edn, Melbourne: F.W. Cheshire

Elkin, A.P. 1943 *Wanted—A Charter for the Native Peoples of the South-west Pacific* Sydney: Institute for International Affairs

Elkins, Caroline 2005 *Imperial Reckoning: The Untold Story of Britain's Gulag in Kenya* New York: Henry Holt

Epstein, A.L. 1969 *Matupit: Land, Politics, and Change Among the Tolai of New Britain* Canberra: The Australian National University Press

Epstein, T.S. 1968 *Capitalism, Primitive and Modern: Some Aspects of Tolai Economic Growth* East Lansing: Michigan State University Press

———— 1969 'The Plan and its assumptions...' *New Guinea* vol. 4, no. 3, pp. 59–63

———— 1969–70 'The Mataungan Affair' *New Guinea* vol. 4, no. 4, pp. 9–14

Errington, Frederick and Gewertz, Deborah 2004 *Yali's Question: Sugar, Culture and History* Chicago and London: The University of Chicago Press

Espie, F.F. 1973 'Bougainville Copper: difficult development decisions' in R.J. May (ed.) *Priorities in Melanesian Development* Papers delivered at the 6th Waigani Seminar Canberra and Port Moresby: Research School of Pacific and Asian Studies, The Australian National University and University of Papua New Guinea, pp. 335–342

Etherington, Norman and Deryck Schreuder (eds) 1988 *The Rise of Colonial Nationalism: Australia, New Zealand, Canada and South Africa first assert their nationalities, 1880–1914* Sydney: Allen and Unwin

Evans, L.T. and J.D.B. Miller (eds) 1987 *Politics and Practice Essays in Honour of Sir John Crawford* Sydney: The Australian National University Press and Pergamon Press

Evatt, H.V. 1935 'The British Dominions as Mandatories' *Proceedings of the Australian and New Zealand Society of International Law* vol. 1, pp. 27–54

———— 1945 *Foreign Policy of Australia: Speeches* Sydney: Angus and Robertson

———— 1946 *Australia in World Affairs* Sydney: Angus and Robertson

Fenbury, David M. 1980 *Practice without Policy: genesis of local government in Papua New Guinea* Monograph no. 13, 2nd edn Canberra: Development Studies Centre, The Australian National University

Ferguson, Niall 2009, 'Forword', in Dambisa Moyo, *Dead Aid: Why Aid Is Not Working And How There Is A Better Way For Africa* New York: Farrar, Strauss and Girou

Finch, John 1997 'From proletarian to entrepreneur to big man: The story of Noya' *Oceania* vol. 68, no. 2, pp. 123–133

Fingleton, Jim 1981 'Policy-Making on Lands' in J.A. Ballard (ed.) *Policy-Making in a New State Papua New Guinea 1972–77* St Lucia: University of Queensland Press, pp. 212–237

———— 1983 'Plantation Redistribution among the Tolai' *Melanesian Law Journal* vol. 11, pp. 99–123

Finnemore, Martha 2005 'Redefining Development at the World Bank' in Frederick Cooper and Randall Packard (eds) *International Development and the Social Sciences: Essays on the History and Politics of Knowledge* Berkeley: University of California Press, pp. 203–227

Finney, Ben R. 1968 'Bigfellow man belong business in New Guinea' *Ethnology* vol. 7, pp. 394–410

———— 1969 *New Guinea Entrepreneurs: Indigenous Cash Cropping, Capital Formation and Investment in the New Guinea Highlands* New Guinea Research Bulletin no. 27, Port Moresby and Canberra: New Guinea Research Unit, The Australian National University

———— 1970 'Partnership in developing the New Guinean Highlands, 1948–1968' *Journal of Pacific History* vol. 5, pp. 117–134

———— 1973 *Big-Men and Business: Entrepreneurship and Economic Growth in the New Guinea Highlands* Honolulu: The University Press of Hawaii

———— 1987 *Business Development in the Highlands of Papua New Guinea* Research Report Series no. 6 Honolulu: Pacific Islands Development Program, East-West Center, University of Hawaii

Firth, Stewart 1972 'The New Guinea Company, 1885–1899: a case of unprofitable imperialism' *Historical Studies* vol. xv, no. 1, pp. 361–377

———— 1978 'Albert Hahl: Governor of German New Guinea' in James Griffin (ed.) *Papua New Guinea Portraits. The Expatriate Experience* Canberra: ANU Press, pp. 28–47

———— 1982 *New Guinea under the Germans* Melbourne: Melbourne University Press

Fisher, Bart 1972 *The International Coffee Agreements: A Study in Coffee Diplomacy* New York: Praeger

Fisk, E.K. 1962 'The Economy of Papua-New Guinea' in D.G. Bettison, E.K. Fisk, F.J. West and J.G. Crawford *The Independence of Papua-New Guinea: What are the Pre-requisites?* Sydney: Angus and Robertson, pp. 25–43

———— 1962 'Planning in a Primitive Economy: Special Problems of Papua New Guinea' *Economic Record* vol. 38, no. 84, pp. 462–478

———— 1964 'Planning in a Primitive Economy; from pure subsistence to the production of a market surplus' *Economic Record* vol. 40, no. 90, pp. 156–174

———— 1965 'The Development of Trade and Specialization in a Primitive Economy' *Economic Record* vol. 41, no. 94, pp. 193–206

———— 1966 'The Economic Structure' in E.K. Fisk (ed.) *New Guinea on the Threshold: Aspects of Social, Political and Economic Development* Canberra: ANU Press, pp. 23–43

———— 1968 'Economic Bases for an Independent New Guinea' in John Wilkes (ed.) *New Guinea…Future Indefinite?* Proceedings of the 34th Summer School, Australian Institute of Political Science Sydney: Angus and Robertson, pp. 5–15

———— 1969 'An Answer to Crocombe—III: How fast do you go?' *New Guinea* vol. 4, no. 2, pp. 64–71

———— 1971 'Labour Absorption Capacity of Subsistence Agriculture' *Economic Record* vol. 47, no. 118, pp. 366–378

———— 1972 'Cold Comfort Farm: The wonderful world of subsistence affluence' *New Guinea* vol. 7, no. 1, pp. 28–39

———— 1972 'Development goals in rural Melanesia' in Marion Ward (ed.) *Change and Development in Rural Melanesia* 5th Waigani Seminar, Canberra and Port Moresby: The Australian National University and University of Papua New Guinea, pp. 9–23

———— 1974 'Rural Development' *New Guinea* vol. 9, no. 1, pp. 51–60

———— 1975 'The neglect of traditional food production in Pacific countries' *Australian Outlook* vol. 29, no. 2, pp. 149–160

———— 1975 'The response of nonmonetary production units to contact with the exchange economy' in L.G. Reynolds (ed.) *Agriculture in development* New Haven: Yale University Press, pp. 53–83

———— 1975 'The subsistence component in national income accounts' *The Developing Economies* vol. 13, no. 3, pp. 252–279

———— 1995 *Hardly ever a dull moment* History of Development Studies no. 5, Canberra: National Centre for Development Studies, The Australian National University

Fisk, E.K. and R.T. Shand 1970 'The Early Stages of Development in a Primitive Economy: The Evolution from Subsistence to Trade and Economic Specialization' in C.R.J. Wharton (ed.) *Subsistence Agriculture and Economic Development* London: Frank Cass and Co., pp. 257–274

Fitzpatrick, Peter 1980 *Law and State in Papua New Guinea* London: Academic Press

———— 1980 'The Creation and Containment of the Papua New Guinea Peasantry' in E. Wheelwright and K. Buckley (eds) *Essays in the Political Economy of Australian Capitalism* vol. 4 Sydney: ANZ Book Co., pp. 85–121

———— 1985 'The Making and Unmaking of the Eight Aims' in P. King, Wendy Lee and Vincent Warakai (eds) *From Rhetoric to Reality? Papua New Guinea's Eight Point Plan and National Goals after a Decade* Waigani: University of Papua New Guinea, pp. 22–31

Font, Mauricio A. 1990 *Coffee, Contention and Change in the Making of Modern Brazil* Cambridge, Mass.: Basil Blackwell

Fowke, John 1995 *Kundi Dan: Dan Leahy's life among the Highlanders of Papua New Guinea* St. Lucia: University of Queensland Press

Gammage, Bill 1998 *The Sky Travellers: Journeys in New Guinea 1938–1939* Melbourne: The Miegunyah Press and Melbourne University Press

Garnaut, Ross 1972 'Problems of Inequality: the social organization v. the state' *New Guinea* vol. 7, no. 3, pp. 52–62

———— 1977 'Urban growth: An Interpretation of Trends and Choices' in R.J. May (ed.) *Change and Movement: readings on Internal Migration in Papua New Guinea* Canberra: Papua New Guinea Institute of Applied Social and Economic Research in association with ANU Press, pp. 71–95

———— 1981 'The Framework of Economic Policy-Making' in J.A. Ballard (ed.) *Policy-Making in a New State: Papua New Guinea 1972–77* St Lucia: University of Queensland Press, pp. 157–211

———— 1984 'The Neo-Marxist Paradigm in Papua New Guinea' in R.J. May (ed.) *Social Stratification in Papua New Guinea* Working Paper no. 5, Canberra: Department of Political and Social Change, Research School of Pacific and Asian Studies, The Australian National University, August, pp. 63–81

Garnaut, Ross, Wright, Michael and Richard Curtain 1977 *Employment, Incomes and Migration in Papua New Guinea Towns* Monograph no. 6, Boroko: Papua New Guinea Institute of Applied Social and Economic Research

Gerritsen, Rolf 1975 *Aspects of the Political Evolution of Rural Papua New Guinea: Towards a Political Economy of the Terminal Peasantry* Canberra Marxist Discussion Group Seminar, 26th October 1975

———— 1981 'Aspects of the political evolution of rural Papua New Guinea: towards a political economy of the terminal peasantry' in R. Gerritsen, R.J. May and M.A.H.B. Walter *Road Belong Development. Cargo Cults, Community Groups and Self-help Movements in Papua New Guinea* Working Paper no. 3, Department of Political and Social Change, Research School of Pacific and Asian Studies, The Australian National University, August

Ghai, Yash P. and Anthony J. Regan 1992 *The Law, Politics and Administration of Decentralisation in Papua New Guinea* Monograph no. 30, Boroko: National Research Institute

Glezer, Leon 1982 *Tariff Politics Australian Policy-Making 1960–1980* Melbourne: Melbourne University Press

Godyn, D.L. 1974 *An Economic Survey of Cocoa in Papua New Guinea Part III village cocoa* Port Moresby: Department of Agriculture, Stock and Fisheries, June

Good, Kenneth and Mike Donaldson n.d. *The Development of Rural Capitalism in PNG: Coffee Production in the Eastern Highlands* Boroko: Institute of Papua New Guinea Studies

Gorringe, K.R. 1966 'The Tolai Cocoa Project, New Guinea' *Cocoa Growers' Bulletin* vol. 6, pp. 23–27

Gray, Geoffrey 1996 '"The next focus of power to fall under the spell of this little gang": anthropology and Australia's post-war policy in Papua New Guinea' *War & Society* vol. 14, no. 2, pp. 101–117

———— 2000 'Managing the Impact of War: Australian Anthropology, WWII and the Southwest Pacific' in Roy M. MacLeod (ed.) *Science and the Pacific War. Science and Survival in the Pacific, 1939–1945* London: Kluwer Academic Publishers, pp. 187–210

———— 2006 'Stanner's War: W.E.H. Stanner, the Pacific War, and its Aftermath' *The Journal of Pacific History* September, vol. 41, no. 2, pp. 145–163

———— 2006 'The army requires anthropologists: Australian anthropologists at war, 1939–1946' *Australian Historical Studies* no. 127, pp. 156–180

Gregory, C.A. 1979 'The Emergence of Commodity Production in Papua New Guinea' *Journal of Contemporary Asia* vol. 9, no. 4, pp. 389–409

———— 1982 *Gifts and Commodities* London: Academic Press

Griffin, James 1973 'Movements for Separation and Secession' in A. Clunies Ross and J. Langmore (eds) *Alternative Strategies for Papua New Guinea* Melbourne: Oxford University Press, pp. 99–130

———— 1975 'Papua New Guinea' *Australian Journal of Politics and History* vol. 21, no. 3, pp. 123–131

———— 1976 'Papua New Guinea' *Australian Journal of Politics and History* vol. 22, no. 1, pp. 115–130

———— 1982 'Napidakoe Navitu' in R.J. May (ed.) *Micronationalist movements in Papua New Guinea* Monograph no. 1, Canberra: Department of Political and Social Change, Research School of Pacific and Asian Studies, The Australian National University, pp. 113–138

———— 1989 '"Someone Who Needed No Pushing": The Making of Sir John Gunther' in Sione Latukefu (ed.) *Papua New Guinea: A Century of Colonial Impact 1884–1984* Port Moresby: National Research Institute and the University of Papua New Guinea, pp. 223–246

———— 2005 'Origins of Bougainville's Boundaries' in Anthony J. Regan and Helga M. Griffin (eds) *Bougainville before the conflict* Canberra: Pandanus Books, Research School of Pacific and Asian Studies, The Australian National University, pp. 72–75

———— 2005 'Movements Towards Secession 1964–76' in Anthony J. Regan and Helga M. Griffin (eds) *Bougainville before the conflict* Canberra: Pandanus Books, Research School of Pacific and Asian Studies, The Australian National University, pp. 291–299

Griffin, James, Nelson, Hank and Stewart Firth 1979 *Papua New Guinea: A Political History* Richmond, Victoria: Heinemann

Griffin, James (ed.) 1978 *Papua New Guinea Portraits The Expatriate Experience* Canberra: ANU Press

Grist, D.H. 1983 *Rice* 6th edn London: Longmans

Grosart, I. 1982 'Nationalism and micronationalism: the Tolai case' in R.J. May (ed.) *Micronationalist movements in Papua New Guinea* Monograph no. 1, Canberra: Department of Political and Social Change, Research School of Pacific and Asian Studies, The Australian National University, pp. 139–175

Grosart, I. and C.F. McColl 1976 'East New Britain' in D. Stone (ed.) *Prelude to Self-Government: Electoral Politics in Papua New Guinea 1972* Canberra: Research School of Pacific and Asian Studies and the University of Papua New Guinea at The Australian National University, pp. 373–399

Grossman, Lawrence S. 1982 'Beer Drinking and Subsistence Production in a Highland Village' in Mac Marshall (ed.) *Through a Glass Darkly: Beer and Modernization in Papua New Guinea* Boroko: Papua New Guinea Institute of Applied Social and Economic Research pp. 59–72

———— 1984 *Peasants, Subsistence Ecology and Development in the Highlands of Papua New Guinea* Princeton University Press

Guest, David 2003 'Enhancing PNG smallholder cocoa production through greater adoption of disease control practices' ACIAR Research that works for developing countries and Australia, retrieved 12 September 2012 at <http://www.aciar.gov.au/project/ASEM/2003/015>

Gunther, Sir John 1958 'The People' in J. Wilkes (ed.) *New Guinea and Australia* Sydney: Angus and Robertson, pp. 48–74

———— 1990 'Post-war medical services in Papua New Guinea: a personal view' in Sir Burton G. Burton-Bradley (ed.) *A History of Medicine in Papua New Guinea: Vignettes of an Earlier Period* Kingsgrove, NSW: Australasian Medical Publishing, pp. 47–76

Gutman, G.O. 1966 'Aspects of Economic Development in Papua and New Guinea' *The Australian Journal of Agricultural Economics* vol. 10, no. 2, pp. 128–141

Hahl, Albert 1980 *Governor in New Guinea* edited and translated by Peter G. Sack and Dymphna Clark Canberra: ANU Press

Hale, Peter R. n.d. c.1977 *Rice Agriculture in the Economy A Series of Review Papers* Port Moresby: PNG Department of Primary Industry

Hanson, L.W., Allen, B.J., Bourke R.M. and T.J. McCarthy 2001 *Papua New Guinea Rural Development Handbook* Canberra: Department of Human Geography, Research School of Pacific and Asian Studies, The Australian National University

Harding, T.G. and P. Lawrence 1971 'Cash Crops or Cargo?' in A.L. Epstein, R.S. Parker, and Marie Reay (eds) *The Politics of Dependence Papua New Guinea 1968* Canberra: ANU Press, pp. 162–207

Hasluck, Paul 1942 *Black Australians. A Survey of Native Policy in Western Australia, 1829–1897* Melbourne: Melbourne University Press

———— 1951 *A Policy for New Guinea Address by the Minister for Territories* Address to the William McGregor Club, Sydney, 20th November

———— 1956 *Australian Policy in Papua and New Guinea* George Judah Cohen Memorial Lecture presented at University of Sydney, 4 October

———— 1958 'Present Tasks and Policies' in J. Wilkes (ed.) *New Guinea and Australia* Presented at 24th Summer School of the Australian Institute of Political Science, Canberra ACT, 25th to 28th January, Sydney: Angus and Robertson, pp. 75–137

———— 1959 'Some Problems of Assimilation' Address to Section F of ANZAAS, Perth

———— 1962 'The Economic Development of Papua and New Guinea' *Australian Outlook* April, vol. 16, no. 1, pp. 5–25

———— 1976 *A Time for Building: Australian Administration in Papua and New Guinea 1951–1963* Melbourne: Melbourne University Press

Hau'ofa, Epeli 1981 *Mekeo: Inequality and ambivalence in a village society* Canberra: ANU Press

Healy, A.M. 1987 'Monocultural Administration in a multicultural environment: the Australians in PNG' in J.J. Eddy, and J.R. Nethercote (eds) *From Colony to Colonizer: Studies in Australian Administrative History* Sydney: Hale and Ironmonger, pp. 207–276

Hegarty, David 1972 'The Territory of Papua and New Guinea' *Australian Journal of Politics and History* August, vol. 18, no. 2, pp. 295–301

———— 1973 'Papua New Guinea' *Australian Journal of Politics and History* vol. 19, no. 3, pp. 438–446

Hide, Robin 1968 'A most just cause of Warre: a lesson to be learned at Merani…' *New Guinea* vol. 3, no. 1, pp. 25–42

———— 1973 *The Land Titles Commission in Chimbu: An Analysis of Colonial Land Law and Practice* New Guinea Research Bulletin no. 50, Port Moresby and Canberra: New Guinea Research Unit, The Australian National University

———— 2003 *Pig Husbandry in New Guinea: A Literature Review and Bibliography* Monograph no. 108, Canberra: Australian Centre for International Agricultural Research

Horner, David 1998 *Blamey: The Commander-in-Chief* St. Leonard's, NSW: Allen and Unwin

Howlett, Diana 1973 'Terminal development: From tribalism to peasantry' in H. Brookfield (ed.) *The Pacific in Transition: Geographical Perspectives on Adaptation and Change* London: Edward Arnold, pp. 249–273

Hudson, W.J. 1970 *Australia and the Colonial Question at the United Nations* Sydney: Sydney University Press

———— 1993 *Australia and the New World Order: Evatt at San Francisco 1945* Canberra: The Australian National University

Hughes, Colin A. 1965 'The Development of the Legislature: The Legislative Councils' in D.G. Bettison, Colin A. Hughes and Paul W. van der Veur (eds) *The Papua-New Guinea Elections 1964* Canberra: The Australian National University, pp. 8–27.

Hughes, Helen 2002 'PNG in need for much more than money' *Executive Highlights* no. 103, Sydney: The Centre for Independent Studies (Published in *The Australian Financial Review* 14 August 2002)

———— 2003 'Aid has failed the Pacific' *Issue Analysis* no. 33, Sydney: The Centre for Independent Studies. Ex-Kiap Network Forum, retrieved 12 September 2005 at <http://exkiap. net?articles/cis20030507-failed-aid/ia33.htm>

———— 2004 *Can Papua New Guinea Come Back From the Brink?* Issue Analysis no. 49, Sydney: The Centre for Independent Studies, 13 July

Hughes, Helen and Windybank, Susan 2005 *Papua New Guinea's Choice: A Tale of Two Nations* Issue Analysis no. 58, Sydney: The Centre for Independent Studies, 31 May

Hughes, Ian 1977 *New Guinea Stone Age Trade: The Geography and Ecology of Traffic in the Interior* Terra Australis 3 Canberra: The Australian National University

———— 1978 'Good Money and Bad: Inflation and Devaluation in the Colonial Process' *Mankind* vol. 11, no. 3, pp. 308–318

Huntington, S.P. 1965 'Political Order and Political Decay' *World Politics* vol. 17, no. 3, pp. 386–430

———— 1968 *Political Order in Changing Societies* New Haven: Yale University Press

Illich, Ivan 1972 'Design for a Convivial Society?' *New Guinea* vol. 7, no. 2, pp. 2–7

Jackman, Harry H. 1988 *Copra marketing and price stabilization in Papua New Guinea: A history to 1975* Pacific Research Monograph no. 17, Canberra: National Centre for Development Studies, The Australian National University

Jackson, Richard 1976 'The Impact of the Introduction of Markets: A Case Study from the Highlands of Papua New Guinea' *Savanna* December, vol. 5, no. 2, pp. 175–182

Jinks, Brian 1981 'The Directorate of Research and Post-War New Guinea' Unpublished Paper presented at Post-War Reconstruction Seminar, Canberra: The Australian National University, 3 August to 4 September

———— 1982 'Australia's Post-War Policy for New Guinea and Papua' *Journal of Pacific History* vol. 17, no. 2, pp. 86–100

———— 1983 'Alfred Conlon, the Directorate of Research and New Guinea' *Journal of Australian Studies* vol. 12, pp. 21–33

Johnson, Chalmers A. 1982 *MITI and the Japanese Miracle: the growth of industrial policy, 1925–1975* Stanford: Stanford University Press

———— 1995 *Japan, Who Governs? The Rise of the Developmental State* New York: Norton

———— 1999 'The Developmental State: Odyssey of a Concept' in Meredith Woo-Cummings (ed.) *The Developmental State* Ithaca: Cornell University Press, pp. 32–60

Joyce, R.B. 1971 *Sir William MacGregor* Melbourne: Oxford University Press

Kaputin, John 1969 'Australia's Carpetbaggers: After the apple—a miserable core?' *New Guinea* vol. 4, no. 1, pp. 35–42

Krasner, Stephen D. 1973 'Business Government Relations: The Case of the International Coffee Agreement' *International Organization* September, vol. 27, issue 4, pp. 495–516

Kay, Geoffrey B. 1976 *Development and Underdevelopment: A Marxist Analysis* London: Macmillan

Kerr, John 1978 *Matters for Judgement: An Autobiography* South Melbourne: Macmillan

Kiki, Albert Maori (Sir) 1971 *Ten Thousand Years in a Lifetime A New Guinea Autobiography* Melbourne: Cheshire

King, David and Nancy Burge n.d. c. 1980 'Cash Crops' in David King and Stephen Ranck (eds) *Papua New Guinea Atlas: A Nation in Transition* Port Moresby: Robert Brown and Associates (Australia) P/L in conjunction with the Geography Department, UPNG pp. 52–53

Kituai, August 1998 *My gun, my brother: the world of the Papua New Guinea police, 1920–1960* Honolulu: University of Hawai'i Press

Kohli, Atul 'Where Do High-Growth Political Economies Come From? The Japanese Lineage of Korea's Developmental State' in Woo-Cumings (ed.) *The Developmental State* Ithaca: Cornell University Press pp. 93–136

Koyati, Peandui 1978 *Coffee growing in the Baiyer River Area of the Western Highlands Province* History of Agriculture Discussion Paper no. 14, Waigani: University of Papua New Guinea and Department of Agriculture, June

Kuabaal, Leo 1976 'Sinasina Open Electorate' in D. Stone (ed.) *Prelude to Self-Government: Electoral Politics in Papua New Guinea 1972* Canberra: Research School of Pacific and Asian Studies, The Australian National University and the University of Papua New Guinea, pp. 350–370

Laracy, Hugh 2005 '"Imperium in Imperio"?: The Catholic Church in Bougainville' in Anthony J. Regan and Helga M. Griffin (eds) *Bougainville before the conflict* Canberra: Pandanus Books, Research School of Pacific and Asian Studies, The Australian National University, pp. 125–135

Larmour, Peter 1991 'Registration of Customary Land: 1952–1987' in Peter Larmour (ed.) *Customary Land Tenure: Registration and Decentralisation in Papua New Guinea* Monograph no. 29, Boroko: National Research Insitute, pp. 51–72

Lawrence, Peter 1964 *Road Belong Cargo: A Study of the Cargo Movement in the Southern Madang District, New Guinea* Manchester: Manchester University Press and Humanities Press

Lea, David A.M. and R. Gerard Ward 1970 'Crop Combinations' in David A.M. Lea and R. Gerard Ward (eds) *An Atlas of Papua and New Guinea* Glasgow: Collins and Longman, pp. 56–57

Leach, Jerry W. 1982 'Socio-historical conflict and the Kabisawali Movement in the Trobriand Islands' in R.J. May (ed.) *Micro-nationalist movements in Papua New Guinea Political and Social Change* Monograph no. 1, Canberra: Research School of Pacific Studies, The Australian National University, pp. 249–289

Leahy, Michael 1936 'The Central Highlands of New Guinea' Royal Geographical Society, published in *Geographical Journal* vol. 87, no. 3, pp. 229–260

Leahy, Michael and Maurice Crain 1937 *The Land That Time Forgot* New York: Funk and Wagnalls

Lee, David 1995 *Search for Security: The Political Economy of Australia's Postwar Foreign and Defence Policy* St. Leonards, NSW: Allen and Unwin

Lee, David and Christopher Watts (eds) 1997 *Evatt to Evans The Labor Tradition in Australian Foreign Policy* St. Leonards, NSW: Allen and Unwin

Lett, L. 1949 *Sir Hubert Murray of Papua* London: Collins

Lewis, David C. 1996 *The Plantation Dream: Developing British New Guinea and Papua 1884–1942* Canberra: The Journal of Pacific History

Leys, Colin 1959 'Socialism and the Colonies: Review' *Fabian Journal* July, no. 28, pp. 20–24

Longayroux, J. 1972 *Hoskins Development: The Role of Oil Palm and Timber* New Guinea Research Bulletin no. 49, Port Moresby and Canberra: New Guinea Research Unit, The Australian National University

Louis, William, Roger 1997 *Imperialism at Bay: The United States and the Decolonization of the British Empire, 1941–1945* Oxford University Press

MacWilliam, Scott 1984 'Electoral Politics and State Power' *Yagl-Ambu* June, vol. 11, no. 2, pp. 33–53

——— 1984 'Nationalism and Social Democracy: Papua New Guinea—Australia Relations Since World War I' *Yagl-Ambu* September, vol. 11, no. 3, pp. 4–28

——— 1985 'Inter-Provincial Comparisons in Coffee Production' *Kofi Tok* July, no. 1, pp. 9–10

——— 1986 'International capital, indigenous accumulation and the state in Papua New Guinea: the case of the Development Bank' *Capital and Class* Summer, no. 29, pp. 150–181

——— 1987 'International Companies and Nationalist Politics in Papua New Guinea' *Journal of Contemporary Asia* vol. 17, no. 1, pp. 19–41 (Previously presented at CSE Annual Conference, Sheffield, July 1986)

——— 1988 'Smallholdings, Land Law and the Politics of Land Tenure in Papua New Guinea' *The Journal of Peasant Studies* October, vol. 16, no. 1, pp. 77–109

——— 1992 'Smallholder Production, the State and Land Tenure' in Peter Larmour (ed.) *Customary Land Tenure: Registration and Decentralisation in Papua New Guinea* Boroko: Papua New Guinea Institute of Applied Social and Economic Research, pp. 9–32

——— 1993 'The Politics of Privatisation: The Case of the Coffee Industry Corporation in Papua New Guinea' *Australian Journal of Political Science* November, vol. 28, no. 3, pp. 481–498

——— 1996 'Papua New Guinea in the 1940s: Empire and Legend' in D. Lowe (ed.) *Australia and the End of Empires: the impact of decolonization in Asia and the South Pacific, 1945–1965* Geelong,Vic.: Deakin University Press, pp. 25–42

——— 1997 'Liberalism and the End of Development: Partington against Hasluck and Coombs' *Island* Issue 70, pp. 79–91

——— 1998 'Plantations and Smallholder Agriculture' in L. Tamakoshi-Zimmer (ed.) *Modern Papua New Guinea* Kirksville, Missouri: Thomas Jefferson Press and University Presses of America, pp. 107–132

——— 2005 'Post-war Reconstruction in Bougainville: Plantations, Smallholders and Indigenous Capital' in Anthony J. Regan and Helga M. Griffin (ed.) *Bougainville before the conflict* Canberra: Pandanus Books, Research School of Pacific and Asian Studies, The Australian National University, pp. 224–238

——— forthcoming 'Conservative Hero or Liberal Developer: Locating Paul Hasluck'

——— forthcoming 'The International Coffee Organisation: Cartel or Development Agency?'

Mair L.P. 1948 *Australia in New Guinea* 1st edn London: Christophers

Marmak, Alexander and Richard, Bedford 1974 'Bougainville's Students' *New Guinea* vol. 9, no. 1, pp. 4–15

Marshall, Mac (ed.) 1982 *Through a Glass Darkly: Beer and Modernization in Papua New Guinea* Monograph 18, Port Moresby: Papua New Guinea Institute of Applied Social and Economic Research

Marx, Karl 1976 *Capital: A Critique of Political Economy* vol. 1 Harmondsworth: Penguin

——— 1978 *Capital: A Critique of Political Economy* vol. 2 Harmondsworth: Penguin

May, Ron 1976 'The New Guinea Research Unit: 1961–1975' in R.J. May (ed.) *Research Needs and Priorities in Papua New Guinea* Monograph no. 1, Port Moresby: Papua New Guinea Institute of Applied Social and Economic Research, pp. 7–14

——— 1998 *Nugget, Pike et al.* Discussion Paper 8/98, Darwin: Northern Australia Research Unit, The Australian National University

——— 2006 *State and Society in Papua New Guinea: the first twenty-five years* ch. 15 'From promise to crisis: a Political Economy of Papua New Guinea' retrieved 16 September 2012 at <http://epress.anu.edu.au/sspng/mobile_devices/ch15.html>

McAuley, James 1952 'White Settlement in Papua New Guinea' *South Pacific* March, vol. 5, no. 12, pp. 250–255

———— 1952 'Mechanization, Collectives and Native Agriculture' *South Pacific* April, vol. 6, no. 1, pp. 276–281

———— 1956 'Economic Development Among the Mekeo' *South Pacific* January/February, vol. 8, no. 10, pp. 217–220

McIntyre, Neil et al. 1963 *Alfred Conlon: A Memorial by some of His Friends* Sydney: Benevolent Society of New South Wales

McKay, D.H. 1987 'Post-War Agriculture' in L.T. Evans and J.D.B. Miller (eds) *Policy and Practice Essays in Honour of Sir John Crawford* Sydney: ANU Press and Pergamon Press, pp. 34–50

McKillop, R.F. 1974 *Problems of Access: Agricultural Extension in the Eastern Highlands of New Guinea* presented at a Seminar, University of Papua New Guinea, November

———— 1981 'Managing Plantations in Papua New Guinea Today: Who Wants to be the Labourer?' in M.A.H. Walter (ed.) *What Do We Do About Plantations?* Monograph no. 15, Boroko: Papua New Guinea Institute of Applied Social and Economic Research pp. 25–32

———— 1981 'Agricultural Policy-Making' in J. Ballard (ed.) *Policy-Making in a New State Paua New Guinea 1972–77* St. Lucia: University of Queensland Press, pp. 238–256

Mikell, Gwendolyn 1989 *Cocoa and Chaos in Ghana* New York: Paragon House

Millmow, Alex 2000 'Revisiting Giblin: Australia's first Proto-Keynesian economist?' *History of Economics Review* no. 31, pp. 48–67

———— 2003 'W. Brian Reddaway—Keynes' emissary to Australia 1913–2002' *Economic Record* vol. 79, no. 244, pp. 136–138

Minns, John 2006 *The Politics of Developmentalism: the Midas states of Mexico, South Korea, and Taiwan* Basingstoke: Palgrave Macmillan

Mitchell, D.D. II 1976 *Land and Agriculture in Nagovisi Papua New Guinea* Monograph no. 3, Port Moresby: Papua New Guinea Institute of Applied Social and Economic Research

Morauta, Louise 1974 *Beyond the Village: Local Politics in Madang, Papua New Guinea* London: University of London Athlone Press and Humanities Press

Morefield, Jeanne 2005 *Covenants without Swords: Idealist Liberalism and the Spirit of Empire* Princeton: Princeton University Press

Morris, Alan and Rob Stewart 2005 *Papua New Guinea Analytical Report for the White Paper on Australia's aid program* Canberra: AusAID, September

Moulik, T.K. 1977 *Bougainville in transition* Monograph no. 7, Canberra: Development Studies Centre, The Australian National University

Moyo, Dambisa 2009 *Dead Aid: Why Aid Is Not Working And How There Is A Better Way For Africa* New York: Farrar, Strauss and Girou

Munnull, J.P. and Densley D.R.J. n.d.c. 1978 *Coffee: Agriculture in the Economy A Series of Review Papers* Konedobu: PNG Department of Primary Industry

Murray, Colonel J.K. 1949 *The Provisional Administration of the Territory of Papua-New Guinea* Brisbane: University of Queensland

———— 1971 'In Retrospect 1945–1952: Papua-New Guinea and Territory of Papua and New Guinea' in K.S. Inglis (ed.) *The History of Melanesia* Canberra and Port Moresby: Research School of Pacific and Asian Studies, The Australian National University and University of Papua New Guinea, pp. 177–208

Muthu, Sankar 2003 *Enlightenment Against Empire* Princeton and Oxford: Princeton University Press

National Statistical Office of Papua New Guinea 2000 '2000 National Census' retrieved 21 September 2012 at <http://www.spc.int/prism/country/pg/stats/2000_Census/census.htm>

Nelson, Hank 1976 *Black White & Gold: Goldmining in Papua New Guinea 1878–1930* Canberra: ANU Press

———— 1993 'Cleland, Sir Donald Mackinnon (1901–1975)' in *Australian Dictionary of Biography* vol. 13, Melbourne: Melbourne University Press, pp 440–441.

Nisbet, Robert A. 1969 *Social Change and History: Aspects of the Western Theory of Development* New York: Oxford University Press

———— 1980 *History of the Idea of Progress* New York: Basic Books

Nixon, Richard M. 1962 *Six Crises* London: WH Allen

Ogan, E. 1971 'Charisma and Race' in A.L. Epstein, R.S. Parker and Marie Reay (eds) *The Politics of Dependence Papua New Guinea 1968* Canberra: ANU Press, pp. 132–161

───── 1972 *Business and Cargo: Socio-economic change among the Nasioi of Bougainville New Guinea* New Guinea Research Bulletin no. 44, Port Moresby and Canberra: New Guinea Research Unit, The Australian National University

───── 1996 'Copra Came Before Copper: The Nasioi of Bougainville and Plantation Colonialism, 1902–1964' *Pacific Studies* March, vol. 19, no. 1, pp. 31–51

Packenham, Robert A. 1966 'Political-Development Doctrines in the American Foreign Aid Program' *World Politics* January, vol. 18, no. 2, pp. 194–235

Palacpac, Alice C. 1976 *World Rice Statistics* Manila: Department of Agricultural Economics, The International Rice Research Institute, April

Pan-American Coffee Bureau c. 1963 *Impact of Coffee on the U.S. Economy* New York: Pan-American Coffee Bureau

Parker, R.S. 1971 'From Dependence to Autonomy' in A.L. Epstein, R.S. Parker and Marie Reay (eds) *The Politics of Dependence Papua New Guinea 1968* Canberra: ANU Press, pp. 315–360

Parker, R.S. and E.P. Wolfers 1971 'The Context of Political Change' in A.L. Epstein, R.S. Parker and Marie Reay (eds) *The Politics of Dependence Papua New Guinea 1968* Canberra: ANU Press, pp. 12–47

Peacock, Andrew 1973 'Opening Address' in R.J. May (ed.) *Priorities in Melanesian Development* Canberra and Port Moresby: Research School of Pacific and Asian Studies, The Australian National University and University of Papua New Guinea, pp. 3–6

Pendergrast, Mark 1999 *Uncommon Grounds: The History of Coffee and How It Transformed Our World* New York: Basic Books

Philipp, P.F., Langness, L.L., von Fleckenstein, F. and M. Evans 1975 *Four Papers on the Papua New Guinea Cattle Industry* New Guinea Research Bulletin no. 63, Port Moresby and Canberra: New Guinea Research Unit, The Australian National University

Pitts, Jennifer 2005 *A Turn to Empire: The Rise of Imperial Liberalism in Britain and France* Princeton: Princeton University Press

Porter, Robert 1993 *Paul Hasluck: A Political Biography* Nedlands: University of Western Australia Press

Premdas, Ralph 1977 'Papua New Guinea in 1976: Dangers of a China Connection' *Asian Survey* January, vol. 17, no. 1, pp. 55–60

Pybus, Cassandra 1999 *The Devil and James McAuley* St Lucia: University of Queensland Press

Quinn, Peter 1981 'Agriculture, Land Tenure and Land Law to 1971' in Donald Denoon and Catherine Snowden (eds) *A time to plant and a time to uproot: A History of Agriculture in Papua New Guinea* Port Moresby: Institute of Papua New Guinea Studies, pp. 171–184

Rabe, Stephen G. 1988 *Eisenhower and Latin America: The Foreign Policy of Anticommunism* Chapel Hill: The University of North Carolina Press

Rattigan, Alf 1986 *Industry Assistance the Inside story* Melbourne: Melbourne University Press

Read, K.E. 1951 'Development Projects in the Central Highlands of New Guinea' *South Pacific* December, vol. 5, no. 10, pp. 202–207

———— 1952 'Land in the Central Highlands' *South Pacific* October, vol. 6, no. 7, pp. 440–449

Reay, M. 1959 'Individual Ownership and Transfer of Land among the Kuma' *Man* vol. lix, pp. 78–82

———— 1959 *Freedom and Conformity in the New Guinea Highlands* Melbourne: Melbourne University Press

———— 1969 'But Whose Estates? The Wahgi smallholders' *New Guinea* vol. 4, no. 3, pp. 64–68

Regan, Anthony J. and Helga M. Griffin (eds) 2005 *Bougainville before the conflict* Canberra: Pandanus Books

Reynolds, W. 1996 'Dr H.V. Evatt: Foreign Minister for a Small Power' in David Day (ed.) *Brave New World: Dr H.V. Evatt and Australian Foreign Policy* St.Lucia: University of Queensland Press, pp. 146–157

Roberts, H. (later Sir Henry ToRobert) 1965 'New Guinea's Leadership: Problems of the Prestige Period' *New Guinea* vol. 1, no. 3, pp. 12–16

Roche, Julian 1992 *The International Rice Trade* Cambridge, England: Woodhead Publishing

Rosberg, Carl G. Jr and John Nottingham 1996 *The Myth of 'Mau Mau': Nationalism in Kenya* Nairobi: East African Publishing House

Ross, Rev William 1936 'Ethnological Notes on Mt Hagen Tribes (Mandated Territory of New Guinea) with special reference to the tribe called Mogei' *Anthropos* vol. 31, pp. 341–363

Rowley, Charles D. 1958 *The Australians in German New Guinea 1914–1921* Melbourne: Melbourne University Press

———— 1968 *The New Guinea Villager: A Retrospect from 1964* Melbourne: F.W. Cheshire

Rowse, Tim 1978 *Australian Liberalism and National Character* Malmsbury, Vic.: Kibble Books

———— 1999 'Coombs the Keynesian' *History of Economics Review* Summer, no. 30, pp. 108–125

———— 2002 *Nugget Coombs: A Reforming Life* Port Melbourne: Cambridge University Press

Ryan, Peter 1971 'The Australian and New Guinea Administrative Unit' in Ken S. Inglis (ed.) *The History of Melanesia* Second Waigani Seminar held at Port Moresby May 30–June 5, 1968, Canberra and Port Moresby: The Australian National University and University of Papua and New Guinea, pp. 531–548

———— 2012 'Papua New Guinea: the almost broken country' Keith Jackson & Friends: PNG Attitude, 6 September, retrieved 11 September 2012 at <http://asopa.typepad.com/asopa_people/2012/09/papua-new-guinea-the-almost-broken-country-nearing-90-peter-ryan-reflects-on-his-association-with-pn.html?cid=6a00d83454f2ec69e20177448bee17970d>

Salisbury, Richard F. 1962 *From Stone to Steel: Economic Consequences of a Technological Change in New Guinea* Melbourne: Melbourne University Press

———— 1970 *Vunamami: Economic Transformation in a Traditional Society* Berkeley and Los Angeles: University of California Press

Schaffer, B. 1965 'Thoughts at Goroka, Sins of the World Bank team' *New Guinea* vol. 1, no. 2, pp. 72–79

———— 1966 'Advising About Development: The Example of the World Bank Report on Papua and New Guinea' *Journal of Commonwealth Political Studies* March, vol. iv, no. 1, pp. 30–46

Schneider, Ben Ross 1999 'The Desarrollista State in Brazil and Mexico' in Meredith Woo-Cummings (ed.) *The Developmental State* Ithaca: Cornell University Press pp. 276–305

Scragg, R.F.R. 1977 'Historical epidemiology in Papua New Guinea' *Papua New Guinea Medical Journal* September, vol. 20, no. 3, pp. 102–109

Shand, R.T. 1969 'An Answer to Crocombe—II: In defence of nucleus estates' *New Guinea* vol. 4, no. 2, pp. 60–63

——— 1965 'The Development of Trade and Specialization in a Primitive Economy' *Economic Record* vol. 41, no. 95, pp. 193–206

——— 1966 'Trade Prospects for the Rural Sector' in E.K. Fisk (ed.) *New Guinea on the Threshold: Aspects of Social, Political and Economic Development* Canberra: ANU Press, pp. 193–206

Shand, R.T. and M.L. Treadgold 1971 *The Economy of Papua New Guinea: Projections and Policy Issues* Canberra: Department of Economics, Research School of Pacific Studies, The Australian National University

Shand, R.T. and W. Straatmans 1974 *Transition from Subsistence: Cash Crop Development in Papua New Guinea* New Guinea Research Bulletin no. 54, Port Moresby and Canberra: New Guinea Research Unit, The Australian National University

Shaw, Barry 1985 *Agriculture in the Papua New Guinea Economy* Discussion Paper no. 20, Port Moresby: Institute of National Affairs

Shenton, Bob 2000 'Obituary' *The Journal of Peasant Studies* July, vol. 27, no. 4, pp. 163–166

Sinclair, James 1984 *Kiap—Australia's Patrol Officers in Papua New Guinea* Bathurst: R Brown and Associates

——— 1995 *The Money Tree: Coffee in Papua New Guinea* Bathurst, NSW: Crawford House Publishing

Singh, Sumer 1967 *A Benefit Cost Analysis of Resettlement in the Gazelle Peninsula* New Guinea Research Bulletin no. 17, Port Moresby and Canberra: New Guinea Research Unit, The Australian National University

——— 1974 *Co-operatives in Papua New Guinea* New Guinea Research Bulletin no. 58, Port Moresby and Canberra: New Guinea Research Unit, The Australian National University

Snowden, Catherine n.d. 'Copra Co-operatives' in Denoon and Snowden (eds) *A time to plant and a time to uproot: A History of Agriculture in Papua New Guinea* Port Moresby: Institute of Papua New Guinea Studies, pp. 185–204

Somare, Michael Thomas (Sir) 1975 *Sana: An autobiography of Michael Somare* Port Moresby: Nuigini Press

Southern, Roger 1974 '"Hagenkofi"—an episode of enterprise in the New Guinea Highland coffee industry' *Yagl-Ambu* vol. 1, pp. 39–53

Spate, O.H.K. 1953 'The Rice Problem in New Guinea' *South Pacific* November/December, vol. 7, no. 6, pp. 731–736

———— 1953 'Changing native agriculture in New Guinea' *The Geographical Review* vol. 43, no. 2, pp. 151–172

———— 1957 'Problems of Development in New Guinea' *South Pacific* July/August, vol. 9, no. 7, pp. 451–456

———— 1972 'Problems and Priorities: Summing up the Sixth Waigani' *New Guinea* vol. 7, no. 2, pp. 50–62

———— 1990 *On the Margins of History from the Punjab to Fiji* History of Development Studies 3, Canberra: National Centre for Development Studies, The Australian National University

Spender, P.C. 1972 *Politics and a Man* Sydney: Collins

Standish, Bill 1976 'New men for an Old Society: the Chimbu Regional Campaign' in D. Stone (ed.) *Prelude to self-Government: Electoral Politics in Papua New Guinea 1972* Canberra: Research School of Pacific and Asian Studies, The Australian National University pp. 308–349

———— 1982 'Elite Communalism: The Highlands Liberation Front' in R.J. May (ed.) *Micronationalist Movements in Papua New Guinea Political and Social Change* Monograph no. 1, Canberra: Research School of Pacific Studies, The Australian National University, pp. 359–413

Stephen, David 1972 *A History of Political Parties in Papua New Guinea* Melbourne: Landsdowne Press

Stewart, R.G. 1992 *Coffee: The Political Economy of an Export Industry in Papua New Guinea* Boulder, San Francisco: Westview Press

Stone, David 1976 'The Political Turning Point: The Birth of the National Coalition Government' in D. Stone (ed.) *Prelude to Self-Government: Electoral Politics in Papua New Guinea 1972* Canberra: Research School of Pacific and Asian Studies and the University of Papua New Guinea at The Australian National University, pp. 529–538

Strathern, Andrew 1971 'Pig Complex and Cattle Complex: Some Comparisons and Counterpoints' *Mankind* vol. 8, no. 2, pp. 129–136

——— 1973 'Political development and problems of social control in Mt Hagen' in R.J. May (ed.) *Priorities in Melanesian Development* Canberra and Port Moresby: Research School of Pacific and Asian Studies, The Australian National University and University of Papua New Guinea, pp. 73–82,

Stuart, R. 1977 *Nuts to You!* Sydney: Wentworth Books

Tennant, Kylie 1970 *Evatt Politics and Justice* Sydney: Angus and Robertson

Thompson, Herb M. and Scott MacWilliam 1992 *The Political Economy of Papua New Guinea: Critical Essays* Manila and Wollongong: Journal of Contemporary Asia Publishers

Tomasetti, W.E. 1970 *Australia and the United Nations: New Guinea Trusteeship Issues from 1946–1966* Bulletin no. 36, Canberra and Boroko: New Guinea Research Unit, The Australian National University, July

Townsend, William H. 1969 'Stone and Steel Use in a New Guinea Society' *Ethnology* vol. 8, no. 2, pp. 199–205

Trainor, Luke 1994 *British Imperialism and Australian Nationalism: manipulation, conflict and compromise in the late nineteenth century* Melbourne: Cambridge University Press

Turner, Mark 1990 *Papua New Guinea: The Challenge of Independence a nation in turmoil* Ringwood, Victoria: Penguin Books

van Beusekom, Monica M. 2002 *Negotiating Development: African Farmers and Colonial Experts at the Office du Niger, 1920–1960* Portsmouth, NH, Oxford and Cape Town: Heinemann, James Currey and David Philip

Vasey, D. n.d. c. 1980 'Subsistence Crop Systems' in David King and Stephen Ranck (eds) *Papua New Guinea Atlas: A Nation in Transition* Port Moresby: Robert Brown and Associates (Australia) P/L in conjunction with the Geography Department, University of Papua New Guinea, pp. 50–51

Vernon, Don 2005 'The Panguna Mine' in Anthony J. Regan, and Helga M. Griffin (eds) *Bougainville before the conflict* Canberra: Pandanus Books, pp. 258–273

von Fleckenstein, F.W. 1975 'Observations on Coffee Marketing in the Eastern Highlands' *Yagl-Ambu* vol. 2, no. 2, pp. 116–132

Voutas, Tony 1981 'Policy Initiative and the Pursuit of Control' in J.A. Ballard (ed.) *Policy-Making in a New State: Papua New Guinea 1972–77* St Lucia: University of Queensland Press, pp. 33–47

Waddell, Robert 1979 'Local Government Policy in Papua New Guinea from 1949 to 1973' *Australian Journal of Politics and History* vol. xxv, no. 2, pp. 186–200

Wade, Robert 1990 *Governing the Market: Economic Theory and the Role of Government in East Asian Industrialization* Princeton: Princeton University Press

Walter, Michael A.H.B. (ed.) 1981 *What Do We Do About Plantations?*Monograph no. 15, Boroko: Papua New Guinea Institute of Applied Social and Economic Research

Ward, A.D. 1972 'Agrarian Revolution Handle with Care' *New Guinea* January, vol. 6, no. 4, pp. 25–34

——— n.d. 'Customary Land, Land Registration and Social Equality' in D. Denoon and Catherine Snowden (eds) *A time to plant and a time to uproot: A History of Agriculture in Papua New Guinea* Port Moresby: Institute of Papua New Guinea Studies for the Department of Primary Industry, pp. 249–264

——— 1983 'The Commission of Enquiry into Land Matters 1973: Choices, Constraints and Assumptions' *Melanesian Law Journal* vol. 11, pp. 1–13

——— 1990 'Time to Make a New Start' in Peter Larmour (ed.) *Customary Land Tenure: Registration and Decentralisation in Papua New Guinea* Monograph no. 29, Boroko: National Research Institute, pp. 177–194

Ward, Marion W. 1970 'Urbanisation—Threat or Promise? *New Guinea* vol. 5, no. 1, pp. 57–62

——— 1975 *Road and Development in Southwest Bougainville* New Guinea Research Bulletin no. 62, Port Moresby and Canberra: New Guinea Research Unit and The Australian National University

Ward, R.G. 1971 *Internal Migration and Urbanisation in Papua New Guinea* New Guinea Research Bulletin no. 42, Population Growth and Socio-Economic Change Papers from the second demography seminar, Port Moresby 1970 Port Moresby and Canberra: New Guinea Research Unit and The Australian National University, pp. 81–107. Reprinted in R.J. May (ed.) 1977 *Change and Movement: readings on Internal Migration in Papua New Guinea* Canberra: Papua New Guinea Institute of Applied Social and Economic Research in association with the ANU Press, pp. 27–51

Watt, Alan 1968 *The Evolution of Australian Foreign Policy 1938–1965* Cambridge: Cambridge University Press

West, F.J 1956 'Colonial Development in Central New Guinea' *South Pacific* September/October, vol. 9, no. 2, pp. 305–313

———— 1958 'Indigenous Labour in Papua-New Guinea' *International Labour Review* vol. 77, no. 2, pp. 89–112

———— 1968 *Hubert Murray The Australian Pro-Consul* Melbourne: Melbourne University Press

West, F.J. (ed.) 1970 *Selected Letters of Hubert Murray* Melbourne: Oxford University Press

Weymar, F. Helmut 1968 *The Dynamics of the World Cocoa Market* Cambridge, Massachusetts: The MIT Press

Wheeler, M.A., Sackett, M.A. and D.R.J. Densley n.d. c.1978 *Coconuts: Agriculture in the Economy A Series of Review Papers* Port Moresby: PNG Department of Primary Industry

White, Harold 2002 'Combining Quantitative and Qualitative Approaches in Poverty Analysis' *World Development* vol. 30, no. 3, pp. 511–522

White, Hugh and Elsina Wainwright 2004 *Strengthening Our Neighbour: Australia and the future of Papua New Guinea* Canberra: Australian Strategic Policy Institute, December

Whitlam, Gough 1985 *The Whitlam Government 1972–1975* Ringwood, Vic.: Penguin Books

Wilkes, J. (ed.) 1958 *New Guinea and Australia* Sydney: Angus and Robertson

Williams, F.E. 1937 'The Natives of Mount Hagen' *Man* vol. 37, pp. 90–96

Williamson, K.R. 1958 'The Tolai Cocoa Project' *South Pacific* July/August, vol. 9, no. 13, pp. 593–600

Wilson, L.D. and G.B.A. Evans 1975 *Sample Survey of Smallholder Coffee Producers* Port Moresby: Department of Agriculture, Stock and Fisheries Rural Economics and Commodity Marketing Branch, February

Windybank, Susan and Mike Manning 2003 *Papua New Guinea on the Brink* Issue Analysis no. 30, Sydney: The Centre for Independent Studies, March 12

Wingti, Paias 1985 'Standing by Our Principles in Tough Times' in P. King, Wendy Lee and Vincent Warakai (eds) *From Rhetoric to Reality? Papua New Guinea's Eight Point Plan and National Goals after a Decade* Waigani: University of Papua New Guinea, pp. 15–21

Wolfers, Edward P. 1967 'The unsettled settlers: New Guinea in Australia 1942–1946' *Journal of the Papua and New Guinea Society* vol. 1, no. 2, pp. 7–15

―――― 1967 'The Political Parties' *New Guinea* vol. 2, no. 3, pp. 10–31

―――― 1967 'The Elections' *New Guinea* vol. 2, no. 4, pp. 67–70

―――― 1968 'The 1968 Elections' *New Guinea* vol. 3, no. 3, pp. 50–61

―――― 1968 'The Emergence of Political Parties in Papua and New Guinea' *Journal of Pacific History* no. 3, pp. 155–159

Woo-Cumings, Meredith (ed.) 1999 *The Developmental State* Ithaca: Cornell University Press

Woo, Jung-en 1991 *Race to the Swift: State and Finance in Korean Industrialization* New York: Columbia University Press

Wood, G.A.R. and R.A. Lass 1989 *Cocoa* 4th edn Longman: Harlow, Essex

World Coffee Information Center (WCIC) 1974 *Thirty-Four Years of US Coffee History* Washington, D.C.: Samuel E Stavisky and Associates

―――― c. 1968 *Economic Impact of Coffee: How the International Coffee Agreement contributes to the progress of developing countries and the United States* Washington, D.C.: Pan-American Coffee Bureau

Worsley, Peter 1968 *The Trumpet Shall Sound: A Study of 'Cargo Cults' in Melanesia* New York: Schocken Books

Wright, Huntley L.R. 2001 'Contesting community: The labour question and colonial reform in the post-war Territory of Papua and New Guinea' *The Journal of Pacific Studies* vol. 25, no. 1, pp. 69–94

―――― 2002 'Economic or Political Development: The Evolution of "Native" Local Government Policy in the Territory of Papua and New Guinea, 1945–1963' *Australian Journal of Politics and History* vol. 48, no. 2, pp. 193–209

―――― 2002 'A Liberal "Respect for Small Property": Paul Hasluck and the "Landless Proletariat" in the Territory of Papua and New Guinea, 1951–63' *Australian Historical Studies* April, vol. 33, no. 119, pp. 55–72

―――― 2002 'Protecting the National Interest: The Labor Government and the Reform of Australia's Colonial Policy, 1942–45' *Labour History* May, no. 82, pp. 65–82

Wu, Yu-Shan 1994 *Comparative Economic Transformations: Mainland China, Hungary, the Soviet Union, and Taiwan* Stanford: Stanford University Press

Index

www.ingramcontent.com/pod-product-compliance
Lightning Source LLC
Chambersburg PA
CBHW061242270326

41928CB00041B/3378